The unimagined community

Manchester University Press

Cultural History of Modern War

Series editors   Ana Carden-Coyne, Peter Gatrell, Max Jones,
Penny Summerfield and Bertrand Taithe

Already published

Carol Acton and Jane Potter   *Working in a world of hurt: trauma and resilience in the narratives of medical personnel in warzones*

Julie Anderson   *War, disability and rehabilitation in Britain: soul of a nation*

Michael Brown, Anna Maria Barry and Joanne Begiato (eds)   *Martial masculinities: experiencing and imagining the military in the long nineteenth century*

Quintin Colville and James Davey (eds)   *A new naval history*

James E. Connolly   *The experience of occupation in the Nord, 1914–18: living with the enemy in First-World-War France*

Lindsey Dodd   *French children under the Allied bombs, 1940–45: an oral history*

Rachel Duffett   *The stomach for fighting: food and the soldiers of the First World War*

Peter Gatrell and Lyubov Zhvanko (eds)   *Europe on the move: refugees in the era of the Great War*

Christine E. Hallett   *Containing trauma: nursing work in the First World War*

Grace Huxford   *The Korean War in Britain: citizenship, selfhood and forgetting*

Jo Laycock   *Imagining Armenia: orientalism, ambiguity and intervention*

Chris Millington   *From victory to Vichy: veterans in inter-war France*

Juliette Pattinson   *Behind enemy lines: gender, passing and the Special Operations Executive in the Second World War*

Chris Pearson   *Mobilizing nature: the environmental history of war and militarization in Modern France*

Jeffrey S. Reznick   *Healing the nation: soldiers and the culture of caregiving in Britain during the Great War*

Jeffrey S. Reznick   *John Galsworthy and disabled soldiers of the Great War: with an illustrated selection of his writings*

Michael Roper   *The secret battle: emotional survival in the Great War*

Penny Summerfield and Corinna Peniston-Bird   *Contesting home defence: men, women and the Home Guard in the Second World War*

Trudi Tate and Kate Kennedy (eds)   *The silent morning: culture and memory after the Armistice*

Spiros Tsoutsoumpis   *The People's Armies: a history of the Greek resistance*

Laura Ugolini   *Civvies: middle-class men on the English Home Front, 1914–18*

Wendy Ugolini   *Experiencing war as the 'enemy other': Italian Scottish experience in World War II*

Colette Wilson   *Paris and the Commune, 1871–78: the politics of forgetting*

https://www.alc.manchester.ac.uk/history/research/centres/cultural-history-of-war/

The unimagined community

Imperialism and culture in South Vietnam

~

DUY LAP NGUYEN

Manchester University Press

Copyright © Duy Lap Nguyen 2020

The right of Duy Lap Nguyen to be identified as the author of this work has been asserted by him in accordance with the Copyright, Designs and Patents Act 1988.

Published by Manchester University Press
Oxford Road, Manchester M13 9PL

www.manchesteruniversitypress.co.uk

British Library Cataloguing-in-Publication Data
A catalogue record for this book is available from the British Library

ISBN 978 1 5261 4396 9 hardback
ISBN 978 1 5261 6250 2 paperback

First published 2020

The publisher has no responsibility for the persistence or accuracy of URLs for any external or third-party internet websites referred to in this book, and does not guarantee that any content on such websites is, or will remain, accurate or appropriate.

Typeset in Minion by
Servis Filmsetting Ltd, Stockport, Cheshire

Per Annalisa

Contents

List of figures	viii
Acknowledgments	ix
Introduction	1
1 Colonialism and national culture	23
2 Vietnamese anti-colonialism and the Personalist critique of capitalism and liberal democracy	51
3 The other Vietnamese revolution: The Strategic Hamlet Campaign and US imperialism	96
4 Psychological warfare, counterinsurgency and the society of spectacle in South Vietnam	153
5 Mass culture in the later Republic	175
6 Surveillance and spectacle in Bùi Anh Tuấn's Z.28 novels	214
7 Image-making and US imperialism: Sovereignty, surveillance and spectacle in the Vietnam War	248
Conclusion	265
Index	273

Figures

2.1 Emmanuel Mounier (courtesy of the Association les Amis d'Emmanuel Mounier). 54
2.2 Ngô Đình Nhu (Office national de radiodiffusion télévision française). 63
2.3 Ngô Đình Diệm (courtesy of Hoover Institution Archives). 74
2.4 Ngô Đình Nhu at the inauguration of the Strategic Village of Củ Chi, March 3, 1962 (courtesy of Harry S. Truman Library & Museum). 83
4.1 Lê Lợi on Sacred Sword Patriotic League propaganda flyer (Joint United States Public Affairs Office). 157
4.2 Thích Quảng Đức's self-immolation (AP Photo/Malcolm Browne). 161
5.1 Sài Gòn traffic, Hàm Nghi Street (John Beck). 177
5.2 Bookstall on Tự Do Street, Sài Gòn, April 1969 (Brian Wickham). 191
5.3 Taping of the daily news on RVN TV, January 1967 (Đài Truyền Hình Việt Nam Cộng Hòa). 193
7.1 IBM computers at the US AID Information Center, 1971 (courtesy of Michigan State University Archives). 252

Acknowledgments

This project has benefited immensely from conversations with numerous friends, family members and acquaintances on history, politics and philosophy, even though these conversations have failed to correct the innumerable faults, omissions and errors that must be contained in this book. I thank Nguyễn Văn Hường, Sean R. Garner, Justin Vandergrift, Đinh Thị Dĩ, Bùi Công Tường, Elaine Woo, Olga Dror, Keith Taylor, Ivan Small, Bradley Davis, Travis Tanner, Travis Workman and Gavin Walker for ideas and causal insights that led me to critical arguments in the course of completing this project. My colleagues at the University of Houston, including Robert Buzzanco, Karen Fang, Cedric Tolliver, Hosam Aboul-Ela and Alessandro Carrera, have been a vital source of both inspiration and encouragement. Special thanks to Julie-Françoise Tolliver for her much-needed advice on earlier drafts of the manuscript. As a fellow at the Pembroke Center at Brown University, I gained a great deal from discussions with Lilia Topouzova and Debbie Weinstein, who were co-participants in the seminar on socialism and postsocialism in 2013. A portion of the project was originally conceived while I was a graduate student at University of California, Irvine, working under the direction of Dina Al-Kassim and Charles Wheeler. Their mentorship, together with that of Neil Larsen and Raul Fernandez, continues to be an invaluable resource. Finally, I would like to thank my editors at Manchester University Press, Emma Brennan and Paul Clarke, for their patience, support and guidance in helping to realize this project.

Introduction

Prologue: A death in November

On September 2, 1963, Ngô Đình Nhu, the brother and chief political advisor to the South Vietnamese president, Ngô Đình Diệm, spoke in secret with the Polish diplomat Mieczysław Maneli to discuss the possibility of peace talks with Hà Nội. In the context of the deteriorating relationship between the Americans and the South Vietnamese, the meeting in Sài Gòn, which was seething "with rumors, plots, and counterplots,"[1] raised US suspicions that Nhu was trying to betray the alliance and forfeit the war.[2]

The crisis was stirred by an incident that occurred several months earlier. On May 8, South Vietnamese soldiers in the city of Huế killed several unarmed civilians opposing a government ban on the public display of Buddhist flags.[3] The episode ignited a wave of political protest during the summer that would come to be symbolized by the famous photograph of Thích Quảng Đức's self-immolation. By "burn[ing] himself in front of reporters," working for the American media, the Vietnamese monk had apparently produced the "first really powerful image to shake the Western world, to momentarily crack through the chain of mediatized simulacra."[4]

Shattering the image of the South Vietnamese government as a "stable, viable and democratic bastion of the Free World,"[5] the photograph would become "a universal symbol of rebellion and the fight against injustice."[6] Taken during the height of the Civil Rights Movement, the picture appeared to provide irrefutable evidence that the Republic of Vietnam (RVN) was a repressive regime, denying equality to its own Buddhist majority. The backlash in the international press would prompt

Introduction

US officials to threaten a withdrawal of support and a complete suspension of aid,[7] at a moment when the insurgency appeared to be fulfilling its pledge to destroy the "dictatorial government of the American lackey, Ngô Đình Diệm."[8]

In less than two months after the meeting in September, Diệm and Nhu were killed in a coup backed by officials at the American embassy. The assassination on November 1 marked the beginning of a tragicomic cycle of changing regimes and incompetent leaders. This ended in April 1975 with the communist victory and the humiliating withdrawal of American forces, after two decades of war that left millions of Vietnamese dead. By that point, the Republic was already widely regarded as a political puppet, manufactured by the world's greatest capitalist power, waging an imperialist war against a poor peasant society. Refracted through political and cultural movements in the US and Europe, the victory against the Americans and the South Vietnamese would be celebrated as a symbol of world revolution: "In the wave of youthful protest against authority… in the 1960s, rejection of old sexual morality and an enthusiasm for the joys of marijuana and LSD became conflated with lunges against capitalism and imperialism, of which Vietnam appeared an exceptionally ugly manifestation."[9]

Viewed from this vantage point, Nhu's response to Maneli during their meeting on September 2 seems utterly strange and inexplicable. After a lengthy "exposition on the philosophy of the cult of personality,"[10] and its role in what he described as the Republic's increasing success in the war, Nhu, unaware that the end had arrived, announced the beginning of a "new phase" of the conflict.[11] For the South Vietnamese, the war, as he explained in his peculiar paradoxical style of speaking, had become a "social revolution" against the communist revolution in the countryside. As a total transformation of society, this revolution, moreover, was not simply a nationalist struggle to overcome communism. On the contrary, nationalism, according to Nhu, was merely an "alibi" exploited by Third World leaders who failed to recognize the "need for social revolution in under-developed countries."[12]

Casting the Buddhist Affair as a mediatized spectacle ("*ce spectacle unique au XXème siècle*"),[13] and an "imperialist plot" (*âm mưu đế quốc*) to crush the social revolution in the name of a Western ideal of democracy,[14] Nhu declared the "war cannot be won with the Americans because they are an obstacle to the revolutionary transformation of society which is the prerequisite of victory."[15] This obstacle was identified in particular with the mechanism of American aid, which Nhu (speaking through

Introduction

a government newspaper organ) had condemned, in unmistakably Marxist terminology, as an instrument of underdevelopment: "Vietnam Not a Guinea Pig for Capitalist Imperialism to Experiment On."[16] The "new phase" of the conflict, therefore, would call for resistance both against communism and American neo-colonialism. The Republic, as Nhu explained to an astonished Maneli, "is fighting against [both] the guerrillas and imperialism."[17]

Even more puzzling, however, than the idea that the South Vietnamese were engaged in an anti-colonial struggle against their American allies was the fact that, for Nhu, the ultimate aim of the social revolution in the South was not to defeat communism. Rather, the goal was the abolition of capitalism. Just as the Americans were now an "obstacle to the revolutionary transformation of society," so the "capitalist regime" in the South "cannot effectively oppose Communis[m]."[18] In another display of his penchant for abstruse dialectical statements, Nhu therefore explained that the anti-communist war was, in fact, an anti-capitalist strategy: "I am really combating communism in order to put an end to materialistic capitalism."[19]

This apparently implausible explanation of the political aims of the South Vietnamese state, which was reputed to be a bastion of democracy, has been taken as "evidence that Nhu was mad," dismissed as a symptom of his opium-induced paranoia, or one of his Machiavellian schemes to preserve his own power.[20] The socialist concepts that Nhu described to Maneli, however, were in fact an integral part of the "philosophy of the cult of personality," or Vietnamese Personalism, which Nhu had developed before the founding of the Republic in 1955 as a "Personalist democracy."[21] This form of democracy, which was viewed as directly opposed to Western liberal democracy,[22] would not be based on individual rights and formal equality, but rather on the communist principle of "to each according to his needs." As Nhu affirmed in the manifesto of the Personalist Labor Party (*Cần lao Nhân vị Cách Mạng Đảng*), the "goal of production must be the satisfaction of needs."[23] Under a Personalist government, "production must serve the people," whereas in a capitalist regime, "it is man who is in the service of the economy."[24] This Marxian principle, moreover, was one that the Republic would attempt to apply in its anti-capitalist war against communism. For Nhu, the struggle against the Marxist insurgency in the South "was never just a security measure," but the "vehicle for a full-scale political and social revolution that would put into practice the long-proclaimed … ideals of the regime's own philosophy of 'personalism.'"[25] This "Marxist Personalism,"[26] therefore, as Nhu pointed out to Maneli, was the intellectual foundation for the counterinsurgency program, the "philosophy of the Strategic Hamlet Campaign."[27]

This commitment to a political theory that seems to so closely resemble the doctrine of the Communist Party suggests a different explanation of the crisis in 1963. From the perspective of Nhu's surprising account of the conflict, the Republic appears not as the first in a series of ill-fated experiments to prop up dependent and decadent political proxy regimes in the war against international communism. Nor were the Ngos, as John F. Kennedy would later remember them, patriots who were deeply devoted to the national cause despite all their flaws. ("They were just tyrants," said an acquaintance to Kennedy, seeing his shock at the news that the two Vietnamese leaders had been brutally killed in the coup. "No," he responded. "They were in a difficult position. They did the best they could for their country."[28]) In Maneli's report, Nhu appears not as a nationalist figure, but something stranger and more paradoxical, an anti-colonial leader, exploiting the wealth of an imperial power in order to wage an anti-capitalist war against communism: "Nhu spoke about his socialist concepts with many of the highest-ranking Western diplomats, and seemed to believe in them. And this during a period when he was drawing millions of dollars from American's 'nonsocialist' treasury."[29]

Seen from this unlikely perspective, the coup in 1963 appears, then, not as an event that marked the demise of an undemocratic regime and an American puppet. If Nhu's socialist concepts were not a sign of insanity, but principles that were actually applied in an anticommunist war against capitalism, then the collapse of the Republic may have been something other than the way it appears in much of the historical record: the defeat a revolutionary attempt to establish a socialist society different than that of the Communist Party. This society, according to Nhu, was in the process of successfully fighting the war against the insurgency,[30] while freeing itself from the economic dependence imposed by its capitalist patron.[31]

This social revolution, however, would never be realized. In the place of a socialist society, "fighting against the guerrillas and imperialism," the Americans, after the coup, would help install a dependent "capitalist regime" that would be unable to "effectively oppose Communis[m]."

A South Vietnamese view of the war

The Unimagined Community presents a political and cultural history of imperialism and capitalism in the South Vietnamese context, from the

Introduction

colonial era to the end of the Vietnam War. As a conceptual frame for the project, the first part of the book reconstructs the ideology that informed the seemingly improbable account of the conflict that Nhu relayed to Maneli during their meeting in 1963. From the point of view of Nhu's Vietnamese Personalism, the war was not a contest between Marxism and nationalism or communism and democracy (as it appears from a Cold War perspective), but an anti-capitalist struggle against Stalinism and US imperialism.

Inspired by a form of French Marxist humanism, this Vietnamese Personalism emerged both as a product of and critical reflection on the history of imperialism. According to this theory, the society that existed prior to the colonial period was radically altered by the introduction of capitalism and bourgeois democracy, which resulted in underdevelopment rather than political and economic modernity. As a "Personalist democracy," the First Republic (*Đệ Nhất Cộng Hòa Việt Nam*, 1954–1963), therefore, would seek to establish a non-Western form of modernity in a social revolution against capitalism and liberal democracy. While this revolution would make use of the "alibi" of nationalism, promoting the development of a South Vietnamese national culture, its ultimate aim was a communitarian form of democracy, based on the "withering away of the state" and the abolition of the form of the nation itself.

This social revolution would be crushed as a result of the coup. Its defeat, however, did not come at the hands of the communists. Nor was its end the result of its own authoritarian tendencies, provoking rebellion by the South Vietnamese masses. Rather, it was defeated by agents of the "imperialist" institutions that it sought to eradicate, institutions with which it was allied in the war against communism. Backed by the American embassy, the coup was carried out by members of an elite urban minority who dominated the underdeveloped capitalist economy, as well as the centralized structures of the state, which the social revolution had been designed to abolish.

After the fall of the First Republic, the South Vietnamese leaders who came into power, avoiding the "need for social revolution in underdeveloped countries," would adopt the ambiguous banner of nationalism and democracy, which covered the absence of any alternative political project. The war, then, would become a conflict between communism and democracy, Marxism and nationalism. What followed, however, in the decade after the coup, would largely confirm the unlikely assertion by Nhu that a "revolutionary transformation of society" was "the prerequisite of victory." Along with the destruction and violence of the war

Introduction

of attrition, which replaced the social revolution in the countryside to establish a non-Western form of modernity, the economic and political liberalism of the later regimes would create an economically dependent urban society.

Extending the Personalist critique of liberal democracy developed in the earlier chapters, the second part of the book, shifting the attention to culture, examines what South Vietnamese writers described as an underdeveloped "postindustrial society" (*xã hội hậu kỹ nghệ*) that emerged in the cities after the fall of the First Republic. From the mid-1960s, a capitalist culture industry, promoting a new *société de consommation*, would diminish the role of journalism, high culture and art, leading communist critics to condemn this development as an American scheme to destroy the national consciousness. This conspiracy, however, was actually an unintended effect of political and economic liberalization, which had been suppressed under the Personalist regime of the early Republic. Instead of providing a medium for imagining the nation (to recall Benedict Anderson's famous account of the role of print capitalism), the culture industry in the South would dispense with the "alibi" of nationalism in an unexpected direction, in the creation of a kind of unimagined community: an urban audience for mass-produced culture that became increasingly detached from the reality of the war in the countryside.

The book concludes with several reflections on another unusual feature of US imperialism during the Vietnam War, related to the rise of mass culture. For Hannah Arendt, this imperialism was that of a liberal democracy whose policymaking was transformed by the practice of "image-making," or the production of mediatized spectacles. Many of these images, which have been celebrated as universal symbols of rebellion in the iconography of the era, take on a more uncertain significance from the perspective explored in this book. The photograph of Thích Quảng Đức's self-immolation, which endures as a powerful image of political protest, would destroy a social revolution against capitalism in the South. The result was a crisis that created the need for a massive American military intervention, which the social revolution had tried to avert. In "a poignant example of resistance to Diem," the "spectacular self-immolation during the 1963 Buddhist crisis stamped an image on the Vietnam War that has never faded away." But the "demise of the Diem regime created the situation that the Buddhists fought to avoid at all costs: increased American involvement in South Vietnam's affairs and expansion of the war."[32]

Introduction

In 1968, the power of the image to propel such unexpected reversals in the course of events was confirmed once again by the strange fate of the Southern insurgency (whose revolution had been reproduced in a non-Stalinist form by the government that the Americans had helped to demolish). During the Tết Offensive, the insurgency was desicively defeated as a result of an enormous military miscalculation by communist leaders. Through the agency of the image, however, this tragic defeat on the battlefield was transfigured as an unprecedented political victory for the communist forces. The Southern insurgency was immortalized by the mediatized representation of the appalling miscalculation that guaranteed its destruction.

On the other hand, for the South Vietnamese, image-making by the international media would have exactly the opposite impact. As Diệm correctly conjectured months before the media coverage of the Buddhist Affair, the "war can only be lost by the American press."[33] But what he could not have imagined perhaps was that, after the coup, the authors of the mediatized representations that helped to bring down the regime would also play a principal part in shaping its historical image: "The anti-Diem faction dominated the [American] press through the efforts of a small group of journalists," including Malcolm Browne, who captured the photo of Thích Quảng Đức. "The significance of this is that those who championed the coup have written the popular history of its aftermath. [These] writings are best understood as an attempt to blame the outcome in Vietnam on everything but the coup."[34]

The sections below present a brief account of this popular history, followed by a more detailed description of the individual chapters of the book.

The South, the war and the myth of the nation

The Vietnam War is often portrayed as the final act in an ancient historical drama, that of the Vietnamese people united in their millennial struggle to achieve independence. For over a thousand years, the Vietnamese, according to the historical fiction, fought to preserve their identity and their national culture against the Chinese, eventually liberating themselves from their colonial masters in the ninth century AD. In the late nineteenth century, the French, following in the footsteps of earlier foreign invaders, conquered the country under the pretext of protecting the followers of their Christian religion. Acting contrary to the ideals of the French Revolution and the Rights of Man, they succeeded

Introduction

in subjugating the Vietnamese masses. To ensure their domination, the imperialists then tried to erase the national culture of their colonial subjects, attempting to civilize a people who "possessed a rich civilization ... when the French were still living in caves."[35]

The colonial era came to a close in 1940, when Indochina was occupied by Japan. At the end of the war, the surrender of the Imperial Army created a political vacuum, allowing the Việt Minh, led by Hồ Chí Minh, to declare independence. This independence, however, would only be won through a long and difficult struggle. In response to the attempt by the French to reestablish control of the colony, the Việt Minh launched an anti-imperialist war, continuing the ancient tradition of resistance to foreign invaders.

Following the defeat of the French at Điện Biên Phủ in 1954, the Americans, mistakenly identifying a war of national independence with the international communist struggle, would become directly involved militarily. Rejecting the Communist Party's legitimate claim to represent the Vietnamese people, the USA, under the pretext of aiding a separate but equally sovereign Vietnamese state, provided support to a series of corrupt and incompetent governments in the South. Lacking a popular base of support, these regimes were forced to employ dictatorial methods to preserve their authority.[36]

The first of these regimes, which existed from 1954 to 1963, was "headed by President Ngo Dinh Diem, an autocratic, nepotistic ruler who valued power more than either his relations with the Vietnamese people or progress in fighting the communists."[37] A representative of the interests of a reactionary colonial-era elite, Diệm, a former mandarin and a Catholic, ruling a country with a Buddhist majority, conducted a campaign of mass repression and terror. Through a draconian program of forced relocation, Diệm attempted to gain "control over the peasants by herding them into 'strategic hamlets.'"[38]

The program was part of a "hodgepodge of ersatz Fascist ... techniques that the regime resorted to in its efforts at political motivation and control," efforts that were directed by Diệm's younger brother Ngô Đình Nhu. Operating largely in the shadows, Nhu, an "admirer of Hitler" as well as communist dictators, "borrowed promiscuously from both right-wing and left-wing varieties of totalitarianism" in order to establish an extensive police apparatus in the South.[39] Controlled by a "proto-Fascist and mentally unstable drug addict," the "Strategic Hamlet Program," however, "as carried out by ... Nhu proved to be a catastrophic failure."[40] The program would stoke deep-seated resentment among the

Introduction

Vietnamese masses, "roused into a fury by an abuse beyond any [they] had previously experienced from this foreign-rooted government."[41] Instead of establishing a "stable, viable and democratic bastion of the Free World,"[42] the policies implemented by Diệm and Nhu would serve to destabilize the political situation, alienating the people, provoking widespread international outrage, and undermining the credibility of the US mission abroad.[43] As a result, the repressive tactics employed by the puppet regime in Sài Gòn could not overcome the communist people's war, which drew its primary base of support from the population itself.

Recognizing this failure, and the unpopular character of the regime they had helped create, US officials supported a coup against Diệm and his brother in November 1963, seeking to replace them with more capable and less authoritarian leaders.[44] But because the new political puppets proved to be as corrupt and incompetent as the ones before them, the situation continued to quickly deteriorate, allowing the insurgency to prevail on the battlefield. Faced with the possibility of imminent defeat, US officials made the fateful decision to expand the American presence. Discarding the political pretences supporting a sovereign national government, fighting a war against communist subversion, the Americans, then, would assume a leading role in the conflict. By the mid-1960s, the repressive program of mass relocation, which was employed unsuccessfully by the puppet regime in the South, was replaced by a high-tech war of attrition.[45] Having failed in its attempt to control the Vietnamese people by proxy, by forcing the peasantry into government camps policed by its political clients, the USA would deploy its immense military apparatus with the aim of killing the enemy as quickly as possible.

The war of attrition, however, in spite of the mass destruction and death, would fail in the end to overcome the insurgency, owing to the superior methods of organization employed in the people's war strategy. Drawing its strength from the indomitable will of the Vietnamese people, rooted in an ancient tradition of resistance to foreign invaders, the insurgency would defeat a vastly superior conventional army, reuniting the nation and restoring the country's independence.

This account of the conflict corresponds to what the Vietnamese Marxist writer and activist Ngô Văn Xuyết has described as a reductive representation of the war that "depicts the North as David bringing down Goliath."[46] In this image, the war appears as a contest between US imperialism and the Vietnamese people, steeped in a heroic tradition of anti-foreign resistance. This depiction of Vietnamese culture relies on what the historian Keith Taylor describes as an enduring fable, repeated in much of the historiography on the Vietnam War: "Most books about the mid-twentieth-century Vietnamese wars provide a prefatory myth about the Vietnamese being a unified people who for millennia have been enemies of the Chinese, and consequently have become experts at resisting foreign aggression."[47] For example, Nguyễn Bá Chung, criticizing the American government for its "amazing ... ignorance" of this nationalist myth, argued that the failure to "take into account ... Vietnam's two thousand year history of hard-fought existence ... is the essence of the Vietnam tragedy."[48] In a more recent work on the war, this 2,000-year history is identified as the source of an indomitable will to resist that enabled the Vietnamese people (who are identified with the communist forces) to overcome a vastly superior army: "Americans had never heard of Vietnam before the late 50s ... but Vietnam had a long ... history that goes back several thousand years." As a result of this national history, "a 'tradition of resistance' had been forever instilled within the Vietnamese and would be used effectively by the communists in the 20th century."[49] "Expelling foreign invaders," therefore, as another writer concludes, "was an ancient Vietnamese custom."[50]

For Ngô Văn, such representations distort the fundamental complicity between the ideals espoused by the American government and those of the communist forces. In the war, the Americans, who had fought to defend capitalism and bourgeois democracy, would be defeated by a Stalinist bureaucracy whose reign would serve only to perpetuate the same institutions in a more authoritarian cast: "The Vietnamese bureaucracy ... with its 'cultivated middle-class' background, master of a hierarchical one-party state, has done nothing but replace the bourgeoisie and the landowners in exploitation of the proletariat and the peasantry." Through the program of collectivization, carried out after the war, the labor and land of the Vietnamese masses would be expropriated as commodities, collectively owned by the bureaucratic elite, who imposed an authoritarian form of state capitalism. In the end, a "Stalinist party came to power through the terrible suffering and sacrifice of millions of peasants, who were rewarded by their renewed enslavement to the nationalist bureaucracy, as a workforce necessary for the primitive accumulation of capital ... for the sole profit of a new variety of moneygrabbers."[51]

In light of this tragic historical outcome, the Vietnam War can be understood as belonging to what Guy Debord has described as a series of spectacular "battles between competing versions of alienated power." During the Cold War, these conflicts pitted the "most advanced economies" against the "state bureaucracy ... of ... countries living under

Introduction

colonialism or semi-colonialism." The antagonists in these battles, who appeared to embody opposing political systems, were, in fact, the "functions of a single tendency that ... is capitalism."[52] Thus, after the war, the bureaucratic elite in Vietnam, having asserted that "socialism differs from capitalism in crucial ways, and proving it by applying its premises to pursue the war successfully ... were converted to the notion ... that all economies ... must surrender to the ... immutable objective laws of the market, whoever is nominally in power."[53]

Outline

This study disputes the representation of the war as a contest between US imperialism and the indomitable will of the Vietnamese people, rooted in a national history of heroic anti-colonial struggle. As I argue in Chapter 1, this ancient tradition was in fact a modern invention, a product of new forms of mass media, introduced by the colonial administration as part of the mission to civilize. This imperial project, moreover, did not simply betray the ideals of the French Revolution and the Rights of Man. Rather, as I argue in Chapter 3, the imperialism of the early colonial state was defined by the attempt to impose a Western ideal of democracy, one that was fundamentally opposed to the structure of Vietnamese civilization.

In the precolonial period, the country, which consisted of a myriad of semi-autonomous village communities, was ruled by a weak imperial court, a nominally absolute legal authority, lacking a modern apparatus of power that could intervene in the daily affairs of its subjects. This civilization, therefore, was that of a despotism whose largely formal prerogative constituted the juridical superstructure of a communal or democratic organization of peasant production, based on a custom or unwritten tradition of village autonomy. During the early colonial era, this organization was transformed by the introduction of capitalism and Western democracy, based on a system of individual rights guaranteed by the colonial administration. Together with the impersonal power of the market economy, these rights, enforced by the disciplinary institutions of a centralized state (such as the police and the colonial prison), served to weaken the authority of the imperial court while undermining the traditional autonomy of the village.

The disciplinary machinery of the colonial government also included a new system of mass education, based on instruction in the vernacular script, and the creation of a modern Vietnamese media, disseminated through print capitalism. These institutions, which enabled a modern bourgeois public sphere to emerge in the colony, were originally established, with the support of the French secret police, as a tool for monitoring the political activities of the colonial population. In the attempt to deploy this modern form of publicity as a technique of surveillance, the French administration, however, would also create the conditions for a new "imagined community" of the nation, and the development of a new national culture.

During the 1920s and 1930s, the vernacular press would be instrumental in spreading the modern mythology of a 2,000-year history of resistance to foreign invasion. As I argue in Chapter 1, this modern tradition was the result of an anti-colonial interpretation of the precolonial past, based on a European conception of national sovereignty. In the interpretation, the legal prerogative of a weak imperial court, whose power was limited by the customary autonomy of the Vietnamese village, was rewritten as the sovereign right of a "people" possessing a distinct national culture, over the territory it had historically occupied. In this nationalist history, the Vietnamese people (who had appeared in the imperial records only as "subjects" (dân) of the "civilized" rule of the king) would become the foundation of a new "popular sovereignty" (dân quyền). Projecting the modern conception of sovereignty into the precolonial past, writers, working in the modern vernacular media, created a new national history of a new national people. In this history, the latter appears as a unified subject, engaged in a 2,000-year struggle to preserve its national heritage against all foreign invaders.

Disseminated through a popular medium that had been created in part as an imperial tool of surveillance, this history was adopted by the elite, inspiring widespread resistance to colonial rule. Thus, the apparently ancient tradition of expelling foreign invaders would be used to oppose the very imperialism that had helped to create it, in establishing the vernacular press as a tool for policing its subjects.

During the Vietnam War, the diffusion of the new national culture would become an integral part of the program employed by the Communist Party to mobilize the Vietnamese masses and instill in them an indomitable will to resist, apparently rooted in ancient tradition. In that sense, the communist people's war strategy was used to create the very "national people" who would fight to defend its immemorial sovereignty against American neo-imperialism.

In historical works on the war, the uncritical acceptance of the modern mythology of an ancient Vietnamese culture has served to discourage a more careful examination of the South Vietnamese side of the conflict.

Introduction

Portrayed as a government that was hopelessly compromised by its collusion with US imperialism, the Republic has been widely regarded as a political puppet, unworthy of the millennial history of foreign resistance invented in the colonial era. As a result, in "much of the writing on the war, the South Vietnamese," as George Herring has noted, "are conspicuous by their absence, and virtually nothing has been done on their dealings with the United States."[54]

This book will address this conspicuous absence by presenting a wide-ranging discussion of South Vietnamese culture as it emerged in the context of the colonial era and the Cold War. In doing so, however, it will also attempt to call into question a fundamental presupposition of both "orthodox" and "revisionist" accounts of the conflict.[55] This assumption is that the Republicanism of the South Vietnamese state was, from beginning to end, that of a nationalist government aimed at establishing a democratic alternative to communism based on the principle of popular sovereignty.[56] In the case of the First Republic, the project proved unsuccessful because of the failure of its president, Ngô Đình Diệm, to implement democratic reform and to broaden the popular base of his government.

This presupposition has served to conceal a remarkable political and social experiment carried out under the shadow of US imperialism. Contrary to the conventional view, the war, for the First Republic, was not an anticommunist crusade undertaken by a regime that was incapable of creating a stable democracy. Rather, as it evolved in its nine years of existence, the early Republic, could be more accurately characterized as a Marxist humanist state, applying a political philosophy known as "Personalism," which espoused a Marxist critique of capitalism and bourgeois democracy.

Chapter 2 examines the intellectual origins of this Vietnamese Personalism through a close reading of the work of the French Catholic philosopher Emmanuel Mounier. Contrary to the caricature of his thought as an incoherent and reactionary religious ideology, the latter was in fact a philosophically rigorous form of Marxist theology, one that appealed, moreover, to anti-colonial leaders from throughout the developing world. In the chapter, the interpretation of Mounier's Marxist critique of capitalism and liberal democracy will provide the broader theoretical framework for this study and its reexamination of the war from a South Vietnamese perspective.

During the First Republic, the philosophy of Personalism, as I explore in Chapter 3, would inform the development of the Strategic Hamlet

Campaign, which was the primary strategy in the struggle against the insurgency. Contrary to existing accounts of the latter, the program was not simply a totalitarian technique of mass repression, developed by foreign advisors such as the British counterinsurgency expert Robert Thompson. Rather, it was conceived by Diệm's brother Ngô Đình Nhu as a "social revolution" (*cách mạng xã hội*), aimed at transforming the entire economic and political structure in the South.

This revolution was supposed to provide an alternative to that of the government's communist rivals. This alternative, however, was not simply a mixture of nationalism, capitalism and liberal democracy, institutions that were inherited from the colonial administration. On the contrary, the leaders of the early Republic were acutely aware of the difficulties of establishing a Western-style democracy and a liberal economy in the context of war and underdevelopment, difficulties that were exasperated by American influence and aid. Instead of seeking to establish a bastion of capitalism and bourgeois democracy, the South Vietnamese leaders, therefore, in devising the Strategic Hamlet Campaign, would attempt to actualize an *alternative version of communism*.

But as such, the war in this earlier phase was not a conflict between socialism and democracy. Rather, as this study contends, it was a *contest between two different forms of anti-colonial communism*. Rejecting the ideals of liberal democracy, which had been introduced as part of the mission to civilize, the early Republican leaders would come to conceive of the conflict as a social revolution against both liberal democracy and the Stalinism of the Communist Party.

Drawing on the historiography invented in the colonial era, Republican leaders presented this Marxist humanist struggle as a modern version of the national myth of the "Southward Advance" (*nam tiến*), the South Vietnamese counterpart to the ancient tradition of resistance to foreign invaders. The revolution, then, in the South, would be cast as the continuation of the process of geographical expansion that, over the course of some 700 years, established the national territory of the Vietnamese people. In contrast, however, to the communist deployment of the modern mythology of an ancient tradition of anti-imperialism, the aim of the second Southward Advance was not the creation of a sovereign national government. Rather, the leaders of the early Republic envisioned a kind of return to a precolonial tradition of village autonomy, modernized on the revolutionary model of a direct "democracy at the base."[57]

This model was partly derived from the Personalist notion of praxis (which Nhu translated as *cần lao*), an act of free individuals, liberated,

Introduction

through their voluntary subjection to a "communal discipline," from the impersonal rule of the market as well as the disciplinary apparatus of the national government. In a "withering of the state," this autonomy, based on a personal discipline that is freely imposed, would serve to preempt the power of the centralized government, creating the conditions for a stateless form of non-Western modernity, superseding the notion of national sovereignty. The early Republic, therefore, would attempt to defeat the insurgency by employing a form of social organization, based on an ancient tradition of village democracy, that could operate independently of the centralized state.

But in that case, the war, as it was waged by the South Vietnamese government, was not simply a nationalist struggle. In contrast to the communist people's war strategy, the dissemination of a national culture, which the early Republic employed as part of its program of "nation-building" (*xây dựng quốc gia*), was not aimed at creating an "imagined community" of the nation. Rather, the nationalist myth of the Southward Advance was used in the program as a means of imagining a stateless form of modern community. During the period of the First Republic, the war, then, was not a conflict in which US imperialism employed a superior conventional army against a people steeped in a long national history of anti-foreign partisan warfare. Rather, it was a contest between two Vietnamese states, applying the same people's war strategy while embracing two different conceptions of communism: one based on the dictatorship of the proletariat and the other oriented toward a socialism without the state.

By 1962, moreover, the revolution to establish this stateless form of democracy had begun to succeed in containing the insurgency in the South. As I argue in Chapters 3 and 4, however, the aim of creating a democracy at the base, or a socialism without the state, would put the leaders of the early Republic directly at odds with the Americans, as well as the South Vietnamese urban elite. For this group, the social revolution seemed like an authoritarian seizure of power by the executive branch, whose program of decentralization threatened the political prerogative of the ministries and military elite in Sài Gòn. In that sense, the goal of creating a democracy at the base, preempting the authority of the centralized government, was directly opposed to the aim, embraced by the Americans and urban elite, of establishing a parliamentary state in the South.

Ultimately, this "misalliance" between the Americans and the leaders of the early Republic would lead to its downfall. In 1963, the regime

Introduction

was overthrown in a coup supported by the American embassy in a misguided attempt to uphold the image of the Republic as a liberal democracy, an image that its leaders had rejected in favor of a stateless form of democracy, and a return to rural autonomy. Contrary to the conventional view, the collapse of the First Republic, therefore, was not a result of its failure to establish a viable parliamentary government. Rather, it was the increasing success of the Strategic Hamlet Campaign (as an alternative version of communism) in superseding the central agencies of the constitutional government and decentralizing the struggle against the insurgency that caused the fall of the First Republic.

But in that case, the early South Vietnamese state was neither a reactionary puppet regime, hired by an imperial power to repress its own population, nor an independent nation that was undermined by its own lack of democracy. Rather, the First Republic, in the years just before its collapse, was something more paradoxical and improbable. It was an anti-Stalinist socialist government, attempting to carry out its own communist revolution against the insurgency, a revolution that would put its objectives at odds with those of its neo-colonial patron, who conspired to overthrow the regime for the sake of liberal democracy.

As I explore in Chapter 4, this contradiction would compromise both the counterinsurgency strategy (which the early Republic conceived as a social revolution rather than a program of pacification), as well as the psychological warfare campaign carried out in the North. For the South Vietnamese, the campaign was to be an extension of the counterinsurgency strategy, a second Southward Advance to reconquer the North. For the Americans, on the other hand, the aim of the program was to employ modern mass communication technologies to discredit the communist government, to undermine its nationalist image and publicize its lack of liberal democracy.

In the end, the coup that defeated the Personalist revolution would produce a profound political crisis, compelling US officials to dramatically expand the American military presence. Having undermined the Marxist humanist program of the early Republic, policymakers in Washington would come to rely on a high-tech war of attrition, employing information and image-making in order to overcome the insurgency. The violence of the war of attrition would result in widespread rural depopulation. The early Republican program of social revolution in the countryside, then, would be replaced by an "urban revolution," aimed at isolating the insurgency by displacing the rural population en masse. In the cities, moreover, the policies implemented by the later Republican

Introduction

governments would help to precipitate the emergence of an enormous consumer society, dependent on American aid. Chapter 5 will look at the rise of a new popular culture, which would become an increasingly pervasive phenomenon in South Vietnamese cities from the mid-1960s, as the violence continued to escalate in the countryside.

This popular culture, and the consumer society from which it emerged, was viewed by the Communist Party as an instrument for enslaving the masses that was far more effective than American psychological warfare campaigns. Having failed to crush the indomitable will of the Vietnamese people (rooted in an ancient tradition of resisting foreign invaders) through the use of superior violence, the Americans attempted to "invade the national culture" through popular media, in order to undermine the will to resist. In the cities, therefore, the "decadent cultural products of American neo-colonialism" were deployed, purportedly, for the purpose of destroying national consciousness. The development of a "neo-colonialism" consumer society would be used to dissolve the national culture, which had previously served as a medium for imagining the nation. Divested of their national identity by the products of a foreign popular culture, urban South Vietnamese would become increasingly indifferent to the revolutionary appeals of the Party.

As I argue in Chapter 5, the development of popular culture, contrary to this communist account of neocolonialism, was not part of a psychological warfare campaign to manipulate the South Vietnamese masses. Rather, it was an unintended outcome of policies implemented by the later Republican governments in accordance with the American aim of establishing a bastion of liberal democracy and free-market capitalism. In the cities, this created a climate of intellectual and cultural freedom, conducive to artistic experimentation and vigorous democratic debate in the media, which were completely unknown in the North.

Because of this liberal tendency, however, the later Republican regimes would largely abandon the project of disseminating a national culture in order to create an imagined community of the nation. This liberalism with regard to the question of culture would lead to the emergence of a largely unregulated market for media in the South. As the violence continued to escalate in the countryside, the market would become almost completely confined to the cities, reinforcing the separation between the rural and urban populations. Freed from the censorship imposed by the early Republic, the market, moreover, would divert the attention of South Vietnamese intellectuals away from the creation of high culture and art toward the production of mass

Introduction

entertainment. This entertainment included new forms of serialized fiction, genres on which the newspapers depended for profits from advertisers, who promoted the products of an underdeveloped society of high mass consumption. During this period, the free market for media would impose a compulsion upon artists to meet the increasing demand for popular fiction, while producing an uneven distribution of culture, which helped to isolate the imagination of rural and urban South Vietnamese. If print capitalism, therefore, during the colonial era, had helped to establish a new national culture, during the war, the unregulated market for media would work to unravel this imagined community. This effect of the media, in the era of high mass consumption and imperial image-making, would realize the aim of the early Republic in a direction that its leaders had never expected. Whereas the First Republic, in its opposition to capitalism and liberal democracy, had imagined a stateless form of community, the liberalism of the later Republic would give rise to an *unimagined community*, as a form of anti-modernity.

Chapter 6 proposes a reading of one of the most successful examples of South Vietnamese serialized fiction from this period of the war: Bùi Anh Tuấn's Ian Fleming-inspired Z.28 novels. Like other popular works from the period, the novels' primary source of appeal is the language of advertising employed in the prose, a phenomenon that became pervasive in South Vietnamese cities during the war. The novels consist of narratives of surveillance composed out of passages modeled on commercials for brand-named commodities. The success of the Z.28 series, however, was not only due to the appeal of its Vietnamese superspy character as a figure of vicarious consumption. In the novels, the character also appears as a symbol for the South Vietnamese state and its precarious position within the broader geopolitics of the Cold War. The frivolous tales of high mass consumption, therefore, set in a world reduced to an advertised image, also suggest a reflection on the place of the nation within the Cold War balance of power. In the Z.28 series, the RVN appears as a state whose autonomy is undermined by the military and economic support it receives from its American ally. The Republic, in other words, is portrayed as a nation whose political sovereignty is threatened by its dependence upon its superpower patron. The American government, then, is characterized in the series as both an ally and an object of political enmity. In the Z.28 novels, the Vietnamese spy appears as a figure who opposes this ambivalent ally not through overt forms of resistance, but rather through the act of consuming

Introduction

American aid in the form of brand-named commodities. Thus, in the novels, the celebration of consumerism implies both an endorsement of the "neocolonial" consumer culture that emerged in the South as well as a repudiation of the imperialism or dependence on American aid that created this culture.

Finally, turning to the American perspective, Chapter 7 presents an analysis of the role of image production in American liberal democracy as a distinguishing feature of US imperialism during the Vietnam War. As the USA took control of the conflict, "image making," which Arendt defined as both the production of media spectacles and the creation of data, would play an increasingly significant part in the campaign against the insurgency. While intelligence and high-tech surveillance were employed in order to detect and destroy an unconventional army, the projection of the image of US omnipotence was used to "persuade" the enemy to surrender the war.

This unconventional army would finally be defeated in 1968. In an enormous strategic mistake, the communist leadership launched a general offensive at Tết that allowed the Americans and South Vietnamese to virtually destroy the entire Southern insurgency. This tragic defeat on the battlefield, however, would become a decisive success for the communist forces on the terrain of the spectacle, turning American public opinion against the Vietnam War.

Notes

1 George Donelson Moss, *Vietnam: An American Ordeal* (London: Routledge, 2016), 109.
2 Fredrik Logevall, *Choosing War: The Lost Chance for Peace and the Escalation of War in Vietnam* (Berkeley: University of California Press, 1999), 7.
3 Robert J. Topmiller, *The Lotus Unleashed: The Buddhist Peace Movement in South Vietnam, 1964–1966* (Lexington: University Press of Kentucky, 2006), 1.
4 Nora M. Alter, "Vietnamese theatre of resistance: Thich Nhat Hanh's metaphysical sortie on the margins," in *Imperialism and Theatre*, ed.J. Ellen Gainor (London: Routledge, 1995), 10.
5 Adrian Jaffe and Milton C. Taylor, "A crumbling bastion: flattery and lies won't save Vietnam," *The New Republic* 144:7 (June 19, 1961), 17.
6 Mark Oliver, "The Full Story of the Burning Monk Who Changed the World," All That's Interesting, allthatsinteresting.com/thich-quang-duc-burning-monk. Last accessed July 27, 2019.
7 Topmiller, *The Lotus Unleashed*, 4.

Introduction

8 Quoted in Nguyen Van Canh, *Vietnam Under Communism, 1975–1982* (Stanford, CA: Hoover Institution Press, 1987), 2.
9 Max Hastings, *Vietnam: An Epic History of a Divisive War 1945–1975* (New York: Harper, 2018), 1.
10 Telegram from the Central Intelligence Agency Station in Saigon to the Agency, September 6, 1963.
11 Secret Telegram from Maneli (Saigon) to Spasowski (Warsaw) [Ciphergram No. 11424], September 4, 1963, History and Public Policy Program Digital Archive, AMSZ, Warsaw; 6/77, w-102, t-625, obtained and translated by Margaret Gnoinska. Published in CWIHP Working Paper No. 45.
12 Memorandum for the Record, Saigon, October 21, 1962.
13 Jacqueline Willemetz, *La République du Viêt-Nam et les Ngô-Đình* (Paris: L'Harmattan, 2013), 66.
14 Meeting Minutes, June 14, 1963, Box 03, Folder 04, Douglas Pike Collection: Other Manuscripts – Intra-Ministry Committee for Strategic Hamlets, Vietnam Center and Archive (hereafter VCA), Texas Tech University.
15 Telegram from the Embassy in Vietnam to the Department of State, Saigon, October 7, 1963, 7 p.m.
16 Quoted in Howard Jones, *Death of a Generation: How the Assassinations of Diem and JFK Prolonged the Vietnam War* (New York: Oxford University Press, 2003), 136.
17 Secret Telegram from Maneli (Saigon) to Spasowski (Warsaw) [Ciphergram No. 11424].
18 Mieczysław Maneli, *War of the Vanquished* (New York: Harper & Row, 1971), 145.
19 Ibid., 145–6.
20 Ellen J. Hammer, *A Death in November: America in Vietnam, 1963* (New York: E. P. Dutton, 1987), 230.
21 In articles that appeared in the paper *Xã hội*, founded by future members of the Cần Lao like Trần Quốc Bửu, Nhu advocated a syndicalism based on the cooperative as an anti-capitalist organization. See Dân Sinh, "Tìm hiểu tổ chức hợp-tác-xã" [Understanding the commune-cooperative organization], *Xã Hội*, September 15, 1953, 23.
22 Piero Gheddo, *Catholiques et bouddhistes au Vietnam* (Paris: Groupe des éditions Alsatia, 1970), 154.
23 *Đảng cương Cần lao Nhân vị Cách mạng Đảng* [Principles of the Cần Lao Personalist Revolutionary Party], folder 29361, Phông Phủ Tổng Thống Đệ Nhất Cộng hòa [Files of the Office of the President, First Republic], Vietnam National Archives No. 2.
24 Quoted in John Corwin Donnell, "Politics in South Vietnam: Doctrines and Authority in Conflict" (Ph.D. dissertation, political science, University of California at Berkeley, 1964), 168.

Introduction

25 Paper – The Political Factor in Pacification: A Vietnam Case Study [Draft], 4. VCA. 21470122001 No Date Box 01, Folder 22. Vincent Puritano Collection.
26 Seth Armus, "Bernanos, Mounier, and Catholic Anti-Americanism," in *National Stereotypes in Perspective: Americans in France, Frenchmen in America*, ed. William L. Chew (Amsterdam: Rodopi, 2001), 348.
27 National Security File, Box 200: Vietnam, 9/22/63 - 10/6/63, CIA Reports. Box 2.
28 Francis X. Winters, *The Year of the Hare: America in Vietnam, January 25, 1963–February 15, 1964* (Athens: University of Georgia Press, 1997), 141.
29 Maneli, *War of the Vanquished*, 120.
30 Willemetz, *La République du Viêt-Nam*, 66.
31 Meeting Minutes (#20), Uỷ-Ban Liên-Bộ Đặc-Trách về Ấp Chiến-Lược tại Dinh Gia Long [Intra-Ministry Committee for Strategic Hamlets], 8. VCA. 1820108001 September 7, 1962. Box 01, Folder 08. Douglas Pike Collection: Other Manuscripts – Intra-Ministry Committee for Strategic Hamlets.
32 Topmiller, *The Lotus Unleashed*, 4.
33 Robert Thompson, *Defeating Communist Insurgency: The Lessons of Malaya and Vietnam* (New York: Praeger, 1967), 100.
34 The Editor, "Review & Outlook: The First Lesson of Vietnam," *Wall Street Journal*, November 2, 1983, 1.
35 Nguyen An Ninh, "La France et l'Indochine," *Europe*, 8:31 (July 15, 1925), 262.
36 George C. Herring, *America's Longest War: The United States and Vietnam, 1950–1975*, 4th ed. (Boston, MA: McGraw-Hill, 2002), 59; David Anderson, *Trapped by Success: The Eisenhower Administration and Vietnam, 1953–61* (New York: Columbia University Press, 1991), 121–33.
37 John Prados, "JFK and the Diem Coup: Declassified Records" (November 5, 2003), nsarchive2.gwu.edu/NSAEBB/NSAEBB101/index.htm. For a similar view of Diệm, see Kathryn Statler, *Replacing France: The Origins of American Intervention in Vietnam* (Lexington: The University Press of Kentucky, 2007), 1, 249–50, 282.
38 Neil Sheehan, *A Bright Shining Lie: John Paul Vann and America in Vietnam* (New York: Vintage, 1989), 124. On Thompson, see David French, *The British Way in Counterinsurgency 1945–1967* (Oxford: Oxford University Press, 2011).
39 Sheehan, *A Bright Shining Lie*, 179.
40 Eric M. Bergerud, *The Dynamics of Defeat: The Vietnam War in Hau Nghia Province* (Boulder, CO: Westview, 1991), 35.
41 Sheehan, *A Bright Shining Lie*, 309–11.
42 Jaffe and Taylor, "A crumbling bastion," 17.
43 Seth Jacobs, *Cold War Mandarin: Ngo Dinh Diem and the Origins of America's War in Vietnam, 1950–1963* (Lanham, MD: Rowman & Littlefield Publishers, 2006), 185.

Introduction

44 James M. Carter, *Inventing Vietnam: The United States and State Building, 1954–1968* (New York: Cambridge University Press, 2008), 13.
45 Gregory Daddis, *Westmoreland's War: Reassessing American Strategy in Vietnam* (New York: Oxford University Press, 2014), 77.
46 Ngo Van, *In the Crossfire: Adventures of a Vietnamese Revolutionary* (Oakland, CA: AK Press, 2010), 121.
47 Keith Taylor, "The Vietnamese Civil War of 1955–75 in Historical Perspective," in *Triumph Revisited: Historians Battle for the Vietnam War*, ed. Andrew Wiest and Michael J. Doidge (New York: Routledge, 2010), 17.
48 Quoted in Phạm Hữu Trác, "Chương trình nghiên cứu người Việt hải ngoại và vụ kiện William Joiner Center." http://talawas.org/talaDB/showFile.php?res=2744&rb=0307. Last accessed July 21, 2019.
49 Lonnie M. Long and Gary B. Blackburn, *Unlikely Warriors: The Army Security Agency's Secret War in Vietnam 1961–1973* (Bloomington, IN: iUniverse LLC, 2013), 17.
50 James F. Dunnigan and Albert A. Nofi, *Dirty Little Secrets of the Vietnam War* (New York: Thomas Dunne Books, 1999), 28.
51 Ngo Van, "Revolutionary witness: Vietnam's history of struggle against imperialism," *The International: Journal of the Workers International to Rebuild the Fourth International*, 17 (January 1996).
52 Guy Debord, *Society of the Spectacle*, trans. Ken Knabb (London: Rebel Press, 1983), 27.
53 Gabriel Kolko, *Vietnam: Anatomy of a Peace* (New York: Routledge, 1997), 9.
54 George C. Herring, "'Peoples quite apart:' Americans, South Vietnamese, and the war in Vietnam," *Diplomatic History*, 14:1 (January 1, 1990), 1.
55 See Gary R. Hess, "Historiography: The unending debate. Historians and the Vietnam War," *Diplomatic History*, 18:2 (Spring, 1994), 239–64.
56 Vũ, Tường, "Nation Building and War: The Republican Experience, 1955–75," Symposium: Vietnam War Revisited, September 14, 2018, Washington, DC National Archives Research Center.
57 See Marguerite Higgins, *Our Vietnam Nightmare* (New York: Harper & Row, 1965), 166–7, 173; and Thompson to McGhie, November 27, 1961, FO371/160119, DV1015/258, PRO; Saigon to Foreign Office, August 1, 1962, FO371/166706, DV1015/166, PRO.

1

Colonialism and national culture

> And the whole triumphant history of culture can be understood as the history of the revelation of culture's insufficiency, as a march toward culture's self-abolition. Culture is the locus of the search for lost unity. In the course of this search, culture as a separate sphere is obliged to negate itself.
>
> Guy Debord

In a 1928 speech, Nguyễn An Ninh, one of the most prominent Vietnamese intellectuals and activists during the colonial era, condemned the French administration for its arrogant attempt to "civilize" a population that already "possessed a rich civilization ... when the French were still living in caves."[1] For Ninh, the mission to civilize was, in reality, a project promoted by the colonial government in order to dissolve the "national culture" (văn hoá dân tộc), depriving the Vietnamese people of the "spiritual inheritance" contained in its long national history. Insofar as this national culture constituted the "soul of the nation" itself (văn hoá là tâm hồn của dân tộc), the imposition of French civilization amounted to a systematic attempt to destroy the very identity of the Vietnamese people.[2]

Ninh's efforts to preserve this identity against the imperial mission to civilize correspond to what Frantz Fanon described as the attempt "to secure a national culture ... against the universal condemnation of the colonizer."[3] In response to the "colonialist theory of a precolonial barbarism," used to convince the colonial subject of its lack of civilization, intellectuals throughout the colonial world engaged in the "quest for a national culture prior to the colonial era."[4]

As Fanon cautioned, however, it would be a mistake to identify this national culture with the "mummified fragments" of a fixed or unchanging tradition. Such a reified conception of culture fails to consider the way in which new "modes of thought, language [and] ... modern techniques of communication ... have dialectically reorganized the mind of the people."[5] As such, it "is not enough to reunite with the people in a past where they no longer exist."[6] Rather, the people require a national history that can be appropriated creatively in response to the needs of the present, a present defined by European imperialism. The "colonized intellectual," therefore, must use "the past ... with the intention of opening up the future, of spurring [the people] into action and fostering hope" in the future, a future in which the people recover their national sovereignty.[7] Without a national culture, tied to a past that can open itself to the future, the people exist only as "individuals without an anchorage, without borders, colorless, stateless, rootless, a body of angels."[8]

As Ninh argued, similarly, the national culture of the Vietnamese people should not be conceived as a civilization that is fixed for eternity. Rather, culture, according to Ninh, consists of "all the potential [tiềm năng] that the nation has left ... in the course of its history," a potential that can be actualized by the people in response to its present condition. The national culture, therefore, is not an unchanging tradition. Rather, it is "eternal" only insofar as it can be appropriated continually as a living tradition by those who inherit it in the present: "To speak of the eternity [sự trường tồn] of a ... culture ... is to speak of the vitality of a people ... And the Vietnamese people have had the vitality to create such a culture."[9]

Civilization and culture

But if the civilizing mission, according to Ninh, was an attempt to subjugate the Vietnamese people by erasing the national history, this history, nevertheless, was a product of European imperialism. As Dương Quảng Hàm pointed out in a pedagogical text that was widely circulated in colonial schools, the Vietnamese people did not possess a national history prior to the introduction of French civilization:

> [N]ational history must be considered among the most important of subjects taught in ... school. This pedagogical truth, so evident all on its own, was nevertheless unknown to Annamites before the arrival of the French. In the traditional Annamite curriculum, in fact, pupils only study the Chinese chronicles: the history of Annam was not mentioned ...[10]

Colonialism and national culture

In spite of its self-evidence, then, the existence of an eternal Vietnamese culture was completely unknown to Annamites prior to the colonial period. Indeed, as Ninh admitted in an earlier speech, delivered in 1923, the very concept of culture could not be conveyed in the "Annamite language," a language that, at the time, possessed no equivalent to the word *culture* in French. In order to speak, therefore, of a Vietnamese culture, Ninh, despite rejecting the claim that the French possessed a superior civilization, was compelled to communicate in the more civilized language of the colonizer:

> I must promise you that it is not for me a matter of pride that I speak with Annamites in French. The Annamite language is still so backward and is far from the level of European languages, of the languages of East Asia. I have tried … to translate into Annamite the word culture and have not succeeded in finding a word … The words *cầm kỳ thi họa* gives us an idea of culture, but an inadequate idea and one at risk of erroneous interpretation. *Cầm* is music, *kỳ* intellectual speculation, *thi* is literature, and *họa*, painting. We would be forced into adopting the composite word *chúng đọc học thức*. Those who can find the correct word might be kind enough to show me forbearance on this previous point.[11]

If the Vietnamese, therefore, had already developed a civilization when the French were living in caves, their language, nevertheless, compared with that of the colonizer, was "still so backwards," insofar as it had not yet developed an expression for *culture*.

The concept of culture, however, which Ninh perceived as the sign of a superior civilization, was a relatively recent invention in the languages spoken in Europe. According to Theodor Adorno, the use of the word "culture" to refer to "so many things lacking a common denominator … such as philosophy … religion, science and art … conduct and mores … and finally … the objective spirit of an age … is scarcely older than Kant." Derived from the Latin *cultura*, which denoted the cultivation of land, the word "culture," beginning in the eighteenth century, would be used "to connote the idea of *niveau* and cultivation … in contrast to the sphere of entertainment."[12] In German, the term *Kultur* came to refer to both the education (or *Bildung*) of the individual, as well as to a society's state of development, a usage that would later inform the meaning of "culture" in English and French.[13]

In the East Asian languages, on the other hand, "the modern notion *wenhua* or culture resulted from the recent history of East-West encounter." According to Lydia Liu, the word *wenhua* was first employed as a translation for "culture" in the early twentieth century, when Chinese intellectuals confronted the threat of European imperialism. In East Asia, therefore, the concept of culture emerged "as a privileged sphere of discourse in a time of colonialist ... expansion."[14]

Prior to this period, the word *wen* – the first character of the compound *wenhua* or "culture" – referred to the cultivated activities of the Confucian elite. *Wen* was used to describe scholar-officials engaged in "civil" administration, as opposed to "military" (*wu*) affairs. Whereas *wen*, as Tze-Ki Hon describes, referred "to a gradual process of education, persuasion, and negotiation that ends in consensus," *wu* "suggest[ed] the direct control of the rulers without any regard for ... the ruled." The word *wen*, therefore, originally denoted rulership through "civil" techniques of control, rather than "coercion based on brute force."[15] Thus, the older usage of *wen* implies an intrinsic connection between the cultural and political spheres, confirming Adorno's assertion that: "Whoever speaks of culture speaks of administration as well."[16]

Combined with the character *hua* (*hoá* in Vietnamese), connoting "the transformation of human behavior," *wenhua* would be used in the twentieth century to refer to the "civil process of transformation whereby ... disparate individuals become a self-conscious group."[17] In the work of Chinese nationalist scholars such as Liu Yizheng, *wenhua* was used to develop a conception of "Chinese culture" as a system that is "open to change ... yet remain[ing] constant." To borrow Fanon's definition of "national culture," Chinese intellectuals, confronting the threat of Western imperialism, rediscovered a national past "with the intention of opening up the future."[18]

In the Vietnamese context, *wenhua* would be adapted in the Vietnamese language in the 1920s and 1930s as *văn hoá*, supplanting Ninh's neologism, *chúng đọc học thức*, as the common expression for "culture." Ninh's unsuccessful attempt to devise a translation for culture, however, remains instructive in the way that it underscores the discrepancy between the modern conception of culture and its counterparts within Vietnamese "civilization." In the passage quoted above, Ninh at first considers, as a translation for *culture* in French, the Sino-Vietnamese expression *cầm kỳ thi họa*, which refers to the "four refined arts" or "leisure time pleasures" of the Confucian literati.[19] This expression, however, is inadequate precisely insofar as these arts are associated with the *civilization* of the scholar-elite, as opposed to a national culture belonging to the Vietnamese people in general. In order to avoid this "erroneous interpretation," therefore, Ninh proposes *chúng đọc học thức* ("reading, studying and thinking together"). Combining a series of common Vietnamese terms, the new expression, as Judith Henchy has noted, connotes a "national pedagogical project," as opposed to an individual process of self-cultivation, separating a group of Sinicized scholar-elite from the commoners, ruled by techniques of "civility" (*văn*).[20]

Colonialism, surveillance and media

During the early colonial era, this older model of civility was gradually eroded by the colonial state in its imperial mission to civilize Vietnamese civilization through the introduction of new forms of modern mass media. By 1918, the French had completely abolished the Confucian examinations through which scholar-officials were recruited to serve in the civil administration of the imperial court. "When the French first arrived ... Confucianism [*nho học*]," as the South Vietnamese philosopher Nguyễn Văn Trung described, "embodied the anti-French spirit of the literati, so they opposed Confucianism, advocated its abolition, because the Chinese script [*chữ nho*] and Confucianism ... were viewed as ... harmful to the policy ... of assimilation."[21] In their place, a system of colonial schools was established in which French and *quốc ngữ*, the Romanized vernacular script developed by Jesuit priests in the seventeenth century, would replace instruction in Chinese characters and the interpretation of classical texts. According to Benedict Anderson, these language policies were "consciously promoted to break ... links with China ... and ... also with the indigenous past ... by making dynastic records and ancient literatures inaccessible to a new generation of colonized Vietnamese."[22] "Initially, the French used the *quốc ngữ* as a weapon of spiritual invasion [*xâm lược tinh thần*], to isolate the people from the ... tradition associated with Confucianism" (*nho học*).[23]

During the same period, the establishment of an indigenous press in the vernacular script was sponsored by the colonial secret police as a means of monitoring the attitudes and activities of organizations opposed to the French.[24] As Louis Marty, the head of the *Sûreté*, explained in a memo, this plan would largely succeed in its goal of creating a modern mass media in the Vietnamese language in order to serve as an instrument of surveillance for the colonial state. Before World War I, "secret societies" that opposed the colonial government had communicated through banners and seals emblazoned with anti-colonial slogans inscribed in Chinese. By 1918, these societies had been replaced by a "no longer secret" "native opposition," "expressed through newspapers written in French and Romanized script."[25]

This new media, however, not only provided a means of publicizing the private political views of the Vietnamese people, it also *produced* the very "public opinion" (*công luận* or *dư luận*) that this media allowed the secret police to surveil.[26] As Anderson noted, "government publication[s] ... [in] *quoc ngu* ... significantly accelerated the spread of this European-invented script, unintentionally helping to turn it ... into the popular medium for the expression of Vietnamese cultural (and national) solidarity."[27] As a vernacular script, this popular medium (which the French had promoted in order to sever the ties between the elite and its traditional modes of civility) was much easier to master than the classical system of characters. By "simplify[ing] the problems of mass education," the *quốc ngữ*, according to David Marr, helped to "bring elite and popular experiences ... together," facilitating its use not only as a means of self-cultivation but also for pursuing a "national pedagogical project."[28] The media, then, which had been originally established in order to "kill the patriotism" of the Confucian elite,[29] would become a means of "saving the nation through a path of culture" (*cứu nước bằng đường lối văn hóa*), promoting "nationalism through language" (*chủ nghĩa quốc gia bằng ngôn ngữ*).[30]

This development was observed with apprehension by the secret police. The creation of a modern indigenous media had not only exposed the old secret societies to the surveillance of the colonial state, it had also begun to unite the disparate groups of "feudal" elite into a broader coalition against the colonial state:

> Annamite society was, before the war, a handful of individuals from which emerged several feudal families. I indicated that these times had passed and that new groupings have been formed ... the most important groups having a newspaper. The new development, considerable, to which I draw your attention, is that these groups, competitors as late as last year, are tending to jam together closely to make up a tightly-knit opposition.[31]

During the colonial era, therefore, a modern sphere of *publicity* was established in part as a technique of *surveillance*, imposed as a means of controlling the very national culture whose condition it also created. This indigenous media – which would constitute, as Anderson famously called it, the "imagined community" of the Vietnamese nation – was originally intended to serve as an instrument to divide and conquer the very national culture it would help to imagine.[32]

Colonialism and national culture

Imprinting popular sovereignty

In the 1920s and 1930s, this national culture, promoted by the colonial state in order to separate the colonial subject from its own civilized past, would serve to create a new Vietnamese "people" (*dân tộc*) by providing the latter with a national history, previously "unknown to the Annamites." This new history was based upon categories derived from Western historiography. Rejecting the traditional view of the state, which emphasized the personal relationship between ruler and subject (*vua-tôi*), historians adopted a modern conception of sovereignty as the right of a national people over the territory that it historically occupied.

Reworking an older imperial discourse of civility, which the French had tried to erase by creating a new indigenous media culture, Vietnamese writers began to refer to the people as *dân*, a term which originally denoted "children of the ruler." In the new national histories written in the vernacular script, the word was first used to "imply a common ethnic identity. The next step," as David Marr describes, "was to give *dân* the meaning 'citizens of the modern state.'"[33] The "people," then, who had appeared in the dynastic records (which had increasingly become inaccessible) only as subjects of the sovereign, would emerge within the new national history as the very foundation of sovereignty itself, a "sovereignty of the people" (*dân quyền*).[34] "Without the people (*nhân dân*)," as the reformist leader Phan Bội Châu observed, "there would be no territory (*đất đai*), [thus] sovereignty (*chủ quyền*) could not be established."[35]

In the literature of the period, moreover, the individuals forming this new sovereign people began to refer to themselves using a new first-person singular: the *tôi*. Derived from the "ruler-subject" relation (*vua-tôi*), the *tôi*, as Marr describes, was "upgraded," politically, during the colonial era, and used to refer to a self that existed independently of its relationship of subordination to the emperor and the imperial court. The *tôi*, then, no longer denoted a subject of the king, but was used instead to signify something more closely resembling what Michel Foucault called the "sovereign subject" or the "enslaved sovereign,"[36] an autonomous individual subordinated to its own moral conscience (to its "tribunal of the heart" (*tòa án lương tâm*), to borrow an expression used by writers during the 1920s and 1930s).[37]

Adopting the modern conception of a sovereign national subject, Vietnamese writers, working in the popular medium of vernacular print, appropriated the past in light of the colonial present as a long historical prelude to the contemporary anti-colonial struggle. Events recorded in dynastic accounts memorializing the deeds of ancient heroes and sovereigns were rewritten as the 2,000-year history of a people united in an ongoing struggle to defend its national sovereignty against all foreign invaders (*truyền thống anh hùng chống ngoại xâm*).[38]

One of the most influential examples of this wholesale revision of the indigenous past was the new nationalist reading of "The Proclamation of the Pacification of the Marauding Ngô" (*Bình ngô đại cáo*), a work that Phạm Văn Đồng described as "the great immortal song of our people" (*khúc ca hùng tráng bất hủ của dân tộc ta*).[39] The text was written by the scholar Nguyễn Trãi for the emperor Lê Lợi, following his victory in 1428 against an occupying army dispatched by the Ming Dynasty.[40] During the colonial era, the "Proclamation" would come to be seen as a Vietnamese "declaration of independence" (*tuyên bố độc lập*), affirming the cultural identity and national sovereignty of the Vietnamese people against Chinese imperialism.[41] The "Proclamation" was "intended as a declaration of independence for the Vietnamese people and as an affirmation of viability of a separate national culture."[42]

In the text itself, however, the "sovereignty" – or "imperial rule" (*đế*) – that Lê Lợi proclaims is not that of a nation-state (*quốc gia*) defined by a unique ethnic identity.[43] This sovereignty, in other words, is not asserted on the basis of a *cultural* difference, separating the Vietnamese people from the empire seeking to dominate it. The text, therefore, does not declare a "popular sovereignty" (*dân quyền*), reflecting the will of an ethnic or national people, a *dân tộc*. Instead of this modern expression, the text refers to *ngã dân*, a term that, according to Liam C. Kelley, "literally means 'my people' … and is thus similar to a European absolute monarch's view of 'my subjects.'"[44] In the text, Lê Lợi is speaking, therefore, not as a representative of a sovereign national people, but as their imperial ruler. This gesture is consistent with the description of the role of the king in official court chronicles: "Heaven created the people and gave them a king in order to guide them, not to serve them."[45]

Furthermore, the text does not invoke a separate and unique Vietnamese "culture" (*văn hóa*), but refers only to individual "customs" (*phong tục*). While customs, as the "Proclamation" asserts, distinguish the territories (or "mountains and rivers") ruled by the two sovereign "kingdoms" or "courts" (*quốc*) ("Vietnam" and "China"), these differences, nevertheless, do not imply a lack of *civilization*: "Our kingdom of Đại Việt is truly a domain of civility [*văn hiến chi bang*]. Just as its territorial areas are distinct, so are the customs of the South and North also different."[46]

Colonialism and national culture

Thus, the sovereignty that Lê Lợi declares is based not on *cultural difference* but on a shared *civilization*, one that exists, so the text asserts, in both northern and southern domains of civility, in spite of the difference in custom between their imperial subjects. In proclaiming the sovereignty of his kingdom, therefore, Lê Lợi does not appeal to the culture created by an indigenous people during the course of its national history. Instead, he evokes a legitimate record of dynastic succession, in order to indicate that his subjects, while they differ in custom from their counterparts in the North, are ruled by a separate but equally civilized court in the South: "It was the Triệu, the Đinh, the Lý and Trần, who in succession built this kingdom [*quốc*]. Even as the Han, the Tang, the Sung and Yuan, each was sovereign [*đế*] in its own domain."⁴⁷

During the early twentieth century, such precolonial texts as the "Proclamation" would be "reinterpreted," as Kelley has argued, from the perspective of the colonial situation, "in order to give people in the present hope for the future."⁴⁸ To borrow Fanon's description of national culture, Vietnamese intellectuals used "the past ... with the intention of opening up the future, of spurring [the people] into action and fostering hope." As Nguyễn Văn Trung pointed out, this hope was identified with the development of the new vernacular media, which the French had employed in order to erase Vietnamese civilization: "Vietnamese ... in a situation in which the nation had been lost, could look to ... the [new system of] writing as a means of ... constructing a future for the people [*xây dựng tương lai dân tộc*] through language and culture." At "the beginning" of the colonial era, then, "patriots opposed [the *quốc ngữ*] because it was used by the colonialists as an instrument of spiritual invasion ... but later we appropriated it, turning it into a tool for inciting patriotism, for cultural education directed especially at the ordinary people" (*tầng lớp bình dân*).⁴⁹

This process of revision would eventually produce what William Turley described as a national "image of heroic resistance to foreign rule," and the "myth of indomitability in the face of superior force."⁵⁰ As an image inspiring hope for the future, this myth of the national past as a perennial war of anti-imperialism, waged by a people whose culture had existed for thousands of years, was largely a projection of the colonial present. As Pierre Asselin has argued:

> The uprisings that took place during the millennium of Chinese domination ... were typically localized ... they were not nationwide resistance efforts fueled by nationalistic ... sentiment. ... The underlying claim that

Vietnamese developed through these resistance efforts ... an acute sense of nationalism ... early in their history is simply untrue. Average Vietnamese at the time were unable to even fathom the meaning of "nation," as their world rarely extended beyond their native villages.⁵¹

In the early twentieth century, however, the nation, which the Vietnamese had previously been unable to fathom, and whose history was formerly "unknown to the Annamites," would be "imprinted" into the minds of the Vietnamese people. "[P]eople," as the reformist intellectual Hoàng Đạo Thành argued, "should be made to learn the nation's literature, and its history":

> [F]or this is how we can get the word, "nation" [quốc gia], imprinted [ấn] in each person's brain. It must be made firm there so that it ... cannot come loose. Thereupon they will view the nation's territory as their own property, and will treat their countrymen as compatriots.⁵²

This process of imprinting the nation was made possible by the creation of a new vernacular media, established by the colonial government in order to monitor public opinion. As Louis Marty observed, it was this development that allowed the Vietnamese to transcend the localized forms of resistance to which they were limited before the establishment of an indigenous press as a technique of surveillance. This press would transform "Annamite society" from a "handful of individuals from ... feudal families" into "a tightly-knit opposition," capable of imagining itself and its national history through the popular medium of print.⁵³ By allowing the Vietnamese to imagine their "countrymen as compatriots," sharing a national culture and history, this print media would create the conditions for the rise of a sovereign national people, a *dân tộc* that had never existed before.

In Vietnam, therefore, the introduction of new "modes of thought, language [and] ... modern techniques of communication" did not simply serve – to recall Fanon's account of national culture – as something that "dialectically reorganized the mind of the people."⁵⁴ Rather, *the people as such* were created as an unintended effect of the new forms of media used to disseminate a national culture, a culture that, according to Ninh, constituted the "soul of the people" as such. In the words of Nguyễn Văn Trung, "patriots took the *quốc ngữ* out of the hands of the colonialists, turning it into a weapon to inspire the national soul [*lòng yêu nước*] [and] to resist the French."⁵⁵ As a result, the "fate of the people [*dân tộc*] became connected to ... great works" of literature. "So long as the great work remains, so do the people" (*Tác phẩm tuyệt hảo còn, dân tộc vẫn còn*).⁵⁶ Insofar as the media that created the national culture was established by the colonial state as a form of mass observation, this soul of the nation, to borrow Foucault's description of the Enlightenment notion of man, was produced as the "correlative of a certain technology of power." "The soul is the effect and instrument of a political anatomy."⁵⁷

National culture and war

By the end of the colonial era, the national culture that had emerged as an unintended effect of the mission to civilize was firmly imprinted in the minds of a majority of the educated elite in Vietnam. This culture is officially recognized in the constitutions adopted by the two Vietnamese states that emerged in the wake of the Geneva Accords in 1954, which divided the nation at the seventeenth parallel. In the Constitution of the Democratic Republic of Vietnam, the culture that had been created by a national history that was previously "unknown to Annamites" is invoked as the historical justification for proclaiming a modern national sovereignty: "In the course of their millennia-old history, the Vietnamese people, working … creatively … to construct and defend their country, have forged a unified national tradition [*truyền thống đoàn kết … của dân tộc*] … that has created Vietnamese culture [*văn hiến*]."⁵⁸ Similarly, in the constitution of the Republic of Vietnam (RVN), the myth of a 2,000-year national history, fabricated during the colonial period for the purpose of inspiring hope for the future, is repeated in the following fashion: The "glorious and eternal future of the Vietnamese nation and people [*Quốc gia và Dân tộc Việt Nam*] … has been guaranteed by the heroic history of our ancestors' struggle."⁵⁹ In the two constitutions, therefore, the legitimacy of the postcolonial state is founded upon the assertion that it fulfills the hope for the future, projected into the precolonial past, in the myth of a people united in its ancient anti-imperialist struggle.

During the Vietnam War, the strategy employed by the communist forces involved the mass dissemination of a vernacular media, originally created as a tool of surveillance, in order to imprint the idea of the nation on the Vietnamese masses. Insofar as the process of imprinting was intended to serve as a means of producing the people as such, this strategy paradoxically amounted to an attempt by the postcolonial state to create the very popular sovereignty upon which it is founded. In this strategy, then, the Vietnamese people appear as both the subject and object of the war. The legitimacy of the state is based on the 2,000-year history of a national culture, which the state itself would impose on the population as a means of creating the national people that constitutes its authority.

In the people's war waged by the communist forces, this cultural struggle was combined with a broader plan for social and economic development, which included the construction of schools and public works programs and the formation of local militias. For the communist forces, the war was not simply an armed insurrection employing unconventional tactics of violence and terror. Rather, the war would also be waged as a social and cultural revolution, mobilizing the masses in the creation of new social and political structures, structures that, in turn, would serve to sustain the insurgency.

The armed struggle was conceived as one component within an integral war waged on a series of interconnected fronts. These included what Hồ Chí Minh called the "cultural front" (*mặt trận văn hoá*), a battlefield in which "the pen is a sharp weapon, the newspaper a revolutionary instrument" ("*cái bút là vũ khí sắc bén, bài báo là tờ hịch cách mạng*").[60] The media, then, as a cultural weapon, would be used to create a "culture of the masses" (*văn hóa quần chúng*): Our "way of speaking ... [writing] newspapers ... all have to conform to this principle: everything from out of the masses" (*từ trong quần chúng ra*)."[61] Derived from the masses themselves, this popular culture would serve to empower the Vietnamese people as a political subject. The "culture of the masses" would be deployed by the Party as a means of molding the masses to serve as an instrument and effect of a political power. Hồ Chí Minh, therefore, called for the "promotion of cultural work in order to train a new people [*đào tạo con người mới*] ... for the national war of resistance."[62] As both a means of empowering the people and a political instrument of the state, imposed upon the population, this "culture for the masses" could be characterized in Foucaultian terms as a technique of "subjectivization."

On the cultural front, then, the "people's war" practiced by the insurgency constituted a form of governmentality that was productive of the very "people" the Party sought to both politically manage and mobilize. As the Dương Thu Hương describes in *Novel without a Name*, this process was one in which the political image of the Vietnamese nation and its glorious national history were embedded in individual memory as a technique of internal repression. Through state propaganda and the staging of political spectacles, the glorious image of the Vietnamese Revolution would be imprinted upon the mind as a form of surveillance, creating a sense of group solidarity, constitutive of a political subject. This solidarity was based on a shared sense of guilt, created by an internalized image

Colonialism and national culture

of the nation, an image that served to control individuals through their own self-supervision, while transforming them into historical subjects, engaged in a glorious national struggle:

> We were drawn toward a great mission, a blinding glory (*vinh quang sáng chói*). The war was not simply a struggle against foreign invaders (*cuộc chiến đấu chống quân xâm lược*). Vietnam had been chosen by history (*đã được lịch sử chọn lựa*) ... As we plunged deeper into the war, the memory of the day we enlisted sank deeper [into our minds]. The more we were tortured by the consciousness of our appalling indifference, the more searing the memory ... We had renounced everything for glory. It was this guilt that bound us to one another ... tightly ...[63]

This technique of governmentality, in which the spectacle of political power is imposed on the masses as an internalized form of surveillance, corresponds to Foucault's account of "the Napoleonic character." In this account, Napoleon appears as a transitional historical figure, combining the spectacular grandeur of the monarchical state with the more mundane techniques of panopticism, which emerged in the era of industrial capitalism. In Foucault's terms, this sovereign figure constitutes:

> the point of junction of the monarchical, ritual exercise of sovereignty and the ... permanent exercise of indefinite discipline. He is the individual who looms over everything with a single gaze which no detail, however minute, can escape ... As a monarch who is at one and the same time a usurper of the ancient throne and the organizer of the new state ... [combining] the necessarily spectacular manifestations of power ... [and] the daily exercise of surveillance, in a panopticism in which the vigilance of intersecting gazes was soon to render useless both the eagle and the sun.[64]

In his account of the cult of personality employed by the Communist Party, the Vietnamese Marxist philosopher, Trần Đức Thảo, paints a strikingly similar portrait of Hồ Chí Minh. Like the Napoleonic character, Hồ was a paradoxical figure who combined the modern ideal of democracy with the "spectacular manifestations of power" associated with the sovereignty of the premodern state. According to Thảo, Hồ's modest demeanor and style did not simply imply a democratic rejection of the ostentatious display of authority, which had been the prerogative of the feudal nobility. On the contrary, Hồ's self-effacing appearance was, in reality, a "self-glorifying publicity" (*sự công khai tự tôn vinh mình*), a "well-crafted work of art [*một công trình nghệ thuật*] ... staged in order to elevate 'Uncle [Hồ]' as an exalted, majestic leader." This image was produced by an elaborate "propaganda machine" (*bộ máy tuyên truyền*), operated by specialists in the Party engaged on the cultural front, producing poetry, proverbs and morality tales to be attributed to the president. Every detail of Hồ's public persona "bore the stamp of a sophisticated psychological method [*phương pháp tâm lý*] for cultivating a leader."[65]

Hồ's humble appearance, therefore, was not a spontaneous sign of humility, one that was opposed to the "ritual exercise of sovereignty." Rather, his popular style was carefully calculated to produce the impression of power, and precisely over the people before whom he appeared to humble himself: "This manner of dressing in order to deliberately create a 'popular' [image] among politicians, or among the people, was a technique for commanding the highest respect" (*một cách tự tôn rất cao siêu*). Hồ's populism, therefore, was an image intended precisely to set him apart from the people, in order to dominate them in the name of their own popular sovereignty: "All of the gestures ... in each picture ... had been carefully researched, meticulously staged from the beginning [*dàn dựng tỉ mỉ từ trước*], so that his image [*hình ảnh*] would not be submerged by the ordinary people around him!"[66]

Like the spectacular manifestations of sovereignty deployed by the Napoleonic regime, Hồ's popular image was the instrument of an absolute power exercised in the name of the people. As the cultivated appearance of a sovereign portraying himself as a peasant (a "'king' [*ông vua*] ... with the ambition of becoming a [modern] revolutionary"), Hồ's "proletarian ... aura" (*hào quang ... vô sản*) was an image imposed by a democratic dictatorship in which the proletariat is dominated by its own representation:

> [H]is common sandals ... the way he would leave a few buttons open on his shirt ... how he would hold his burning cigarette ... these were ways of displaying that he had been chosen. These details created an ... aura of the proletarian revolution [*hào quang của cách mạng vô sản*]! His cheap, ordinary looking pith helmet, made of shoddy fabric, was precisely his crown![67]

In the cult of personality, through which Hồ established himself as a proletarian king, a "self-glorifying publicity," borrowed from an older imperial statecraft, was projected by a modern propaganda machine as a means of imposing a panoptic surveillance on the population at large. The Party, as Thảo explains:

> wanted to elevate 'Uncle [Ho],' to make him stand out ... just like an eagle, flying above the top of Thái Sơn ... looking down at the political landscape below with suspicious, contemptuous eyes, with the most exact gaze, pen-

etrating the mind of each individual ... in order to distinguish supporters and potential enemies ...⁶⁸

Like the Napoleonic character, then, Hồ appears as a figure combining the "spectacular manifestations of power ... [and] the daily exercise of surveillance," serving as the image of an absolute sovereign who "looms over everything with a single gaze which no detail ... can escape."

In the *Society of the Spectacle*, Debord refers to this technique of state power as the "concentrated spectacle," a form of domination that "belongs essentially to bureaucratic capitalism." The technique entails the projection of an "imposed image of the good," embodied in a single individual who, elevated to the status of an "absolute star" with whom "[e]veryone must magically identify," functions as an internalized form of repression.⁶⁹ In North Vietnam, this function was fulfilled by the figure of Hồ Chí Minh: "everything worthy, everything good, everything that has value ... must belong to "Uncle [Hồ],' to the Party."⁷⁰ By "giv[ing] an acceptable meaning to ... absolute exploitation," this absolute celebrity serves as "the guarantee of totalitarian cohesion." In Debord's analysis, then, the cult of personality is the spectacle deployed by a totalitarian state to impose a universal surveillance: "Wherever the concentrated spectacle rules, so does the police."⁷¹

Democracy, discipline and the second Southward Advance

The Republic of Vietnam was established in 1955 by its first president, Ngô Đình Diệm, in a fraudulent referendum that removed the puppet emperor Bảo Đại from his position as head of the State of Vietnam.⁷² Contrary to what many have argued, Diệm's presidency was not engineered by the American government.⁷³ Nor was he "unknown even in Vietnam" before his purportedly sudden appearance on the political scene.⁷⁴ Rather, he was recognized by both Bảo Đại and Hồ Chí Minh as a capable and talented leader. Diệm, therefore, as Edward Miller argues, had neither been "plucked from obscurity nor installed in office by the United States."⁷⁵

While Diệm, moreover, during his exile in the early 1950s, succeeded in establishing contact with prominent American leaders, his brother, Ngô Đình Nhu, would become an important political figure in the South. Contrary to the pervasive image of the Vietnamese leader as "a proto-Fascist and mentally unstable drug addict,"⁷⁶ a "Vietnamese Rasputin,"⁷⁷ who had "something frightening in his face, an air of Machiavellian mystery and cynical vanity, wicked intelligence and calculated malice,"[78] Nhu had lived an ascetic existence prior to beginning his political career.[79] Trained at the prestigious École Nationale des Chartes, Nhu, who was the school's first Annamite student, graduated third in his class.[80] While working as an archivist in Hà Nội, he was evaluated by Paul Boudet, director of the Indochinese Archives and Libraries Department, as "a young civil servant of the highest quality, combining the virtues of resoluteness and straightforwardness with a wide culture and impeccable professional abilities."[81] In the 1950s, Nhu, inspired by the writings of French syndicalist thinkers, would become one of the most effective political organizers in the country, establishing the Cần Lao Party, which would play a significant role in Diệm's ascendance to power.[82] As the British correspondent Michael Field recalled, Nhu "was undoubtedly one of the most astute Vietnamese politicians of his generation. It was probably Ngo Dinh Nhu who created the situation in 1954 in which his elder brother was the most obvious candidate for the premiership."[83]

Moreover, in spite of its undemocratic beginnings, Diệm's "Personalist" Republic, according to the US Ambassador Frederick Nolting, was not a fascist dictatorship. Rather, it was a government that employed authoritarian measures in an effort to create the conditions for a modern democracy: "I never felt that [Diệm] wanted to maintain an autocracy." He "was dedicated to the long range aim of a self-representative … democratic system," while recognizing that "you had to build the infrastructure of democracy before … [democracy] would mean anything … and strangely enough, I think his brother Nhu was even more anxious to introduce self-government measures, although he had the reputation of being just the reverse."[84]

Dedicated to the long-range goal of democracy, Diệm, then, in the early part of his presidency, proposed a program of "national discipline" (kỷ luật quốc gia) as a means of building the infrastructure for a representative government. At a National Assembly meeting in 1957, Diệm defined this "disciplined national freedom" (kỷ luật quốc gia tự do ưng thuận) as a self-imposed form of civic surveillance:

> [T]he characteristic of civilized nations is the establishment of a discipline by themselves which they observe freely and loyally. If the authorities must intervene each moment to watch the conduct of each one and punish the infringements of the rules … where would freedom be? There is only one way of avoiding that intervention: each one must accept this discipline and see to it that his compatriots do the same. … If to that sense of discipline we add a sense of sacrifice … then I can assure you that although we are at

Colonialism and national culture

present a backward country ruined by a prolonged war, we can occupy in ... short time a good place among the Asian countries in the competition for economic development.[85]

For Diệm, then, "national discipline," as a form of surveillance that is internalized by the masses ("each one must accept this discipline" and observe their own conduct), was not merely a negative technique of repression. Rather, it was a constitutive condition of both political freedom and economic development, which in "civilized nations" is based on a self-imposed vigilance, observed "freely and loyally" by each individual.

The program of national discipline to establish a Western-style democracy would be accompanied by the creation of what Nhu described as a "'mixed economy,' i.e., partly state and partly private control." This economy, as Nhu explained to US officials in the 1950s, would constitute a "third way" between "communism ... [and] western liberal capitalism" (adding, however, that the latter "doctrine was associate[d]" in the developing world "with colonialism"). Just as national discipline, then, would be employed by the state to achieve the "long range aim of a self-representative ... democratic system," so, in the plan for constructing a "mixed economy," a "system of state control" would be used to develop a Western-style liberal economy based on free private enterprise.[86]

In this program to develop the nation, the internal connection that the Ngos emphasized between freedom and discipline, economic liberalism and centralized planning would appear to conform to Foucault's characterization of the "dark side" of the European Enlightenment and the parliamentary state. In the eighteenth and nineteenth centuries, the establishment of a popular sovereignty, a "representative regime" in which "the will of all of ... form[s] the fundamental authority of sovereignty" was supported by the "development of ... disciplinary mechanisms."[87] The rise of the constitutional state, based on the sovereign will of the people, was tied to the emergence of a "panoptic machine," deployed in the prison, the school and the factory, subjecting the masses to a universal surveillance. The democratic expansion of the right to representation was dependent, therefore, upon a "despotic" technique of mass visibility, affording a "single individual" an "instantaneous view of a great multitude."[88] The "'Enlightenment', which discovered the liberties, also invented the disciplines."[89]

For Diệm, similarly, discipline was not simply a technique of repression that is employed exclusively by authoritarian states. Rather, the connection between the liberties and disciplines is also inherent in liberal democracy:

> [D]iscipline is necessary [not] only in planned economies. Even in countries believing in liberalism, this discipline is indispensable, because in the present state of affairs all economic activity is subject to the exigencies of technique which is imposed upon each of us and prevents him from acting too independently.[90]

For Diệm, then, the representative form of the "civilized" state, inherited from the European Enlightenment, is not a democracy that is devoid of all despotism. Rather, this form of democracy presupposes a "disciplined freedom" in which the sovereignty of the people is based upon their subjection to a disciplinary technique of mass observation.

This paradoxical notion of constitutional government, as founded on a national people, subjectivized by a state that embodies its popular sovereignty, was widely dismissed by critics of the regime as "diemocracy," as authoritarian rule disguised as democracy. For many observers, as Catton points out, the Republic's attempts to mobilize the Vietnamese masses, "in an imitation of the 'Front' strategy employed by the Communists," "were more reminiscent of politics in a people's republic than a democracy; they were creations of the state rather than reflections of the popular will."[91] Meanwhile, Nhu's attempt to apply the techniques of socialist planning in order to create a Western-style liberal economy sparked rumors that his clandestine political party, the Cần Lao, "was trying to monopolize all business and industry in the country."[92]

But if the "diemocracy" of the early Republic was not simply a cover for authoritarian rule, but a political program "dedicated to the long-range aim" of a representative government, the program, nevertheless, would appear to imply what Dipesh Chakrabarty has called a "historicist" denial of the modernity of non-Western peoples. Thus, while the Ngos, as Philip Catton has noted, extolled the egalitarian virtues of the Vietnamese peasantry, they also "believed that it would take time before they could ... assume the responsibilities of citizenship."[93] But in that case, the program to establish an infrastructure for a Western-style democracy would appear to entail a "recommendation to the colonized to wait," repeating the familiar imperialist gesture of consigning the colonized to an "imaginary waiting room of history."[94]

This Western ideal of modernity, defined by a doctrine of "western liberal capitalism ... associate[d] ... with colonialism," and by an enlightened form of democracy, based on the modern apparatus of discipline, is one that Diệm and his brother, however, would come to repudiate. During the course of the war, the Ngos, under the pressure of both the insurgency and US imperialism, would come to espouse a more radical notion of democratic self-government and economic organization, one that was more closely aligned with the political philosophy proclaimed as the Republic's ideological basis. By the 1960s, the Ngos would view the establishment of a constitutional government, "adopting institutions of parliamentary democracy from [Western] liberal states" as only a preliminary stage in a broader Personalist revolution. The transformation in the political superstructure, effected in the 1955 Referendum, would be accompanied by a "second revolution, building a genuine democracy in the infrastructure. This was the Strategic Hamlet Program ... also known as the rural revolution."[95]

This program entailed a strategy similar to the one employed by the insurgency in the South, a strategy that Catton describes as "an anti-Communist version of a 'people's war,' based on a militarily and politically mobilized population."[96] Like the communist program of social revolution, the counterinsurgency campaign would combine tactics of irregular warfare with the creation of a new social and political order, pursuing a policy of pacification through social and economic development. The strategy, then, was not "just a security measure against the VC [Viet Cong]; it was the vehicle for a full-scale political and social revolution."[97]

Just as the war, moreover, was portrayed by the communists as a continuation of the 2,000-year "struggle of the Vietnamese people against foreign invaders" (chiến đấu chống quân xâm lược), so the counterinsurgency program would be set "within a panoramic vision of the nation's historical development."[98] This vision, however, would underline an aspect of the national history, invented during the colonial era, that was deemphasized in the communist account of the latter: the nam tiến or the "Southward Advance."[99]

In the early twentieth century, writers who were reworking the precolonial past from the perspective of the colonial present began to conceive of the history of the Vietnamese people in terms of two interrelated phenomena. According to Li Tana, historians "suggested that all Vietnamese history before the nineteenth century can be summed up in two phrases: Bắc cự (resistance to the North, meaning China) and Nam tiến (expansion to the South). If Bắc cự aimed at insuring Vietnamese survival in regard to China, then Nam tiến was necessary for Vietnamese development."[100] The nam tiến, then, refers to the myth of the "march to the south" by the Vietnamese people, who, in the course of seven centuries, resisted Chinese imperialism while expanding their national sovereignty over the territory extending from the Red River to the Mekong Delta.

But just as the idea of the *bắc cự* had emerged from a wholesale revision of the indigenous past as a national history of resistance to foreign invaders, so, in the myth of *nam tiến*, a series of contingent events was rewritten as a "linear progression," leading to the establishment of a sovereign Vietnamese nation. In the *nam tiến*, a succession "of different episodes responding to particular events" was transformed into an historical teleology, an "essentialized preordained sequence by which the 'Vietnam' of the 10th century became the 'Vietnam' of today."[101]

Appropriating this part of the national history (as it was imagined in the colonial era), Republican leaders conceived of the counterinsurgency strategy as an historical and geographical extension of the Southward Advance. As Ngô Đình Nhu explained in an interview, Republican leaders sought to "position the strategic hamlet policy within the historical movement of the Vietnamese People [*vận động lịch sử của Dân tộc Việt Nam*] over these past two thousand years."[102] For Nhu, programs such as the agrovilles and Strategic Hamlet Campaign (*Ấp Chiến lược*) were not merely security measures, used to contain the insurgency in the countryside. Rather, they represented the "next frontier in the story of struggle, [a new] ... stage of Vietnamese history," an historical sequel to the Southward Advance. In that sense, "the national policy of strategic hamlets," as Nhu described, would be "the quintessence of our truest traditions."[103]

In this historical sequel, the march south (as the quintessential nationalist myth of an ancient Vietnamese people, fulfilling its manifest destiny by expanding its territorial sovereignty) would be accompanied by a "march toward progress" or political and economic modernity. As a modern reenactment of the Southward Advance, the campaign of forced relocation would realize "our truest traditions," while at the same time establishing "an authentically Vietnamese route to modernity."[104]

This ideal of modernity, however, would no longer be that of a Western democracy, for which the South Vietnamese would be required to wait. The Strategic Hamlet Program, in other words, was not an autocratic means for establishing what Nolting described as "the long-range aim of a self-representative ... democratic system." Unlike its American ally, the Republic was not committed to the goal of creating a bastion of liberal democracy. Rather, like their counterparts in the Communist Party, the Republican leaders would come to repudiate the latter as a bourgeois

Colonialism and national culture

ideology, one that they would seek to abolish by means of a revolutionary transformation of the economic and political infrastructure in the South. This transformation was identified by the creation of a "real democracy from the base," which was directly opposed to both free-market capitalism and liberal democracy.[105]

In contrast, however, to the revolution waged by the Communist Party, the ultimate aim of this program, as it evolved under the combined pressure of the insurgency and US imperialism, was not the establishment of a socialism controlled by the state. For the leaders of the early Republic, such a socialism remained within the framework of a Western modernity in which the establishment of individual rights required the development of a disciplinary apparatus deployed by a centralized state. South Vietnamese leaders, therefore, would attempt to create a stateless form of modernity based on a direct "democracy from the base."[106] To that end, the Ngos would pursue the apparently contradictory program of employing the discipline or dictatorial power of the central government to establish a decentralized system of politically autonomous rural communities. This autonomy, in turn, would serve to dissolve the centralized power that was used to create it.

In contrast to the role of disciplinary power in Foucault's account of the dark side of modernity, the aim of the Republican program of national discipline was not the creation of a representative regime supported by a system of panoptic surveillance. The object, in other words, was not to establish a popular sovereignty based upon the subjection of the people to the disciplinary mechanisms of the state and the capitalist economy. The "national people" (*dân tộc*) that the Republican leaders attempted to mold through their program of national discipline, then, would not be the citizens of a liberal democracy, endowed with individual rights (rights that were abrogated by the extrajuridical forms of coercion deployed by the government). Rather, the goal of the early Republic was to create a stateless community of "persons" (*nhân vị*), liberated by means of a "communal discipline" (*kỷ luật tập thể*) from the impersonal rule of the market as well as the sovereignty of the state and its power of discipline.[107] "National discipline," then, would serve to establish a decentralized system of direct democracy and communal production, whose political autonomy would preempt the authority of the national government. The stateless community, created through the program of national discipline, would serve, therefore, to *dissolve the nation itself*, along with the principle of national sovereignty, as an inheritance of the colonial government.

The unimagined community

If the war, then, was portrayed by the Communist Party as an attempt to realize the myth of a 2,000-year struggle for national sovereignty, for the Republican leaders, on the other hand, it was a second Southward Advance toward a non-nationalistic form of modernity. In this program, the dissemination of a national culture through the vernacular media would be used as a means of imagining a stateless form of community, beyond the idea of the nation. Toward the end of the early Republic, moreover, South Vietnamese leaders would attempt to utilize this stateless community as an instrument for opposing the American government, whose intervention, in the early 1960s, would begin to assume the character of a neocolonial enterprise.

Notes

1 Nguyen An Ninh, "La France et l'Indochine," *Europe*, 8:31 (July 15, 1925), 262. On Nguyễn An Ninh's career, see Hue-Tam Ho Tai, *Radicalism and the Origins of the Vietnamese Revolution* (Cambridge, MA: Harvard University Press, 1992).
2 Nguyễn An Ninh, *Tuyển Chọn Các Tác Phẩm* [Selected Works] (Thành phố Hồ Chí Minh: Nhà Xuất Bản Trẻ, 1996), 56, 81.
3 Frantz Fanon, *The Wretched of the Earth*, trans. Constance Farrington (New York: Grove Press, 1963), 152.
4 Ibid., 148.
5 Ibid., 225.
6 Ibid., 160–3.
7 Ibid., 167.
8 Ibid., 155.
9 Nguyễn An Ninh, *Tuyển Chọn Các Tác Phẩm*, 81.
10 Dương Quảng Hàm, *Leçons d'histoire d'Annam* (Hanoi: Le Van TAN, 1936), 5.
11 Quoted in Judith Henchy, "Performing Modernity in the Writings of Nguyễn An Ninh and Phan Văn Hùm" (Ph.D. dissertation, University of Washington, 2005), 61–2.
12 Theodor W. Adorno, *The Culture Industry: Selected Essays on Mass Culture* (London: Routledge, 1991), 107.
13 Philip Durkin, "Etymology, World History, and the Grouping and Division of Material in Historical Dictionaries," in *The Oxford Handbook of Lexicography*, ed. Philip Durkin (Oxford: Oxford University Press, 2016), 243; Alexandre de Rhodes's *Dictionarium Annamiticum Lusitanum et Latinum*, which was the first trilingual Vietnamese–Portuguese–Latin dictionary, published in Rome in 1651, does not contain an entry for "culture" in either Latin or Vietnamese.

14 Lydia Liu, *Translingual Practice: Literature, National Culture, and Translated Modernity – China, 1900–1937* (Stanford, CA: Stanford University Press, 1995), 240.
15 Tze-ki Hon, *The Allure of the Nation: The Cultural and Historical Debates in Late Qing and Republican China* (Leiden and Boston, MA: Brill, 2015), 85.
16 Adorno, *The Culture Industry*, 107.
17 Ibid.
18 Tze-Ki Hon, "Cultural identity and local self-government: A study of Liu Yizheng's 'History of Chinese Culture,'" *Modern China*, 30:4 (October 2004), 518.
19 Nguyễn Đình Hoà defines *Cầm kỳ thi họa* (in Chinese, *Qin Qi Shu Hua*) as "the four sophisticated pastimes," *Vietnamese–English Student Dictionary* (Carbondale: Southern Illinois University Press, 1971), 57. Under the Nguyễn dynasty in the nineteenth century, *cầm kỳ thi họa* was viewed as "vehicles for the Way" (*văn dĩ tái đạo*). Phương Lựu, "*Khái quát về quan niệm văn học Nho giáo ở Việt Nam*" [Outline of Confucian literary concepts in Vietnam], in *Nho giáo ở Việt Nam* [Confucianism in Vietnam] (Hà Nội: Nhà xuất bản khoa học xã hội, 2006), 393–427.
20 See Liam Kelley, "Vietnam as a 'domain of manifest civility' (*Văn Hiến Chi Bang*)," *Journal of Southeast Asian Studies*, 34:1 (2003), 63–76. *Việt Nam văn hóa sử cương* [An Outline of Vietnamese Culture] (Huế: Quan Hải tùng thư, 1938), by historian and lexicographer Đào Duy Anh was perhaps the most influential attempt during the colonial period to expound the new concept of culture. Đào Duy Anh's text draws on the work of the Chinese Marxist historian Yang Dongchun, who rejected the exclusive identification of culture with the noble civilization and "scholarly ideas" of the Confucian elite. According to Yang Dongchun, this narrow conception of culture implied that "savage peoples" (*dã man dân*) were devoid of culture, which he argued was clearly untrue. For Đào Duy Anh, similarly, culture is not "by nature something lofty and special." Rejecting what Ninh referred to as the "erroneous" identification of culture with the forms of civility practiced by the Confucian literati, Đào Duy Anh argued that "'culture' simply refers to all of the means of life of human beings, and therefore we can say: Culture is life [*văn hóa tức là sinh hoạt*]." See Liam Kelley, "Đào Duy Anh and ROC Intellectual Influence in Colonial Vietnam." https://leminhkhai.wordpress.com/2016/12/02/dao-duy-anh-and-roc-intellectual-influence-in-colonial-vietnam/. Last accessed July 21, 2019.
21 Nguyễn Văn Trung, *Chữ Văn Quốc Ngữ Thời Kỳ Đầu Pháp Thuộc* [The Quốc Ngữ Script in the Early French Colonial Period] (Sài Gòn: Sơn Nam Xuất Bản, 1974?), 119.
22 Benedict Anderson, *Imagined Communities: Reflections on the Origin and Spread of Nationalism* (New York: Verso, 2006), 128.
23 Nguyễn Văn Trung, *Chữ Văn Quốc Ngữ*, 119.

24 CAOM, Indo/GGI/65409: Letter from Governor General to Minister of Colonies, September 15, 1915. See also Nguyễn Văn Trung, *Chủ nghĩa thực dân Pháp ở Việt Nam: Thực chất và huyền thoại* [French Colonialism in Vietnam: Reality and Myths] (Saigon: Nam Sơn, 1963), 231.
25 CAOM (Aix). Indochine. Gouvernement Général 7 F22. L'Administrateur Chef du Service de la Sûreté à M. le Gouverneur de la Cochinchine. "Objet: Sûreté Politique." Saigon, April 2, 1921.
26 Shawn McHale, *Print and Power: Confucianism, Communism, and Buddhism in the Making of Modern Vietnam* (Honolulu: University of Hawaii Press, 2004), 34.
27 See also David Marr, *Vietnamese Tradition on Trial, 1920–1945* (Berkeley: University of California Press, 1984), 137.
28 Ibid., 183.
29 Nguyễn Văn Trung, *Chữ Văn Quốc Ngữ*, 119–20.
30 Ibid., 123.
31 CAOM (Aix). Indochine. Gouvernement général 7 F22. L'Administrateur Chef du Service de la Sûreté à M. le Gouverneur de la Cochinchine. "Object Sûreté Politique." Saigon, April 2, 1921.
32 See Benedict Anderson's discussion of the role of print media in the rise of nationalism in Vietnam in Anderson, *Imagined Communities*, 130.
33 Marr, *Vietnamese Tradition on Trial*, 172.
34 See Liam C. Kelley, "Imagining the Nation in Twentieth-Century Vietnam," presented at the fourth Engaging with Vietnam: An Interdisciplinary Dialogue Conference in Honolulu, November 8, 2012.
35 Phan Bội Châu, *Phan Bội Châu toàn tập*. Volume 3 [Complete Works] (Huế: Nhà xuất bản Thuận hóa, 2001), 68.
36 Michel Foucault, *The Order of Things: An Archaeology of the Human Sciences* (London: Routledge, 1974), 312.
37 See Neil L. Jamieson, *Understanding Vietnam* (Berkeley and Los Angeles: University of California Press, 1993), 172.
38 See, for example, Phạm Quỳnh Phương, *Hero and Deity: Trần Hưng Đạo and the Resurgence of Popular Religion in Vietnam* (Chiang Mai: Mekong Press, 2009) and Liam C. Kelley, "From moral exemplar to national hero."
39 Phạm Văn Đồng, *Về văn hóa và văn học nghệ thuật* [On Culture and Literary Arts] (Hà Nội: Nhà xuất bản Văn học, 2006), 381.
40 According to Alexander Vuving, texts like Lý Thường Kiệt's "Mountains and Rivers of the Southern Court" (*Nam quốc sơn hà nam*) and Nguyễn Trãi's "Proclamation of the Pacification of the Marauding Ngô" (*Bình Ngô đại cáo*), written in the tenth and fifteenth centuries, were not "declarations of independence" (*Tuyên ngôn độc lập*). They expressed concepts of "polity" that were different from the one proclaimed in Hồ Chí Minh's declaration in 1945. See Alexander Vuving, "The references of Vietnamese states and the mechanisms of world formation," *Asien*, 79 (April 2001), 62–86.

41 *Tuyên ngôn độc lập năm 1945 của Chủ tịch Hồ Chí Minh: những giá trị và ý nghĩa thời đại* [President Hồ Chí Minh's 1945 Declaration of Independence: values and meanings of the times] (Hà Nội: Nhà xuất bản Chính trị Quốc gia, 1996), 44.
42 Indochina Monographs – Intelligence. VCA. 1070821001 January 1, 1982. Box 08, Folder 21. Glenn Helm Collection.
43 Trãi Nguyễn, *Thơ văn Nguyễn Trãi* [Poetry of Trãi Nguyễn], (Hà Nội: Văn Học, 1980), 25.
44 Liam C. Kelley, "Who Were the Representatives of the People in the 'Bình Ngô đại cáo'?" https://leminhkhai.wordpress.com/2016/08/08/3-the-bndc-series-who-were-the-representatives-of-the-people-in-the-binh-ngo-dai-cao/. Last accessed July 21, 2019.
45 Quoted in Bửu Lịch, "Les idéologies dans la République du Sud Vietnam 1954–1975" (Ph.D. dissertation, Université de Paris VII, 1983/1984), 36.
46 Trãi Nguyễn, *Thơ văn Nguyễn Trãi*, 25.
47 Ibid.
48 Liam C. Kelley, "From moral exemplar to national hero: the transformations of Trần Hưng Đạo and the emergence of Vietnamese nationalism," *Modern Asian Studies*, 49:6, 1989.
49 Nguyễn Văn Trung, *Chữ Văn Quốc Ngữ*, 127.
50 William S. Turley, *The Second Indochina War: A Concise Political and Military History*, 2nd ed. (Lanham, MD: Rowman & Littlefield, 2009), 9, 10. See also Patricia M. Pelley, *Postcolonial Vietnam: New Histories of the National Past* (Durham, NC: Duke University Press, 2002), 159.
51 Pierre Asselin, *Vietnam's American War: A History* (Cambridge: Cambridge University Press, 2018), 17–18.
52 Hoàng Đạo Thành, *Việt sử tân ước toàn biên* [Complete Compilation of the New Testament of Việt History] (1906), A. 1507., tự 1a-1b.
53 CAOM (Aix). Indochine. Gouvernement Général 7 F22. L'Administrateur Chef du Service de la Sûreté à M. le Gouverneur de la Cochinchine. "Object Sûreté Politique." Saigon, April 2, 1921.
54 Fanon, *The Wretched of the Earth*, 225.
55 Nguyễn Văn Trung, *Chữ Văn Quốc Ngữ*, 120.
56 Ibid., 123.
57 Michel Foucault, *Discipline and Punish: The Birth of the Prison* (New York: Vintage, 1977), 30.
58 Mộng Lang Trần, *Hiến pháp Việt Nam: từ năm 1946 đến năm 2001* [Vietnamese Constitutions: 1946–2001] (Thành phố Hồ Chí Minh: Nhà xuất bản Thành phố Hồ Chí Minh, 2002), 126.
59 Văn An Lê, *Tổ-chức hành-chánh Việt-Nam* [Administrative Organization in Vietnam] (Sài Gòn: Học-viện quốc-gia hành-chánh, 1963), 96.

60 Huy Đỗ, Hữu Ái Lê, *Tìm hiểu tư tưởng văn hóa nghệ thuật Hồ Chí Minh* [Understanding Hồ Chí Minh's thinking on culture and art] (Hà Nội: Nhà Xuất Bản Khoa Học Xã Hội, 1995), 82, 60.
61 *Tư tưởng Hồ Chí Minh về Đảng cộng sản Việt Nam* [Thoughts of Hồ Chí Minh on the Vietnamese Communist Party] (Hà Nội: Chính trị quốc gia, 2008), 94.
62 Quoted in *Tư tưởng Hồ Chí Minh về phát triển văn hóa và con người* [Thoughts of Hồ Chí Minh on Cultural and Human Development] (Hà Nội: Nhà xuất bản Chính trị quốc gia, 2005), 295.
63 Dương Thu Hương, *Tiểu thuyết vô đề* [Novel Without a Name] (Stanton, CA: nhà xuất bản Văn Nghệ, 1991).
64 Foucault, *Discipline and Punish*, 217.
65 Trần Đức Thảo, *Những lời trăn trối* [Final Testaments] (Arlington, VA: Tổ hợp Xuất bản Miền Đông Hoa Kỳ, 2014), 264.
66 Trần Đức Thảo, *Những lời trăn trối*, 264–5.
67 Ibid., 265.
68 Ibid.
69 Debord, *Society of the Spectacle*, 32.
70 Trần Đức Thảo, *Những lời trăn trối*, 262.
71 On RVN efforts to create a cult of personality for Diem, see John C. Donnell, "National renovation campaigns in Vietnam," *Pacific Affairs*, 32 (March 1959), 56–63.
72 Christopher Goscha, *Vietnam: A New History* (New York: Basic Books, 2016), 290.
73 See, for example, Seth Jacobs, *America's Miracle Man in Vietnam: Ngo Dinh Diem, Religion, Race, and U.S. Intervention in Southeast Asia* (Durham, NC: Duke University Press, 2004), 52–6.
74 John Osborne, "The tough miracle man of Vietnam," *Life*, 42 (May 13, 1957), 157. On Diệm's early career as an administrator, see Bernard Fall, *The Two Viet-Nams* (New York: Praeger Publishers, 1967), 239.
75 Edward Miller, *Misalliance: Ngo Dinh Diem, the United States, and the Fate of South Vietnam* (Cambridge, MA: Harvard University Press, 2013), 20–1.
76 Eric M. Bergerud, *The Dynamics of Defeat: The Vietnam War in Hau Nghia Province* (Boulder, CO: Westview Press, 1991), 35.
77 Stephen Kinzer, *Overthrow: America's Century of Regime Change from Hawaii to Iraq* (New York: Times Books, 2006), 153.
78 Joseph Buttinger, *Vietnam: Vietnam at War* (London: Pall Mall Press, 1967), 1150.
79 Lương Khải Minh and Cao Thế Dung, *Làm thế nào để giết một tổng thống? tập 1* [How to kill a president, vol. 1] (Sài Gòn: Nhà xuất bản Hòa Bình, 1970), 194–5.
80 Willemetz, *La République du Viêt-Nam*, 18.

81 Đào Thị Diến. "*Nhà lưu trữ Việt Nam thời kì 1938–1946.*" [Ngô Đình Nhu: Vietnamese Archivist 1938–1946]. Tạp chí Nghiên cứu và Phát triển *[Journal of Research and Development]*, 6–7:104–5 (2013), 239.
82 Văn Luận Cao, *Bên giòng lịch sử* [Riding Our History Currents], *1940–1965* (Sài Gòn: Trí Dũng, 1972), 180–9. See also John L. Sorenson and David K. Pack, *Unconventional Warfare and the Vietnamese Society* (China Lake, CA: U.S. Naval Ordinance Test Station, 1964), 4. On Nhu's organizing activities, see Hà Kim Phương, "Tìm Hiểu Ngô Đình Nhu Trong Khía Cạnh Một Nhà Trí Thức." [Understanding Ngô Đình Nhu as an Intellectual] Luutruvn.com, February 11, 2015, luutruvn.com/index.php/2015/11/02/tim-hieu-ngo-dinh-nhu-trong-khia-canh-mot-nha-tri-thuc/#_ftnref15. Last accessed July 21, 2019. On Nhu's involvement in the conferences on Christian social doctrine, organized during the 1950s by Fernand Parrel, which informed Nhu's views on Personalism, see Trịnh Trấn Nguyễn O.P. "*Lớp Huấn Luyện Xã Hội Công Giáo.*" [A Lesson on the Christian Social Doctrine]. *Đạo Binh Đức Mẹ* [The Legion of Mary], August 1952, 8, 13.
83 Michael Field, *The Prevailing Wind: Witness in Indochina* (London: Methuen, 1965), 152.
84 "Vietnam: A Television History; America's Mandarin (1954–1963); Interview with Frederick Nolting, 1981." 04/30/1981. WGBH Media Library & Archives. July 21, 2019. http://openvault.wgbh.org/catalog/V_A2513CA622CC4C8E8454EB2B1F7F5A0C. Last accessed July 21, 2019.
85 *President Ngo Dinh Diem on Democracy (Addresses relative to the Constitution)* (Saigon: Press Office, 1958), 31–2.
86 Memorandum of a Conversation, Saigon, January 30, 1958. See also Ngô Đình Nhu, "Industrialization: prerequisite to self-sufficiency," *Times of Vietnam Magazine*, 5:18 (May 5, 1963), 4–5.
87 Foucault, *Discipline and Punish*, 222.
88 Ibid., 216–17.
89 Ibid., 222.
90 *President Ngo Dinh Diem on Democracy*, 31.
91 Philip Catton, *Diem's Final Failure* (Lawrence: University Press of Kansas, 2002), 14.
92 Despatch From the Chargé in Vietnam (Elting) to the Department of State, Saigon, July 30, 1959.
93 Catton, *Diem's Final Failure*, 49.
94 Dipesh Chakrabarty, *Provincializing Europe: Postcolonial Thought and Historical Difference* (Princeton, NJ: Princeton University Press, 2000), 8.
95 Phạm Văn Lưu, *Chính Quyền Ngô Đình Diệm 1954–1963: Chủ Nghĩa và Hành Động* [The Government of Ngô Đình Diệm 1954–1963: Theory and Action.] (Melbourne: Centre For Vietnamese Studies Publications, 2017), 30–1.

96 Catton, *Diem's Final Failure*, 90. See also Tùng Phong (Ngô Đình Nhu). *Chính Đề Việt Nam* [Political Solution for Vietnam] (Saigon: Nhà xuất bản Đồng-Nai, 1965), 266.
97 Paper – The Political Factor in Pacification: A Vietnam Case Study [Draft], 4. VCA. 21470122001 No Date. Box 01, Folder 22. Vincent Puritano Collection.
98 Catton, *Diem's Final Failure*, 118.
99 Claudine Ang, "Regionalism in southern narratives of Vietnamese history: The case of the 'Southern Advance'" [*Nam Tiến*], *Journal of Vietnamese Studies*, 8:3 (Summer 2013), 8.
100 Tana Li, *Nguyen Cochinchina: Southern Vietnam in the Seventeenth and Eighteenth Centuries* (Ithaca, NY: Cornell University, SEAP Publications, 1998), 19.
101 Ibid. On the myth of the *nam tiến*, see Brian Zottoli, "Reconceptualizing Southern Vietnamese History from the 15th to 18th Centuries: Competition along the Coasts from Guangdong to Cambodia" (Ph.D. dissertation, University of Michigan, 2011), 3, 13, 393–9.
102 Cuộc nói chuyện than mật với cán bộ ấp chiến lược của ông cố vấn chính trị Ngô Đình Nhu [A Friendly Talk by the Political Counselor to Cadres in the Strategic Hamlet Campaign], folder 21760/02, Phủ Tổng thống đệ nhất Việt Nam Cộng hòa [Files of the Office of the President, First Republic], Vietnam National Archives No. 2.
103 See Nhu's account of the *nam tiến* in Tùng Phong (Ngô Đình Nhu), *Chính Đề Việt Nam*, 245–52.
104 Catton, *Diem's Final Failure*, 118.
105 *Press interviews with President Ngo Dinh Diem, Political Counselor Ngo Dinh Nhu* (Saigon: Republic of Vietnam, 1963), 71.
106 Ibid.
107 Tùng Phong (Ngô Đình Nhu), *Chính Đề Việt Nam* [Political Solution for Vietnam], 391.

2

Vietnamese anti-colonialism and the Personalist critique of capitalism and liberal democracy

Personalism: Between capitalism and communism

The stateless conception of communism espoused by the leaders of the early Republic was partly derived from the philosophy of Personalism, developed by the French philosopher Emmanuel Mounier. This philosophy, which is commonly treated in a cursory manner in the historical scholarship on the war, was widely dismissed by US officials as "muddle-headed" and "vague,"[1] a "mish-mash of ideas," "not coherent enough to be readily summarized."[2] The theory, as Frances Fitzgerald described, was an "incomprehensible hodgepodge having something to do with state power, the dignity of the Person (as opposed to the individual)."[3]

As the official philosophy of the early Republic, Personalism was deemed to be too "esoteric" (as though a lack of complexity were the mark of a superior state ideology, as Stalinism and liberalism have undoubtedly demonstrated).[4] On the other hand, Jean-Marie Domenach, editor of the Personalist journal *Esprit*, condemned the use of Personalism by the South Vietnamese government as an opportunistic "attempt to fill the regime's ideological vacuum," betraying Mounier's profound philosophical work.[5] Similarly, in a memorandum issued in exile by officers who participated in the failed coup against Diệm in 1960, Vietnamese Personalism is characterized as an "odious, lying ... doctrine," "hastily and arbitrarily" put together by "opportunists and highly-paid priests."[6] Devoid of any real political principles, the South Vietnamese leaders, therefore, turned opportunistically to an incoherent political doctrine taken from the foreign religion of their former colonial masters in order to justify the oppression of their own population: "In the hands of Nhu and Diem, personalism supplied an intellectual foundation for an authoritarian regime that alienated Catholics nearly as badly as South Vietnam's Buddhist majority."[7]

Personalism, moreover, is typically characterized as a "third way" between "Marxist collectivism and Western individualistic capitalism,"[8] an "unsystematic *mélange* of 'third force' ideas," seeking a "middle-ground" between communism and liberal democracy.[9] This superficial description, however, has served to conceal the radically anti-capitalist character of Mounier's political philosophy. From the Personalist perspective, capitalism was in fact a far greater danger than communism: "Thus, the evil of capitalism is incorrigible, the Soviet evil is curable."[10] Mounier's critique of the Soviet Union, moreover, was not that it failed to incorporate the positive elements of capitalism and liberal democracy. On the contrary, the problem was that it was incapable of completely abolishing the capitalist system and its political superstructure. Therefore, as the philosopher Lucien Sève noted, Mounier's "third way" was more directly aligned with Marxism than Western individualistic capitalism: "What characterizes [Mounier's] third way" is not that it is "situated ... at an equal distance between ... two poles." Rather, it is "much closer to Marxism." The "factor that unites currents ... like the existentialism of Sartre and his disciples and the personalism of Mounier and his followers ... [is] precisely that they define themselves ... with reference to Marxism."[11] As Sève's description suggests, then, Mounier's "Marxist Personalism" was a form of Marxist humanist thought,[12] a category more often associated with the work of thinkers such as Jean-Paul Sartre, György Lukács and Henri Lefebvre.[13]

Therefore despite its connection to Catholicism, Personalism, in many of its French and the Vietnamese forms, was not a conservative ideology (as it was in the USA, where Personalism was appropriated as a critique of the secularism and moral decay of modern society).[14] "We are a reactionary regime, you have been told," said Nhu sarcastically in an interview with *Le Monde*, "are you aware of the fact that we take our inspiration from the thinkers of the Western Left, particularly the French? I don't want to name names [he laughed] or compromise anybody. ... But you must realize that we base ourselves on personalism!"[15] And despite Diệm's reputation as "an aloof doctrinaire Roman Catholic mandarin," the doctrine to which he strictly adhered appears to have been a politically radical one: "Some say that we are prone to a theory close to Communism," according to Nhu.

In Vietnam, moreover, Personalism was not merely confined to the Vietnamese Catholic community. During the colonial period, its admirers included people such as Xuân Diệu and Huy Cận, two of the most prominent figures in modern Vietnamese poetry, both of whom would join the Communist Party. While neither accepted Catholicism, their criticisms of Confucianism, and of the traditional family for its suppression of the individual, were informed by Mounier's defense of the "person" in his *Manifeste sur le personalisme.*[16] This affirmation of the individual (or the *tôi*) would become an integral part of the concept of modernity articulated the Self-Strength Literary Group (*Tự Lực văn đoàn*), the most influential cultural movement to emerge during the colonial era.

Although Catholicism was regarded as a foreign influence, its followers having served as a "fifth column" for the French imperial forces during the conquest, Personalism, as a Catholic philosophy, was in fact an explicitly anti-colonial doctrine.[17] Like Marxism, the doctrine attracted leaders from throughout the colonial Empire, who adapted the foreign philosophy to develop a range of anti-colonial nationalisms. Léopold Senghor's *"voie africaine du socialisme,"* for example, a *"socialisme à hauteur d'homme,"* was based on Mounier's ideal of the person.[18] Mounier, moreover, was the *"maître à penser de* Michel Aflaq," the Syrian philosopher credited with the development of *Ba'athism*.[19] Aflaq's ideal of an "Arab nationalism based on the values of Islam," therefore, was inspired by Mounier's radical Christian philosophy. And for the Syrian-Lebanese Egyptian philosopher René Habachi, Personalism provided an alternative to the vulgar materialism of Soviet communism, which denied the spiritual nature of man.[20]

Mounier's Personalism, however, was never intended as an alternative to Marxism itself. In fact, he "dissociated himself from any attempts to 'go beyond Marxism,'"[21] arguing that "[a]nti-Communism … is the … sufficient crystallizing force for a return of Fascism."[22] Mounier's criticism of communism, moreover, was marked by a conspicuous failure to unequivocally condemn the excesses of Stalinism.[23] "Until the end of his life, Mounier never critiqued Soviet policy without also explaining that America was just as bad."[24] In contrast, his rejection of Western individualistic capitalism was uncompromising and clear: "[W]e hold … all manner of liberalism, in horror, for it is the greatest and most evil fraud in history,"[25] the "most cunning and cruel hoax of all."[26] In Mounier's work, then, Personalism is presented as a Marxist critique of communism, one that, in contrast to the liberal account of totalitarianism in postwar American politics, identifies fascism with capitalism and bourgeois democracy, rather than the communist state and the command economy.

2.1 Emmanuel Mounier (courtesy of the Association les Amis d'Emmanuel Mounier).

The alienation of labor and the inalienable Rights of Man

According to William Rauch, "this assimilation of ... democracy to totalitarianism under the control of occult capitalist powers was common fare for French social critics during the early nineteen thirties."[27] In Mounier's work, the "occult operations" of the capitalist economy are attributed to the fetishism of commodities:[28] "Marx used to say of capitalism that it [is based on] the reduction of things to commodities."[29] In an encyclical titled *Laborem Exercens*, Pope John Paul II reiterates Mounier's (Marxist) criticism of capitalism, describing the latter as a society in which "work was understood and treated as a sort of 'merchandise' that the worker ... sells to the employer."[30] Reduced to a commodity, labor – and the subjects employed to perform it – becomes what Marx referred to as an "*alienable* ... object ... subjected to the slavery of egoistic need and to the market."[31] In the process, the "motley ... ties that bound m[e]n" together are "pitilessly torn asunder," leaving "no other nexus between man and man than naked self-interest [and] callous 'cash payment.'" The exchange of commodities, including labor as an alienable object, is established in place of earlier forms of community and communal production. The result, according to Mounier, is a dehumanizing inversion of the means and ends of society. Money, as a means of exchange, becomes the aim of production itself, subordinating the worker to its impersonal power. In the process, capital develops the attributes of a subject or sovereign: "It is not money that is at the service of the economy and labor, it is the economy and labor that are at the service of money. The first aspect of this sovereignty is the primacy of capital over labor."[32]

In this inversion, the dehumanization (or *dépersonnalisation*) of labor is accompanied by a transformation of things (money and capital) into an impersonal subject, a modern-day idol or fetish that dominates individuals. While people, therefore, are reduced to alienable objects, money acquires the "anonymous power" to act as an autonomous agent, imposing its will upon individuals who have been "depersonalized" by the alienation of labor.[33] Subjected to what Mounier describes, with reference to Marx, as the "mystifications into which man has been inveigled by social constructions derived from his material conditions,"[34] humanity is ruled by a sovereign economy that humanity itself has created: "It is not the economy that it at the service of man, but man who is at the service of the economy."[35]

As Mounier argued, however, the sovereignty of the capitalist economy, which "hardens class distinctions and alienate[s] ... man," cannot be opposed by means of a political program proclaiming the sovereignty of the people.³⁶ For Marx, as Mounier points out, this popular sovereignty presupposes a bourgeois conception of man as an abstract legal persona possessing inalienable rights, rights that serve to perpetuate the economic alienation upon which this legal conception depends. In bourgeois society, the "practical application of man's right to liberty is man's right to private property," the right to freely dispose of one's merchandise, including the labor of others, "without regard to other men."³⁷ In the Rights of Man, the alienation of labor is legally ratified as the inherent and inalienable right of free individuals as "sovereign proprietors" (*souverain propriétaire*).³⁸ This right, therefore, serves to hypostatize and eternalize a historically determinate system of market production, mediated by the commodity form, in which the sale and purchase of labor for profit preempts direct cooperation by workers within a community. The "so-called ... *droits de l'homme* as distinct from the *droits du citoyen*, are nothing but the rights ... of egoistic man, of man separated ... from the community."³⁹ In Mounier's terms, the rights of man, which belong to a capitalist "civilization now breaking up before our eyes,"⁴⁰ are "restricted to the assurance that these egoisms should not encroach upon one another, or on their betterment as a purely profit-making association."⁴¹ For Marx, the exercise of this freedom was based upon the mutual subservience of individuals to a sovereign economy in which "independent producers of commodities ... acknowledge no authority other than that of competition, of the coercion exerted by the pressure of their reciprocal interests."⁴²

Following Marx, moreover, Mounier argued that the self-imposed tyranny of capitalist production (based on the alienation of labor as an inalienable right) is reinforced by the right to political representation or popular sovereignty established in democratic regimes. As Marx describes in "On the Jewish Question," the liberal state is not simply a political instrument that serves the interest of the ruling class by protecting its property. On the contrary, the right to representation, which the state guarantees to all of its citizens, is based on a "political annulment of private property" as a "qualification for ... suffrage," allowing the "non-property owner ... [to] become the legislator for the property owner."⁴³ As Marx argues, however, this right to equal representation presupposes the economic inequality, created by the private pursuit of self-interest, that it serves to politically nullify:

> The state ... declares that birth, social rank, education, occupation, are non-political distinctions ... proclaim[ing] that every member of the nation is an equal participant in national sovereignty ... Nevertheless, the state ... only exists on the presupposition of their existence; it ... asserts its universality only in opposition to these elements of its being.[44]

Rather than abolishing all private property, then, the political right to equal representation perpetuates what Mounier called "an anonymous system of possession, guaranteed by the state," a system based upon egoistic self-interest, adjudicated by the state in the interest of all.[45] As the embodiment of a universal self-interest, the liberal state constitutes a paradoxical form of "communal being": it is the "political community" of egoistic individuals who are "separated ... from the community" and communal production, or the direct association of the producers.[46] Insofar as the free interaction of self-interested sovereign proprietors, however, is precisely what subordinates them to the sovereignty of the capitalist economy, the right to equal representation, or popular sovereignty, serves to perpetuate the tyranny of production for profit. In Mounier's words, the "sovereignty of the public," which he condemned as the "absolutism of the majority,"[47] preserves "an anarchic sovereignty of free individuals" that engenders the "dictatorship of capital."[48] Far from liberating humanity from the clutches of tyranny, the Declaration of the Rights of Man and of the Citizen, according to Mounier, merely ratify the despotic rule of the capitalist economy.

Echoing Marx's reproach to the "foolishness of those socialists ... who want to depict socialism as the realization of the ideals of bourgeois society articulated by the French Revolution,"[49] Mounier, therefore, argued that, the "revolution of '89 was not a popular revolution but a bourgeois revolution."[50] During the 1930s in Europe, moreover, the rights proclaimed in this bourgeois revolution, based on the fetishism of production for profit and the "illusion of popular sovereignty," would lead to economic collapse and the rise of fascism by means of electoral democracy. Fascism, then, according to Mounier, was not a betrayal of the principles of the French Revolution. On the contrary, it was a product of the "occult operations" of the capitalist economy and its parliamentary system of representative government. For Mounier, this implied that capitalism could not be abolished by appealing to the principles that belong to its own political superstructure, since the "electoral machinery" of bourgeois democracy presupposes the very private ownership that it nullifies as a qualification for suffrage.

The liberation of labor in the image of God: Christian theology against capitalism

Affirming the "*anticapitalisme ... des années 1930,*" Mounier, therefore, proposed the "Personalist revolution" as a program for liberating humanity from the tyranny of both production for profit and majority rule in liberal democracy. This Catholic anti-capitalism, however, was not merely a reactionary assertion of an old religious morality against the evils produced by the secular institution of the free market economy. Mounier's Personalist program was in fact far more ambitious in scope, seeking a sort of dialectical reconciliation between a premodern tradition of Christian theology and a modern conception of man, derived from Marx's early humanist writings. Thus, while Mounier emphatically rejected "reactionary forms of ... anti-capitalism" which advocated a return to a "precapitalist economy," his Marxist criticism of capitalism was couched in an explicitly theological language.[51]

For Mounier, the occult operations of the capitalist economy, and its dehumanization of labor and persons, were the product of a "pagan" heresy that "attributes to man the eminent domain of God, a God of greed and not of love."[52] Capitalism, then, is a non-Christian form of modernity, one in which God's divine right of dominion, usurped by a bourgeois humanity, is degraded into a mere right of possession, the right to freely dispose of nature and other individuals as alienable objects.

This inalienable right of man, however, as Mounier argued, is distinct from the "*a priori* and absolute right of property" accorded to God in the Christian religion.[53] In contrast to the sovereign right of kings, as well as to the bourgeois right of sovereign proprietors, the "sovereign dominion" (*Souverain Domaine*) of God is not derived either from conquest or legal exchange. God "does not have to conquer the world, he made it." Therefore God holds a sovereign dominion over all things by "virtue of his creation and providence."[54]

This divine act of creation is distinct from the act of production, narrowly understood as the transformation of nature to satisfy human needs and desires. Creation cannot be the product of an instrumental activity, a property that fulfills God's desires, since this would imply a lack or deficiency within the creator. As a perfect being, God "desires nothing, is jealous of nothing."[55] Unlike the commodity, moreover, creation cannot be conceived as an object that can be legally owned, exploited or alienated by a sovereign proprietor. Insofar as the whole of creation is made in the image of God, the Creator exists *within* the sovereign dominion that he also possesses as property, even while he transcends the world that he owns by virtue of the absolute right of creation: God "is everything that is, but he is not in the world."[56]

In God, therefore, being and possession converge: "Having and Being are conjoined."[57] As both the subject and object of the act of creation, God exists *as* the world he possesses, and he possesses the world that he is. But since God exists in the world he creates and possesses, the relationship between creation and the Creator is not one of greed or desire, but *love*, not *avidité* but *amour*.

In capitalism, on the other hand, this reciprocity between being and possession, which defines God's sovereign dominion, is reduced to a relation of "having": "The modern liberal and commercial world, in breaking with these [Christian] perspectives, has revived ... a certain pagan tradition that empties its being ... as both possessor and object."[58] In bourgeois society, then, man, in assuming the right of Sovereign Dominion (and reducing the latter merely to having), becomes "*un Dieu qui serait avidité et non pas amour.*"[59]

For Mounier, therefore, the heresy committed by capitalism, as a non-Christian form of modernity, is not that it situates man in the position of God. On the contrary, capitalism, as a system based on a pagan conception of nature and man as mere objects and instruments, is condemned for its failure to elevate man to the Christian ideal of *imago Dei*, the image of God as both subject and object of the act of creation: The "error of ... capitalism [is that] ... man is ... treated ... as an instrument and not in accordance with the true dignity of his work – that is to say ... he is not treated as subject and maker ... as the true purpose of the whole process of production."[60]

According to Mounier, this Christian conception of man as the image of God is largely consistent with the atheistic notion of freedom that Jean-Paul Sartre proposed in his existentialist humanism. Like Sartre's definition of freedom, creation is an act of production in which the subject realizes itself in the process of transforming the object. However, in failing to recognize that this subjective freedom is constrained by the object upon which it imposes itself (an object, nature, that is simultaneously humanized in the process of labor), the existentialist notion of man falls short of the Marxist conception of praxis:[61] "To make, [and] in making to make oneself, and to be nothing but what one has made oneself, this formula, in which Sartre wants to comprehend the whole of man, is very nearly the Marxian one."[62] For Mounier, therefore, the Marxist conception of praxis, in contrast to the Sartrean notion of freedom, more closely corresponds to the Christian idea of humanity as the image of God's act of creation: "The supreme value that is claimed, by Marxism, for man's practical activity (*praxis*), is a kind of secularization of the central value that the Christian tradition claims for work."[63] In its secular theory of praxis, therefore, Marxism paradoxically discovers a Christian form of modernity, one that accords with the Christian ideal of man as *imago Dei*. In Mounier's account of the latter, human *praxis* becomes the foundation for a philosophical anthropology, the ontological basis of all knowledge and action, assuming the position of God within Christian theology: "The person stands at the summit of being, and all being is subject to a process of personalization. Hence, the metaphysics of the person will provide the ultimate criteria for all *praxis*."[64]

If Mounier's "Personalist revolution," then, constitutes a "third way" between capitalism and communism, it is one in which the Marxist conception of praxis (as a secularization of the Christian idea of creation) is opposed to the reduction of labor to instrumental activity, which persists in both capitalism and official state communism. Mounier, therefore, proposed an organization of praxis, constitutive of autonomous "persons" liberated from the tyranny of the market as well as from the dictatorship of the proletariat, which perpetuates the *capitalist* institution of wage labor that alienates work: by "socialism we mean the following: The abolition of the proletarian condition [and] the supersession of the anarchic economy of profit by an economy directed to the fulfilment of ... personal needs."[65]

From the Personalist perspective, however, such a socialist society, based on "an economy directed to the fulfillment of ... personal needs," on the first principle of the person, cannot be realized within the framework of a "falsely liberal regime of capitalist democracy."[66] Since this "illusion of popular sovereignty" is based on an individual liberty that engenders the despotism of capital, it precludes the possibility of a revolutionary transformation of labor, founded on the direct association of persons within a community, as opposed to an unregulated system of production for profit. This communal production, therefore, cannot be founded on the freedom of egoistic individuals, separated from the community, a freedom of "negation, refusal to associate ... the liberty to oppose."[67] Rather, the praxis that defines the person is identified with what Mounier calls a "responsible liberty," or personal discipline.[68]

In praxis, the subject is liberated from the external compulsion to labor for profit by freely adopting a personal discipline, a *"discipline personnelle librement décidée."*[69] For Mounier, then, praxis is a process of subjectivation in which the subject masters itself as an object of internal compulsion while simultaneously mastering nature: The "vital link of all humanist action" is the "mastery which man exercises over matter as over himself."[70] In Mounier's conception of praxis, therefore, the act of self-discipline, as a Vietnamese Personalist manual describes, constitutes the incorporeal soul of the humanist subject, made in the image of an eternal God:

> The corporeal part of the man is annihilated when man dies but the soul remains, immortal. To have the soul is ... to have self-mastery or independence, and an understanding of self and the capacity to guide one's own direction ... Freedom does not mean one does whatever one wishes ... that is the mistaken concept of freedom. Freedom in the Personalist conception means the right way.[71]

As in Foucault's account of the Enlightenment notion of man, Mounier's humanist subject "is the effect and instrument of a political anatomy." Its personal liberty, resembling the image of God, is the effect of an internal surveillance, a discipline that imprisons the body (the "corporeal part of ... man"), producing an incorporeal subject that is free from external compulsion: the "free man ... is able to impose discipline upon himself, but will not take it blindly from anyone else."[72] For Mounier, this "responsible liberty," or freedom from external compulsion (by means of internal repression), constitutes "the basis of authentic sovereignty," which "lies in ... the middle term between freedom and organization."[73]

This sovereign subject, nevertheless, is distinct from the abstract subject of rights that Foucault identifies with the modernity of the constitutional state and Western liberal democracy. For Foucault, this liberal subject is subordinated to a "disciplinary technology of labor," which emerged in the industrial factory to "calculate power with minimum expenditure and maximum efficiency." This form of discipline, therefore, was "one of the basic tools for the establishment of industrial capitalism and the corresponding type of society."[74] On the other hand, Mounier's Christian ideal of the Person is one that converges with the concept of autonomy within the anarchist tradition, autonomy as a law (*nomos*) that is given to oneself (*autos*).[75] In Mounier's Personalist program, this autonomy or responsible liberty is opposed to both capitalism, as the tyranny of production for profit, and the principle of majority rule that defines the constitutional state: "In the place of capitalist tyranny is established, not an irresponsible parliamentary ... democracy, but an organic democracy in which each is the sanction and source of responsibility."[76]

The unimagined community

The person, therefore, becomes the "sanction and source" of an internalized discipline, forming the foundation for a decentralized form of direct communal production, free from the external compulsion of the capitalist state and the bourgeois economy.

For Mounier, however, this organic democracy, based on a responsible liberty, cannot be established by recourse to the "irresponsible" institution of representative bourgeois democracy. Capitalism cannot be abolished by means of its own political superstructure, since its "electoral machinery" presupposes a system of market production based on the interaction of free individuals that preempts the direct association of labor. Rather, following Marx's dictum that "changes in the economic foundation lead … to the transformation of the … superstructure,"[77] Mounier argued that "the liberal stage of democracy … will … be superseded. … [o]nly on the foundation of a new social structure."[78] In this new social structure, the "tyranny" of an anarchic capitalist economy, along with the "oppression" of the "overly centralized apparatus" of the parliamentary state, would be suppressed by the creation of "decentralized [political] communities" (*communautés décentralisées*), with a "decentralized economy" based on the principle of the Person.[79] While the Person, in this new social structure, would be subject to the bonds of the community, internalizing its discipline, this discipline, as a condition of personal freedom, would constitute a "collective [form of] control, not statist, but decentralized" (*contrôle collectif, non étatiste, mais décentralisé*).[80]

Colonialism, capitalism and the Rights of Man in French Indochina

"[T]he difference between Indochina and us is Descartes."[81]

In South Vietnam, this Marxist humanism, which would mostly remain an intellectual and academic tradition in France,[82] was adopted as official state doctrine by the early Republican government.[83] The individual who was chiefly responsible for the development of the doctrine and its political and military application was Ngô Đình Nhu, "*père du personnalisme viêtnamien.*"[84]

Contrary to the conventional caricatures of the latter as "Confucianism in another guise," as a feudal ideology used to perpetuate the rule of "Personalist mandarins," Nhu's "Oriental Personalism" (*Chủ nghĩa nhân vị phương Đông*) was in fact an appropriation of Mounier's thought, "adapted to an Asian society emerging from colonialism into the modern world."[85]

2.2 Ngô Đình Nhu (Office national de radiodiffusion télévision française).

As an anti-colonial form of French humanist Marxism, Nhu's personalism, then, was perhaps more closely related to the work of figures such as Frantz Fanon and Aimé Césaire, whose discourse on colonialism was influenced by Sartre's existentialist humanism.[86] This connection has been obscured by the emphasis placed on the Christian character of Personalism, which made it possible, especially after the Buddhist protests against Diệm's "Catholic regime,"[87] to ignore Nhu's Marxist rejection of capitalism and liberal democracy: "[M]y Personalism ... has no relationship to the Christian Personalism taught by the Catholic organizations in ... Vietnam. ... [T]he Personalism ... I advocate is a militant democracy ... [aimed at] modifying the superstructure of the present government."[88] As Nhu emphasized, moreover, the practical application of this doctrine would require a thorough knowledge of Marxism: "our cadres must clearly grasp the theory and historical development of Marxist-Leninist theory ... There must be lessons on communist principles of organization."[89] For Pentagon analysts, these organizational methods, which played an indispensible part in Diệm's rise to power,[90] made it difficult to distinguish the political aims of the *Cần Lao* Party from those of its communist counterparts.[91]

For US officials, therefore, the main problem with Personalism was not its Catholicism, but its "acceptance of the Marxist critique of capitalism," which "cause[d] the Vietnamese (and the French) to perceive the ... political systems of the West through a Marxist prism."[92] According to the economist Milton Taylor, for example, Personalism was an incoherent amalgam "of Papal encyclicals and kindergarten economics," Christian theology combined with a dogmatic belief in socialist planning, contrary to a rational understanding of the market economy.[93]

For Mounier, of course, this market economy was based on an egoistic conception of man that he described, in Marxian terms, as the "ideology and the prevailing structure of Western bourgeois society in the 18th and 19th centuries. Man in the abstract, unattached to any natural community, the sovereign lord of a liberty unlimited and undirected." This critique of liberal democracy was one that Nhu would encounter in France, as a student at the École des Chartes.[94] In Nhu's "Oriental Personalism," Mounier's depiction of bourgeois society would be appropriated as a critique of Western civilization itself: "Occidental countries had for their *structure* ... Capitalism ... for their *ideology* ... Liberalism."[95] In the Occidental ideology of liberalism, "man conceived as an individual, like in free capitalism, is an abstract man."[96] For Nhu, following Mounier, this free individual, separated from direct communal production, engendered the tyranny of production for profit and its "depersonalizing" effect upon individuals: "The capitalists ... have trampled on human dignity ... to build a career of wealth on the blood of laboring [Cần lao] people" ("*Bọn tư bản ... đã ... chà đạp lên phẩm giá con người ... xây dựng sự nghiệp giàu sang trên xương máu của dân chúng Cần lao*").[97]

This view of capitalism, with its apparently crude combination of "Papal encyclicals and kindergarten economics," a view that was derived in fact from the Marxian critique of political economy, informed the economic and political policies of the early South Vietnamese state: The "official Personalists in the Vietnamese Government ... remained at heart Marxists ... [i]n their concern over the human damage caused by ... rampant ... *laissez-faire* ... capitalism."[98] Thus, according to Nguyễn Ngọc Thơ, who served as the national economy secretary, the goal of the South Vietnamese state was to establish a "Personalist economic system" based on "economic cooperation practiced under the organizational form of cooperatives." This socialist system would "avoid the liberalism of the Capitalistic system with its cyclical evils of unemployment and economic crises."[99]

Against the depersonalizing inversion in capitalism – whereby money, as a means of exchange, becomes the aim of production itself – Nhu, repeating Mounier's slogan, proclaimed that the "goal of production must be the satisfaction of needs."[100] Affirming the principle of Personalist socialism, Nhu declared that "production must serve the people," in contrast to the inhuman condition in capitalism, where "it is man," in Mounier's words, "who is in the service of the economy."[101]

This capitalist economy was imposed upon the Vietnamese population by the early colonial administration, accompanied by an "ambitious French liberalization" of indigenous law, which introduced the "individual as a legal abstraction."[102] Instead of refusing to recognize the humanity of its Vietnamese subjects, the early colonial administration had attempted to grant them their inalienable rights, rights that had been denied by the imperial court and its *régime tyrannique*. Embracing a "social revolutionism," the early colonialists conceived of the imperial project as an extension of the French Revolution.[103] In the colony, therefore, the Rights of Man were applied in order to limit the political tyranny of the imperial state, as well as the "domestic tyranny" of the traditional family.

As the early colonialists would quickly discover, however, the attempt to establish these inalienable rights would weaken the very foundation of the non-Western society they intended to liberate: "In traditional Vietnam, the individual was not really ontologically separate from his or her family. The notion of the distinct, civic 'individual' – ... the fundament of all Western law – was absent."[104] By applying the "so-called rights of man ... the rights of egoistic man ... separated ... from the community,"[105] the French, therefore, would unwittingly erode the traditional bonds of community that prevailed in the precolonial period.[106]

Prior to this period, the country had consisted of a "myriad of scattered, thriving, semi-autonomous communes,"[107] governed by an imperial court whose seemingly absolute power was, in reality, largely spectacular, limited to the "ritual exercise of sovereignty": the coronation, the public execution and so on.[108] As Tạ Văn Tài suggests, the imperial state was a sovereignty that was almost completely devoid of "discipline," in the Foucaultian sense of the latter as the "daily exercise of surveillance," operating invisibly at the everyday level: "The Vietnamese dynastic state was a relatively weak polity, without the ability to reach deeply into all spheres of life because it did not have at its disposal mass communications means and a large police force or prison system."[109] Owing to the weakness of the imperial court and its tyrannical rule, village "notables managed local affairs, and the family was the fundamental unit of disciplinary 'jurisdiction.' ... Early French visitors were struck by the remarkably decentralized nature of social organization."[110]

In the precolonial period, the family and the semi-autonomous village exercised a discipline that preempted the role of the centralized government. Lacking the disciplinary apparatus of the modern state, the despotism of this "weak polity," then, was never extended over the entire territory of the "nation." The "emperor," as James Barnhart explains, "ruled intangibly over people, rather than concretely over territory; authority in peripheral areas (and even the exact location of international borders) was hazy."[111] Contrary, moreover, to the nationalist myth of the Vietnamese people, as united in a 2,000-year struggle to defend its national territory and culture against all foreign invaders, the subjects of the emperor were not a *national* people. Although "foreign invasion might touch off impassioned resistance, this could hardly be called 'nationalism.' Lines of allegiance to the emperor ran vertically from collective villages to the (idealized) person of the sovereign ... rather than horizontally among fellow citizens in a well-delimited nation-state."[112] The sovereignty, then, of the imperial court was not that of the "European conception of territorial sovereignty," which was not "introduced until Western colonization in the nineteenth century."[113]

In the twentieth century, the increasingly nationalist character of the anti-colonial struggle was a result of the spread of indigenous media. As the French secret police had observed, the latter helped to transform "Annamite society" from a "handful of individuals from ... feudal families" into "a tightly-knit opposition," united by a new national culture.[114] This supposedly ancient national culture, which was "unknown to the Annamites," would later be invoked by the two postcolonial states in Vietnam as the basis for claiming national territorial sovereignty.

This sovereignty, however, is distinct from that of the imperial court, whose weak tyrannical rule was only *ideally* extended over the territory that nominally belonged to the emperor, a weakness expressed in the traditional adage "*phép vua thua lệ làng*" ("the right of the emperor gives way to the customs of the village").[115] In the precolonial period, therefore, a despotic centralized state, which lacked the power of discipline, presided over a decentralized form of directly associated production based on the family. As a Republic of Vietnam government publication describes, the "social and political organization of Vietnam consisted of two

Vietnamese anti-colonialism

opposing and superimposed systems. At the bottom there was popular, autonomous ... democracy; at the top was the absolute monarchy which was highly centralized thanks to its mandarin system." The "Vietnamese nation," therefore (as the text continues, anachronistically applying the concept of the nation), "was like a federation composed of numerous and small communal states," autonomous "village commune[s], which ... sprang up spontaneously and adapted [themselves] to the extremely centralized system of the oriental absolute monarchies."[116] "Viewed from the top," this "nation," as Barnhart describes, "was a highly centralized system, based on formal procedure and extensive statutory texts; from the bottom, it was extremely decentralized, informal, and relatively undocumented."[117] "Vietnamese society," therefore, "was characterized by both a highly developed autocracy and remarkable degree of democracy."[118]

In terms of the relationship between the base and the superstructure, between the economic foundation and the legal and political order, the system was exactly the opposite of the one imposed by the French. In bourgeois democracy, the formal equality, guaranteed by the state, conceals the existence of concrete inequality within civil society, a contradiction that, according to Marx, is characteristic of capitalism. In contrast, the absolute sovereignty accorded to the Vietnamese emperor was merely a *formalized* tyranny, an abstraction disguising the "concrete weakness of imperial power," and the democratic organization of communal production.[119] In Nhu's terms, the official autocracy of the imperial state was limited, in reality, by the "democratic nature of the autonomous organization [tổ chức tự trị] of the village and [its] independence ... in relation to the central government."[120] Whereas the democratic "rights that the liberal State grants to its citizens are abrogated," as Mounier argued, "by the facts of their economic ... existence," the despotic authority of the Vietnamese court was abrogated by the economic autonomy of its imperial subjects. "The Rights of the emperor give way to the customs of the village."

If the emperor, then, as Lê Lợi proclaimed, exercised a "civilized" sovereignty over his "subjects" (*ngã dân*) (see Chapter 1), this formalized privilege was subordinate, nevertheless, to the village and its extrajuridical "customs" (customs that had not yet been canonized as part of a national culture that could serve as the basis for a "popular sovereignty" (*dân quyền*)). In contrast, therefore, to the *legal* right of the king (*phép vua*), the "democracy and autonomy in the village," as Diệm pointed out, was not a "written law" (*luật lệ thành văn*). Rather, it was a "customary practice [*phong tục tập quán*] passed down from one generation to the next," an extrajuridical form of autonomy that preempted the people's subjection under the law of the emperor.[121]

But as such, the autonomy of the emperor's subjects, in relation to his nominally absolute power, cannot be identified with the inalienable right of freedom belonging to an abstract individual. In Europe, as Diệm pointed out, the establishment of this juridical freedom had coincided, historically, with the development of new forms of coercion and techniques of control: "[I]n liberalism ... discipline is indispensable ... all economic activity is subject to the exigencies of technique which is imposed upon each of us and prevents him from acting ... independently."[122] During the era of industrial capitalism, these disciplinary techniques were deployed, in Foucault's terms, for the purpose of "extract[ing] time and labor from ... bodies."[123] Adapted to the colonial context, the new forms of discipline provided "the French [with]... capacities to control and to coerce never dreamed of by previous [Vietnamese] rulers," which "meant that traditional village obligations to the ruler ... taxes, corvée service, and military service ... could now be enforced with unprecedented efficiency."[124] On the other hand, in the precolonial period, as Diệm pointed out, "there was never an excessive centralization of power ... to enable conscription of labor-power" on a continual basis.[125] Lacking the power to impose a "daily exercise of surveillance," the "Annamite state," as one French observer acknowledged, "intervenes only on rare occasions ... It is indolent by nature."[126] Prior to the colonial period, therefore, the imperial court was as a formalized despotism that, while denying the rights of its subjects, was largely devoid of the modern power of discipline. In contrast to the *citizens* of a modern constitutional state, whose individual liberties entailed the creation of a panoptic machine, the *subjects* of the Vietnamese court preserved an autonomy that was never legally recognized, and therefore was never completely subjected to the disciplinary apparatus of the state.

As Charles Le Myre de Vilers, the first civilian governor of Indochina, lamented, this system of imperial tyranny and peasant autonomy, underlying Vietnamese civilization, was undermined by the political and economic liberalization carried out by the colonial regime. While the imposition of capitalism and liberal democracy liberated the people from the personal rule of a weak tyrannical sovereign, it also subjected the peasantry to the impersonal reign of the market.[127] "The French," according to Nhu, "have broken up the organization of our social infrastructure" (*tổ chức xã hội hạ tầng*), introducing capitalism in order to "replace an economic system based on the traditional village," and the "democratic

Vietnamese anti-colonialism

nature of [this] autonomous organization."[128] By liberalizing Vietnamese civilization, the French had precipitated a process of mass dispossession and proletarianization, unraveling the older organization of communal production, while creating the conditions for a system of formalized freedom based on the tyranny of production for profit:

> [T]he small proprietors tend to disappear ... while the proletariat develops; the municipal oligarchy, the essential base of the political constitution of Annam, no longer functions as it did traditionally ... Unconsciously, we have destroyed Annamite civilization, without putting anything in its place; we are marching towards a sort of social revolution.[129]

Vietnamese Personalism and anti-colonialism

This account of the civilizing mission departs from the conventional characterization of European colonialism in postcolonial theory as a hypocritical enterprise that "preached ... Enlightenment humanism" while denying the latter in practice.[130] In the Declaration of Independence, announced by Hồ Chí Minh in 1945, colonialism is condemned, in similar terms, as a glaring contradiction to the Rights of Man, proclaimed by a supposedly enlightened French Republic:

> The Declaration of ... 1791 on the Rights of Man and the Citizen ... states: "All men ... remain free and have equal rights." ... Nevertheless ... the French imperialists, abusing the standard of Liberty, Equality, and Fraternity ... have acted contrary to the ideals of humanity. They have built ... prisons ... impoverished our people, and ... mercilessly exploited our workers.[131]

In Le Myre de Vilers' account, on the other hand, the "destruction of Annamite civilization" was not the result of the colonial state "abusing the standard of Liberty [and] Equality." The "program" imposed by the early colonial government was "not to conquer in order to exploit the vanquished ... but, on the contrary, to try and instill the new subjects with [our] ideas," "calling them to enjoy the rights of the citizen."[132] By acting, however, in accordance with Republican principles (rather than "contrary to the ideals of humanity"), French colonialism "unconsciously" created a dispossessed peasantry, which could be exploited as wage labor for profit.[133] Deprived of its traditional function by a liberalization of Vietnamese law, aimed at the protection of individual freedom, the "municipal oligarchy" of the semi-autonomous village would be replaced by a modern apparatus of discipline: the police, the prison and the colonial school. In this "ruse of Reason," the contradictions to the Rights of Man, perpetrated by colonialism, emerge as the unintended result of policies that were "decisively shaped by [Enlightenment] doctrines which were, at base, anti-colonial."[134]

French colonialism, therefore, was not defined by a refusal to extend the inalienable rights of man to the colonial subject. On the contrary, the civilizing mission was an attempt to repeat the French Revolution in the non-Western world, imposing an abstract conception of man as the individual bearer of a formalized freedom that undermined an autonomous form of communal production. In Le Myre de Vilers' account, colonialism, then, is described, paradoxically, as a social revolution that, by imposing the political freedoms belonging to bourgeois society, unwittingly reproduced the economic conditions that led to the French Revolution: the creation of a dispossessed class, excluded from communal production.

For Nhu, this history of imperialism implied that the anti-colonial struggle could not simply repeat the ideals of the European Enlightenment, waging its revolution in the name of the same Rights of Man that had undermined Vietnamese civilization. The Personalist revolution, in other words, could not be carried out in the name of an Occidental ideology of liberalism, rooted in the structure of capitalism: "Our justice has to be based on … the theory of Personalism [and recognize] the situation of underdevelopment. [We] cannot follow the old system of justice left by the French because the European notion of freedom is not consistent with the Asian."[135] This aspect of Vietnamese Personalism distinguished the doctrine from the more orthodox anti-colonialism of Vietnamese Marxists who, to borrow the writer Phạm Quỳnh's description, were "rebels in the French style, for French Reasons."[136] These rebels, as Daniel Guérin predicted in 1930, would one day overthrow the "Western bourgeoisie," using its own ideology to oppose imperial rule:

> What is paradoxical about the intellectual evolution, parallel to the economic evolution, of the Orientals is that … the Europeans taught them the ideas that they are now using against their masters. … [T]he Western bourgeoisie brought about its own negation and fashioned its own gravediggers in a … striking manner. Where did these young Annamites learn about the rights of man, if not in Republican France?[137]

For Vietnamese Personalists, on the other hand, the paradox of imperialism was not that it contradicted the ideals of bourgeois democracy by refusing to recognize the inalienable rights of the colonial subject, rights that the French Revolution had declared universal. Rather, the paradox was that the inalienable rights that the French had applied in the colony, the rights of "egoistic man ... separated ... from the community," had served to establish the alienation of labor and the impersonal reign of the market. Instead of "negating" the Western bourgeoisie in the name of its own political principles, Nhu, therefore, rejected the Occidental ideology of liberalism that emerged from the structure of capitalism, which colonialism had established in the process by protecting the individual rights of its subjects:

> Under colonial domination, man is subjected to money and power. Such a regime favors the egoistic type of man ... Against colonialism ... the Vietnamese Personalist and communitarian revolution conceives of human value as independent of money ... and as residing in ... responsibility.[138]

For Nhu, then, the aim of the anti-colonial struggle, as a communitarian revolution, was not to realize the Rights of Man, denied to the colonial subject, the rights of a Western "egoistic man," subordinated to the anonymous power of money. The humanism, or "human value," which Nhu evokes in this passage, therefore, is directly opposed to the Enlightenment humanism to which Hô and other anti-colonial leaders appealed in order to condemn the hypocrisy of the colonial project. Instead, Nhu would propose a socialist humanism based on Mounier's conception of praxis, as an act of "responsible liberty," "*une discipline personnelle librement décidée.*"[139]

Labor and praxis

The expression in Vietnamese that Nhu invented in order to translate this notion of praxis was "*cần lao*," which was incorporated into the name of his political party, the Đảng Cần Lao Nhân Vị.[140] Although the latter is usually translated as the "Personalist Labor Party," Nhu wanted to distinguish the expression *cần lao* from "labor" or *lao động*. For Nhu, *lao động*, which was "used in the communist party name (*Đảng Lao Động Việt Nam*) ... implies labor under the pressure of an external authority." In contrast, *cần lao* "derives from a classical expression meaning a willingness to work without coercion, which can be translated as 'diligence.'"[141]

Like the concept of "culture" (*văn hoá*), moreover, "labor" or *lao động* is a modern expression whose use in the indigenous media that emerged in the colonial era coincided with the development of a capitalist economy and the process of mass dispossession. The word *lao động*,

The unimagined community

for example, does not appear in Auctore J. L. Taberd's 1838 *Dictionarium Latino-Anamiticum*. In the dictionary, moreover, *lao*, the root of *lao động*, is defined not as labor, but *fessus* or "tired," exhausted from physical exertion.¹⁴² In Đào Duy Anh's 1932 *Chinese-Vietnamese Dictionary* (*Hán-Việt từ điển*), on the other hand, *lao động* is explicitly identified with proletarian labor, defined as a "person who is hired to work by a capitalist" (*người làm thuê cho một nhà tư bản*), an "*ouvrier*."¹⁴³

In the ideology of the Vietnamese Communist Party, this modern form of production for profit is conflated with creative activity as such, thereby naturalizing a particular form of external compulsion inherited from the Occidental structure of capitalism. Instead of abolishing capitalism, therefore, the Communist Party, in accordance with its official state socialism, merely sought to collectivize the proletarian labor or *lao động* that constitutes the very foundation of capitalism, as a society in which work is "treated as 'merchandise' that the worker ... sells."¹⁴⁴ In this collectivized form of commodified labor, which supplanted the earlier system of decentralized communal and household production, the worker sells his labor power as merchandise to the state instead of to a private employer or capitalist. In that sense, "the dictatorship of the proletariat," as a Republican government publication described, is "the proletariat under a dictatorship."¹⁴⁵

If Nhu, then, "equated the 'evil' of capitalism with that of communism," the equation was based on a Personalist critique of the Soviet Union as a collectivized version of capitalism. In the latter, the Party, in organizing the process of production for profit, usurps the role of the capitalist class in securing the exploitation of labor: "Capitalism on one side and communism on the other side are profitable for only one class."¹⁴⁶ To borrow Marx's critique of the Proudhonist conception of the socialist state, the collectivization of proletarianized labor creates a "papacy of production," one in which the Communist Party emerges as the "despotic ruler of production and trustee of distribution."¹⁴⁷ Thus, instead of founding a new socialist society, the Vietnamese Communist Party established a collective regime of commodity production, one in which the alienation of *lao động* or labor is monopolized by what the Vietnamese Marxist philosopher Trần Đức Thảo referred to as a "red capitalist state" (*nhà nước tư bản đỏ*): The "people labor so that they [the communist leaders] ... can be satiated, free and happy" (*nhân dân lao động để cho họ được ... ấm no, tự do, hạnh phúc*).¹⁴⁸

For Nhu, this implied the need for a liberation of human activity from the domination of *lao động* or labor, imposed under both capitalism and communism (or, more precisely, under the liberal and collectivized forms of capitalist production, which Nhu characterized as systems based upon "competing 'Western' philosophies").[149] This liberation was identified with *cần lao*, as "a willingness to work without coercion." In the political philosophy of Personalism, "labor [*lao động*]," as Nguyễn Đức Cung describes it, "becomes diligence [*cần lao*] when it is no longer the slave of profit, as in capitalism, or a slave to the rule of the party, as in the communist regime."[150]

Thus, for Diệm, the "first task" of the South Vietnamese state "was the creation ... of institutions that could protect [the person] from the abstract power of market forces on one side and the impersonal state on the other."[151] Drawing on Mounier's work, Nhu referred to these anti-capitalist institutions as a real "infrastructure of democracy": "[O]ur Government aims at one major objective: the establishment of a truly democratic infrastructure."[152]

Vietnamese Personalism and American liberal democracy

As numerous critics have argued, however, this "infrastructure of democracy" did not appear to include any of the institutions most commonly associated with democracy. According to Milton Taylor, the Vietnamese Personalist democracy in the South that the US supported, contrary to the claims of the American government, was not a "stable, viable and democratic bastion of the Free World." Having established itself through a fraudulent referendum in 1955, Diệm's democratic republic appeared to more closely resemble a communist police state:

> [The regime] maintains a secret police ... and detains some 40,000 political prisoners in concentration camps. Arrests are made arbitrarily, detention is indefinite, fair trial procedures are unknown, the safeguards of ... juries and legal defense are virtually ignored, and almost all law is by edict ... The press is controlled as thoroughly as in the Soviet Union.[153]

Because of this lack of democracy, "most Americans, who have never heard of personalism," as the US ambassador, Frederick Nolting, explained to Diệm, "think that it means glorifying your person as head of state."[154] For US observers, therefore (who "found personalism vague and confusing, particularly as articulated by Nhu"),[155] the regime's ideology was simply an elaborate cover for authoritarian rule disguised as democracy, for "diemocracy." Diệm's Personalist democracy was "theoretically

2.3 Ngô Đình Diệm (courtesy of Hoover Institution Archives).

a parliamentary democracy but actually a personal dictatorship under Ngo Dinh Diem."[156]

Contrary to Philip Catton's description, however, the Ngos' attempt to build an "'infrastructure of democracy,' which was not ... synonymous with the promotion of Western-style liberties," did not imply a "loose definition of 'democracy.'"[157] Rather, the project was based on a Marxist humanist critique of bourgeois democracy, a critique in which "all manner of liberalism" was regarded as "the greatest and most evil fraud in history."[158] This Marxist humanism, therefore, was directly opposed to the Enlightenment humanism embodied in the Rights of Man, rights that, in the colonial era, had undermined Vietnamese civilization.

In Mounier's work, this fraudulent humanism is identified with the United States, and with the "economic subservience" that it sought to impose through the "Trojan horse" of the Marshall Plan as an imperialist program of economic liberalization.[159] While "Christians, like ... Mounier ... refused to oppose communism ... they denounced

Vietnamese anti-colonialism

the Marshall Plan and NATO for incorporating Western Europe into an American protectorate and destroying hope for an autonomous future."[160] Already in the 1930s, however, writers affiliated with Mounier's journal *Esprit*, which was one of the most influential French publications among intellectuals in the early Republic,[161] "developed [the] ... formula of anti-liberalism as anti-Americanism": "Since an America divorced from capitalism simply could not exist," the United States was a society that "could never move beyond ... liberal individualism."[162] Thus, Mounier's Marxist humanism, which was adopted by Diệm as the official philosophy of the South Vietnamese state, was also a form of French anti-Americanism.

For the French Personalists, moreover, the intractable character of American liberalism was matched by its naivety, by the vulgar and simplistic appeals that it used in support of "the greatest ... fraud in history." In American liberal individualism, the egoism of the old bourgeoisie was combined with the crass materialism of US consumer society, which the communist poet Louis Aragon described in 1951 as a degraded "civilization of bathtubs and Frigidaires."[163] In its foreign policy doctrine, moreover, the humanism of the European Enlightenment was replaced by a specious endorsement of liberal democracy, which, devoid of any real philosophical foundation, resembled the advertising that pervaded American culture. For the communists and Christian anti-capitalists such as Mounier, therefore, the Marshall Plan was part of a *"coca-colonisation"* of Europe. In this new imperialist doctrine, the inalienable right to individual liberty was simply repackaged, embellished with the image of freedom of choice in consumer society.[164]

In Vietnam, according to existential philosopher Nguyễn Văn Trung (who was also influenced by Mounier's thought), this *coca-colonisation* had supplanted the civilizing mission. Whereas the French had tried to educate the colonial elite in the lofty ideals of the French Revolution, the Americans appealed democratically to the Vietnamese "masses ... via mass media such as television, cinema, popular music, and magazines."[165] "The dominance of the American Empire," therefore, as Lý Chánh Trung argued similarly, has a "thoroughly different character than the dominance of classical empires." US imperialism sought to impose "a prefabricated freedom produced in America and imported here under the brands 'Coca' or 'Pepsi' Cola."[166]

If Diệm's Personalism, from the perspective of his American advisors, appeared to embody a "loose definition of 'democracy,'" for the Ngos the form of democracy endorsed by the American government was merely the latest variety of a completely fraudulent liberalism. Indeed, for the Ngos, the program that the USA proposed for creating a "bastion of the Free World" was an absurdly simplistic solution: The protection of individual rights and the establishment of a representative government, inclusive of oppositional parties, would naturally lead to a stable democracy that, based on the support of the people, would be capable of overcoming the communists. "The Americans," as the journalist Marguerite Higgins described, "who believed that more civil liberties were the sure answer to Vietnam's problems used to accuse Ngo Dinh Diệm and his brother ... of being 'as bad as Communists.'"[167] "We are advised," as Nhu explained, "that we must 'have the people with us,' a 'good' political system, a parliamentary regime, and so on' to beat the Communists."[168]

However, as Nhu pointed out, criticizing the "fallacies of the liberal position on Communism," the insurgency in the South was being effectively fought by a communist organization deprived of all the purported advantages of bourgeois democracy. Since the "Communists, of course, rejected ... political tolerance," Nhu, who had an "acute appreciation of Communist tactics,"[169] did not "see any necessary relationship between liberty and political participation ... and substantive popular support."[170] On the contrary, the establishment of a "good" parliamentary system, according to Nhu, "the kind of democratic government preached by Western liberals," would be antithetical to the aim of obtaining substantive support from the people.[171]

For Nhu, the problem with imposing a parliamentary system, however, was not that the country "lacked an indigenous democratic tradition,"[172] having known only what General Maxwell Taylor referred to as the "oriental despotic tradition."[173] Rather, the problem was that this despotic tradition was based on an entirely different form of democracy, one that was directly opposed to that of a liberal democratic regime.

Like the popular sovereignty invested in the parliamentary state, the despotic imperial court was viewed in the precolonial period as "the ideal embodiment of authority," granted the "exclusive right to formulate and execute laws" on behalf of the people.[174] However, in the case of the precolonial court, these laws, which were supposed to express the universal interest of all, were seen as *opposed* to the autonomy of the household and the village ("The laws of the emperor give way to the customs of the village"), to the democratic organization of communal production. This democratic tradition, therefore, was based not upon the ideal of equal representation under the law (which Diệm dismissed, using Mounier's terms, as a mere "supremacy of number"). Rather, it was based on the *suspension, avoidance or nullification of law*. A "cardinal mandate of the [Vietnamese political and juridical] system was to discourage litigation, and solve problems through local mediation. The proper realm of justice was not in the court, but outside it."[175] In that sense, the democratic autonomy of the traditional village, therefore, was directly opposed to the popular sovereignty of the parliamentary state, based on a legal ideal of equality that precludes the possibility of a "justice" outside the law.[176] As such, liberal democracy, as an Occidental ideology, precludes the communitarian form of democracy concealed beneath an "oriental despotic tradition" that was largely formal in nature.

Modernity and Personalism: Personal freedom and the discipline of communal production

> "You and I want totally different futures for Vietnam. Can you guarantee you will not try and impose a dictatorship of the proletariat here?" – Ngô Đình Diệm

Contrary to Catton, moreover, the Oriental Personalism espoused by the Ngos did not embody a contradictory view of the peasantry, as the inheritors of an authentic "primeval democracy" (*dân chủ sơ khai*) who were, nevertheless, unprepared to fully participate in a modern democracy.

> [A]t the same time as romanticizing peasants, the Ngos ... regarded them as ignorant and backward. "You have seen the Montagnard ... The Chams. The Cao Dai. The Hoa Hao [Diệm said]. The primitive villages where the ancestors rule – as they do most places in Vietnam. Tell me ... what can parliamentary democracy mean to a Montagnard, when his language does not even have a term to express it?[177]

While the Ngos, therefore, according to Catton, extolled the egalitarian virtues of the Vietnamese peasantry, they also "believed that it would take time before they could ... assume the responsibilities of citizenship."

Diệm's refusal, however, to establish a parliamentary state was not based on what Dipesh Chakrabarty has called a "historicist" denial of the modernity of non-Western peoples, consigning them, in a familiar colonial gesture, to an "imaginary waiting room of history."[178] In Vietnam, the imperialism of the civilizing mission, in its early stages at least, was not defined by a "recommendation to the colonized to wait." On the contrary, it was precisely the imperial administration's attempt to recognize the modernity of its colonial subjects, granting the Rights of Man to the Vietnamese peasantry, which had "destroyed Annamite civilization."[179]

If the peasants, therefore, according to Diệm, were ignorant of the advantages of parliamentary democracy (an Occidental ideology that Mounier called the "most evil fraud in history") it was not because they were still waiting to realize a fraudulent Western modernity: "Diem was not conforming to Western standards of democracy," which was "really the heart of the case against him." The "assumption that Occidental-style democracy was ... the answer to ... Vietnam's problems ... was an assumption with which Ngo Dinh Diem disagreed on both practical and philosophical grounds."[180]

For the Ngos, then, the non-parliamentary form of democracy of the Vietnamese peasantry provided the precedent for an entirely different form of modernity. This non-Western modernity, which the Ngos attempted to put into practice in their Personalist program, would serve to restore the ancient tradition of "primeval democracy" that had once been the foundation of Vietnamese civilization: "[W]e must build up slowly, beginning with the villages. There is a tradition of democracy and autonomy in the Village."[181] The revolution, then, would recover an ancient rural autonomy that had been undermined by "colonial domination ... and subjected to money and power." At the same time, the program would serve to establish "a new society," a "revolutionary [society] aimed at destroying the ancient social foundations based on feudal and colonialist influences."[182]

In this Vietnamese form of modernity, then, the ancient tradition of communal production, detached from the impersonal rule of the market, would be freed simultaneously from the feudal bonds of the family and the traditional hierarchy of the village, to be replaced by a free association of persons.[183] As Diệm insisted, however, this free association would be distinct from the system of individual liberties guaranteed in American-style liberal democracy: "we are not going back to a sterile copy of the mandarin past. But we are going to adapt the best of our heritage to the modern situation. The Americans have a ... society built on entirely different ideas of the priorities and values."[184] "But it is impossible – a delusion – to think that a solution for Asia consists in blindly copying Western models."[185] Thus, the modern form of democracy envisioned by the leaders of the early Republic would neither be a "sterile copy" of the precolonial past, with its despotic tradition of imperial rule, nor a blind imitation of the American model, based on the right of individual liberty: "President Ngo dinh Diem rejects both absolute individualism and absolute state power."[186] Instead, the "revolution" would "reconcile tradition and democracy" by restoring the ancient autonomy of the village on the modern foundation of a free association of persons.[187]

This concept of modernity corresponds to Marx's account of a postcapitalist form of society. In the *Grundrisse*, Marx defines the possibility of a postcapitalist society in relation to capitalist and precapitalist social formations. Whereas precapitalist societies were based on "relations of personal dependence" – "the patriarchal relation, the community of antiquity, feudalism" – capitalism is characterized by an individual freedom that engenders the alienating power of money and capital: The "general exchange of activities and products, which has become a vital condition for each individual – their mutual interconnection – here appears as something alien to them, autonomous, as a thing." In capitalism, therefore, "Personal independence [is] founded on objective dependence"; the mutual interaction between free individuals creates an economy that operates independently of their personal will, controlling them as an impersonal sovereign.[188]

On the other hand, a postcapitalist society would be a "community of free individuals ... with the means of production in common, in which the labour ... of ... individuals is consciously applied as the combined labour ... of the community."[189] In *Capital*, this postcapitalist form of production, liberated from the objective domination of money and the commodity form, is identified with the organization of labor in precapitalist modes of production, "spontaneously developed [at] ... the threshold of the history of civilized races." Like the "patriarchal ... peasant family," production in a postcapitalist society would constitute a form of "labour in common or directly associated labour." But whereas the division of labor within household production is based upon the hierarchy of the family, inherited from tradition, communal production in a postcapitalist society would be organized "in accordance with a definite social plan."[190] This plan, then, is opposed to both the principle of production for profit, in which individual freedom is founded on the impersonal power of capital, as well as the "relations of personal dependence" underlying the traditional family. In contrast to the latter, the plan would be the creation of a "community of free individuals," individuals whose freedom is subordinated to communal production: "Free individuality, based on the universal development of individuals and on their subordination of their communal, social productivity as their social wealth."[191]

This postcapitalist society, in which an ancient mode of communal production is "consciously applied as the combined labour ... of the community," corresponds to Mounier's notion of "responsible liberty." Just as Marx's conception of "free individuality" paradoxically implies its subordination to communal production, so "responsible liberty," according to Mounier, constitutes a "middle term" between the individual and the community: "Democracy is not the supremacy of the number, which is a kind of oppression. It is nothing but the search for the political means destined to guarantee all persons in a community the right to free development and maximum responsibility."[192] For Mounier, then, democracy cannot be identified with the popular vote, with a "*démocratie quantitative, parlementaire et irresponsable*," based on the right "of egoistic man … separated … from the community" and subject to the tyranny of production for profit. Freedom, in other words, cannot be understood, as in bourgeois society, in purely negative terms, as the "refusal to associate … the liberty to oppose."[193] Rather, freedom is the right to fully develop one's individual abilities in fulfilling the social obligations imposed by a community, whose aim is the freedom of individual persons. Drawing upon this Personalist conception of freedom, Nhu argued that a "Person [*Nhân vị*] who is not associated with the community is merely a cover for selfish individualism" (*một hình thức che đậy cá nhân chủ nghĩa quy về vị kỷ*). Conversely, a "community that is detached from the Person is a collectivism that conceals the enslavement of human beings."[194]

In Nhu's Oriental Personalism, this responsible liberty, embodied in a free individuality subordinated to the community, is translated as *cần lao*, or "willingness to work without coercion." *Cần lao*, then, refers to a communal compulsion that is freely imposed on the self in order to develop its personal freedom. In the Personalist government that Diệm sought to establish, this responsible liberty is opposed to the liberal democracy prescribed by the American government. Repeating Mounier's formula, Diệm affirmed that "democracy is [not] … the supremacy of numbers. Democracy is essentially a permanent effort to find the right political means for assuring to all citizens the right of free development and of maximum initiative, responsibility, and spiritual life."[195]

Unlike their American counterparts, then, the Ngos were not committed to the aim of creating a bastion of capitalism and liberal democracy based upon popular sovereignty and the protection of individual freedom. On the contrary, their goal was to develop a democratic organization of communal production, modernizing a primeval democracy that, in replacing the structure of capitalism, would dissolve its political superstructure. Thus, the Ngos demanded a "real democracy from the base (first of all the level of the village …) against formal and liberal democracy," a real democracy founded on "communitarian labor ... and justice based on a social plan ... rather than ... submission to the capitalist order."[196]

For prominent figures in the French Personalist movement, this political program represented a "travesty of the philosophy of Emmanuel Mounier."[197] According to Jean-Marie Domenach, Mounier's work was intended as a "'philosophical matrix' and by no means an ideology or system of government."[198] Nevertheless, the goal of establishing a "real democracy from the base" in the place of a fraudulent "formal or liberal democracy" would appear to conform to Mounier's appeals to abolish the bourgeois system of government: the "liberal stage of democracy ... will surely soon be superseded ... on the foundation of a new social structure." This prescription, moreover, is consistent with Marx's account of social revolution, in which "changes in the economic foundation lead ... to the transformation of the ... superstructure," instead of vice versa.

In accordance with Mounier's Marxist prescription, therefore, the "major objective" of the South Vietnamese state was not to establish a "good" parliamentary system, one that recognizes the will of the people expressed in the popular vote. On the contrary, the aim was to *supersede* the parliamentary system as such through the creation of an anti-capitalist "infrastructure of democracy" that would completely transform the political superstructure of liberalism. For Nhu, the strategy to be employed in this social revolution against capitalism and liberal democracy was the Strategic Hamlet Campaign: "In the movement of the strategic hamlets, a revolutionary movement starting from the base ... it is inevitable that the whole superstructure will be profoundly modified, with or without elections."[199]

This open disdain for the electoral machinery of the parliamentary state was matched, therefore, by an equally adamant commitment to the establishment of a democracy at the base. Thus Nhu, at an intraministerial committee meeting on November 8, "reprimanded provincial and district chiefs for not holding honest elections for chiefs of strategic hamlets, fearing that a VC [Viet Cong] or reactionary would be elected." As Nhu explained, "Free, secret elections of the hamlet chief and hamlet council are the key to the success of the strategic hamlets." By providing the means with which to "institute basic democracy ... on a local scale which the people can understand," the Strategic Hamlet Campaign would preempt the role of the parliamentary state and its centralized form of electoral democracy: "Through the Strategic Hamlet Program, the Government intends to give back to the hamlets the right of self-government with its own charter and system of community law."[200] Because of the program, hamlet leaders for "the first time ... were selected by ballot in most of South Vietnam." [201]

In Vietnam, then, Personalism "found its concrete expression in the programme of Strategic Hamlets."[202] As a modern reenactment of the Southward Advance, the program would serve to restore an ancient form of democracy, while replacing its traditional bonds with a new social plan based on the principle of a free association of persons liberated from "submission to the capitalist order."[203] In that sense, "the national policy of strategic hamlets" would embody the "quintessence of our truest traditions" in the form of a "perfectly revolutionary policy aimed at destroying ancient social foundations based on feudal influences." Thus, Nhu, while speaking openly "about his socialist concepts with … the highest-ranking Western diplomats," [204] never "hid … his ambition to reestablish the traditional commune (or village) autonomy in the millennium-old society of Việt Nam," an autonomy which had been undermined by the sovereignty of the capitalist economy.[205]

If the Strategic Hamlet Program, then, was "an anti-Communist version of a 'people's war' strategy," used by the insurgency in the South,[206] for Nhu, its "architect and prime mover,"[207] it was also, and more fundamentally, an anti-capitalist struggle: "I am anti-communist from the doctrinal point of view. I am not anti-communist from a political point of view or from a human point of view. I consider the communists as brothers. I am not in favor of a crusade against communism."[208]

For Nhu, then, the war was not a crusade against communism itself, but against the Stalinist doctrine espoused by the Vietnamese Communist Party. This doctrine affirmed the capitalist institution of proletarian labor or *lao động*, which was opposed to the Marxist conception of the person as a free individual, subordinated to the community and communal production. For the Ngos, therefore, Personalism was not an anti-communist doctrine, but a communism that was more anti-capitalist than the vulgar Marxism adopted by the Communist Party: "I am really combating communism in order to put an end to materialistic capitalism."[209]

As the Marxist historian Gabriel Kolko observed, the Vietnamese Communist Party was made up "overwhelmingly [of] men who mastered a simple litany of phrases and had an astonishingly superficial theoretical … capacity. … [N]one incorporated Marxist or Leninist doctrines into their thinking in any meaningful way and, more important, very few even attempted to do so."[210] This superficial theoretical capacity

2.4 Ngô Đình Nhu at the inauguration of the Strategic Village of Củ Chi, March 3, 1962 (courtesy of Harry S. Truman Library & Museum).

was ridiculed in South Vietnamese radio broadcasts during the war: The *"Lao Dong* Party is the single Communist Party in the … 'socialist camp' which did not have … any party-theoretician." Its leaders and "theorists," including Trường Chinh and Hồ Chí Minh, were men who needed "a lot of quotations to make clear what [they] want … to say" because they did "not understand much of the subject."[211] Compared with this superficial understanding of Marxism, the Ngos believed that Personalism, as a communist doctrine, was "capable of counterbalancing the type of primitive Marxism that the Vietminh was trying to 'sell' to the Vietnamese."[212]

But in that case, the war, as it was waged in the early Republic, was not a conflict between communism and democracy or Marxism and nationalism. Rather, it was a contest between two different visions of anti-colonial communism, Stalinist and Marxist humanist.[213] As Diệm emphasized in a speech: "The current struggle of the Vietnamese people is not only a struggle for national independence. It is … a social revolution for the economic independence of Vietnamese farmers and laborers."[214] For Nhu, moreover, this social revolution, which would be carried out through the Strategic Hamlet Campaign, would serve as "the first stage of de-colonization."[215]

Notes

1. Thomas L. Ahern, *CIA and the House of Ngo: Covert Action in South Vietnam, 1954–1963* (Washington, DC: Center for the Study of Intelligence, 2000), 108, 157.
2. Anthony Trawick Bouscaren, *The Last of the Mandarins; Diem of Vietnam* (Pittsburgh, PA: Duquesne University Press, 1965), 56–7.
3. Frances Fitzgerald, *Fire in the Lake: The Vietnamese and the Americans in Vietnam* (New York: Vintage, 1972), 127–8.
4. Michael Field, *The Prevailing Wind: Witness in Indo-China* (London: Methuen & Co. Ltd., 1965), 313.
5. Quoted in Angelo Del Boca and Mario Giovana, *I figli del sole, Mezzo Secolo di nazi-fascismo nel mondo* [The Children of the Sun: A Half-Century of Nazi-Fascism] (Milan: Feltrinelli editore, 1965), 334.
6. Quoted in Wilfred G. Burchett, *The Furtive War: The United States in Vietnam and Laos* (New York: International Publishers, 1963), 82.
7. James C. Dobson, Jr., "Diem, Ngo Dinh," in *Encyclopedia of Modern Christian Politics*, vol. 1, A–K, ed. Roy P. Domenico and Mark Y. Hanley (London: Greenwood Press, 2006), 170.
8. Chester A. Bain, *Vietnam: The Roots of Conflict* (Englewood Cliffs, NJ: Prentice-Hall, Inc., 1967), 118.
9. John C. Donnell, "National renovation campaigns in Vietnam," *Pacific Affairs*, 32 (March 1959), 77–80.
10. Bửu Lịch, "Les idéologies dans la République du Sud Vietnam 1954–1975" (Ph.D. dissertation, Université de Paris VII, 1983/1984), 90.
11. Lucien Sève, "Les troisième voies," *La Pensée*, 92 (July–August 1960), 44.
12. Like Sartre's existentialist Marxism, Personalism was based on a philosophical anthropology derived from what Jacques Derrida described as a French "anthropologistic reading of Hegel, Husserl, and Heidegger." This reading, "which furnished the best conceptual resources to postwar French thought… was the common ground of Christian or atheist existentialisms [and] … of personalisms of the right or the left, of Marxism in the classical style." (Jacques Derrida, *Margins of Philosophy*, trans. Alan Bass (London: The Harvester Press, 1982), 117). Thus, Sartre, in his search for method, would attempt to synthesize existentialism and Marxism on the basis of an anthropological interpretation of Martin Heidegger's notion of *Dasein* as "projection": "From the day that Marxist thought will have taken on the *human dimension* (that is, the *existential project*) as the foundation of anthropological Knowledge, existentialism will … [be] surpassed … by the totalizing movement of philosophy." (Sartre, *Search for a Method* (New

York: Vintage, 1968), 181.) Jean Lacroix, one of Mounier's principal collaborators at the journal *Esprit*, makes a similar philosophical gesture in his Personalist synthesis of existentialism and Marxism. Drawing in part on Alexandre Kojève's anthropological account of the *Phenomenology of Spirit*, Lacroix identifies "l'homme marxiste" with the concept of the Person and the existentialist conception of man. (*Marxisme, existentialisme, personnalisme: présence de l'éternité dans le temps* [Marxism, existentialism, personalism: presence of eternity in time] (Paris: Presses universitaires de France, 1966)). Such humanist interpretations of Marxism (which Michel Foucault characterized as "the kind of Marxism that agonizes over the… alienation" of man (Michel Foucault, *Remarks on Marx: Conversations with Duccio Trombardori* (New York: Semiotext(e) Books, 1991), 86.) would be challenged by communist philosophers, trained at the École Normale Supérieure, who were influenced by the work of Jean Cavaillès. These philosophers included, most notably, Trần Đức Thảo, who developed a dialectical materialist reading of Edmund Husserl's phenomenology, and Louis Althusser, whose Marxist theory of knowledge was based on Cavaillès' philosophy of science. According to Derrida, this work occupies an important but largely unrecognized position within a still unwritten "genealogy of the Rue d'Ulm philosophers" (i.e., the work of Derrida, Foucault, Lyotard, Bourdieu, etc.: Jacques Derrida, *Negotiations: Interventions and Interviews, 1971–2001*, ed. Elizabeth Rottenberg (Stanford, CA: Stanford University Press, 2002), 148–9.

13 Edward Francis Rice, *Emmanuel Mounier and Esprit, 1932–1938* (Madison: University of Wisconsin, 1967), 76. See also Bửu Lịch, "Les idéologies dans la République du Sud Vietnam," 36. For a discussion of Mounier's relationship to the French Communist Party, see Donald Wolf, "Emmanuel Mounier: A Catholic of the Left," *The Review of Politics*, 22:3 (July 1960), 324–44.

14 Seth Armus, *French Anti-Americanism (1930–1948): Critical Moments in a Complex History* (Lanham, MD: Lexington Books. 2007), 66. See also Zeev Sternhell, *Neither Right nor Left: Fascist Ideology in France* (Princeton, NJ: Princeton University Press, 1983), 75; and Michael Gauvreau, "Catholicism in Quebec: Confronting Modernity," in *Contemporary Quebec: Selected Readings and Commentaries*, ed. Michael D. Behiels and Matthew Hayday (Montréal: McGill-Queen's University Press, 2011), 130. On American personalism and Marxism, see Gerard Gagnon, "Le Personnalisme Américain" (Ph.D. dissertation, University of Ottawa, 1956), 191.

15 Quoted in Jean Lacouture, *Le Vietnam entre deux paix* (Paris: Éditions du Seuil, 1965), 37. The interview was supposed to appear in two January issues of *Le Monde* (see Donnell, "Politics in South Vietnam," 92).

16 Donnell, "Politics in South Vietnam," 172.

17 On Vietnamese Catholicism and radical politics, see Charles Keith, *Catholic Vietnam: A Church from Empire to Nation* (Berkeley: University of California Press, 2012), 1–10.

18 See Leopold Senghor, *African Socialism* (New York: American Society of African Culture, 1959) [pamphlet], and Nadia Yala Kisukidi, "L'influence vivante du personnalisme de Mounier sur la philosophie esthétique et la poésie de Léopold Sédar Senghor," *COnTEXTES* [online], December 2012. https://journals.openedition.org/contextes/5592. Last accessed September 14, 2019.
19 Bichara Khader, *Le Monde arabe expliqué à l'Europe: histoire, imaginaire, culture, politique, économie, géopolitique* (Paris: Harmattan, 2009), 208.
20 See Majid Fakhry, *A History of Islamic Philosophy*, 3rd ed. (New York: Columbia University Press, 2004), 386.
21 Seth Armus, "Primacy of the Spiritual: French Resistance to America and the Formation of French Identity" (Ph.D. dissertation, State University of New York: Stony Brook, 1998), 112.
22 Emmanuel Mounier, "Débat à Haute Voix," *Esprit*, 119:2 (1946), 165.
23 Tony Judt, *Past Imperfect: French Intellectuals, 1944–1956* (Berkeley and Los Angeles: California University Press, 1992), 155.
24 Armus, *French Anti-Americanism*, 81.
25 Emmanuel Mounier, "Rupture entre l'ordre chrétien et le désordre établi" [The Rupture between the Christian Order and the Established Disorder], *Esprit*, 6 (March 1933), 875.
26 Emmanuel Mounier, *Liberté sans condition* (Paris: Editions du Seuil, 1946), 218. Seth Armus argues that Mounier only turned "after the war, into a trendy *marxisant*," and that this served to cover over the fact that "Mounier and many of his followers [were] quite comfortable in a collaborationist France." (Seth Armus, "The Eternal enemy: Emmanuel Mounier's *Esprit* and French anti-Americanism," *French Historical Studies*, 2 (Spring 2001), 288.) During the war, Mounier, despite his fundamental opposition to fascism and antisemitism, initially found common cause with the Vichy government in its "refusal of the liberal order." This has led scholars like Zeev Sternhell to argue that Mounier's Personalist critique of liberal individualism "shared ideas and political reflexes with Fascism." (Zeev Sternhell, "Emmanuel Mounier et la contestation de la démocratie libérale dans la France des années trente," in *Revue française de science politique*, 34ᵉ année, n°6, 1984, 1144.)
27 William Rauch, *Politics and Belief in Contemporary France* (The Hague: Martinus Nijhoff, 1972), 90.
28 Emmanuel Mounier, *Œuvres*, vol. 1 (Paris: Éditions du Seuil, 1961), 469.
29 Emmanuel Mounier, *Personalisme*, 7th ed. (Paris: Les Presses universitaires de France, 1961), 30.
30 Pope John Paul II, *On Human Work: Encyclical Laborem Exercens* (Washington DC: Office for Publishing and Promotion Services, United States Catholic Conference, 1981), 15. See also Nguyễn Đức Cung's discussion of the text in relation to Vietnamese Personalism in "*Từ Ấp Chiến Lược Đến Biến Cố Tết Mậu Thân: Những Hệ Luỵ Lịch Sử Trong Chiến Tranh*

Việt Nam" [From the Strategic Hamlet to the Tet Offensive: Historical Falsehoods in the Vietnam War]. http://kilopad.com/Tieu-su-Hoi-ky-c12/doc-sach-truc-tuyen-tu-ap-chien-luoc-den-bien-co-tet-mau-than-b3591/chuong-7-1-1-van-de-y-thuc-he-chinh-tri-ti7. Last accessed July 21, 2019.
31 Karl Marx, "On the Jewish Question," in *Early Writings*, trans. Rodney Livingstone and Gregor Benton (London: Penguin Books, 1992), 241.
32 Mounier, *Œuvres*, vol. 1, 271.
33 Mounier, *Personalisme*, 106.
34 Ibid., 16.
35 Mounier, *Œuvres*, vol. 1, 271.
36 Ibid., 289.
37 Marx, "On the Jewish Question," 229.
38 Mounier, *Œuvres*, vol. 1, 426.
39 Marx, "On the Jewish Question," 229.
40 Mounier, *Personalisme*, 35.
41 Ibid., 35.
42 Marx, *Capital: A Critique of Political Economy*, vol. 1 (Chicago: Charles H. Kerr & Co., 1915), 477.
43 Marx, "On the Jewish Question," 219.
44 Ibid.
45 Mounier, *De la propriété capitaliste à la propriété humaine* (Paris: Desclée de Brouwer, 1936), 27.
46 Marx, "On the Jewish Question," 220.
47 Quoted in Rauch, *Politics and Belief*, 91.
48 Mounier, *Personalisme*, 114.
49 Karl Marx, *Grundrisse: Foundations of the Critique of Political Economy* (London: Penguin, 1973), 248.
50 Quoted in Sternhell, *Neither Right nor Left*, 281.
51 Emmanuel Mounier, *Manifeste au service du personnalisme* (Paris: Aubier, Éditions Montaigne, 1936), 145.
52 Mounier, *De la propriété capitaliste*, 36.
53 Ibid., 35.
54 Ibid., 15.
55 Ibid.
56 Ibid., 16.
57 Mounier, *Œuvres*, vol. 1, 423.
58 Ibid., 21.
59 Ibid., 36.
60 Pope John Paul II, *On Human Work*, 16.
61 According to Jean Lacroix, Personalism, therefore, is a humanism or philosophical anthropology based on a "mutual copenetration of subject and object": Jean Lacroix, *Marxisme, existentialisme, personnalisme*, 109.

62 Mounier, *Personalisme*, 75.
63 Ibid., 30.
64 Eileen Cantin, *Mounier: A Personalist View of History* (New York: Paulist Press, 1973), 30.
65 Ibid., 106.
66 Edmond Hameau, "La Propriete littéraire: Les Droits d'Auteur," *Esprit: revue internationale*, 19 (April 1934), 161.
67 Mounier, *Personalisme*, xviii.
68 Ibid., ix.
69 Mounier, *Manifeste*, 232.
70 Emmanuel Mounier, *Be Not Afraid: A Denunciation of Despair* (New York: Sheed and Ward, 1962), 161.
71 Trần Hữu Thanh, *Cuộc cách mạng nhân vị, Đối Đáp* [The Personalist Revolution: Questions and Answers] (Saigon: Phạm Thanh Giản, 1955), 26.
72 Mounier, *Personalisme*, 63.
73 Ibid., 114.
74 Michel Foucault, *Society Must Be Defended: Lectures at the College de France, 1975-76* (New York: Picador, 2003), 36.
75 Murray Bookchin, *Social Ecology and Communalism* (Oakland, CA: AK Press, 2006), 91.
76 Mounier, *De la propriété*, 121.
77 Marx, "A Contribution to the Critique of Political Economy," *Early Writings*, 426.
78 Mounier, *Personalisme*, 115.
79 Emmanuel Mounier, *Révolution personnaliste et communautaire* (Paris: F. Aubier, 1935), 198.
80 Ibid., 218.
81 Archives Nationales, Paris. AJ-16-2708.
82 William S. Lewis, *Louis Althusser and the Traditions of French Marxism* (Lanham, MD: Lexington Books, 2005), 135.
83 Nguyễn Xuân Hoài, "Chế độ Việt Nam cộng hòa ở miền Nam Việt Nam giai đoạn 1955-1963" [The Republic of Vietnam regime in South Vietnam (1955-1963)] (Dissertation, Ho Chi Minh City: University of Social Sciences and Humanities, 2011), 43-47.
84 Bửu Lịch, "Les idéologies dans la République du Sud Vietnam," 36.
85 Keith Taylor, *A History of the Vietnamese* (Cambridge: Cambridge University Press, 2013), 556.
86 Simon Gikandi, "Poststructuralism and Postcolonial Discourse," in *The Cambridge Companion to Postcolonial Literary Studies*, ed. Neil Lazarus (Cambridge: Cambridge University Press, 2004), 100.
87 Đỗ Mậu, *Việt Nam máu lửa quê hương tôi* [Vietnam: My Country of Blood and Fire] (California: Nhà Xuất bản Hương Quê, 1986), 800-1.

88 *Press interviews with President Ngo Dinh Diệm, Political Counselor Ngo Dinh Nhu* (Saigon: Republic of Vietnam, 1963), 68.
89 Meeting Minutes (#36), Uỷ-Ban Liên-Bộ Đặc-Trách về Ấp Chiến-Lược tại Dinh Gia Long [Intra-Ministry Committee for Strategic Hamlets], 15–16. VCA. 1820204001 February 1, 1963. Box 02, Folder 04. Douglas Pike Collection: Other Manuscripts – Intra-Ministry Committee for Strategic Hamlets.
90 Field, *The Prevailing Wind*, 152.
91 Congress, House, Committee on Armed Services, "Major Trends in South Vietnam," 1956 French Withdrawal – 1960, in United States – Vietnam Relations. 1945–1967. d. Volume IV, Book 10 of 12, 1192.
92 Donnell, "National renovation campaigns in Vietnam," 469. See also Economic and Social Development, 15. Michigan State University Archives & Historical Collections, Wesley R. Fishel Papers (UA 17.95). Box 1192, Folder 35.
93 Quoted in Bernard B. Fall, "Review: *Problems of Freedom in South Vietnam*," *International Journal*, 17:4 (Fall 1962), 436.
94 Nguyên Thái, *Is South Vietnam Viable?* (Manila: Carmelo and Bauermann, 1962), 129.
95 Quoted in Ahern, *CIA and the House of Ngo*, 157.
96 "Personalism – Vietnamese Specialists; also Others Somewhat Relevant," VCA. January 1, 1953. Folder 14, Box 03. John Donnell Collection. See also Bernard Fall, "Book Review, *Problems of Freedom: South Vietnam Since Independence*," *Journal of Asian Studies*. VCA. February 1, 1963. Folder 11, Box 12. Douglas Pike Collection: Other Manuscripts – American Friends of Vietnam.
97 Tuyên ngôn Cần lao Nhân vị Cách mạng Đảng [Manifesto of the Cần Lao Personalist Revolutionary Party], folder 29361, Phông Phủ Tổng Thống [Files of the Office of the President], Vietnam National Archives No. 2.
98 Donnell, "National renovation campaigns in Vietnam," 135, 469. References to the economic literature of the period in South Vietnamese journals such as *Quê Hương* include works by leftist critics of capitalism and political liberalism. See Nguyễn Như Cường, "*Công nghiệp hóa và phát triển kinh tế*" [Industrialization and Economic Development]. *Quê Hương*, 9 (March 1960). Among these works are the writings of dependency theorists and Marxist thinkers such as the Trinidadian economist Frederic Clairmont, who, in *Economic Liberalism and Underdevelopment*, defines liberalism as faith in the "impersonal functioning of an unfettered market": Frederic Clairmont, *Economic Liberalism and Underdevelopment: Studies in the Disintegration of an Idea* (New York: Asia Publishing House, 1960), 7.
99 Quoted in M. N. Trued, "South Viet-Nam's industrial development center," *Pacific Affairs*, 33:3 (September 1960), 259.
100 Đảng cương Cần lao Nhân vị Cách mạng Đảng [Principles of the Cần Lao Personalist Revolutionary Party].

The unimagined community

101 Quoted in Donnell, "National renovation campaigns in Vietnam," 168.
102 James Barnhart, "Violence and the Civilizing Mission: Native Justice in French Colonial Vietnam, 1858–1914" (Ph.D. dissertation, University of Chicago, 1999), 231.
103 Alexander Woodside, *Community and Revolution in Modern Vietnam* (Boston, MA: Houghton Mifflin, 1976), 8.
104 Barnhart, "Violence and the Civilizing Mission," 190.
105 Marx, "On the Jewish Question," 229.
106 See Tùng Phong (Ngô Đình Nhu), *Chính đề Việt Nam* [Political Solution for Vietnam] (Sài Gòn: Nhà xuất bản Đồng Nai, 1964).
107 Barnhart, "Violence and the Civilizing Mission," 591. See also Maurice Barruel, *De la Substitution progressive des tribunaux français aux tribunaux indigènes en IndoChine (thèse)*. In-8° (1905), 214, and Nhu's account of the federal structure of the precolonial Vietnamese "nation" in Directorate General of Information (RVN), *Viet Nam's Strategic Hamlets* (Saigon, 1963), 3.
108 Foucault, *Discipline and Punish*, 217.
109 Tạ Văn Tài. "The Vietnamese tradition of human rights," *Indochina Research Monograph #4* (Berkeley: University of California, 1988), 43.
110 Barnhart, "Violence and the Civilizing Mission," 12.
111 Ibid., 110.
112 Ibid., 111.
113 Yoshiharu Tsuboi, *L'Empire Vietnamien face à la France et à la Chine* (Paris: L'Harmattan, 1987).
114 CAOM (Aix). Indochine. Gouvernement Général 7 F22. L'Administrateur Chef du Service de la Sûreté a M. le Gouverneur de la Cochinchine. "Objet: Sûreté Politique." Saigon, April 2, 1921. See also David Marr, *Vietnamese Anticolonialism, 1885–1925* (Berkeley: University of California Press, 1972), 213.
115 See Minh Võ Vũ Đức Minh, *Ngô Đình Diệm và Chính Nghĩa Dân Tộc* [Ngô Đình Diệm and the National Cause] (California: Hồng Đức, 2008), 129.
116 Nguyen Dang Thuc, "Democracy in traditional Vietnamese society," *Vietnam Culture Series*, 4 (Department of National Education, 1961), 5–6.
117 Barnhart, "Violence and the Civilizing Mission," 132.
118 Ellen Hammer, *The Struggle for Indochina, 1940–1955* (Stanford, CA: Stanford University Press, 1954).
119 Barnhart, "Violence and the Civilizing Mission," 113.
120 Nhu, *Chính Đề Việt Nam*, 28. On the "autonomous organization" of the traditional village, see Vũ Quốc Thúc's *L'économie communaliste du Vietnam* (Hanoi: Presse Universitaire, 1951), which is the primary source on the topic in *Chính Đề Việt Nam*.
121 Quoted in Nguyễn Ngọc Tấn, "Chủ-Nghĩa NHÂN-VỊ: Con Đường Mới, Con Đường của Tiến Bộ?" [Personalism: A New Road, A Road of Progress], (*Hội Người Việt Quốc Gia* (2007)), 149. See also *The Village Council as an*

Vietnamese anti-colonialism

Institution in Vietnam, 4. VCA. 2321511005 January 19, 1959. Box 15, Folder 11. Douglas Pike Collection: Unit 06 – Democratic Republic of Vietnam.
122 President Ngo Dinh Diem on Democracy (Addresses relative to the Constitution) (Saigon: Press Office, 1958).
123 Foucault, Society Must Be Defended, 35.
124 See also Vietnamese Tradition on Trial, 3.
125 Address of Ngo Dinh Diem before a luncheon, May 14, 1957. Michigan State University Archives & Historical Collections Wesley R. Fishel Papers (UA 17.95). Box 1193, Folder 56.
126 Barruel, De la Substitution progressive des tribunaux français, 214.
127 Clive Christie, Ideology and Revolution in Southeast Asia 1900–1980 (Richmond: Curzon Press, 2001), 149.
128 Tùng Phong (Ngô Đình Nhu), Chính Đề Việt Nam, 397.
129 Charles Marie Le Myre de Vilers, Les Institutions Civiles De La Cochinchine, 1879–1881: Recueil Des Principaux Documents Officiels (Paris: E. Paul, 1908), 137. In the Mekong Delta, this process of proletarianization had in fact preceded the arrival of the French. By the early eighteenth century, "Vietnamese settlement in the Mekong" was characterized by a "regime of large landholders and a mobile peasantry" (Taylor, A History of the Vietnamese, 464).
130 Chakrabarty, Provincializing Europe, 4.
131 Spencer C. Tucker (ed.), Encyclopedia of the Vietnam War: A Political, Social, and Military History, vol. 3 (Santa Barbara, CA: ABC-CLIO, 1998), 889.
132 Le Myre de Vilers, Les Institutions Civiles De La Cochinchine, 50.
133 Ibid., 140–1.
134 Barnhart, "Violence and the Civilizing Mission," 241.
135 Meeting Minutes (#34), Uỷ-Ban Liên-Bộ Đặc-Trách về Ấp Chiến-Lược tại Dinh Gia Long [Intra-Ministry Committee for Strategic Hamlets], 21. VCA. 1820203001 January 4, 1963. Box 02, Folder 03. Douglas Pike Collection: Other Manuscripts – Intra-Ministry Committee for Strategic Hamlets.
136 Scott McConnell, Leftward Journey: The Education of Vietnamese Students in France, 1919–1939 (New Brunswick, NJ: Transaction, 1989).
137 Daniel Guérin, Ci-gît le colonialisme: Algérie, Inde, Indochine, Madagascar, Maroc, Palestine, Polynésie, Tunisie – Témoignage Militant (Paris: Mouton, 1973), 427.
138 Tan Phong (Ngô Đình Nhu), "Ấp Chiến lược: một thực hiện mới của chính phủ để diệt cong và xây dựng nông thôn" [Strategic Hamlets: A New Government Policy for Exterminating the Communists and Rural Reconstruction], Quê Hương, 37 (1962), 41–2.
139 Mounier, Manifeste, 232.
140 See Edmund S. Wehrle, "'No more pressing task than organization in Southeast Asia': The AFL-CIO approaches the Vietnam War, 1947–1964," Labor History, 42:3 (2001), 277–95.

141 Taylor, *A History of the Vietnamese*, 556–7.
142 J. L. Taberd and Pierre Joseph, Georges, Pigneau de Béhaine, "Lao," *Dictionarium Latino-Anamiticum* (Fredericnagori vulgo Serampore: ex typis J. C. Marshman, 1838), 255.
143 Đào Duy Anh. *Hán-Việt từ điển* [Chinese-Vietnamese Dictionary] (Hà Nội: Nhà xuất bản văn hoá thông tin, 2005), 334.
144 Pope John Paul II, *On Human Work*, 15. On the Communist Party's conception of a socialist economy, see Lê Duẩn, *Cách mạng xã hội chủ nghĩa ở Việt Nam* [The Socialist Revolution in Vietnam] (Hà Nội: Nhà Xuất Bản Sự Thật, 1963), 311.
145 Phuc Thien, *President Ngo-Dinh-Diem's Political Philosophy* (Saigon: Review Horizons, 1956), 8.
146 Quoted in Edward Doyle and Stephen Weiss, *A Collision of Cultures* (Boston, MA: Boston Publishing Co., 1984), 19.
147 Marx, *Grundrisse*, 15.
148 Trần Đức Thảo, *Những lời trăng trối*, 61.
149 Paper – The Political Factor in Pacification: A Vietnam Case Study [Draft], 5. VCA. 21470122001 No Date. Box 01, Folder 22. Vincent Puritano Collection.
150 Nguyễn Đức Cung, "*Từ Ấp Chiến Lược Đến Biến Cố Tết Mậu Thân: Những Hệ Luỵ Lịch Sử Trong Chiến Tranh Việt Nam.*"
151 Christie, *Ideology and Revolution in Southeast Asia*, 148.
152 Quoted in Donnell, "National renovation campaigns in Vietnam," 578–9.
153 Jaffe and Taylor, "A crumbling bastion," 17.
154 Quoted in Joseph Buttinger, *Vietnam: Vietnam at War: A Dragon Embattled*, vol. 2 (London: Pall Mall Press, 1967), 1139.
155 Jerome T. French, "Politics and National Development in Vietnam – 1954–1960," Pol. Sci. 287A, 9. VCA. No Date. Folder 39, Box 01. John B. O'Donnell Collection.
156 Robert Vincent Daniels, *Year of the Heroic Guerrilla: World Revolution and Counterrevolution in 1968* (Cambridge, MA: Harvard University Press, 1996), 21. See also George C. Herring, *America's Longest War: The United States and Vietnam, 1950–1975*. 4th ed. (Boston, MA: McGraw-Hill, 2002), 77.
157 Philip Catton, *Diem's Final Failure* (Lawrence: University Press of Kansas, 2002), 49.
158 Quoted in Armus, *French Anti-Americanism*, 66. See also Sternhell, *Neither Right nor Left*, 290–1.
159 André Véran, "Visages Americains du Plan Marshall," *Esprit*, 144 (April 1948), 551–2.
160 Richard F. Kuisel, *Seducing the French: The Dilemma of Americanization* (Berkeley: University of California Press, 1993), 42–3.
161 Đào Trung Đạo, "Nguyễn Văn Lục hay Trần Trọng Đăng Đàn: Ai là con hoang của Sartre?" [Nguyễn Văn Lục or Trần Trọng Đăng Đàn: Who is the

Bastard Child of Sartre?] *Talawas* (August 23, 2004), talawas.org/talaDB/showFile.php?res=2666&rb=0301.
162 Armus, *French Anti-Americanism*, 67.
163 Quoted in Alessandro Brogi, *Confronting America: The Cold War between the United States and the Communists in France and Italy* (Chapel Hill: The North Carolina University Press, 2011), 168.
164 Kuisel, *Seducing the French*, 38.
165 Quoted in Hiên Thu Lương, "Vietnamese Existential Philosophy: A Critical Appraisal" (Ph.D. dissertation, Temple University, 2009), 6.
166 Lý Chánh Trung, "Tự do Pepsi-Cola" [Pepsi Cola Freedom]. *Tin Sáng* (October 19, 1970).
167 Higgins, *Our Vietnam Nightmare*, 293.
168 Quoted in Donnell, "National renovation campaigns in Vietnam," 521.
169 Ray S. Cline to Maxwell D. Taylor. Document, Central Intelligence Agency "Possible Rapproachment Between North and South Vietnam [sic]." VCA. September 26, 1963. Folder 04, Box 01. David Lifton Collection.
170 Quoted in Donnell, "National renovation campaigns in Vietnam," 520–1.
171 See *Press interviews with President Ngo Dinh Diệm*, 68.
172 George Donelson Moss, *Vietnam: An American Ordeal* (New York: Routledge, 2016), 72.
173 Letter from the President's Military Representative (Taylor) to the President, Washington, November 3, 1961.
174 Barnhart, "Violence and the Civilizing Mission," 105.
175 Ibid., 127.
176 Phuc Thien, *Ngo Dinh Diem of Viet-Nam* (Saigon: Press Office, Presidency of the Republic of Viet-Nam, 1957), 18.
177 Catton, *Diem's Final Failure*, 49.
178 Chakrabarty, *Provincializing Europe*, 8.
179 Le Myre de Vilers, *Les Institutions Civiles De La Cochinchine*, 137.
180 Higgins, *Our Vietnam Nightmare*, 165.
181 Quoted in ibid., 166.
182 Tan Phong (Ngô Đình Nhu), *Ấp Chiến lược*, 41.
183 Bửu Lịch, "Les idéologies dans la République du Sud Vietnam," 65.
184 Higgins, *Our Vietnam Nightmare*, 166.
185 Ibid., 173.
186 Phuc Thien, *President Ngo-Dinh-Diem's Political Philosophy* (Saigon: Review Horizons, 1956), 6.
187 Nguyễn Hữu Chí, "Vai trò hương ước trong quốc sách Ấp Chiến lược" [The role of village conventions in the national policy of strategic hamlets], *Quê Hương*, 46 (1963), 18–19.
188 Marx, *Grundrisse*, 157–8.
189 Karl Marx, *Capital: A Critique of Political Economy*, vol. 1 (Chicago: Charles H. Kerr & Co., 1915), 90.

190 Ibid., 89–90.
191 Marx, *Grundrisse*, 157–8.
192 Mounier, *Œuvres*, vol. 1, 623.
193 Mounier, *Personalisme*, xviii.
194 Quoted in Nguyễn Văn Minh, *Dòng họ Ngô Đình: Ước mơ chưa đạt* [The Ngô Đình Family: Dreams Unrealized] (Garden Grove, CA: Hoàng Nguyên Xuất Bản, 2003), 425–6.
195 *President Ngo Dinh Diem on Democracy*, 15.
196 Gheddo, *Catholiques et bouddhistes au Vietnam*, 154.
197 Georges Chaffard, *Les Deux Guerres Du Vietnam: De Valluy À Westmoreland* (Paris: La Table Ronde, 1969), 296.
198 Bửu Lịch, "La Première République Du Viêt-Nam," VIET NAM Infos Le Bulletin d'lInformation Économique Politique Culturelle sur le Viet Nam, Infos Numéro 39. N.p., December 15, 2006. May 25, 2018.
199 Ngô Đình Nhu, "Viet Nam, le cerveau de la famille," interview by Raoul Goulard. *Cinq colonnes à la une*. RTF Télévision. Saïgon: October 3, 1963.
200 Report, A Report on Counter-Insurgency in Vietnam, VCA. 23970128002 July 20, 1962, Box 01, Folder 28, Rufus Phillips Collection.
201 Bert Fraleigh, "Counterinsurgency in Vietnam: The Real Story," in *Prelude to Tragedy: Vietnam, 1960–1965*, ed. Harvey Neese and John O'Donnell (Annapolis, MD: Naval Institute Press, 2001), 102.
202 *Press interviews with President Ngo Dinh Diệm*, 69.
203 Nguyễn Công Luận, *Nationalist in the Viet Nam Wars: Memoirs of a Victim Turned Soldier* (Bloomington: Indiana University Press, 2012), 219.
204 Maneli, *War of the Vanquished*, 120.
205 Nguyen Công Luan, *Nationalist in the Viet Nam Wars*, 219.
206 Catton, *Diem's Final Failure*, 90.
207 VCA. Booklet – Vietnam's Strategic Hamlets. VCA. 23970130054 February 1963. Box 01, Folder 30. Rufus Phillips Collection. See also Memorandum from the Director of the Vietnam Task Force (Cottrell) to the Assistant Secretary of State for Far Eastern Affairs (Harriman)," Washington, April 6, 1962, [Source: Department of State, Vietnam Working Group Files: Lot 67 D 54, Pol. 7. Secret.] in FRUS: Vietnam 1962. Vol. II, 311.
208 Ngô Đình Nhu, "Viet Nam, le cerveau de la famille."
209 Maneli, *War of the Vanquished*, 145–6.
210 Gabriel Kolko, *Vietnam: Anatomy of a Peace* (New York: Routledge, 1997), 27.
211 Hanoi Badly Needs Theoreticians (First Script). VCA. 0720122004 No Date. Box 01, Folder 22. John Donnell Collection.
212 Quoted in Anthony Marc Lewis, "Re-examining our perceptions on Vietnam," *Studies in Intelligence*, 17:4 (1973), 1–62.

213 See Văn Lưu Phạm and Ngọc Tấn Nguyễn, *Đệ nhất Cộng hòa Việt Nam 1954–1963: Một cuộc cách mạng* [The First Republic: A Revolution] (Melbourne: Centre for Vietnamese Studies, 2005).

214 Quoted in La Valeur Universelle de la Liberté: Reflets Du Personnalisme en Asie à la fin du XXe siècle, 17. VCA. 0720314008 No Date. Box 03, Folder 14. John Donnell Collection.

215 Speech Transcript – Friendly Talk to the Militants by Political Counsellor NGO-DINH-NHU, 4. VCA. 23970131033 April 17, 1963. Box 01, Folder 31. Rufus Phillips Collection.

3

The other Vietnamese revolution: The Strategic Hamlet Campaign and US imperialism

The Strategic Hamlet Campaign, the Vietnamese village and council democracy

"'All power to the soviets' must once again be our slogan, but literally this time, without the Bolshevik ulterior motives."

Situationist International

The difference between the two forms of communism espoused by the early Republic and the Communist Party was not simply a matter of theory or doctrine. Contrary to the caricature of Nhu as an "intellectual and an aristocrat" who "made no attempt to conceal his lack of interest in the needs of the Vietnamese people," Nhu's apparently incomprehensible conception of Personalism was one that emphasized praxis:[1] "the Personalism ... I advocate is a militant democracy in which freedom is ... the fruit of [an] ... unceasing conquest of living reality, not in an ideal context, but in a given geopolitical condition."[2] Despite its "diffuseness and its lack of discernible application to day to day problems," Nhu's Vietnamese Personalism, as a CIA memorandum reported, was a doctrine that was "quite aware of the need to descend from the plain of philosophy in order to make the problem attractive to the peasants who are the main target."[3]

Nhu's philosophy, moreover, was not a theory that, "in practice," according to Robert Shaplen, "was whatever Nhu wanted it to be."[4] Although the Strategic Hamlet Campaign began as a philosophical "pipedream," partly inspired by Mounier's writings, the theory, beginning in 1962, would be confirmed by strategies developed spontaneously by local officials, whose concrete experience was used to revise the original plan for the program:

The other Vietnamese revolution

> [Nhu] had originated the strategic hamlet program, [but] it was only an idea, a "pipe-dream" ... until the last four months. Since that time he has been making constant trips to the provinces ... During his ... trips, all ceremonies were eliminated ... Most of his time was consumed by visits ... meetings with ... hamlet ... province [and] ... district chiefs and committees. These discussions often lasted as long as five hours. He found the trips ... exhilarating because he had been able to test out his theories about strategic hamlets through actual experience.[5]

If Personalism, therefore, compared to the Party's primitive Marxism and its "simple litany of phrases," seemed like a "poorly expressed doctrine" that "was above the illiterate peasantry," the doctrine, nevertheless, was to be proven concretely.[6] For Diệm, the doctrine demanded "putting into practice" a form of "democratic life" that exists "only where a concrete democratic experience exists." This experience, however, cannot be identified with either the exercise of individual rights or participation in the popular vote. "Our democracy," as an editorial in the official Republican newspaper explained, "is not of the parliamentary type, but no doubt it is a democracy."[7] Insofar as the right to political representation in the parliamentary state presupposes the private interests of egoistic individuals, "separated ... from the community," liberal democracy, from the perspective of Personalism, precluded the possibility of direct communal production, liberated from the tyranny of production for profit.

For Nhu, the communal organization of labor, required for the creation of a "democracy at the base," was distinct, however, from the form of collective production, or *lao động*, imposed by the Communist Party. In the latter, the capitalist alienation of work is preserved and monopolized by the state, which becomes the despotic ruler of a proletarianized labor. In Personalism, this vulgar conception of socialism is rejected in favor of an alternative model of communism.

In *Understanding America* (*Tìm hiểu nước Mỹ*), Lý Chánh Trung, one of the leading philosophers in the South affiliated with Personalism, draws on Hannah Arendt's analysis of the Paris Commune and the Russian workers' councils to propose a "non-communist" theory of "socialist revolution" (*cách mạng xã hội chủ nghĩa không cộng sản*) in third world societies.[8] For Arendt, the workers' councils, which would "make their appearance in every genuine revolution throughout the nineteenth and twentieth centuries ... were utterly neglected by statesmen, historians, political theorists, and, most importantly, by the revolutionary tradition itself." Within the revolutionary tradition, these autonomous organizations, which were the "spontaneous organs of the people ... outside of all revolutionary parties ... entirely unexpected by ... their leaders," were viewed as "temporary organs in the revolutionary struggle."[9] In orthodox Marxism, the workers' councils or soviets were regarded as merely a transitional stage in the revolutionary struggle to establish a communist society based on the collectivization of labor under the central authority of the communist party. Because the "self-government of the Communes," "each a small power structure of its own ... [was] clearly a danger for the centralized state power," these temporary organs were dissolved, in the end, by the Bolsheviks.[10] Thus, Lenin, having declared "All Power to the Soviets!" would later "sacrifice ... the new institutions of freedom, the soviets, to the party which he thought would liberate the poor."[11]

In contrast to this Marxist tradition, Marx himself regarded the council as a means of abolishing the alienation of labor in capitalism: The "working class government," created by the Paris Commune, constituted the "political form at last discovered under which to work out the economical emancipation of labor."[12] In the form of the council, the "smashed state machine" and its disciplinary apparatus is superseded by a "fuller democracy," based on directly elected governing bodies, and of the "abolition of the standing army," replaced by a popular militia. In this way, democracy was "transformed from bourgeois into proletarian democracy; from the state ... into something which is no longer a state proper."[13] For syndicalist thinkers, moreover, like Georges Sorel, who regarded the soviet commune as a political form capable of supplanting the "arrogant bourgeois democracies," the revolutionary project was conceived "not in terms of the replacement of one... elite by another but as a process diffusing authority down into the workers' own organizations."[14]

The Marxist tradition, however, viewing these organizations as only a transitional stage, "failed to understand [that] ... the council system ... [was] an entirely new form of government, with a new public space for freedom ... constituted ... during the course of the revolution itself."[15] Thus, in the history of the Vietnamese Communist Party, the new political form of the council, as it emerged, for example, in the Nghệ Tĩnh soviets in 1930, is portrayed as an "imperfectly conscious" organization of workers, lacking the leadership of the Party.[16] Yet, despite the lack of "communist party encouragement," the Nghệ Tĩnh uprising, as David Marr describes, spontaneously "create[d] alternative social institutions, including the village administrator committees, self-defense units, *quoc ngu* schools, and welfare networks."[17] During the Great Depression, Vietnamese peasants and workers, faced with the collapsing value of land, labor and basic commodities, demanded autonomy from the money economy imposed by the French, together with the corrupt feudal regime that collected its taxes.[18] Like the workers' councils in Russia, therefore, the Nghệ Tĩnh soviets constituted a "new body politic ... outside of the parties," creating "alternative village institutions," opposed to the impersonal domination of capital as well as the traditional hierarchies of feudal society. "The most subtle lesson of Nghệ Tĩnh," therefore, according to Marr, "had to do with problems of leadership" rather than with the peasantry and its "imperfectly conscious" revolutionary organizations. During the uprising, the "Communist Party ... had been unable to adequately predict, plan, or coordinate events at the provincial level, much less implement a viable national strategy."[19]

The political form of the council, moreover, as Arendt pointed out, was also abandoned by the American Revolution, which established a representative government, incapable of the "rational formation of opinion," instead of adopting a system of "elementary republics." According to Arendt, this system, devised by Thomas Jefferson, was a form of council democracy that "exceeded" even "the sections of the Parisian Commune and the popular societies [created] during the French Revolution."[20] Based on the ideal of agrarian democracy, Jefferson's plan of elementary republics was designed to promote direct democratic engagement in the political process by preserving the economic independence of farmers against industrial capitalism and finance. For Jefferson, "debt ... and factory work ... could rob men of the economic autonomy essential for republican citizens."[21]

Jefferson would find support for his ideal of democracy in an unlikely source, the work of Pierre Poivre, a French missionary and colonial administrator whose writings on agricultural methods in Asia and Africa became popular in the American colonies prior to the Revolution.[22] In *Voyages d'un Philosophe* (1768), a work that stimulated Jefferson's interest in Southern Vietnam,[23] Poivre provides an account of the precolonial village in Đàng Trong: "I never saw any country where the progress of population was so remarkable."[24] The territory of Đàng Trong (which Poivre refers to as "Cochinchina") was annexed as part of the *nam tiến* or Southward Advance in the seventeenth century, a process that extended the autonomous organization of the Vietnamese village to what is today known as South Vietnam. Despite being subjected to the tyrannical rule of the emperor, who was "vain, ignorant, lazy, miserly, superstitious,"[25] the peasants in Cochinchina enjoyed the status of "free cultivators." In the semi-autonomous Vietnamese villages, "[f]reedom and property form the basis of abundance, and good agriculture."[26]

Despite his disdain for the tyrannical prince, Poivre believed, nevertheless, that his imperial subjects were far more productive and free than the slaves within France's colonial empire. Poivre, therefore, proposed the autonomy of the South Vietnamese village as a model for France's American colonies, where the institution of plantation slavery was preserved by a purportedly enlightened monarchical government:

> After what I have seen in Cochinchina, I cannot doubt that free cultivators, to whom the lands of America would have been divided ... could have produced double the quantity that it procures from the slaves. What has Europe ... so enlightened in the rights of humanity, gained ... by authorizing ... the daily outrages made on human nature in our colonies, in permitting the degradation of men ... as beasts of burden?[27]

Whereas the French, therefore, after the conquest of Indochina, would enact the alienable rights of man against the tyranny of the Vietnamese emperor, Poivre, writing a century earlier, had proposed the autonomy of the South Vietnamese village as a justification for the abolition of slavery.

In the American Revolution, however, which began shortly after Poivre published his travelogue, the institution of slavery would be allowed to persist, while Jefferson's republican councils were abandoned in favor of representative government.[28] The American Revolution, therefore, was marked, in Arendt's terms, by the "failure of the founders to incorporate the township and the town-hall meeting into the Constitution."[29] This failure would help establish a worldwide revolutionary tradition, extending from Robespierre and Lenin to Mao and Lê Duẩn, in which the various manifestations of council democracy were regarded as temporary organs, to be dissolved by the centralized state.

For Lý Chánh Trung, it was this abandoned political form of the American Revolution that provided the model for a non-communist socialist revolution in the South, a revolution that was directly opposed to the liberalism prescribed by the American government.[30]

The kibbutz and the Strategic Hamlet Campaign

"[T]he *political state disappears* in a true democracy."

Marx

For Ngô Đình Nhu, the models for the form of council democracy that would be applied in the Strategic Hamlet Campaign included the Soviet Commune: the "first science of organizing mass movements is based on

The other Vietnamese revolution

the Soviet organization of the Communists in Russia" (*khoa học đệ nhất về tổ chức phong trào quần chúng là tổ chức theo phương pháp Xô Viết của Cộng sản ở Nga*).³¹ The model, however, was amended by concrete experience, using techniques developed spontaneously by local officials in the struggle against the insurgency:

> The strategic hamlet program … grew out of a variety of security and political measures adopted by local officials, acting to a considerable extent on their own initiative … The government of … Ngo Dinh Diem, recognizing the effectiveness of these scattered efforts responded quickly and threw its entire resources behind the development of a national strategic hamlet program, drawing on its knowledge of the communist insurgencies in Malaya and Indochina and even the kibbutz program in Israel.³²

The program, therefore, emerged out of a combination of history, theory and practice: "Thus the strategic hamlet policy was born from the revolutionary conscience in its direct confrontation with a concrete historical society, our own."³³ But if the program was originally based on security measures invented by local officials to fight the insurgency, its direct historical models, as the report suggests, were not the counterinsurgency campaigns employed in the struggle against communism.³⁴ Rather, the program was inspired by the *insurgencies themselves*. According to Nguyễn Xuân Hoài, the Strategic Hamlet Campaign was conceived as a "mass organization of communists aimed at attacking communists" (*tổ chức đoàn thể của những người cộng sản nhằm mục đích tấn công lại những người cộng sản*).³⁵ These models, moreover, which informed the design for a "real democracy from the base," for a modernized form of the traditional Vietnamese commune, included the Israeli kibbutz or workers' cooperatives:³⁶

> Ngô Đình Nhu, strategist of the First Republic, built the regime on a communist model [*theo mô hình cộng sản*]. The Communists took Marxist-Leninism as their foundation, while the First Republic adopted Personalism, based on the French philosophy of Emmanuel Mounier … The Communists had the Nghệ Tĩnh Soviets, while the First Republic had … the Strategic Hamlet Program, based on the Israeli *kibbutz*.³⁷

According to James Horrox, the kibbutz, for its early adherents, was an attempt to create a "commune of communes," drawing on the neglected experiments in council democracy, which had been excluded from the revolutionary tradition.³⁸ For Arendt, the kibbutz was a "rigorous realization of social justice within [a] small circle," a democratic organization of culture and labor based on a "genuine contempt for material wealth, exploitation and bourgeois life." Like the workers' councils and soviets, this democratic organization, however, was not a representative government. On the contrary, the kibbutzniks were "too decent for [parliamentary] politics," which "they gladly left to the politicians – on condition they were ... left alone with their own social organization."[39] In the tradition of Jewish anarchist thought that informed the kibbutz, this antagonism toward liberal democracy was rooted in an opposition to capitalism. The communards of the early kibbutzim rejected what Emma Goldman called "the dream of capitalist Jewry ... for a Jewish state machinery to protect the privileges of the few against the many." "At stake," therefore, as Horrox explains, "was nothing less than the opportunity to transform the Jewish mobilization around Palestine into a project for the social liberation of all peoples, a project that could only be achieved under the banner of *stateless socialism*."[40]

In an interview with *Reader's Digest*, Nhu (perhaps unaware of the magazine's anti-communist stance) would describe the Strategic Hamlet Program in similarly grandiose terms, as an anti-capitalist form of postcolonial modernization: "My ambition is that the fortified hamlets may thus form a new approach to the saving of civilization. It is better than the Indian system of trying to get progress as a gift of the capitalist societies."[41] In Nhu's Personalist program for a "real democracy from the base," the politically and economically autonomous form of the council (*hội đồng xã*), which had emerged outside the state, would become the major objective of the South Vietnamese government.[42] The state and its centralized power, therefore, would be used to establish a socialism without the state, based on a decentralized program of communal production, modeled on such organizations as the Israeli kibbutz: "Our primary task ... is complete the political, economic ... and social revolution, advancing within each Strategic Hamlet and from the Strategic Hamlets to the Central Authority" (*từ các Ấp Chiến Lược chuyển phát lên Trung Ương*).[43]

As Nhu reminded officials at an interministry meeting on the Strategy Hamlet Campaign, this ideal of a stateless democracy distinguished the Personalism of the Republic from the primitive Marxism espoused by the Communist Party. For the latter, the creation of a decentralized system of semi-autonomous "communes" (*xã bộ*) was regarded as a "temporary organ," a means towards the ends of establishing a collective regime of *lao động* or labor under the central authority of a socialist government. (For this reason, according to Kolko, the "absolute necessity of decentralizing the war organization throughout the provinces" was continually in

The other Vietnamese revolution

conflict with the "centralizing pretensions and ... elitist organizational theory" of the Communist Party.)[44] For the Party, the withering of the state, then, was a task to be accomplished only "after ... the proletarian revolution [*cách mạng vô sản*], which means that people in the present must ... sacrifice themselves for ... the future."[45] For Nhu, on the other hand, the ideal of a democracy at the base, which would dissolve the functions of the constitutional state, was the aim of the revolution itself: "That is right. I agree with Marx's final conclusion: the state must wither away – this is a condition for the final triumph of democracy. The sense of my life is to work so that I can become unnecessary."[46]

According to Robert Thompson, however, the emphasis placed on the creation of hamlets "all over the country," without any apparent "strategic direction," was indicative of the fact that the "Vietnamese tended to confuse the means with the end."[47] As Nhu argued, on the other hand, such views were based upon the assumption that the Strategic Hamlet Campaign was only a temporary security measure, as opposed to an end in itself or a means without ends: "The Americans and the Vietcong imagine that the strategic hamlets are purely military institutions that will be liquidated as unnecessary once victory is achieved. The Americans and the Vietcong are both wrong."[48] The aim of the Strategic Hamlet Campaign was in fact exactly the opposite. The program was not simply an instrument of the state to be "liquidated as unnecessary" once victory was achieved and the government had accomplished its purpose. The hamlets were not purely military organizations, but rather "basic institutions of direct democracy" which, in a "final triumph of democracy," would allow the state itself to be liquidated and its personnel to be rendered unnecessary: "The sense of my life is to work so that I can become unnecessary." Insofar as the establishment of a stateless form of democracy was the ultimate goal of the revolution itself, the possibility of a socialist future (which the Communist Party proposed to postpone until after the dictatorship of the proletariat was secure) was one that, for Nhu, was *already present* in the political form of the hamlet. Whereas the Party, therefore, believed that "people in the present must ... sacrifice themselves for ... the future," "[f]or us ... people in the present possess the same value of those in the future. Therefore, we propose to savor whatever we attain in our struggle" (*đặt vấn đề tranh đấu tới đâu hưởng tới đó*).[49]

This aspect of the Strategic Hamlet Campaign conforms to Mounier's account of the *révolution personnaliste et communautaire*, as a revolution for which there "are no necessary stages: the most Marxist revolutions have shown they know how to do without them" ("*Il n'y a pas d'étapes nécessaires: les révolutions les plus marxistes ont montré qu'elles savaient s'en passer*").[50] Contrary to Frances Fitzgerald, therefore, Nhu (who supposedly "lacked the rigorous analysis of Marxism") had not "misinterpreted" Mounier's work "as a doctrine of the corporate state in which the alienated masses would find unity through ... authoritarian social organizations." Rather, Nhu's Strategic Hamlet Campaign was in fact an attempt to realize in practice the communitarian Marxism that Mounier opposed to that of "the massive Soviet state."[51] Like liberalism, this state, according to Nhu, embodied an Occidental ideology whose development historically coincided with capitalism: "The leadership bureaucracy of the Communists, organized according to the dictatorship of the Party [*độc tài Đảng trị*], is also a ... bureaucracy that the West created, contemporaneous with Communist theory." [52]

Between dictatorship and democracy

> The obvious result of the Nhus' fascination with communism was a government which in many ways was patterned after the Communists'. One Frenchman who also knew the Hanoi government very well called South Vietnam "the only Anti-Communist people's Democratic Republic in the world." "All they need to do is change the flags, and overnight South Vietnam would be a communist country."[53]

The concept of democracy, embodied in the Strategic Hamlet Campaign, was directly opposed to the one prescribed by the American government during the war, a government that had abandoned the Jeffersonian ideal of a direct democracy, based on a system of independent elementary republics. The "Vietnamese and Americans," as William Nighswonger pointed out, "often meant different things when saying the same words." "Ngo Dinh Nhu and the Americans were not really saying the same things in describing the intent of the strategic hamlet program."[54]

For the Americans, the aim of the program, in accordance with the broader objective of creating a "stable, viable and democratic bastion of the Free World," was to win popular support for the regime by demonstrating the benefits of capitalism and liberal democracy. As Edward Lansdale explained, describing his approach to counterinsurgency, "I took my American beliefs with me into these Asian struggles, as Thomas Paine would've done."[55] As a practitioner of what Arendt referred to as the global policy of image-making (see Chapter 7), Lansdale, who adapted his experience in advertising to psychological warfare, had not only helped to successfully stage an anti-communist counterinsurgency war in the Philippines,[56] but had also applied his formidable skills in propaganda and public relations to engineering Ramon Magsaysay's presidential campaign. Using modern techniques of mass persuasion to bring Magsaysay to power in the nation's first "clean elections,"[57] Lansdale, having disproven the communist slogan that "bullets not ballots" were needed for political change, had led Filipinos "to American-style democracy."[58]

The form of democracy, however, that Lansdale sought to impose in his personal struggles in Asia completely diverged from the one that Nhu had in mind in designing the Strategic Hamlet Campaign. For Nhu, the aim was not to establish an Asian society based on the principles of Thomas Paine (a figure in the American Revolution who, as Arendt describes, assumed that the "inalienable political rights of all men" were universal and eternal).[59] On the contrary, Nhu was committed to creating a real democracy from the base, freed from the inalienable liberties of the egoistic individual, which served only to ratify the alienation of labor inherent in the Occidental structure of capitalism. The aim, then, for Nhu, was not to win rural support for the South Vietnamese state, as it developed toward becoming a stable, representative government, but to supersede the liberal stage of democracy through the establishment of a democratic (and anti-capitalist) infrastructure of communal production. This goal, moreover, would not be accomplished, as in American-style democracy, through a public relations campaign to influence the South Vietnamese peasantry. Rather, Nhu's democracy at the base would be established through the same dictatorial methods employed by the Communist Party:

> [While US] advisors ... hoped to duplicate the genuine and successful appeal to popular support which had won against the Huks in the Philippines ... Nhu was ... dreaming of a new era of popular support for the regime drawn from the grassroots by the same techniques of human engineering the communists had employed in China.[60]

Thus, Nhu, despite the doctrinal differences with the Communist Party, endorsed democratic centralism (*dân chủ tập trung*) as a means of realizing his own communist doctrine:[61] As Ellen Hammer described, Nhu was "prepared ... to establish an authoritarian regime in order to direct a ... social revolution."[62] Under Nhu's direction, therefore, the South Vietnamese state would employ authoritarian means towards the ends of creating a stateless society (as opposed to a dictatorship of the proletariat), freed from the authority of the centralized government. Thus, the "diemocracy" that prevailed in the South (the "democratic one-man-rule" of Ngô Đình Diệm) was defined, in Edward Miller's terms, by the use of "dictatorial methods ... for democratic ends."[63] In Nhu's account of the Strategic Hamlet Campaign, these methods in fact are identified with the very "revolutionary movement starting from the base" that would lead to the creation of a new democratic society, liberated from the impersonal rule of the state as well as the market.[64]

The dictatorial methods included not only the suppression of individual liberty, censorship of the media, the mass incarceration and torture of political prisoners, and tampering with democratic elections. In order to carry out his *"révolution vietnamienne communautaire,"* Nhu would also resort to what Bửu Lịch describes as *"les methodes de regroupement ... autoritaires,"* to the mass relocation of the Vietnamese people in a second Southward Advance toward a non-capitalist form of modernity.[65]

This forced relocation would be accompanied by the creation of a network of mass surveillance based on the clandestine system of cells (*chi bộ*) and techniques of mass organization similar to the one that had been successfully employed by the communists.[66] Comprising the members of Nhu's "Personalist Labor Party," who occupied key positions in the military, the police, the educational system and the media, this network of surveillance would connect the villages to the highest levels of administration.[67] Together with the strategy of forced relocation, this clandestine organization, according to the official account of the war produced by Hà Nội, would be successfully used to isolate the insurgency:

> As they built ... "strategic hamlets" the enemy also organized a network of intelligence agents and informants to expose our followers ... drive our ... guerrillas away, pushing our armed revolutionary forces back into isolated ... areas ... where they could be ... destroyed. This was a poisonous ... scheme combining political, economic, and social tactics.[68]

In the program, moreover, the establishment of a network of intelligence was coordinated with the creation of "basic institutions of direct democracy," schools and organizations for the development of civic and cultural literacy. Surveillance, then, was combined with what Mounier described as the development of "new systems of education and political procedure corresponding to the altered conditions of society."[69] These institutions would be built in syndicalist fashion by the community itself, which would form its own social bonds of self-discipline and mutual aid, fostering a "'communitarian' spirit" (*"tinh-thần 'communitaire'"*) through the communal endeavor[70] to create the conditions for a new democratic society.[71] The discipline of communal production, in turn, would serve to engender a sense of personal diligence or *cần lao*, a "willingness to work without coercion," based on an internalized form of "auto-surveillance,"[72] a *discipline personnelle librement décidée*."[73] The act of communal production, therefore, was one in which the people participated in what Diệm referred to as the "establishment of a discipline by themselves which they observe freely and loyally." As a condition of personal freedom, "each one must accept this discipline and see to it that his compatriots do the same."[74] "The regime inside the strategic hamlet should be revolutionary, but the revolution," as Nhu emphasized, "should be inside each individual."[75]

As a revolutionary principle "aimed at destroying ... feudal influences," this personal autonomy, founded on the discipline of communal production, was opposed to what Marx referred to as the "relations of personal dependence" within the traditional family. This Personalist ideal of freedom, however, cannot be equated with the individual liberty that prevails in bourgeois society, a "personal independence" that, according to Marx, is "founded on objective dependence," on the sovereignty of the market and the tyranny of production for profit. "Our union," as Trần Lệ Xuân (or Madame Nhu) explained, "will never be a disordered collection of individuals each following the sole aim of personal interest. Our union [draws] its strength from unity and discipline."[76]

While the hamlets were connected to the leadership in Sài Gòn through a clandestine system of cells, the creation of local governing councils, presiding over an autonomous communal production, would allow for initiative at the level of the individual village. As Robert Thompson described, "contact between the government and the people is being re-established together with an elementary form of local democratic administration in the election of hamlet and village councils."[77] The Strategic Hamlets, therefore, would provide the foundation for a Personalist democracy in which a secret parallel government, a "state within a state," would direct a decentralized system of autonomous local production and governance.[78]

For Nhu, however, the primary purpose of this organization was not to overcome communism in the name of liberal democracy. On the contrary, like the revolutions and workers' cooperatives that informed its design, the program would be used to completely abolish a "colonial domination" in which "man is subjected to money and power": "In the larger scheme of Ngo Dinh Nhu's thought, this would ideally be the beginning of a self-generating form of Vietnamese democracy that, from the countryside, would eventually overcome the poisonous residue of a French colonialism that was still strong among urban intellectuals."⁷⁹

But as such, Diệm and Nhu's Personalist democracy was not simply a personal dictatorship disguised as parliamentary government. Nor was the Strategic Hamlet Campaign an attempt to use communist tactics for non-communist ends. Rather, the aim was to provide the Vietnamese people with a *better* communist revolution than that of the Communist Party: "Therefore, this is neither a simple military formula aimed at countering the armed efforts of the communists … nor a simple anticommunist tactic which could be imported from abroad," like the counterinsurgency program that Robert Thompson devised in Malaya.⁸⁰ Rather, the goal of the Strategic Hamlet Campaign would correspond to Marx's prescription for social revolution, whereby "changes in the economic foundation lead … to the transformation of the whole immense superstructure": "To build a new society … to live by his own means, to work in his own security and with his own strength, starting from the infrastructure of the hamlets … to pervade all the superstructure of the State – is not this the profound and real aspiration of our people?"⁸¹

The primary objective of the Strategic Hamlet Campaign, therefore, was not to overcome communism, but to carry out a more radical revolutionary struggle. As Nhu emphasized, in eerily prescient terms, only a real revolution, aimed at transforming the entire infrastructure and superstructure of Vietnamese society, could rescue the Republic from ruin: "Victory or defeat … will depend upon whether we can realize democracy … We must carry out a real revolution [*cuộc cách mạng thực sự*] so that the people in the hamlets can clearly see a radical change [*thay đổi căn bản*] … [O]therwise, we will undoubtedly be [branded as] traitors to the nation, to the people and the revolution."⁸²

The Southward Advance as an anti-nationalist myth of the Vietnamese nation

In the hamlets, moreover, the new civic and cultural organizations created by the community would be used to disseminate a new national media for the purpose of "imprinting" the Republican version of the national history in the minds of the masses. "If national consciousness" (*ý thức quốc gia*), as Nhu emphasized, "is ingrained [*ăn sâu*] in the minds of the people … then not even the great invading powers … could destroy the will … of a whole nation."⁸³ "In the information field," as one US study reported, "considerable progress had been made in 1962 …

The other Vietnamese revolution

in conjunction with the national strategic hamlet program." Before this period, the "circulation of the daily newspapers [had] generally ... been confined to the major cities ... due ... to the economics of publishing in Vietnam and ... the extensive efforts of the Communists to prevent widespread distribution and reading of newspapers in rural areas." Because of these efforts, the private sector in the South, engaged in print capitalism, had been unable to distribute its media outside the cities. Circumventing the mechanism of the market, "the GVN [Government of Vietnam] ... embarked on the ambitious project of establishing a district news sheet in every district," "carrying local news to the more remote areas." District newspaper centers were equipped with mimeograph machines and radio receivers, used to transcribe news broadcast from Saigon. Combining national news with local reports, district editors printed newsletters, which were then distributed by motorbike. In 1962, moreover, the National Cinema Center produced twenty-five films about the Strategic Hamlet Campaign, which were screened by mobile units; these also distributed tapes and printed materials produced by the government.[84] In the local schools established as part of the program, these films, along with educational programming on the national culture and history, were incorporated into an "*enseignement audio-visuel.*"[85] This mass dissemination of the national media would serve to further bridge the divide between the rural and urban populations, creating "a highly organized society" of "persons" (*nhân vị*), "full of all kinds of media, communications ... [and] high culture."[86] "The goal," according to Nhu, was to employ modern technology in order "to develop a common culture in the hamlet" (*phát triển văn hóa chung tại thôn ấp*).[87]

As a modern reenactment of the nationalist myth of the Southward Advance, the Strategic Hamlet Campaign, then, would allow the South Vietnamese state to extend its control of the territory through the mass dissemination of a national culture. "Ingrained" with a sense of its Manifest Destiny, the South Vietnamese people (as the historical subject of a second Southward Advance) would serve, paradoxically, as the very foundation of the constitutional state that created it. The legitimacy of the Republic, therefore, was founded on a national people or *dân tộc*, created by the Republic itself through its program of nation-building.

Like the national history that the Communist Party had claimed to inherit, the history adopted by the South Vietnamese state celebrated an ancient tradition of "resisting foreign invaders" (*chống ngoại xâm*), invented in the colonial era.[88] In this history, moreover, a European conception of political sovereignty as the right of a "people" (*dân tộc*), possessing a distinct national culture over the territory that it historically occupied, was projected into the precolonial past. In contrast to the communist version, however, the national history devised by the South Vietnamese state would underline the connection between the tradition of resisting foreign invaders and the tradition of the Southward Advance, the *bắc cự* and the *nam tiến*: "Since the founding of the country," according to Nhu, "two events have completely dominated the nine hundred years of the Vietnamese nation ... contact with China and the Southward Advance."[89] Whereas the tradition of resisting foreign invaders would culminate in the communist version, of course, in the war to "expel the American invaders" (*đánh đuổi giặc Mỹ xâm lược*), for Nhu, this history would be realized authentically in the Strategic Hamlet Campaign, as a second Southward Advance to modernity: "I have constantly sought to 'situate' the policy of Strategic Hamlets. I fixed it in our intimate reality in the historical movement of the Vietnamese people undertaken more than 2,000 years ago."[90]

But if this history appears, in Nhu's account, as a "preordained sequence by which the 'Vietnam' of the 10th century became the 'Vietnam' of today,"[91] the end of this teleology, nevertheless, was not a Vietnamese nation endowed with a Western ideal of territorial sovereignty. Rather, in this teleology, the "nation" (*quốc gia*) recovers a primeval democracy that preceded the European conception of national sovereignty, which had been introduced by the colonial state. Nhu's account of the national history, then, would seem to be marked by an unresolved tension. On the one hand, the Southward Advance, like the tradition of resisting foreign invaders in the communist account of the history, appears as a millennial struggle to realize a national sovereignty that was projected into the precolonial past. On the other hand, it appears as the spontaneous multiplication of an economically and politically autonomous form of community, which was supplanted by the Western conception of sovereignty. Modernized on the model of council democracy (excluded as a "temporary organ" from the revolutionary tradition), the "autonomous organization of the village and its independence from centralized government" would seem to suggest a stateless form of non-Western modernity.[92] But insofar as the Ngos had sought to restore an ancient tradition of communal autonomy in a modernized form, their nation-building program embodied a nationalism that was directly opposed to the Western ideal of the nation-state, inherited from the colonial era.

For Nhu, however, the creation of this stateless democracy required dictatorial means, employed by a "*régime fort ... transitoire et temporaire*,"

The other Vietnamese revolution

which would serve as a "*préparation, une propédeutique à la véritable démocratie.*"[93] In the Strategic Hamlet Campaign, the centralized power of the state would be utilized, despotically, to create the conditions for a direct mass democracy and economic decentralization, liberated from the tyranny of production for profit. An authoritarian program of mass relocation and centralized planning would be utilized, then, to establish a national system of independent communities, in which political freedom and economic autonomy were founded upon a self-imposed discipline. At a meeting with the International Control Commission in 1963, Nhu, reiterating the paradox of "controlled liberty," described this dialectic of despotism and democracy in the following manner: "I am temporarily curtailing freedom to offer it in unlimited form. I am strengthening discipline to do away with its external bonds. I am centralizing the state in order to democratize and decentralize it. As you have noted, I am a proponent of the Hegelian dialectics."[94]

As these apparently contradictory statements would appear to imply, the unlimited freedom that Nhu proposed to achieve by "strengthening discipline" was not the individual freedom of a liberal subject of rights (a subject that, according to Foucault, is subordinated by the disciplinary techniques of the state and the industrial factory). If the Strategic Hamlet Campaign entailed the use of dictatorial methods for a democratic end, the end that the Ngos had in mind was not a representative government based on popular sovereignty. As Phạm Văn Lưu describes, the establishment, in the 1955 Referendum, of a constitutional state in the South, "adopting the institutions of parliamentary democracy from [Western] liberal states," was, in fact, only a preliminary stage in a broader Personalist revolution. Using the expansive powers of the presidency, granted by the Republican constitution (in violation of the norms of liberal democracy), Diệm would attempt to carry out a "revolution ... within the superstructure" ([c]uộc cách mạng ... xảy ra trên thượng tầng cấu trúc) of the state. In a "first step toward democratizing the national apparatus" (dân chủ hóa các guồng máy quốc gia), Diệm would use his "vast emergency powers" in an authoritarian manner,[95] to limit the authority of the ministries within the central government. This revolution in the national superstructure in Sài Gòn was directly connected, however, to a "second revolution, building a genuine democracy in the infrastructure. This was the Strategic Hamlet Program ... also known as the rural revolution." While the first revolution would serve to dissolve the centralized power of the parliamentary state, the second, in building a system of semi-autonomous villages, would create the economic and political infrastructure for a "democratization from the bottom up" (*dân chủ hóa ... từ dưới bùng lên*).⁹⁶ (Hence Nhu's apparently contradictory claim: "I am centralizing the state in order to democratize and decentralize it.")⁹⁷

As such, the authoritarian methods employed by the early Republic, in implementing its Personalist revolution, were not conceived as mere emergency measures, temporarily suspending democracy for the sake of a future parliamentary state. Rather, the aim (in accordance with Marx's prescription) was to abolish the very form of the state by deploying its own despotic power to realize a democracy at the base, in the form of a decentralized system of communal production and political self-organization: The "strategic hamlets are the basic institutions of direct democracy. When they developed and flourished ... the state itself – as Marx said – will wither away."⁹⁸ The "democratic movement starting from the base," therefore, would completely "revise" the institutions of liberal democracy as the legal and political superstructure of capitalism: "All of this will end by 'making the present superstructure crack' ... Thus the eventual modification of the present regime is not unexpected, but is in keeping with the very logic of the Strategic Hamlet movement."⁹⁹ "The essential issue," therefore, as Nhu reminded officials at a meeting of the intra-ministry committee on the Strategic Hamlets, was not simply to contain the communist insurgency in the countryside. Rather, "our task is to complete the political revolution ... developing at the level of the hamlet ... and from the hamlet to the national superstructure" (*nhiệm vụ ... của chúng ta là phải hoàn thành cuộc cách mạng chính trị ... đang phát triển tại ấp ... từ ấp chuyển lên thượng tầng cơ sở quốc gia*).¹⁰⁰ By creating an autonomous form of production and governance, the program, then, would serve to abolish the very centralized power that had initiated the program in a dialectical movement leading to its own dissolution: The "Strategic Hamlet Programme by its internal logic ... cannot fail to limit the powers of Central agencies, and even the presidential powers. It is the whole government system which, proceeding by the democratic and revolutionary movement starting from the base, is being unavoidably altered little by little."¹⁰¹

In this movement, therefore, the state assumed the paradoxical role of a sovereignty seeking to create the conditions for its own disappearance. Indeed, for Diệm, the outcome of the war would depend almost entirely upon whether the Republic could succeed in creating an autonomous system of rural communities that was capable of superseding the sovereignty of the central government. Echoing the communist slogan "All power to the soviets," Diệm declared that "real power lies in the villages and not in the cities ... The Central Government is nothing without the support of the people in the villages. This has long been understood by Asian and African Communists."[102] The "Personalist revolution" (*cuộc Cách mạng Nhân vị*), therefore, "must turn to the people as the basis of organization" (*quay về cơ sở nhân dân mà tổ chức*).[103]

By late 1963, this process of decentralization had progressed to the point that the movement, according to Nhu, had begun to exceed his authority. This authority had become subordinate to the autonomous power of the villages, a power that Nhu identified with democracy itself: "I do not control this Government. Rather is it the Strategic Hamlet movement which, little by little, has generated the procedures of control, that is democracy."[104]

But as such, the "nation" that Nhu proposed to imprint in the minds of the South Vietnamese masses by means of an official national media was not a sovereign national government representing the will of the people. Rather, this media would be used to imagine a stateless form of community, a *dân tộc* or a "national people" whose autonomy – established in a second Southward Advance toward modernity – would serve to annul the sovereignty of the constitutional state, which had been inherited from the colonial government. The goal, therefore, of the Strategic Hamlet Program, as Nhu explained at an intra-ministerial meeting, was not to "call [the people] to become a part of the national community [*cộng đồng quốc gia*]." Rather, the hamlet, as an autonomous collective of "persons [*nhận vị*] ... is more important than the national community" (*quan trọng hơn cộng đồng quốc gia nữa*). This "issue must be clearly understood, because otherwise ... the community of the nation, its unity [*đoàn thể*] ... would destroy the individual [*hủy diệt cá nhân*]," along with the political autonomy of the hamlet as a collective of Persons.[105] In the Hamlet Program, therefore, a "national discipline" would be deployed by the state in order to dissolve the "national community." For Nhu, moreover, it was precisely the anti-nationalist character of the Strategic Hamlet Campaign, as a national strategy, that defined its importance from a global perspective. As "a solution to the central problem of underdevelopment in the XX century," the program "has a world significance that overflows the borders of Viet-Nam."[106]

A communist revolution against the communist revolution

For many observers, however, such statements, with their abstruse dialectical formulas,[107] merely exemplified "Nhu's internally contradictory personalist system."[108] Even for officials within the Republican government, such as Trần Văn Minh, the use of authoritarian means to create a stateless society seemed like the "*degenerescence de la démocratie personnaliste en dictature.*" Nhu, the "*promoteur des 'Hameaux stratégiques,' théoricien du 'Personnalisme,'*" had devolved from "*Mounier à Himmler.*"[109] For its critics, therefore, Personalism was a "nebulous ideology ... under which the fascism of the Ngos disguises itself."[110] Instead of restoring a primeval democracy in a modernized form, the Strategic Hamlets, according to Charles Fourniau, had in reality destroyed the autonomy of the Vietnamese village, replacing it with the concentration camp:

> The autonomy of the Vietnamese commune is one of the foundations of Vietnamese ... society ... Traditionally, imperial authority ended at the bamboo hedge ... American experts ... understand nothing of this deep root of Vietnamese civilization ... and they invented this criminal stupidity of "strategic hamlets," which were based on the displacement of the population from their villages and their "concentration in artificial agglomerations."[111]

Contrary to Fourniau, however, the program had not been invented by American experts, or foreign advisors such as Robert Thompson, who had developed the blueprint for the anticommunist counterinsurgency campaign in Malaya. According to Maxwell Taylor, Thompson, "like all the rest of us," contributed "very little" to the design of the Strategic Hamlet Campaign, which was "Nhu's own project." While American advisors were "too much oriented toward conventional war," Thompson's experience in counterinsurgency was not applicable to the Vietnamese context: The "Malaysian affair was never on the scale of Viet-Nam ... [I]t ... was really a police operation of going out and catching bandits, and it was operated on that scale."[112] Contrary, therefore, to what a study by the United States Operations Missions described as a "policeman's" view of the Strategic Hamlet Campaign, the program was not a purely repressive mechanism of mass surveillance and discipline. This "fallacy," which "owes much to the British experience in Malaya ... may best be understood by its *reductio ad absurdum* ... hypothesizing a country where ... three fourths of the population are in concentration camps, with the other fourth set to guard them."[113] Based on an "essentially negative concept of control," the policeman's view of the Strategic Hamlet Campaign "totally overlooks the necessity for a powerbase within the country," or what Arendt referred to, with regard to the strategy employed by the communist insurgency, as a

The other Vietnamese revolution

"superior organization of power" (see Chapter 7). The program, therefore, was not merely a negative technique of repression, but a "positive" form of control, "implemented by the people themselves ... keeping them so well organized and busy on worthwhile efforts that any aberrant behavior is at once noticed and corrected."[114] The aim, then, was to establish a system of "*auto-surveillance*" and "*auto-défense*" that would serve to preempt direct intervention by the state, and its cumbersome military and disciplinary apparatus.[115] While the creation of an "autonomous ... infrastructure of ... guerilla militias" (*hạ tầng cơ sở ... từ tục ... dân quân du kích*) would allow the regime to "reduce the number of regular military personnel," the system of auto-surveillance increasingly supplanted the role of state security forces: "Previously, we carried out arbitrary arrests of suspects who were transferred to the police, today, with the Strategic Hamlets, the suspects are naturally dealt with on the spot."[116]

Contrary, then, to the policeman's view of the program, the Strategic Hamlet Campaign was not a tool of repression, implemented by American experts who understood "nothing of this deep root of Vietnamese civilization." Rather, it was initiated by Nhu, who "moved in advance and independently of American planners," and whose "strong dislike for Americans ... made him more committed than ever to the personalist principle of self-sufficiency," or communal autonomy.[117]

By 1963, moreover, the campaign appeared to be close to achieving decisive success. In a letter to a former classmate at the École des Chartes, Nhu reported "*progrès ... sur les communistes dans tous les domains,*" as a result of the Strategic Hamlet Campaign. "*Grâce à ce système nous penser* [sic] *gagner cette sale guerre.*"[118] In March of that year, Thompson, who had argued with Nhu over the design of the hamlets, noted an "air of optimism," which did "not just apply to the President, [and] Counselor Nhu ... Province chiefs are now very different men from the harassed officials of a year ago":

> Confidence in strategic hamlets is steadily growing, and there is now little reluctance on the part of the population to be regrouped. Many have requested it; voluntarily without any question of assistance or compensation ... Given a steady and methodical advance of the ... program ... the end might come quicker than many people forecast.[119]

For Thompson, moreover, the program had proven to be more effective as a form of people's war than the one being waged by the communist forces: "If ... the Vietcong by the end of this year fail to find a solution to the ... programme, they will then have lost any chance of regaining control of their 'popular bases.'" By creating its own autonomous system of popular bases, the Hamlet Campaign confronted the communist forces with the very dilemma that the Americans would eventually face, of having to destroy the village in order to save it: "The Vietcong are ... faced with a dilemma. If they attack the hamlets, they are attacking the people whose support they must have to win the war."[120] As Diệm explained in an interview, this had been precisely the aim of the program: the "Communist strategy seeks mainly to mobilise the peasant masses to surround the cities. Thanks to the Strategic hamlets – a strategic revolution – it is rather we [who] ... mobilise the peasant masses against the Communists."[121] In this strategic revolution, the "people," as a communist observer lamented, "were being used to oppose the revolution."[122]

This account of the increasing success of the Strategic Hamlet Campaign is consistent with both North Vietnamese sources and assessments by US intelligence. According to the official military history of the People's Army of Vietnam, the strategy had created "a network of intelligence agents and informants to expose our followers ... [driving our] guerrillas away, pushing our armed revolutionary forces back into isolated ... areas ... where they could be ... destroyed."[123] In a report on their fact-finding mission, presented to President Kennedy in October 1963, Robert McNamara and Maxwell Taylor noted "unanimous agreement that the strategic hamlet program is sound in concept, and generally effective in execution." It was "the view of the vast majority of military commanders consulted that success could be achieved ... by the end of ... 1964."[124]

According to Albert Fraleigh, moreover, one of the few American specialists who played a significant role in the program, the effectiveness of the program as a counterinsurgency measure was matched by its success as an instrument of social revolution. The program had quickly "decentralized Vietnamese government ... and brought rapid political, social and economic progress throughout the rural areas by early 1963." As Fraleigh noted, however, this "fact was never well reported by the news media which preferred sensational war stories."[125] This problem, as Nhu suggested in an interview, was the result of reluctance on the part of American leaders to publicize the success of a program that so closely resembled the communist revolution that they sought to suppress: "For some reason which I do not understand, they do not tell the American people about it, although they are convinced that therein lies the real solution to the problems of under-development generally, into the problems of South Vietnam in particular."[126] Owing to the lack of publicity,

The other Vietnamese revolution

the perception of the Strategic Hamlet Campaign, in the international media as well as among South Vietnamese in the cities, was directly at odds with intelligence studies and official reports on the program. "In all the provinces ... I visited, the ... chiefs," as one US advisor observed, "were executing the program":

> This was so much at variance with what I had heard before arriving in Vietnam that I made a special effort to verify my observations. Rumors of rural discontent with the program were rife in Saigon, but were difficult to pin down to a particular province. ... [U]nhappiness over the program ... has not been as widespread as is supposed.

By 1962, the success of the program (which would earn Nhu recognition as "the only serious theorist of the guerilla warfare in the noncommunist world") had compelled the Communist Party to pursue a political settlement.[127] During a national radio broadcast, Hồ Chí Minh publicly hinted at the possibility of an end to the war with the South.[128] The message was repeated in a new year's greeting published in January in the North Vietnamese newspaper *Nhân Dân*. Although "socialist forces," according to Hồ, "are superior to the imperialist forces," the "forces of peace prevail over the forces of war." The "unification of Vietnam is something sacred to all Vietnamese. Representatives of the two sides could meet, discuss [and] find the best way to achieve peace and reunify the country."[129] Moreover, in a secret communication with Nhu, the North Vietnamese prime minister, Phạm Văn Đồng, declared that "everything is negotiable," expressing "a sincere desire to end hostilities ... on a completely realistic basis."[130] These overtures, as Cao Xuân Vỹ suggests in his account of a secret meeting between Nhu and Phạm Hùng, the head of the Party's Central Office in the South, had been prompted by concerns in the leadership over the progress of the Strategic Hamlet Campaign: "There was one thing they were ... afraid of, the Strategic Hamlet Program. They wanted to know who had advocated it and what was its purpose."[131] Together, these developments, by 1963, had persuaded the Ngos "that the realization of [their] grand designs for South Vietnam was within ... grasp."[132]

The Strategic Hamlets against American aid

> For the Americans personalism was a murky concept they would never understand any more than they would understand Nhu, but then, Nhu would never understand the Americans.[133]

The unimagined community

For the Ngos, however, the larger objective of the Strategic Hamlet Campaign was not to defeat the communist insurgency, which they considered "*comme des frères*."[134] Rather, the aim was to completely transform the structure of capitalism and liberal democracy, which had been introduced by the French.[135] The infrastructure and superstructure of capitalism would be replaced by a "real democracy ... at the level of the village ... against formal and liberal democracy." This real democracy would be created "through communitarian labor ... and based on a social plan ... rather than ... submission to the capitalist order."[136]

While capitalism, in the colonial era, had undermined the traditional autonomy of the villages, in the cities it had created a Westernized urban petite bourgeoisie,[137] landlords who exploited the dispossessed peasantry and merchants whose "unscrupulous speculations" inflated the prices of grain and imported commodities.[138] This "small but vocal bourgeoisie" made up the "bulk of the membership" of such groups as the Vietnamese Nationalist Party (Việt Nam Quốc Dân Đảng) and the Indochinese Constitutionalist Party (Đảng Lập hiến Đông Dương), who supported Western-style democracy and the protection of civil liberties. With few ties to the majority of the population in the countryside, such political parties mainly "spoke for the interest of the affluent bourgeoisie in Saigon and the landlord class." Their "primary concerns were to promote the interests of indigenous merchants and to achieve equal pay for equal work for Vietnamese employees with their European counterparts."[139] As such, the demand for economic equality and majority rule was part of the politics of an elite urban minority who played a disproportionate role in the state, while monopolizing the profit created in the capitalist economy in the colony. The democracy that these political parties demanded, therefore, was that of a parliamentary government that, to recall Marx's critique of the liberal state, represented the universal interests of egoistic individuals engaged in production for profit. Against the liberal economy underlying this bourgeois democracy, Diệm declared in a speech at the National Assembly that "the time is gone when one had only to produce in order to sell, and only to sell in order to make profits,"[140] just as the "time is gone when democracy can be defined in terms of political and parliamentary liberties."[141]

After the Geneva Accords, the tyranny of majority rule, based on production for profit, was exacerbated by American economic assistance, which Diệm had partly inherited from the economic accord signed between Bảo Đại and the American government.[142] At the time, the Ngos had subscribed to the "pessimistic tendency" among Southern officials "to accept the disadvantages of the American presence because it was necessary for our survival." This relationship, however, which would come into conflict with the Personalist aims of the early Republic, was one that Nhu would later repudiate ("I have changed ... my ideas since the period 1954–1956"), putting himself in the implausible position of an anti-capitalist and anti-colonial leader, funded by the world's greatest imperialist power: "Nhu spoke about his socialist concepts with many of the highest-ranking Western diplomats, and seemed to believe in them. And this during a period when he was drawing millions of dollars from America's 'nonsocialist' treasury."[143] Yet, despite its implausible character, the program that Nhu had envisioned initially was precisely a socialist revolution supported by the world's most powerful capitalist country: "[W]e have to utilize the time in which we have [American] means to ... build a guerilla infrastructure [hạ tầng cơ sở du kích] ... in order to wage a real revolution."[144]

The capitalist form of economic assistance provided by America's non-socialist treasury was designed to promote economic development while winning political support for the Republic.[145] As with the Marshall Plan in Europe, the aid in Vietnam was provided in the form of American dollars, which were sold to licensed importers, who in turn would use them to purchase products from the USA and allied nations.[146] By fixing the exchange rate between the dollar and the Vietnamese đồng, thereby subsidizing the costs of these products, the program would supply the country with both capital goods for development and luxury items, which would reduce the inflationary effect of the aid.[147]

In practice, however, the aid program would serve to constrain and distort economic development.[148] Only a tiny portion of the urban elite was engaged in the industrial sector.[149] And because under the program products could only be purchased from American companies, the cost of capital goods, in spite of the subsidy, remained prohibitively high for potential local investors.[150] Meanwhile, the early Republic's attempt to establish a socialist economy based on industrial planning was frustrated by US officials' refusal to fund long-term development projects, and its policy of providing capital equipment only to private enterprises.[151] To many American specialists, Diệm's Personalist program for economic development seemed like socialist dogma. The plan, according to one US study, was merely an expression of the "familiar urge to want to ... control all facets of the economy from the center" and "an attitude of ... mistrust toward the entrepreneur ... and a hostility toward high profits."[152]

As Nhu complained, on the other hand, the Americans were only attracted to projects that promised to yield an immediate profit, assuming that profits from free enterprise were a reliable measure of economic stability: "[T]hey only want to launch projects that bring a 100% dividend in the very first year."[153] For Nhu, it was the criterion of immediate profit employed in the program, rather than socialist planning, that precluded the possibility of economic development.

Yet, in spite of the evidently adverse effects of the aid, the Americans insisted dogmatically on the doctrine of free-market capitalism. Responding to criticisms that the program was poorly adapted to conditions in the developing world, Leland Barrows, chief of the US Operations Mission, asserted that the doctrine would remain American policy regardless of whether it actually worked: "[W]e Americans consider this kind of undertaking [planning] … to be uneconomic. Perhaps on this point we are somewhat doctrinaire, but such is our economic philosophy so far."[154] As another official acknowledged, however, this philosophy was one that was rightly rejected by Nhu and "those Vietnamese who must cope with the problems … of American aid": "It is sad but true: the laws and regulations of the American aid program were simply not written for … effective implementation in underdeveloped countries."[155]

Diệm's Personalist doctrine, therefore, was directly opposed to the dogma of free-market capitalism underlying the American aid program. "American authorities," according to Vũ Quốc Thúc, Diệm's economic advisor, were "systematically hostile to … any measure of state control or interference in the field of economic activity. How, then, can the Vietnamese government expect to integrate American aid into its Five-Year Plan?" As a result of this systematic hostility to socialist planning, economic development in the South, despite the enormous infusion of aid, lagged behind North Vietnam, where foreign assistance was given without the liberal economic constraints imposed upon the Republic.[156]

For Nhu, therefore, the greatest threat to Southern economic autonomy was not the socialist model of planning, which the communists sought to impose, but the freedom of the capitalist market, which the Americans required as a condition for aid: The communists "see in freedom an obstacle to [industrialization] and we must see that freedom does not impede [our own] economic progress."[157] Like Mounier's personalism, therefore (for which, "*le mal capitaliste est incurable, le mal soviétique guérissable*"),[158] the "third way" pursued by the South Vietnamese state in its economic policy was closer to Soviet-type collectivism than free-market capitalism.

The other Vietnamese revolution

Instead of developing a productive economy, the dogma of liberalism reinforced the tendency among the Vietnamese urban elite toward "unconstructive activities as usury, speculative trading in commodities" and land speculation. Since the "yearly profit on these operations [was] ... far more than ... an industrial project," American aid, based on the principle of high profits and free enterprise, benefited the urban elite who had acquired their fortunes in the colonial era through speculation and rent.[159] The liberal capitalism imposed on the South through the aid program, which freed the economy from the tyranny of Soviet-style collectivism, created what Nguyễn Cao Kỳ would later describe as the economic oligarchy of importers of foreign consumer commodities: a "small minority of local capitalists, speculators and middle men have profited [from] the program, thus creating a new class of profiteers who have contributed to an increase in social injustice and conflicts within Vietnamese society."[160]

This class of importers would function as intermediaries for the flow of American aid in the form of consumer commodities, commodities that the Americans believed would ensure popular support for the regime. By "supplying the Vietnamese middle-class with goods they wanted and could afford to buy,"[161] the program, as Barrows explained, would be "a source of loyalty" to the regime. Despite its adverse effect on development, these goods would guarantee support "from the army, the civil servants and professional people, who were able to obtain better clothes, better ... furnishings ... than they had before."[162]

Supplied with consumer goods through the intermediary of an oligarchy of importers, this new middle class, accustomed to a Westernized culture that remained alien to the countryside, would be increasingly inclined toward American-style democracy.[163] Unaware of the danger of dependence on American aid, "some of our ... upper class," according to Nhu, "rely on American aid ... and think that they are Americans, not understanding that they are Vietnamese" (*không hiểu mình là Việt*), living in an underdeveloped society.[164] This upper class included the members of the military and political elite who were "French educated, French appointed, and ... more French than Vietnamese in culture and habits. ... The fathers of many of these officers were landowners, high officials, or wealthy members of the Saigon bourgeoisie."[165] On the one hand, as Albert Fraleigh described, the political class, having risen through the ranks of "a highly centralized government," "a government in the French tradition" inherited from colonialism, embraced the "typical viewpoints of a French civil servant":

The unimagined community

We are also dealing with people who ... are not really interested in looking downward toward helping their own people but in looking upward and carrying out an overall directive ... conceived by people at the central level who have scarcely been out in the countryside and know their own people.[166]

Owing in part to its political loyalty to American aid, the military and political class (which did not "appear to have any appreciable support outside intellectual-elite circles in Saigon")[167] became increasingly critical of what the writer Minh Võ described as "the lack of democracy according to the notion of American democracy, of the Caravelle group (*dân chủ theo quan niệm dân chủ của Mỹ, của nhóm Caravelle*).[168]

While this highly centralized government had created a political class that, adopting the "viewpoints of a French civil servant," was detached from the Vietnamese masses, the hierarchical structure of the Republican army encouraged a similar attitude among the elite in the military. Organized on "conventional lines to defeat a foreign invader and to occupy ... a foreign country," this structure, which discouraged initiative at the bottom, "created a warlord outlook in the senior commanders" with regard to the population they were supposed to protect.[169]

As Thompson noted, moreover, the US commitment to maintaining this ineffective and costly conventional force would only increase the problems produced by the Commodity Import Program: "To pay the recurrent expenditure on the armed forces, the South Vietnamese government was committed to accepting indefinite American aid on a large scale, including the import of subsidized consumer goods in order to generate local piastre funds to pay the army wage bill."[170]

While the flow of commodities engendered political support from the new middle class, who increasingly favored liberal democracy, it would simultaneously serve to undermine economic stability.[171] "The flood of imports," as Duong Van Mai Elliott described, "heavily damaged the few small industries that were still sputtering along."[172] "Thus, the commercial import program," as one study concluded, "has not served to induce substantial economic development in Vietnam ... because the cheap availability since 1954 of a large variety of Western-made products has tended to dampen the development of competing local manufactures."[173]

For Diệm, as Catton points out, the result was a gilded underdevelopment in which the abundance of consumer commodities concealed the destruction of the country's industrial basis: the "importation of consumer, rather than capital, goods created the illusion of prosperity while hampering the development of local industry."[174] Insofar as the Republican army, which was incapable of fighting an irregular war against the insurgency, was the main beneficiary of the counterpart funds created by the sale of consumer commodities by the class of importers, its existence was the primary cause of economic dependence.

Given that the very design of the aid program was based on the dogma of free market capitalism and liberal democracy, *no* amount of aid could have created a self-sufficient economy. The aid program, therefore, as Vũ Quốc Thúc argued, was directly opposed to the Personalist principle of economic autonomy: "The commercial aid program should not be designed with a view to providing the Counterpart Funds with as many Vietnamese *piastres* as possible, but instead must help Vietnam to achieve its short-and medium-range economic development programs." By providing the country with as much money as possible, but only on the condition that it be used to make profit, the Americans created a capitalist economy dominated by loyal oligarchical interests, interests that would corrupt every branch of the government, the police and the military. According to Phan Quang Đán, a political leader who opposed Diệm's regime, "The U.S. Commercial Import Program – which costs us nothing … brings luxury to our ruling group and middle class, and luxury means corruption."[175]

Like the Americans who created it, this class of importers was hostile to the attempts by Diệm's Personalist government to abolish the tyranny of production for profit, as well as to its "semi-socialist, strongly paternalistic economic and social welfare programs."[176] Clamoring for clean elections, freedom of the press and the protection of civil liberties, this "small minority of local capitalists" would attempt to assert its economic and political interests by demanding majority rule.[177] As Diệm argued, however, this spurious form of democracy was merely a cover for oligarchical interests that perpetuated economic underdevelopment and extreme inequality, which threatened to undermine the Republic:

> [T]here is not a single one among them who is really democratic. These people … who talk of waging a war with ifs and buts are, of course, very much appreciated by the communists and also by a … Western press which totally ignores the phenomenon of underdevelopment and … believes in a homogeneous world.[178]

For Diệm, therefore, the liberal democracy demanded by the urban elite and their American patrons was directly connected to economic dependency. This dependency, however, was in part the result of Diệm's own political naivety in having accepted American aid. The program would effectively undermine the political sovereignty of the South Vietnamese state, a sovereignty that Diệm had proclaimed as the very principle of his Personalist republic: "without economic independence, the country's political independence would lack substance."[179] As a result of the program, the Southern economy was transformed into a subsidized market for American consumer commodities, just as the European economies, according to the Personalists, had been reduced to "economic subservience" by the "Trojan horse" of the Marshall Plan.[180] Through the aid program, "South Viet Nam," according to the communist economist Nguyễn Xuân Lai, was "definitively ... integrated into the dollar bloc, with all the ensuing consequences: ... [T]he Americans could freely ... repatriate their profits without any limitation or control. Diem had sacrificed monetary autonomy behind a façade of independence."[181]

For Diệm, of course, this autonomy could not be restored through the establishment of the sort of "stable, viable and democratic bastion of the Free World" that the Americans wanted. On the contrary, such a policy would only perpetuate economic dependency and undermine political stability. Rather, the Ngos, toward the end of their lives, believed that autonomy would only be possible by detaching the country from American aid, destroying its loyal oligarchical interests and completely transforming the economic and political structure of the nation. "Nhu has made statements about pending economic change that neither the wealthy or the Americans will like. He has been promoting discussions on how to survive without American aid [sic]."[182]

However, in the absence of any other available source of outside assistance, this economic autonomy could not be achieved through industrial planning, which had been precluded by the constraints imposed under the Commodity Import Program.[183] Instead, the Ngos, largely in secret, would develop an entirely different approach, one that appeared, in fact, to be unrelated to the aim for achieving economic autonomy, even to the members of their own administration. "[B]ig industrial enterprises," as Vũ Quốc Thúc remarked with annoyance, "have been postponed ... [by a] ... sudden change in government policy ... [F]or some undivulged reason, industrialization has become less important than land development and the creation of agrovilles!"[184]

Thus, the Ngos had abandoned the impossible program of centralized planning under the constraints of American aid and its liberal economic agenda, in Nhu's terms, "of trying to get progress as a gift of the capitalist societies."[185] In the attempt to restore the nation's autonomy, the Ngos sought to establish instead a decentralized system of communal production and council democracy, which seemed on the surface to be only an authoritarian program of mass relocation: "According to Nhu, the U.S. might well reduce its military as well as economic aid. For this reason, the GVN must ... stand independent of the US ... Nhu commented that the GVN was in a position to assert itself because of the tremendous success of the Strategic Hamlet Program."[186]

The "Strategic hamlets," therefore, "were designed not only as a response to the communist insurgency, but also as a response to the threat of American interference in Vietnamese domestic affairs."[187] Nhu "viewed the strategic hamlets as a means to defeat communism while, at the same time, overcoming the problems of an underdeveloped country."[188] The aim of the program, in other words, was to create a "guerrilla infrastructure" for "fighting against the guerrillas and imperialism," for freeing the Republic from the grips of the Communist Party as well as dependence on American power and influence.[189]

Decentralization and the urban elite

By 1963, the success of the program as both a security measure and a mechanism of social and economic transformation had increased support for the Ngos in the countryside, encouraging them to continue expanding for the program.[190] From "an organizational standpoint the results were impressive. Virtually the entire bureaucracy from the national level on down reoriented its activities to the hamlet program."[191]

This reorientation, however, was not only aimed at overcoming the insurgency in the South. Rather, Nhu also "seized upon the Strategic Hamlets as a unique means of ... bypassing and isolating the inhospitable urban political climate." Since the program, "by its internal logic," as Nhu argued, "cannot fail to limit the powers of Central agencies, and even the presidential powers,"[192] the establishment of a decentralized network of local self-government would proceed "even to the point of bypassing the Saigon-level ministry."[193] "Under the decentralization procedure funds are provided directly to the provinces, rather than through the ministries, for civil measures to establish [the] ... hamlets and for a wide range of local development programs."[194] These measures, in turn, would serve to create the conditions for a new leadership to emerge, democratically, "from the bottom up," within the decentralized villages, preempting the role of the political elite in Sài Gòn. According to one intelligence study: "Inspired leadership is generally lacking in the central government":

The unimagined community

In some provinces, however, this kind of leadership is being generated from the bottom up, by such efforts as the strategic hamlet program. Understanding that only through inspired leadership can the war be won, the President and other officials in Saigon appear not only willing but eager to see such leadership developed.[195]

Leading the local hamlet militias, this new class of cadre, in Nhu's design for the program, would reduce the need for the army, decentralizing the war against the insurgency while decreasing the Republic's dependence on American aid as well as the military elite it supported: Nhu "appreciated that if the programme was successful, it would be possible to build up on the peasant a base of political power which would more than counterbalance that of the army."[196]

As William Colby noted, however, the "idea of a new popular elite coming out of the villages" would create a "contradiction" between the regime and the "elites in the cities."[197] The program to establish a democracy at the base in the countryside was opposed to the interests of this group, who, according to Nhu, belonged to an urban comprador class that had previously served as a "go between for the colonialists and the Vietnamese people."[198] In that sense, the Strategic Hamlet Campaign can be conceived as a kind of class struggle against an urban petite bourgeoisie that, as Colby explained, had "not [been] eliminated as they were in the North" by the Communist Party.[199]

From the perspective of this urban elite, on the other hand, the process of decentralization, aimed at creating a democracy at the base, appeared to be exactly the opposite: an authoritarian concentration of power that, in bypassing the ministries and the military command, eliminated democratic protections on the executive branch.[200] This provided the pretext for the political class in Sài Gòn (which consisted "of ... small groups gathered around leaders having little or no real organization and but few direct followers")[201] to criticize the regime in the name of democracy and majority rule. "They ... turned on Diem," as Colby explained, "because... he had changed the old systems to their detriment ... Then they got intoxicated... by the idea that if we just have more democracy everything will be all right."[202] Speaking on behalf of the urban elite, US officials, therefore, condemned Ngô Đình Diệm for his undemocratic refusal to "delegate responsibilities to trusted and capable ministers" and "to appoint talented men to the cabinet."[203]

The increasingly vocal demands for liberal reform were not, however, the result of a popular backlash against the repression deployed in the Strategic Hamlets Campaign. "The implementation of the program did stir some local grievances that may have found their way back to the cities," but the "urban political agitation that overthrew Diem was ... wholly unconnected with the pacification effort per se."[204] Indeed, Diệm's support in the countryside, "where the Communist ... movement challenges the government's control of its population," was, "ironically," far greater than in the "urban areas, particularly the capital city of Saigon, where the government is most secure militarily."[205] Rather, the political opposition to Diệm in the cities was a consequence, paradoxically, of the increasing success of the program in creating a system of autonomous rural communities. Insofar as the Strategic Hamlet Campaign was based on the Personalist principle of a democracy from the base that would "limit the powers of Central agencies," its design was directly opposed to the democratic inclusion of "trusted and capable ministers" from among the urban elite (who were generally lacking in inspired leadership). As Thompson argued, moreover, the generals who would carry out the coup against Diệm were not representatives of the Vietnamese people. Rather, they were the members of an elite urban minority whose interests were directly opposed to the Personalist project to empower the people in order to decentralize the war against insurgency: "All efforts to encourage [Diệm] to broaden the base of his government and attract more popular support were meaningless in a situation in which the reality of political power lay not with the people but with the army."[206] Thus, in demanding the democratic inclusion of the urban elite in positions of power in the army and the central bureaucracy, the Americans, according to Diệm, were "trying to crush the social revolution" in the "name of liberty" itself.[207]

This fundamental contradiction between the Personalism of the early Republic and the liberal democracy promoted by the urban elite and their American allies would culminate, tragically, in the Buddhist affair in 1963 (see Chapter 4). In response to the events in Sài Gòn, a minority within the Kennedy administration, with "well-known compulsions ... to depose Diem," sidestepped other senior officials, sending a cable to the US ambassador, Henry Cabot Lodge Jr., expressing support for a coup.[208] Lodge, then, using the ultimate threat of a complete suspension of aid and the withdrawal of American forces, presented US demands for democratic reform, including free elections and freedom of the press, and constraint in the use of police and security.[209] Despite the potentially disastrous consequences of an end to the American intervention, these demands were firmly denied by the Ngos: "Diem/Nhu have displayed no ... desire to change the traditional methods of control through police action."[210] Instead, they "responded to the suspension [by] ... fight[ing] rather than submit[ing] to U.S. policy directives," and calling for a withdrawal of American forces.²¹¹

For Lodge, this meant that it would be impossible to persuade Diệm and Nhu to implement democratic reforms "without precipitating an economic collapse" and undermining the whole war effort.²¹² Since the aid, according to Lodge, had to continue in order for the war to be won, his conclusion was that only a coup could save the Republic.²¹³ The regime, therefore, had to be overthrown in order to keep the economy from collapsing.

The Ngos' refusal to comply with US demands has been attributed to "Nhu's erratic behavior" during the crisis and his penchant for "Machiavellian tactics."²¹⁴ Fredrick Logevall, for example, argues that Nhu, aware that "Washington was determined to remove him from power," may have been trying to carry out the "not so crazy" scheme of demanding a US withdrawal, while negotiating a truce with communist leaders. Playing his "only trump card," Nhu hoped to "secure increased leverage" by "blackmail[ing] the Kennedy administration into retreating from its efforts to reform the Ngo family." If this strategy failed, then a peace deal with Hà Nội would at least allow the regime to avoid the imminent coup: "The idea that Nhu and his brother could long have survived in power following any kind of deal with Hanoi seems … doubtful, but … [t]he prospect of … twelve or eighteen months in power following an accord would look quite appealing if the alternative might be an ouster within weeks."²¹⁵

Logevall's hypothesis, however, assumes that the willingness, on the communist side, to negotiate peace was primarily due to the threat of an American military escalation. Given this presupposition, Nhu's demands for a US withdrawal can only be understood as a desperate and cynical wager.²¹⁶ While the communists, in 1962, had concluded "that the large-scale increase in the American advisory presence … had made an important difference on the ground," Nhu, fearing a coup, was insisting that "there were too many Americans in South Vietnam."²¹⁷ Determined to protect his position, Nhu, then, was willing to sever relations with the powerful patron upon which his nation depended for its very survival. Nhu's "only trump card," therefore, was to pretend that he was deliberately forfeiting the war in order to temporarily preserve his dictatorial power.

Contrary to Logevall, however, what had made the "important difference on the ground" was not the American advisory presence (which, according to Nhu, was "absolutely incapable of fighting a guerrilla

The other Vietnamese revolution

war").²¹⁸ Rather, the "big factor in this improvement," as Arthur Dommen has noted, "was the strategic hamlet program launched at the start of 1962." Although the "resurgence of the [South Vietnamese] army, helped by new [American] helicopter tactics, placed the Viet Cong on the defensive," it was the Strategic Hamlet Campaign that was chiefly responsible for the fact that "the war was going better in 1962 and 1963." (And indeed, the American tactics, as Nhu emphasized, had failed to "eradicate at the roots the subversive war waged by the enemy,"²¹⁹ which could only be overcome by employing the same subversive style of warfare.)²²⁰ The program had proven to be "such a success" that "captured documents and letters in late 1962 described severe lack of food, medicine, and recruits; generally low morale; desertions; and fear of attack."²²¹

The willingness on the part of communist leaders to negotiate a political settlement during this period, then, cannot be attributed to the American presence alone. According to the writer Minh Võ, the Strategic Hamlets were in fact "more successful than American bullets and bombs" (*đã thành công hơn bom đạn của Mỹ*) in pushing the North to consider a truce.²²² As Marguerite Higgins observes, this peace offer, moreover, was completely withdrawn when the threat of an American military escalation (which had supposedly inspired it) had become a reality: "In midsummer 1963," when the "Viet Cong were unable to seize ... for more than twenty-four hours any strategic hamlet," "Ho Chi Minh publicly hinted in a radio broadcast at a negotiated modus vivendi with South Vietnam." "In midsummer 1965," after Johnson had ordered an increase in US military ground forces, while the Viet Cong had succeeded in seizing "hundreds of strategic hamlets," "Ho Chi Minh rebuffed all offers of unconditional discussions on the grounds that the Viet Cong victory was certain."²²³

Contrary to Logevall's suggestion, therefore, the Party's receptiveness to a peace accord deal was not simply a response to the possibility of a "lengthy stalemate ... with the Vietcong controlling ... the countryside and the Diem regime maintaining its grip on the cities."²²⁴ Instead, it was prompted by the growing success of the social revolution in the countryside, a "rural revolution" that revealed the leaders of the early Republic had comprehended the role of the people's war strategy, which the Party believed would guarantee victory.²²⁵ Logevall's account of the crisis leaves out what Trần Lệ Xuân called the "seldom told other story ... that the war is being won in ... the countryside where the vast majority of the Vietnamese people live. And for Americans to understand Vietnam, it is necessary to know that it is in the countryside, not the cities, that the war will be won or lost."²²⁶ As Nhu insisted, therefore, the US could not prevail by committing more American soldiers who were "incapable of fighting a guerrilla war."²²⁷ On the contrary, as Albert Fraleigh observed, "adding more equipment and American military advisors… was a conventional American response that would doom counterinsurgency in Vietnam."²²⁸ Nor could the war be resolved through a truce with Hà Nội, backed by either the threat of an American military escalation or the promise of political neutrality. Rather, only a social revolution in the countryside against the communist insurgency could bring about a successful end to the conflict: No "government could possibly negotiate with Hanoi either openly or secretly, except after having won a guerrilla war and not in terms of neutralization."²²⁹

But as such, Nhu's apparently erratic behavior was not simply a desperate attempt to pursue peace with the enemy in order to avoid being deposed in a coup, supported by the foreign power whose presence had supposedly prompted the peace deal to begin with. Rather, as Nhu explained to the Polish diplomat, Mieczysław Maneli, at a meeting to discuss "Ho Chi Minh's declaration as to a ceasefire," the Republic had begun a "new phase" of the war, "fighting the guerrillas and [US] imperialism" simultaneously.²³⁰ Instead of forfeiting the war by "unilaterally" signing a treaty "behind the back of the Americans," Nhu had resolved to fight the guerrillas while resisting American efforts to undermine South Vietnamese sovereignty.²³¹

This twofold struggle, as Nhu explained in a lengthy exposition on Personalism and counterinsurgency, would rely upon the same strategy of social revolution that had motivated the ceasefire proposal: "Maneli asked what was the next step and Nhu … replied, 'continue building strategic hamlets.'"²³² In the new phase of the conflict, therefore, the Republic would continue building strategic hamlets in order to win the guerrilla war, while fighting the underdevelopment produced by the aid provided by "America's 'nonsocialist' treasury."

In the cities, this aid had created an inchoate political elite who had little support in the countryside, an urban minority who monopolized profits in the liberal economy, while dominating the centralized agencies of the constitutional state: "Underdevelopment means that parties tend to lack organization and defined programs are largely city-based, and tend to depend heavily on the personalities of their leaders, who come from the small intellectual elite."²³³ Seeking to "bypass … and isolat[e] … th[is] inhospitable urban political climate," the Ngos attempted to utilize the Strategic Hamlet Campaign as a tool of counterinsurgency, as well as

The other Vietnamese revolution

"a solution to the central problem of underdevelopment": the "fortified hamlets ... thus form a new approach ... better than ... trying to get progress as a gift of the capitalist societies."[234]

For the communist leadership, it was this approach to fighting both the insurgency and underdevelopment that constituted the primary threat to its people's war strategy, which the Party believed would ensure certain victory:

> By establishing strategic hamlets ... the enemy would then have the conditions for amassing manpower and material resources to build additional forces, increase military strength, employ the civil guard and militia forces ... to attack the revolution.[235]

On the other hand, for Lodge and other US officials, the fear was that the "tremendous success" of the program had convinced the regime that the social revolution could also be used as a means of resisting American interference, imposed through the leverage of economic assistance:

> Within the last few days the Minister of Civic Action [Ngô Trọng Hiếu] said to one of my (very few, alas!) highly reliable sources: "We don't need the Americans any more even in the economic field, as we can confront our economic problems with our own resources." Present suspension of Commodity Import Program may give GVN a chance to decide whether Hieu is right.[236]

Thus, according to a US State Department report, the real danger, during the 1963 crisis, was not that the suspension of aid would destroy the economy, but that:

> Ngo Dinh Nhu will ... consider present aid pressures as a welcome excuse to bring about changes in the rural scene and perhaps in the whole economy. These changes will be based on his desire to get the Americans out of the countryside ... and his belief that [he has] ... a strong political base.[237]

The real danger, then, was that the suspension of aid could justify the attempt to create an entirely different kind of economy, a Personalist economy freed from American influence, and based on a different form of democracy than the one that the Americans were demanding.

This Personalist economy, however, would not correspond to the earlier program that the Ngos had proposed to US officials in the 1950s, a program for developing a "'mixed economy,' i.e., partly state and partly private control." In this earlier scheme, a "system of state control" would be used to develop a capitalist economy based on free private enterprise.²³⁸ In light of the threat of a suspension of aid, the South Vietnamese, however, considered adopting a more "drastic policy [that] would involve changing everything," taking "stronger measures to ... bring about economic development, curb privileges, and promote more social justice."²³⁹ In contrast to the earlier program, these measures would not simply provide a "third way" between "communism ... [and] western liberal capitalism" (a "doctrine" which, as Nhu explained to US officials, was "associate[d] historically with colonialism").²⁴⁰ Rather, like Mounier's Personalism, the new measures would be much closer to Marxism: "Now if ... aid is reduced," explained Nhu, "we shall have to do what the Communists have done," citing the example of Algeria, where the state had nationalized industries and pursued centralized planning.²⁴¹

But because a centralized system of state control was opposed to the principle of personal autonomy (just as liberal capitalism is contrary to the Personalist ideal of community), this planning would have to be adapted to the requirements of a different kind of communist doctrine. At an intra-ministry meeting in January 1963, Nhu reminded officials that "we established the Strategic Hamlet Campaign not only to solve the security problem, but to deal with all aspects of the economy, culture and society." Whereas "our economic program" had previously been "*directed from top to bottom* (from the Central Authority to the local level)," "economic theory" must now follow the "path of the Personalist Revolution" (*đường lối Cách Mạng Nhân Vị*). Calling for a "revolution in the economy," Nhu underscored the need to "integrate the Strategic Hamlet Campaign with the program of economic development." In this way, the struggle against both the insurgency and underdevelopment would be "*directed*," democratically, "*from bottom to top*."²⁴²

For Nhu, then, the project of employing centralized planning to develop a Western-style liberal economy (which had proven to be impossible under the auspices of American aid) was only a preliminary stage in a broader political and economic revolution. Just as the constitutional government established in 1955, adopting "parliamentary democracy from liberal states," would be superseded by a "democratization from the bottom up," so the program of using state control to create a modern capitalist economy would be replaced by a decentralized form of economic development.

Arguing that American aid was "superfluous," Nhu, therefore, "constantly emphasized the need for hamlet self-sufficiency." This self-sufficiency was perceived as an immediate threat to the influence that the USA maintained through its program of economic assistance (a

The other Vietnamese revolution

program that only perpetuated dependence). Thus, the CIA warned that the changes that Nhu intended to carry out in the countryside "could severely limit our influence in the rural areas. ... Once these actions are taken, [it] will be extremely difficult for us to get this influence back even if we resumed the Commercial Import Program."[243]

The Ngos' refusal of American aid and American-style democracy, then, was not based on a desire to preserve their dictatorial power, even at the cost of destroying the nation's economy. Rather, it was rooted in the "tremendous success of the Strategic Hamlet Program" as a means of transforming the "rural scene and perhaps ... the whole economy."[244]

According to Lucien Conein, Lodge's liaison officer during the coup, Nhu, convinced that the hamlets provided the means of achieving political and economic autonomy, had intended to use the suspension of aid to "go into the program that he had originally planned, which was to ... insist that the Americans get out."[245] Because the "strategic hamlets proved to be successful," making it seem like "a sure thing that the NLF [National Liberation Front] will not achieve further ... victories," the Ngos, as Ramchundur Goburdhun, chair of the International Control Commission, reportedly stated, would "strive to make the Americans withdraw."[246] Thus, in a seemingly "improbable ... development," "Diem and Nhu might have made some rational calculation to terminate the alliance, almost at the same moment as Kennedy," who ordered a suspension of aid in an effort to force the regime to liberalize the Republic.[247] For Nhu, in particular, the decision to end the alliance was based upon the conviction that the aims of the American government were directly opposed to the Personalist revolution, which he believed was the only approach that could ensure success in the war against the insurgency: "The war cannot be won with the Americans because they are an obstacle to the revolutionary transformation of society which is the prerequisite of victory."[248]

In this revolution, a "supersession of the anarchic economy of profit" through the establishment of an autonomous form of communal production would simultaneously lead to a supersession of liberal democracy. In Nhu's terms, the goal was to "build a new society ... starting from the infrastructure of the hamlets ... to pervade all the superstructure of the State."[249] Unlike the Americans, then, the aim of the South Vietnamese state was not to create a bastion of liberal democracy and free-market capitalism. On the contrary, they wanted to abolish both through the establishment of a "*démocratie réelle par la base ... contre la démocratie ... liberale ... et ... la soumission à l'ordre capitaliste.*"[250]

Beginning "from the infrastructure of the hamlets," the "revolution in the countryside," as Diệm described in a speech in 1963, "will advance toward urban areas,"[251] to remove the oligarchical interests demanding majority rule and liberal democracy: the "Strategic Hamlet program necessarily entails the vast revision of the state's superstructure, since a movement which starts from the base ... cannot fail to produce considerable changes in the institutions of the country."[252] The Ngos, therefore, according to Catton, "envisioned that the effects of the Hamlet program would cleanse the rest of the body politic as well, especially the French trained urban elite for whom the Ngos felt particular contempt."[253]

Destroying democracy in the name of democracy

In the end, this anti-capitalist and anti-colonial revolution, waged using authoritarian methods with the aim of creating a democracy from the base, would be defeated by US imperialism in a misguided effort to save the image of the South Vietnamese state as a liberal democracy. The coup was carried out by members of the officer corps, who belonged to an elite urban minority, demanding more "talented men to the cabinet," as the basis for creating a truly popular government. During the coup, however, the conspirators, ironically, would be compelled to assassinate Diệm precisely because he had too much popular support from the peasant majority because he was "too much respected among simple, gullible people in the countryside":

> The top generals who decided to murder Diệm and his brother were scared to death. The generals knew very well that having no talent, no moral virtues, no political support whatsoever, they could not prevent a spectacular comeback of the president and Mr. Nhu if they were alive.[254]

Fearing that supporters of the former regime would oppose their illegitimate power, the generals, then, proceeded to destroy the network of autonomous organizations that Nhu had created through the Strategic Hamlet Campaign:

> The political apparatus was not only deprived of its leadership ... after the *coup*; it was purposely dismantled as a sign of the break with the past. ... Some of its physical aspects remained, but ... the Strategic Hamlet lay gutted politically and organizationally after November 1963.[255]

In an effort, moreover, to ensure that the coup was perceived by the public as an act undertaken in the name of democracy, the generals,

The other Vietnamese revolution

trying to "hide their guilt in having been servants of the CIA" (*che giấu bộ mặt lem luốc bỉ ổi làm tay sai cho* CIA), "deliberately painted the image of the Personalist ... Party as an evil tool of the regime."[256] Immediately after the coup, the generals, with the help of US intelligence, carried out a psychological warfare campaign to defame the early Republic and to proclaim a new era of liberal democracy. Hundreds of thousands of leaflets, distributed throughout the countryside, announced that the "dictatorial, family ruling regime of Ngo Dinh Diem is being replaced by a truly free and democratic regime. A new page of our people's history begins."[257] Cast as a totalitarian instrument of mass repression, the Marxist humanist program of social revolution, which had won widespread support in the countryside as an alternative to the communist insurgency in the South, was systematically undermined. The "implementation of the theory of Personalism was suspended" by the new Republican leaders. In addition, "the hired thugs":

> ... erased the countless works that *Cần Lao* members had contributed toward the construction of the Republic ... [They] ... hunted down *Cần Lao* members and personnel connected with the former regime ... at the same time destroying the anti-communist network that had been created through ... the Strategic Hamlets, which had been quickly progressing ...[258]

The collapse of the program, therefore, as US intelligence studies affirmed, was not the result of a superior strategy devised by the communist insurgency in the South. Rather, the Personalist revolution in the countryside, which was in the process of creating a democracy at the base, was undermined by "urban political agitation," encouraged by the Americans, that was "wholly unconnected with the pacification effort per se."[259] "The fact was that the Buddhist crisis in 1963 crystallized urban opposition to Diem and Nhu and ultimately brought them down, bringing down also the Strategic Hamlet." "The Strategic Hamlet," therefore, "was primarily a casualty and not a cause of the fall of the House of Ngo."[260]

Thus, the social revolution undertaken by the early Republic, aimed at establishing a non-Western form of modernity, founded on a democracy at the base, would be undermined by the Americans, acting in accordance with their own ideals of liberal democracy. "History," as Marguerite Higgins observed:

> may well write that in Vietnam ... there were good Americans, the idealistic Americans ... who in their ... zeal to impose their own Western concepts of right and wrong ... did Vietnam in – but only for its own good. ... What had happened? Very simple. The good Americans had acted on the

very false assumptions that ... a ... country that had never ... experienced nationhood or known peace could nonetheless develop "instant democracy" and operate responsibly in the middle of a war ... to make responsible parliamentary government possible.[261]

This account of the coup, however (as a result of the conflict between the early Republic and the political ideology of its American allies), does not acknowledge the Marxist critique of liberal democracy espoused by the Ngos. For the latter, the aim was not the establishment of a "responsible parliamentary government" (which Mounier had described as a "*démocratie ... parlementaire et irresponsible*"). Such a democracy, which was supported by an elite urban minority that "in the name of liberty [was] trying to crush the social revolution," precluded the possibility of economic and political decentralization, which the Ngos believed was required in order to win the war in the countryside.[262] This contradiction between the politics of the urban elite and the need to implement a program of social reform that could establish stability in the countryside was one that Nhu had sought to resolve, dialectically, in his authoritarian attempt to abolish the authority of the state: "I am centralizing the state in order to democratize and decentralize it."[263]

As a result of the coup, however, this contradiction would continue to plague the South Vietnamese state until the end of the war. After the collapse of the First Republic, the attempt to "make responsible parliamentary government possible," in accordance with American policy, would coincide with the collapse of the counterinsurgency program in the countryside. For the later Republican regimes:

> [u]rban politics alone determined the fate of governments and politicians, generally for reasons not immediately connected with the struggle against the VC [Viet Cong] in the countryside. No regime had a stake of political self-interest in pressing pacification ... and consequently, the political "input" from the central government level was if anything a negative one for the pacification effort.[264]

Having "deliberately painted the image of the Personalis[m] ... as an evil tool of the [former] regime," the urban elite had no "means of inducing popular political support" in the countryside. The new leaders, according to Huỳnh Văn Lang, a former member of the Cần Lao, "were inadequate. They couldn't hold on the people [*nắm dân*]. ... The First Republic devoted all of its effort [to this], and it succeeded in the Strategic Hamlet Campaign, but it was destroyed as soon as it started."[265] As a

The other Vietnamese revolution

result, the Americans, who "had no way of providing either mass or elite political organizations or essential political apparat[i]," were compelled to "provide ... the basic ... ideology of the post-Diem pacification programs," since "the Vietnamese were unable to do so," after the coup. Like the program of free-market capitalism and liberal democracy that the USA promoted among the urban elite, the "American philosophical approach" to counterinsurgency "was ... closely geared to the resources [that] the U.S. was best able to supply – the material ones." Thus, in the post-Diem pacification programs, the "materialist approach of using economic ... benefits as the primary means of inducing popular political support" would replace the Personalist principles of political autonomy and economic self-sufficiency. In "the absence of alternative philosophies and resources, the ideological content of pacification inevitably gravitated toward the American view," to the goal of creating a bastion of capitalism and liberal democracy.

Notes

1 David Halberstam, *The Making of a Quagmire* (Lanham, MD: Rowman & Littlefield Publishers, 1988), 51.
2 *Press interviews with President Ngo Dinh Diệm, Political Counselor Ngo Dinh Nhu* (Saigon: Republic of Vietnam, 1963), 68.
3 Marshall S. Carter, "Memorandum for the Secretary of Defense on the Strategic Hamlet Program," 1–2. VCA. 0410693005 July 13, 1962. Box 06, Folder 93. Central Intelligence Agency Collection.
4 Memorandum from the Special Consultant for Counterinsurgency, United States Operation Mission (Phillips) to the Acting Director of the Mission (Fippin), Saigon, June 25, 1962.
5 Ibid.
6 Stephen B. Croker, "Comparative Investigation of Counterinsurgency," 105. Research Paper, Georgetown University. VCA. January 18, 1965. Folder 18, Box 01. Vincent Puritano Collection.
7 *Times of Vietnam*, December 13, 1958, 1, 8.
8 Chánh Trung Lý, *Tìm Hiểu Nước Mỹ* (Saigon: Nguyễn Du, 1969). On Lý Chánh Trung on his politics, see Bùi Văn Phú, "GS. Lý Chánh Trung Có Là Trí Thức Cánh Tả?" [Was Professor Lý Chánh Trung a left-wing intellectual?], *BBC News Tiếng Việt*. BBC News, BBC, March 18, 2016, www.bbc.com/vietnamese/forum/2016/03/160318_bui_van_phu_ly_chanh_trung. Last accessed July 21, 2019.
9 Hannah Arendt, *On Revolution* (New York: Penguin Books, 1986), 249.
10 Ibid., 245.
11 Ibid., 66.

12 Karl Marx, *The Civil War in France* (New York: International Library Publishing, 1900), 48.
13 V. I. Lenin, *State and Revolution* (Chicago: Haymarket Books, 2016), 18.
14 Georges Sorel, *Sorel: Reflections on Violence*, ed. J. Jennings (Cambridge: Cambridge University Press, 1999), xviii.
15 Arendt, *On Revolution*, 249.
16 David Marr, *Vietnamese Tradition on Trial, 1920–1945* (Berkeley: University of California Press, 1984), 386.
17 Ibid., 385.
18 Samuel Popkin, *The Rational Peasant: The Political Economy of Rural Society in Vietnam* (Berkeley: University of California Press, 1984), 135.
19 Marr, *Vietnamese Tradition*, 385.
20 Arendt, *On Revolution*, 64.
21 Fern K. Willits, Gene L. Theodori and Michael W. P. Fortunato, "The Rural Mystique in American Society," in *Reinventing Rural: New Realities in an Urbanizing World*, ed. Alexander R. Thomas and Gregory M. Fulkerson (Lanham, MD: Lexington Books, 2016), 39.
22 Alfred Owen Aldridge, *The Dragon and the Eagle: The Presence of China in the American Enlightenment* (Detroit, MI: Wayne State University Press, 1993), 150.
23 Tran My-Van, *A Vietnamese Royal Exile in Japan: Prince Cuong De (1882–1951)* (London: Routledge, 2005), 18.
24 Pierre Poivre, *Voyages d'un philosophe, ou, Observations sur les mœurs et les arts des peuples de l'Afrique, de l'Asie et de l'Amerique* (Londres: J. De Ville, & L. Rosset, 1769), 80. For a discussion of Poivre's relation to Jeffersonian democracy, see "L'idéologie de la démocratie agraire américaine," *Cahiers de l'I.S.M.E.A. Série Histoire de la pensée économiques* (Grenoble: Presses universitaires de Grenoble, 1995), 431. See also Manuela Albertone, *National Identity and the Agrarian Republic* (Farnham: Ashgate, 2014), 146.
25 Pierre Poivre, *Voyage de Pierre Poivre en Cochinchine*, in *Revue de l'Extrême-Orient*, tome III (Paris: E. Leroux. 1887), 85.
26 Poivre, *Voyages d'un philosophe*, 94.
27 Ibid., 94.
28 Arendt, *On Revolution*, 236.
29 Ibid.
30 Bửu Lịch, "Les idéologies dans la République du Sud Vietnam 1954–1975" (Ph.D. dissertation, Université de Paris VII, 1983/1984), 102.
31 Báo cáo (mật) về công cuộc khẩn thiết phát động một "Phong trào quần chúng" [Secret Report on the Urgent Need to Launch a "Mass Movement"]. Folder 29257. *Phủ Tổng Thống Đệ Nhất* [Files of the Office of the President]. Vietnam National Archives No. 2.

32 "Strategic Hamlets." George C. Denny to Acting Secretary. Department of State, Bureau of Intelligence and Research. VCA. July 1, 1963. Folder 18, Box 15. Douglas Pike Collection: Unit 06 – Democratic Republic of Vietnam.
33 Ngo Dinh Nhu, *Friendly Talk to the Militants* (Saigon: Nha Tổng Giám Đốc Thông Tin, 1963), 6.
34 See also Meeting Minutes. VCA. 1820308002 August 30, 1963. Box 03, Folder 08. Douglas Pike Collection: Other Manuscripts – Intra-Ministry Committee for Strategic Hamlets.
35 Nguyễn Xuân Hoài, "*Đảng Cần lao Nhân vị*" [The Cần Lao Personalist Party] Luutruvn.com, January 4, 2016. http://luutruvn.com/index.php/2016/04/01/dang-can-lao-nhan-vi/. Last accessed July 21, 2019.
36 "Information Report, Republic of Vietnam – Analysis of the Strategic Hamlets Program and the Montagnard Situation – CIA Research Reports," 4. VCA. July 16, 1962. Folder 0253, Box 0003. Vietnam Archive Collection.
37 *Như Áng Mây Bay: Cuộc đời của Đại Lão Hòa Thượng Thích Đôn Hậu* [Like The Floating Clouds: The Life of the Venerable Thích Đôn Hậu], 2010. Thư Viện Hoa Sen, https://thuvienhoasen.org/a7894/chuong-11-trong-long-phap-nan-1963. Last accessed July 11, 2019. See also Minh Võ, *Ngô Đình Diệm và Chính Nghĩa Dân Tộc*, 93.
38 James Horrox, *A Living Revolution: Anarchism in the Kibbutz Movement* (Edinburgh: AK Press, 2009), iii.
39 Hannah Arendt, "Zionism Reconsidered," in *The Jewish Writings*, ed. Jerome Kohn and Ron H. Feldman (New York: Schocken Books, 2007), 349–50.
40 Horrox, *A Living Revolution*, iii.
41 Charles Stevenson (Washington Editor, *Reader's Digest*), "Notes on Interview with Ngo Dinh Nhu." 1962 (unpublished draft), quoted in Nighswonger, *Rural Pacification in Vietnam*, 73.
42 Meeting Minutes (#26), Uỷ-Ban Liên-Bộ Đặc-Trách về Ấp Chiến-Lược tại Dinh Gia Long [Intra-Ministry Committee for Strategic Hamlets], 24. VCA 1820201001 November 1, 1962. Box 02, Folder 01. Douglas Pike Collection: Other Manuscripts – Intra-Ministry Committee for Strategic Hamlets.
43 Meeting Minutes (#36), Uỷ-Ban Liên-Bộ Đặc-Trách về Ấp Chiến-Lược tại Dinh Gia Long [Intra-Ministry Committee for Strategic Hamlets].
44 Kolko, *Anatomy of a Peace*, 5.
45 Meeting Minutes (#36), *Uỷ-Ban Liên-Bộ Đặc-Trách về Ấp Chiến-Lược tại Dinh Gia Long* [Intra-Ministry Committee for Strategic Hamlets], 14. On the Party's views on the dictatorship of the proletariat, see Lê Duẩn, *Hăng hái tiến lên dưới ngọn cờ của Cách mạng Tháng Mười vĩ đại* [Moving Proudly Forward Under the Great Banner of the October Revolution] (Hà Nội: Nhà xuất bản sự thật,1969), 54.
46 Maneli, *War of the Vanquished*, 145–6.
47 Thompson, *Defeating Communist Insurgency*, 142.
48 Maneli, *War of the Vanquished*, 145.

49 Meeting Minutes (#36), Uỷ-Ban Liên-Bộ Đặc-Trách về Ấp Chiến-Lược tại Dinh Gia Long [Intra-Ministry Committee for Strategic Hamlets], 14.
50 Mounier, *Révolution personnaliste et communautaire*, 25.
51 Emmanuel Mounier, "Prague." *Œuvres*, vol. 4 (Paris: Éditions du Seuil, 1950), 160.
52 Tùng Phong (Ngô Đình Nhu), *Chính Đề Việt Nam* [Political Solution for Vietnam], 379.
53 Halberstam, *The Making of a Quagmire*, 26.
54 Nighswonger, *Rural Pacification in Vietnam*, 59, 219.
55 Edward Geary Lansdale, *In the Midst of Wars: An American's Mission to Southeast Asia* (New York: Fordham University Press, 1991), xxxi.
56 Armed Forces Staff College Lecture – Military Psychological Operations, 4–5. VCA. 12050107009 January 7, 1960. Box 01, Folder 07. Vladimir Lehovich Collection.
57 Max Boot, *The Road Not Taken: Edward Lansdale and the American Tragedy in Vietnam* (New York: Liveright Publishing Corporation, 2018), 157–9.
58 Robert Manning, "Our Best-Known Covert Operative," *New York Times* (February 26, 1989).
59 Arendt, *On Revolution*, 45.
60 Nighswonger, *Rural Pacification in Vietnam*, 304.
61 *Đảng cương Cần lao Nhân vị Cách mạng Đảng* [Program of the Cần Lao Personalist Revolutionary Party], folder 29361, Phông Phủ Tổng thống Đệ Nhất [Files of the Office of the President]. Vietnam National Archives No. 2. On the Party's view on violence and the dictatorship of the proletariat, see Outline of Materials Used in Ideological Training. VCA. 2322510015 March 1972. Box 25, Folder 10. Douglas Pike Collection: Unit 06 – Democratic Republic of Vietnam, 19–21.
62 Hammer, *The Struggle for Indochina*, 307.
63 Edward Miller, *Misalliance: Ngo Dinh Diem, the United States, and the Fate of South Vietnam* (Cambridge, MA: Harvard University Press, 2013), 156.
64 See *Press interviews with President Ngo Dinh Diệm*, 71.
65 Bửu Lịch, "Les idéologies dans la République du Sud Vietnam," 46.
66 *Điều lệ Cần lao Nhân vị Cách mạng Đảng* [Regulations of the Cần Lao Personalist Revolutionary Party], folder 29361, Phông Phủ Tổng Thống Đệ Nhất Cộng hòa, Vietnam National Archives No. 2. On the NLF cell structure, see Duy Lap Nguyen, "The *Kiểm Thảo* and the Uses of Disposable Time in the National Liberation Front," *Public Culture*, 20:2 (May 1, 2008), 375–94.
67 See VCA. 23130005001 January 1, 1963. Box 30, Folder 005. Douglas Pike Collection: Unit 05 – National Liberation Front. See also Fall, *The Two Viet-Nams*, 250.
68 *Victory in Vietnam: The Official History of the People's Army of Vietnam, 1954–1975*, trans. Merle L. Pribbenow (Lawrence: University Press of Kansas, 2002), 109.

69 Emmanuel Mounier, *Personalisme*, 7th ed. (Paris: Les Presses universitaires de France, 1961), 115.
70 Meeting Minutes (#26), Uỷ-Ban Liên-Bộ Đặc-Trách về Ấp Chiến-Lược tại Dinh Gia Long [Intra-Ministry Committee for Strategic Hamlets], 26. VCA 1820201001 November 1, 1962. Box 02, Folder 01. Douglas Pike Collection: Other Manuscripts – Intra-Ministry Committee for Strategic Hamlets.
71 Dân Sinh, "Tìm hiểu tổ chức hợp-tác-xã" [Understanding the commune-cooperative organization]. *Xã Hội*, September 15, 1953, 23. See also Meeting Minutes (#34), Uỷ-Ban Liên-Bộ Đặc-Trách về Ấp Chiến-Lược tại Dinh Gia Long [Intra-Ministry Committee for Strategic Hamlets], 7. VCA. 1820203001 January 4, 1963. Box 02, Folder 03. Douglas Pike Collection: Other Manuscripts – Intra-Ministry Committee for Strategic Hamlets.
72 Willemetz, *La République du Viêt-Nam*, 35.
73 Mounier, *Manifeste au service du personnalisme*, 232.
74 "Opening of the National Assembly, October Session," October 7, 1957.
75 "Vietnam Counterinsurgency – The Diem Era: Strategic Hamlet," 177. VCA. January 1, 1956. Folder 01, Box 01. Douglas Pike Collection: Unit 01 – Assessment and Strategy.
76 Quoted in Bửu Lịch, "Les idéologies dans la République du Sud Vietnam," 39.
77 "Letter from Mr. Rice and Enclosures – RE: Your Meeting with Robert Thompson – Vietnam Working Group, Bureau of Far Eastern Affairs," 1. VCA. March 29, 1963. Folder 0238, Box 0002.
78 *Đảng quy Cần lao Nhân vị Cách mạng Đảng* [Rules of the Cần Lao Personalist Revolutionary Party], folder 29361, Phông Phủ Tổng thống Đệ Nhất [Files of the Office of the President]. Vietnam National Archives No. 2.
79 Taylor, *History of the Vietnamese*, 581.
80 Ngo Dinh Nhu, *Friendly Talk to the Militants*, 6.
81 Ngo Dinh Nhu, "Strategic Hamlets, Basis for Total Revolution." Address to the National Institution of Administration, Saigon, August 23, 1962 (described in *Viet Nam's Strategic Hamlets* (Saigon: Vietnam Directorate General of Information, 1963), 5).
82 Meeting Minutes (#20), Uỷ-Ban Liên-Bộ Đặc-Trách về Ấp Chiến-Lược tại Dinh Gia Long [Intra-Ministry Committee for Strategic Hamlets], 8. VCA. 1820108001 September 7, 1962. Box 01, Folder 08. Douglas Pike Collection: Other Manuscripts – Intra-Ministry Committee for Strategic Hamlets.
83 Tùng Phong (Ngô Đình Nhu), *Chính đề Việt Nam* [Political Solution for Vietnam], 242.
84 South Vietnam: The Formative Years, 16. VCA. 2391113003 No Date. Box 11, Folder 13. Douglas Pike Collection: Unit 11 – Monographs.
85 Meeting Minutes (#26), Uỷ-Ban Liên-Bộ Đặc-Trách về Ấp Chiến-Lược tại Dinh Gia Long [Intra-Ministry Committee for Strategic Hamlets], 29. VCA 1820201001 November 1, 1962. Box 02, Folder 01. Douglas Pike Collection: Other Manuscripts – Intra-Ministry Committee for Strategic Hamlets.

86 Minh Võ, "Ông Cao Xuân Vỹ Kể Việc Ông Ngô Đình Nhu Bí Mật Gặp Ông Phạm Hùng Ở Khu Rừng Tánh Linh Bình Tuy" [Cao Xuân Vỹ Describes Ngô Đình Nhu's Secret Meeting with Ông Phạm Hùng at Tánh Linh Bình Tuy Forest]. *Diễn Đàn Việt Thức*, June 14, 2012, https://tinyurl.com/y6j2x2q2. Last accessed July 21, 2019.
87 Meeting Minutes (#34), Uỷ-Ban Liên-Bộ Đặc-Trách về Ấp Chiến-Lược tại Dinh Gia Long [Intra-Ministry Committee for Strategic Hamlets], 7. VCA. 1820203001 January 4, 1963. Box 02, Folder 03. Douglas Pike Collection: Other Manuscripts – Intra-Ministry Committee for Strategic Hamlets.
88 Tùng Phong (Ngô Đình Nhu), *Chính-đề Việt-nam*, 240.
89 Ibid., 234.
90 Ngo Dinh Nhu, *Friendly Talk to the Militants*, 4.
91 Tana Li, *Nguyen Cochinchina: Southern Vietnam in the Seventeenth and Eighteenth Centuries* (Ithaca, NY: Cornell University, SEAP Publications, 1998), 19.
92 Tùng Phong (Ngô Đình Nhu), *Chính-đề Việt-nam*, 120.
93 Bửu Lịch, "Les idéologies dans la République du Sud Vietnam," 74.
94 Maneli, *War of the Vanquished*, 145.
95 Christopher Goscha, *Vietnam: A New History* (New York: Basic Books, 2016), 299.
96 Phạm Văn Lưu, *Chính Quyền Ngô Đình Diệm 1954–1963: Chủ Nghĩa và Hành Động* [The Government of Ngô Đình Diệm 1954–1963: Personalism and Action] (Reservoir, Vic: Centre For Vietnamese Studies Publications, 2017), 30–1.
97 Maneli, *War of the Vanquished*, 145.
98 Ibid., 145–6.
99 *Press interviews with President Ngo Dinh Diệm*, 57.
100 Meeting Minutes (#35), Uỷ-Ban Liên-Bộ Đặc-Trách về Ấp Chiến-Lược tại Dinh Gia Long [Intra-Ministry Committee for Strategic Hamlets], 13. VCA. 1820203002 January 18, 1963. Box 02, Folder 03. Douglas Pike Collection: Other Manuscripts – Intra-Ministry Committee for Strategic Hamlets.
101 *Press interviews with President Ngo Dinh Diệm*, 70–1.
102 Ibid., 22.
103 *Đề án cải tổ đoàn thể Phong trào Cách mạng Quốc gia*, December 17, 1962 [Reforming the National Revolutionary Movement], Folder 29362, phông Phủ Tổng thống, Vietnam National Archives No. 2.
104 *Press interviews with President Ngo Dinh Diệm*, 71.
105 Meeting Minutes (#35) Intra-Ministry Committee for Strategic Hamlets, 13.
106 *Press interviews with President Ngo Dinh Diệm*, 69. See also Meeting Minutes (#20), Uỷ-Ban Liên-Bộ Đặc-Trách về Ấp Chiến-Lược tại Dinh Gia Long [Intra-Ministry Committee for Strategic Hamlets], 4. VCA. 1820108001 September 7, 1962. Box 01, Folder 08. Douglas Pike Collection: Other Manuscripts – Intra-Ministry Committee for Strategic Hamlets. On the

The other Vietnamese revolution

Strategic Hamlet Program and underdevelopment, see Hoàng Khánh, *Tìm hiểu quốc sách ấp chiến lược* [Understanding the Strategic Hamlet Strategy] (Saigon: Nguyễn-Bá-Tòng, 1962).

107 Memorandum: The Situation in South Vietnam, 6 November 1963, Box 06, Folder 91, Central Intelligence Agency Collection, VCA.
108 Nighswonger, *Rural Pacification in Vietnam*, 59, 77.
109 Hélène Tournaire and Robert Bouteaud, *Livre jaune du Viet-Nam* (Paris: Librairie académique Perrin, 1966), 221.
110 Letter from Nguyen Van Hung to President John F. Kennedy, September 4, 1963. MSU Archives & Historical Collections. Wesley R. Fishel Papers (UA 17.95). Box 1184, Folder 37.
111 Charles Fourniau, "Les traditions de la lutte nationale au Vietnam," *La Pensée*, 125 (January–February 1966), 84.
112 Maxwell D. Taylor, recorded interview by Larry Hackman, December 29, 1969, 61–2, Robert Kennedy Oral History Program of the John F. Kennedy Library.
113 Notes on Strategic Hamlets from Office of Rural Affairs – USOM – Saigon, 3. VCA. 2130303013 January 1, 1963. Box 03, Folder 03. Douglas Pike Collection: Unit 02 – Military Operations.
114 Ibid., 4.
115 Willemetz, *La République du Viêt-Nam*, 35–6.
116 Meeting Minutes (#34), Uỷ-Ban Liên-Bộ Đặc-Trách về Ấp Chiến-Lược tại Dinh Gia Long [Intra-Ministry Committee for Strategic Hamlets], 15–19. VCA. 1820203001 January 4, 1963. Box 02, Folder 03. Douglas Pike Collection: Other Manuscripts – Intra-Ministry Committee for Strategic Hamlets.
117 Nighswonger, *Rural Pacification in Vietnam*, 82–3.
118 Quoted in Willemetz, *La République du Viêt-Nam*, 35–6.
119 Letter from Mr Rice and Enclosures – RE: Your Meeting with R.G.K. Thompson, Head of the British Advisory Mission – Vietnam Working Group, Bureau of Far Eastern Affairs, 28 March 1963, Box 0002, Folder 0209, Sam Johnson Vietnam Archive Collection, VCA. See also Thompson Sees South Vietnamese Waging Stable War Against North's Protracted War, October 1971, Box 21, Folder 06, Douglas Pike Collection: Unit 01 – Assessment and Strategy, VCA.
120 Letter from Mr Rice and Enclosures. See also Booklet – Vietnam's Strategic Hamlets, February 1963, Box 01, Folder 30, Rufus Phillips Collection, VCA.
121 *Press interviews with President Ngo Dinh Diệm*, 43. On this strategy, see also Memo re: Meeting with Ngo Dinh Nhu on 17 December 1962, 2. VCA. 23970201052 December 18, 1963. Box 02, Folder 01. Rufus Phillips Collection.
122 A Party account of the revolutionary movement in South Vietnam from 1954 to 1963, 34.

The unimagined community

123 *Victory in Vietnam*, 109.
124 Memorandum for the President (The Secretary Of Defense Washington) – Subject: Report of McNamara-Taylor Mission to South Vietnam, 557–60. VCA. 2130313002 October 2, 1963. Box 03, Folder 13. Douglas Pike Collection: Unit 02 – Military Operations. See also Rufus Phillips's assessment of the program in "A Report on Counterinsurgency in Vietnam," August 31, 1962. Folder 3, Box 9, Hilsman Papers, National Security Files, John F. Kennedy Presidential Library.
125 "Bert Fraleigh, Draft – The Story of America's Counterinsurgency Efforts in Vietnam in the Early 1960s." VCA. 23970130040 January 1966. Box 01, Folder 30. Rufus Phillips Collection, 2.
126 *Press interviews with President Ngo Dinh Diệm*, 69.
127 Margaret K. Gnoinska, *Poland and Vietnam, 1963: New Evidence on Secret Communist Diplomacy and the "Maneli Affair,"* Cold War International History Project, Woodrow Wilson International Center for Scholars (2005), 20.
128 Higgins, *Our Vietnam Nightmare*, 300.
129 *Hồ Chí Minh toàn tập* [Collected Works], Vol. 9 (Hà Nội: Nhà xuất bản Sự Thật, 1989), 272.
130 Maneli, *War of the Vanquished*, 115–23. See also Nguyễn Văn Châu, *Ngô Đình Diệm và Nỗ lực hòa bình dang dở* [Ngô Đình Diệm and The Incomplete Effort for Peace], Nguyễn Vy Khanh dịch (Los Alamitos, CA: Nhà xuất bản Xuân Thu, 1989), 159–60.
131 Minh Võ, "Cao Xuân Vỹ Kể Việc Ông Ngô Đình" [Cao Xuân Vỹ Describes Ngô Đình Nhu's Secret Meeting].
132 Miller, *Misalliance*, 278. See also Orrin Schwab, *Defending the Free World: John F. Kennedy, Lyndon Johnson, and the Vietnam War, 1961–1965* (Westport, CT: Praeger, 1998), 41.
133 Gerald Hickey, *Window on a War: An Anthropologist in the Vietnam Conflict* (Lubbock: Texas Tech University Press, 2002), 6.
134 Minh Võ, "Cao Xuân Vỹ Kể Việc Ông Ngô Đình Nhu" [Cao Xuân Vỹ Describes Ngô Đình Nhu's Secret Meeting].
135 Ngô Đình Nhu, "Sự góp cực của người Công giáo vào hòa bình ở Việt Nam" [The Contribution of Catholics to Peace in Vietnam], *Xã Hội* (February 1953), 5, 14, 18–22.
136 Gheddo, *Catholiques et bouddhistes au Vietnam*, 154.
137 *Press interviews with President Ngo Dinh Diệm*, 4.
138 *President Ngo Dinh Diem on Democracy (Addresses relative to the Constitution)* (Saigon: Press Office, 1958), 27.
139 William Duiker, *U.S. Containment Policy and the Conflict in Indochina* (Stanford, CA: Stanford University Press, 1994), 19. See also "Politics in an Underdeveloped State, the Colonial Imprint," Michigan State University Archives & Historical Collections, Wesley R. Fishel Papers (UA 17.95).

Box 1193, Folder 39, 5. http://vietnamproject.archives.msu.edu/fullrecord.php?kid=6-20-193. Last accessed July 21, 2019.
140 President Ngo Dinh Diem on Democracy, 29.
141 Press interviews with President Ngo Dinh Diệm, 37.
142 Memorandum for The Record from Office for Rural Affairs/USOM – re: Rural Affairs Meeting with Counselor Nhu on 29 May 1963. VCA. 23970130017 June 8, 1963. Box 01, Folder 30. Rufus Phillips Collection, 1.
143 Maneli, *War of the Vanquished*, 120.
144 Meeting Minutes (#20), Uỷ-Ban Liên-Bộ Đặc-Trách về Ấp Chiến-Lược tại Dinh Gia Long [Intra-Ministry Committee for Strategic Hamlets], 8.
145 Nguyễn Xuân Lai, "Economic Gears and Levers," *Vietnamese Studies*, 31 (1966): *Glimpses of American Neo-Colonialism*, 84.
146 Arthur Z. Gardiner, "Aspects of Foreign Aid" (Department of State Publication, 1961), 9–10.
147 "An Analysis of the Commodity Import Program in Vietnam and Proposals for Change in Administrative Controls, 29 February 1963." VCA. 6-20-EF-116-UA17-95_000183 29 February 2, 1968. Box 1192, Folder 2; Michigan State University Archives & Historical Collections. Wesley R. Fishel Papers, 28.
148 Economic and Social Development, 36. Michigan State University Archives & Historical Collections Wesley R. Fishel Papers (UA 17.95). Box 1192, Folder 35.
149 Economic and Social Development, 27. This problem would persist throughout the war. See Nguyễn Đức Cường, "Building a Market Economy during Wartime," in *Voices from the Second Republic of South Vietnam (1967–1975)*, ed. K. W. Taylor (Ithaca, NY: Cornell, 2014).
150 C. J. Zwick, Charles A. Cooper, Hans Heymann and Richard H. Moorsteen, *U.S. Economic Assistance in Vietnam: A Proposed Reorientation* (Santa Monica, CA: RAND Corporation, September 16, 1964), 75.
151 Economic and Social Development, 37. On Personalism and centralized planning in the Republic, see Milton C. Taylor, "South Viet-Nam: Lavish aid, limited progress," *Pacific Affairs*, 34(3) (1961), 251.
152 Zwick et al., *U.S. Economic Assistance in Vietnam*, 25. See also Taylor, "South Viet-Nam: Lavish aid, limited progress," 252.
153 "Article on the Much Debated Interview of Counsellor Ngo Dinh Nhu from the *Times of Viet Nam*," VCA. 1780119019 June 7, 1958. Box 01, Folder 19. Douglas Pike Collection: Other Manuscripts – American Friends of Vietnam.
154 Quoted in Nguyễn Xuân Lai, "Economic Gears and Levers," 132.
155 Article on the Much Debated Interview of Counsellor Ngo Dinh Nhu. See also Taylor, "South Viet-Nam: Lavish aid, limited progress," 243.
156 Vũ Quốc Thúc, "National planning in Vietnam," *Asian Survey*, 1:7 (September 1961), 7–8. See also Economic Development Under Conditions of Guerrilla

The unimagined community

Warfare: The Case of Viet Nam, 4 April 1962, VCA, Box 02, Folder 03, Douglas Pike Collection: Unit 11 – Monographs.
157 Quoted in John C. Donnell, "National renovation campaigns in Vietnam," *Pacific Affairs*, 32 (March 1959).
158 Bửu Lịch, "Les idéologies dans la République du Sud Vietnam," 90.
159 Vũ Quốc Thúc, "National planning in Vietnam," 5. See also Nhu's description of the urban elite in Despatch From the Chargé in Vietnam (Elting) to the Department of State, Saigon, July 30, 1959, FRUS, 1958–1960, vol. 1, 85, and Zwick et al., *U.S. Economic Assistance in Vietnam*, 23.
160 "Ky Says U.S. Economic Aid Has Failed," *New York Times* (July 5, 1970).
161 See Robert Scheer, *How the United States Got Involved in Vietnam* (Santa Barbara, CA: Center for the Study of Democratic Institutions, 1970), 51.
162 George McT. Kahin, *Intervention: How America Became Involved in Vietnam* (New York: Anchor Books, 1986), 116, 29.
163 Economic and Social Development, 36. Diệm's political opponents were not all enamored with liberal democracy and American aid. As Edward Miller points out, for example, the militant Buddhist leaders who opposed the Personalist Revolution of the early Republic, while criticizing the American intervention, were inspired by a Buddhist-revival nationalism. (Edward Miller, "Religious revival and the politics of nation building: re-interpreting the 1963 'Buddhist crisis' in South Vietnam," *Modern Asian Studies*, 49:6 (November 2015), 1903–62.)
164 Meeting Minutes (#21), Uỷ-Ban Liên-Bộ Đặc-Trách về Ấp Chiến-Lược tại Dinh Gia Long [Intra-Ministry Committee for Strategic Hamlets], 5. VCA. 1820108002 September 14, 1962. Box 01, Folder 08. Douglas Pike Collection: Other Manuscripts – Intra-Ministry Committee for Strategic Hamlets.
165 Arthur J. Dommen, *The Indochinese Experience of the French and the Americans: Nationalism and Communism in Cambodia, Laos, and Vietnam* (Bloomington: Indiana University Press, 2001), 284.
166 Interview – Mr. Bert Fraleigh, 34–5. VCA. 23970216021 February 3, 1967. Box 02, Folder 16. Rufus Phillips Collection.
167 Memorandum from the Director of the Bureau of Intelligence and Research to the Acting Secretary of State, Washington, May 3, 1960.
168 *Ngô Đình Diệm và Chính Nghĩa Dân Tộc*, 83. See also John Osborne, "The Tough Miracle Man of Vietnam: Diem, America's newly arrived visitor, has roused his country and routed the Reds," in *Life*, 42, (May 13, 1957), 175. For a succinct description of the Ngos' view on the "liberal opposition" of the Caravellistes, see William Colby, "William E. Colby on Vietnam, Interview I." Recorded interview by Ted Gittinger, June 2, 1981. The Lyndon Baines Johnson Library Oral History Program (transcript copies available from the LBJ Library Oral History Program, University of Texas at Austin), 11.

The other Vietnamese revolution

169 Thompson, *Defeating Communist Insurgency*, 59–60.
170 Ibid., 163.
171 Kahin, *Intervention*, 86.
172 Duong Van Mai Elliott, *The Sacred Willow: Four Generations in the Life of a Vietnamese Family* (New York: Oxford University Press, 1999), 261.
173 Economic and Social Development, 37–8.
174 Catton, *Diem's Final Failure*, 31.
175 Quoted in Kahin, *Intervention*, 86–7.
176 Donnell, "National renovation campaigns in Vietnam," 100.
177 "Politics in an Underdeveloped State," 27.
178 "Diệm's War or Ours?" *Eyewitness*. CBS. December 29, 1961.
179 Saigon to State, July 30, 1957, 751G.11/7–3057, CDF 55–59, RG 59, USNA.
180 Ngô Công Đức, Secretary-General of the Socialist Opposition bloc in the National Assembly of South Vietnam, asserted that the chief purpose of American aid was to divide the Vietnamese among themselves. The USA had transformed the South Vietnamese market into a one-way consumers' market. "The United States played the role of an international banker who mediated the importation of commodities between Vietnamese businessmen and global suppliers." Report to the Congress of the United States: Survey of the Management and Operation of the Commercial Import Program for Vietnam, CIP folder, Box 3, NSF KL, LBJL.
181 Lai, "Economic Gears and Levers," 86.
182 Paul Kattenburg, "Ngo Dinh Nhu's Possible Reactions to Aid Withholding," October 18, 1963. VCA. F038300020280 October 24, 1963. Box 0002, Folder 0280.
183 Vũ Quốc Thúc, "National planning in Vietnam," 7.
184 Ibid., 4.
185 Stevenson, "Notes on Interview with Ngo Dinh Nhu," quoted in Nighswonger, *Rural Pacification in Vietnam*, 73.
186 CIA telegram, "Comments of Ngo Dinh Nhu on Possible Change in U.S. Policy towards South Vietnam," August 15, 1963. VCA. F038300020280 October 24, 1963. Box 0002, Folder 0280, 2.
187 Taylor, *A History of the Vietnamese*, 581.
188 "Memorandum from the Special Consultant for Counterinsurgency, United States Operation Mission (Phillips) to the Acting Director of the Mission (Fippin)," Saigon, June 25, 1962. Washington National Records Center, RG 84, Saigon Embassy Files: FRC 67 A 677, 350. Counterinsurgency Plan. Secret. Copies were sent to the Ambassador; the Deputy Chief of Mission; Chief, MAAG; Chief, MACV; and Chief, OSA.
189 "Secret telegram from Maneli (Saigon) to Spasowski (Warsaw) [Ciphergram No. 11424]," September 4, 1963, History and Public Policy Program Digital Archive, AMSZ, Warsaw; 6/77, w-102, t-625, obtained and translated by Margaret Gnoinska. Published in CWIHP Working Paper No. 45.

The unimagined community

190 Higgins, *Our Vietnam Nightmare*, 37.
191 "The Political Factor in Pacification: A Vietnam Case Study [Draft]," 11–12. VCA. 21470122001 No Date. Box 01, Folder 22. Vincent Puritano Collection, 5–6.
192 Press interviews with President Ngo Dinh Diệm, 70–1.
193 The Political Factor in Pacification, 8.
194 Some General Operating Patterns of VC Political Cadres. 5–6. VCA. 2310908007 June 1970. Box 09, Folder 08. Douglas Pike Collection: Unit 05 – National Liberation Front. See also Interview – Mr. Bert Fraleigh, 6. VCA. 23970216021 February 3, 1967. Box 02, Folder 16. Rufus Phillips Collection.
195 Report, A Report on Counter-Insurgency in Vietnam, 21. VCA. 23970128002 July 20, 1962. Box 01, Folder 28. Rufus Phillips Collection. See also Meeting Minutes (#26), Uỷ-Ban Liên-Bộ Đặc-Trách về Ấp Chiến-Lược tại Dinh Gia Long [Intra-Ministry Committee for Strategic Hamlets], 28. VCA 1820201001 November 1, 1962. Box 02, Folder 01. Douglas Pike Collection: Other Manuscripts – Intra-Ministry Committee for Strategic Hamlets.
196 Thompson, *Defeating Communist Insurgency*, 126.
197 Colby, "William E. Colby on Vietnam," 19–20.
198 Memorandum of Conversation, Gia Long Palace, Saigon, December 1, 1962, 11:30 a.m.
199 Colby, "William E. Colby on Vietnam."
200 Booklet – The Strategic Hamlet Program in Kien Hoa Province, South Vietnam, 715–17. VCA. 23970133011 No Date. Box 01, Folder 33. Rufus Phillips Collection.
201 "Politics in an Underdeveloped State," 20.
202 Colby, "William E. Colby on Vietnam."
203 Gregory A. Olson, *Mansfield and Vietnam: A Study in Rhetorical Adaptation* (East Lansing: Michigan State University Press, 1995), 45.
204 The Political Factor in Pacification, 11.
205 "Politics in an Underdeveloped State," 45.
206 Thompson, *Defeating Communist Insurgency*, 58–9.
207 *Times of Vietnam*, July 7, 1960, 1.
208 Jones, *Death of a Generation*, 319. There is an extensive historiography on the 1963 coup. For a useful account of the debates within the Kennedy administration, see Andrew Preston, *The War Council: McGeorge Bundy, the NSC, and Vietnam* (Cambridge, MA: Harvard University Press. 2006), 113–28.
209 "Papers of John F. Kennedy. Presidential Papers," 2. National Security Files. Meetings and Memoranda. Meetings on Vietnam: General, September 1963," "Papers of John F. Kennedy. Presidential Papers," National Security Files. Series 06. Meetings and Memoranda.
210 "Telegram from the Ambassador in Vietnam (Lodge) to the Department of State Saigon," October 30, 1963–6:30 p.m. Department of State, Central Files, POL 26 S VIET Top Secret; Flash; Eyes Only.

The other Vietnamese revolution

211 Ann L. Hollick, *U.S. Involvement in the Overthrow of Diem, 1963: A Staff Study Based on the Pentagon Papers* (Washington DC: US Government Printing Office, 1972), 13.
212 "Telegram from the Embassy in Vietnam to the Department of State Saigon," September 19, 1963, 4 p.m. Department of State, Central Files, POL 15 S VIET. Top Secret; Immediate; Eyes Only. Received at 7:04 a.m. and passed to the White House at 8:35 a.m.
213 See Richard Starnes, "Viet-Nam Aid Cut Carries Risk," Associated Press article (October 24, 1963).
214 Jones, *Death of a Generation*, 345.
215 Logevall, *Choosing War*, 7.
216 Here, Logevall, who acknowledges that it "remains to be determined what Ngo Dinh Nhu hoped to achieve with his gambit," follows the analysis of F. A. Warner, head of the British South-East Asia Department. Warner argued that in "the long run, the only thing that can save Nhu and Diem would be an accommodation with North Vietnam." Logevall, *Choosing War*, 7.
217 Ibid., 9, 14.
218 Telegram from the Embassy in Vietnam to the Department of State, Saigon, October 7, 1963, 7 p.m.
219 "The strategic hamlet and military policy," *Times of Vietnam Magazine*, October 28, 1962, 38–9.
220 Meeting Minutes (#19), Uỷ-Ban Liên-Bộ Đặc-Trách về Ấp Chiến-Lược tại Dinh Gia Long [Intra-Ministry Committee for Strategic Hamlets]. VCA. 1820107002 August 31, 1962. Box 01, Folder 07. Douglas Pike Collection: Other Manuscripts – Intra-Ministry Committee for Strategic Hamlets, 4–9.
221 Dommen, *The Indochinese Experience of the French and the Americans*, 501.
222 Minh Võ, *Ngô Đình Diệm và Chính Nghĩa Dân Tộc*, 248, note 16.
223 Higgins, *Our Vietnam Nightmare*, 300.
224 Logevall, *Choosing War*, 9.
225 In an interview in 1964, Madame Nhu claimed that it was the Strategic Hamlet Program that had compelled the insurgents to initiate peace talks, and that the Ngos were only "two fingers away from victory." *Le Nouveau Candide* (February 6–13, 1964), 5.
226 The Truth about Vietnam. October 28, 1963. 2003C87.204. Commonwealth Club of California records. Hoover Institution Archives, Stanford, CA.
227 Telegram from the Embassy in Vietnam to the Department of State, Saigon, October 7, 1963, 7 p.m. See also William Egan Colby, *Lost Victory: A Firsthand Account of America's Sixteen-Year Involvement in Vietnam* (Chicago: Contemporary Books, 1989), 98–100.
228 Fraleigh, "Counterinsurgency in Vietnam," 112–13.
229 Telegram from the Central Intelligence Agency Station in Saigon to the Agency, September 6, 1963, History and Public Policy Program Digital Archive, US Department of State, Foreign Relations of the United States,

The unimagined community

1961–1963, vol. 4: Vietnam August – December, 1963 (Washington DC: Government Printing Office, 1991), 125–6. Published in CWIHP Working Paper No. 45. On Nhu's negotiations with the Communists and his views on neutrality, see Miller, *Misalliance*, 308–11.

230 Secret Telegram from Maneli (Saigon) to Spasowski (Warsaw) [Ciphergram No. 11424].
231 Telegram from the Central Intelligence Agency Station in Saigon to the Agency, September 6, 1963.
232 Ibid.
233 Politics in an Underdeveloped State, the Colonial Imprint (undated), 47. Box 1193, Folder 39; Michigan State University Archives & Historical Collections.
234 Stevenson, "Notes on Interview with Ngo Dinh Nhu," quoted in Nighswonger, *Rural Pacification in Vietnam*, 73.
235 A COSVN Standing Committee Account of the Situation in South Vietnam from the end of 1961 to The Beginning of 1964. 2320113002 April 20, 1964. Box 01, Folder 13. Douglas Pike Collection: Unit 06 – Democratic Republic of Vietnam. VCA. Accessed March 4, 2019.
236 Telegram from the Embassy in Vietnam to the Department of State, Saigon, October 7, 1963, 7 p.m.
237 Forrestal to Paul M. Kattenburg, October 24, 1963. VCA. F038300020280 October 24, 1963. Box 0002, Folder 0280, 1.
238 Memorandum of a Conversation, Saigon, January 30, 1958.
239 Memorandum from Michael V. Forrestal of the National Security Council Staff to the President's Special Assistant for National Security Affairs (Bundy) Washington, October 21, 1963.
240 Memorandum of a Conversation, Saigon, January 30, 1958. See also Ngô Đình Nhu, "Industrialization: PreRequisite to Self-Sufficiency," *Times of Vietnam Magazine* 5, no. 18 (5 May 1963): 4–5.
241 Memorandum from Michael V. Forrestal of the National Security Council Staff to the President's Special Assistant for National Security Affairs (Bundy), Washington, October 21, 1963.
242 Meeting Minutes (#34), Uỷ-Ban Liên-Bộ Đặc-Trách về Ấp Chiến-Lược tại Dinh Gia Long [Intra-Ministry Committee for Strategic Hamlets]. VCA. 1820203001 January 4, 1963. Box 02, Folder 03. Douglas Pike Collection: Other Manuscripts – Intra-Ministry Committee for Strategic Hamlets.
243 Forrestal to Paul M. Kattenburg, October 24, 1963, 2.
244 CIA telegram, "Comments of Ngo Dinh Nhu on Possible Change in U.S. Policy towards South Vietnam," August 15, 1963. For a South Vietnamese account of the success of the program, see Hoàng Thanh Hoài, *Chiến Tranh Việt Nam* [The Vietnam War] (Sài Gòn: Nhà Xuất bản Trí Dũng, 1973), 223.
245 Quoted in Ann L. Hollick, *U.S. Involvement in the Overthrow of Diem, 1963*, Part 56, Issue 3. See also Robert Trumbull, "U.S. Prestige Tied to Saigon

Dispute; Strong Impact in Asia Seen If Diem Resists Pressure," *New York Times*, September 3, 1963.
246 Secret Telegram from Maneli (Saigon) to Spasowski (Warsaw) [Ciphergram No. 5295], April 24, 1963, History and Public Policy Program Digital Archive, AMSZ, Warsaw, 6/77, w-102, t-625, obtained and translated by Margaret Gnoinska. Published in CWIHP Working Paper No. 45. https://digitalarchive.wilsoncenter.org/document/118948. Last accessed July 21, 2019.
247 Winters, *The Year of the Hare*, 141.
248 Telegram from the Embassy in Vietnam to the Department of State, Saigon, October 7, 1963, 7 p.m.
249 Ngo Dinh Nhu, "Strategic Hamlets, Basis for Total Revolution," 5.
250 Bửu Lịch, "Les idéologies dans la République du Sud Vietnam," 35.
251 *Press interviews with President Ngo Dinh Diệm*, 69.
252 Ibid., 56.
253 Catton, *Diem's Final Failure*, 49.
254 Quoted in Higgins, *Our Vietnam Nightmare*, 215.
255 "The Political Factor in Pacification," 11–12.
256 Phạm Quang Trình. "*Cần Lao Nhân Vị Cách Mạng Đảng qua lời trối trăng của ông Cố vấn Ngô Đình Nhu.*" [The Cần Lao Revolutionary Personalist Party in Counselor Ngô Đình Nhu's Final Words." https://tinyurl.com/y3yafzoz. Last accessed July 21, 2019.
257 ACTIV, Headway Addenda, II CORPS 061601H – 131600H NOV 1963, C8.
258 Phạm Quang Trình, "*Cần Lao Nhân Vị Cách Mạng Đảng qua lời trối trăng của ông Cố vấn Ngô Đình Nhu.*"
259 The Political Factor in Pacification, 11.
260 Ibid., 10–11. While the Strategic Hamlet Program was plagued by corruption and poor implementation, its collapse cannot be attributed to this factor alone, or to the insurgency and its success in exploiting this weakness. Although "[o]ver-expansion of construction and poor quality of defenses," as one study observed, were "contributory reasons … for the failure of the Strategic Hamlet Program," this was largely true "only on the initial phase of the program." The problem of poor implementation, moreover, "does little to explain why the entire program collapsed" when "Diem and Nhu departed the scene," Pentagon Papers [Part IV. B. 2.] Evolution of the War. Counterinsurgency: Strategic Hamlet Program, 1961–63, National Archives and Records Administration, National Archives Identifier, 5890494. The primary cause of the program's collapse appears to have been the purge of Cần Lao cadre following Diệm's assassination. According to Robert McNamara, the "political control structure extending from Saigon down into the hamlets disappeared following the November coup. Of the 41 incumbent province chiefs on November 1, 35 have been replaced … Scores of lesser officials were replaced. Almost all major military commands

have changed hands twice since the November 2. The faith of the peasants has been shaken by the disruptions in experienced leadership and the loss of physical security" (Memorandum from the Secretary of Defense (McNamara) to the President, Washington, March 16, 1964). "When the Ngo brothers died," according to another report on the program, "Strategic Hamlets died along with them." On the origin of the program, 180. Vietnam Counterinsurgency – The Diem Era: Strategic Hamlet. VCA. 2120101001 No Date. Box 01, Folder 01. Douglas Pike Collection: Unit 01 – Assessment and Strategy.

261 Higgins, *Our Vietnam Nightmare*, 287–9.
262 *Times of Vietnam*, July 7, 1960, 1. See also Phillips to Brent, May 1, 1963, in FRUS 1961–3, 3:256–8.
263 Maneli, *War of the Vanquished*, 145.
264 The Political Factor in Pacification, 12.
265 Huynh Van Lang, "Huynh, Lang Van," Vietnamese in the Diaspora Digital Archive (ViDDA). https://vietdiasporastories.omeka.net/items/show/110. Last accessed July 20, 2019.

4

Psychological warfare, counterinsurgency and the society of spectacle in South Vietnam

The Sacred Sword Patriotic League: Between revolution and liberal democracy

In the early stage of the war, then, the primary strategy used by the South Vietnamese state in its anti-communist struggle was a socialist revolution that the Ngos had also sought to employ as an instrument of anti-imperialism against the Americans. The irreconcilable conflict, however, between the aims and objectives of the South Vietnamese and their ally, between the ideal of a "*démocratie reelle par la base*" and American liberal democracy, was not merely confined to the counterinsurgency program. This "misalliance" was one that would also inform the psychological warfare campaigns carried out by the USA and the South Vietnamese state.

In an effort to reproduce the people's war waged in the South by the communist forces, US and Republic of Vietnam (RVN) intelligence organizations attempted to manufacture a "network of resistance" in the North, directed against the government in Hà Nội.[1] One of the most elaborate of these psychological warfare campaigns was the Sacred Sword Patriotic League (*Mặt trận Gươm Thiêng Ái Quốc*, SSPL).[2]

The program employed a range of tactics, including the dissemination of a national media through modern forms of mass communications for the purpose of "implanting the idea of an anti-communist organization in the minds of the people in North Vietnam" (*thử cấy trong tâm trí người dân Miền Bắc ý niệm một tổ chức chống cộng*).[3]

The idea for the organization was developed on the basis of information gathered from interviews with defectors in the *Chiêu hồi* program. Through this intelligence, American operatives were able to uncover the nationalist myth of a 2,000-year history of anti-imperialist struggle, which had been created during the colonial era through a vernacular media, disseminated as a form of surveillance. In Robert Chandler's *War of Ideas: the U.S. Propaganda campaign in Vietnam*, the nationalist mythology of an ancient tradition of "resisting the north" (*bắc cự*), which would be adapted for the psywar campaign, is retold in the following fashion:

> No less than fifteen times during the last 900 years the people (of Vietnam) responded to the call to arms, frustrating invasion attempts by superior Chinese and Mongol forces. Each time a trespasser [appeared] … the peasants threw themselves into the conflict, routing the invaders and preserving independence. The resistance most remembered by the Vietnamese was the successful overthrow of the … Chinese … in 1428. Le Loi … the "Prince of Pacification" … led the people in a decade of incessant guerrilla warfare that evicted the intruders. His leadership became legendary over the following centuries; repeated by word-of-mouth from one generation to the next.[4]

The SSPL, then, would receive its name from a fable about Lê Lợi, who Chandler, along with his native informants, anachronistically credited with having developed an anti-colonial form of partisan warfare in the fifteenth century.[5] In the legend, Lê Lợi acquires a sword belonging to a dragon king who inhabits a lake in Hà Nội. After using the magical weapon to defeat the Ming army in 1428, Lê Lợi returns the sword to its owner, throwing it into the lake, which is renamed the "Lake of the Restored Sword" (*Hồ Hoàn Kiếm*).

The story appealed to the American agents involved in the program because of its resemblance to the Arthurian legends and because of Lê Lợi's depiction within the nationalist history as an ancient practitioner of the modern art of political propaganda (*tuyên truyền*). Having discovered the fable of an ancient nationalist figure, widely revered as the "exemplar of Vietnamese resistance to foreign domination," US intelligence agents set out to create their own twentieth-century version of the modern mythology: "Five hundred years later the sacred sword returned to Vietnam." In this sequel to the nationalist fable, the sacred sword would be "wielded by psychological warriors, men who fought with ideas instead of weapons, propaganda instead of bullets."[6]

Combining elements from the lives of real Vietnamese leaders, American agents, working with their Vietnamese counterparts, invented a sort of postcolonial work of historical fiction, one that they believed would be more compelling than the nationalist narratives devised by

Psychological warfare

the Democratic Republic of Vietnam (DRV) as well as the RVN. In the history created for the SSPL, its founding members were former French resistance leaders affiliated with the Việt Minh and the Vietnamese Nationalist Party (*Việt Nam Quốc Dân Đảng*). During the communist wave of repression in 1953, which enabled the Party to consolidate its power in the North, the future leaders of the SSPL were forced to flee to Nghệ An and Hà Tĩnh, the native provinces of Hồ Chí Minh and Lê Lợi. At a secret conference held in April 1953 in a clandestine base in the highlands, the SSPL was founded and Lê Quốc Hùng was elected as its first president.[7] In the historical fiction, therefore, the leader of the SSPL would share the same surname as Lê Lợi, the greatest in the pantheon of premodern national heroes, created during the colonial era.[8] The name Lê Quốc Hùng ("Lê the national hero") was also supposed to resemble the pseudonym, Nguyễn Ái Quốc ("Nguyễn the patriot"), used by Hồ Chí Minh at the Versailles Conference in 1919, where he presented a petition calling for the immediate independence of the Annamite people.

After the terror unleashed by the land reform in the North in 1954, the SSPL attempted to rally the peasantry, staging a revolt in Nghệ An, which was ruthlessly crushed by the Party. The organization was then forced underground, forming secret cells and establishing training facilities located in liberated zones where the Front, according to the fictional history, had established an autonomous non-communist society within the national territory of the DRV.[9]

To reinforce the appearance of the SSPL as a legitimate nationalist organization, agents involved in the program also concocted a political ideology, which emphasized the ancient tradition of resistance to imperial rule. In the SSPL's propaganda, both North and South Vietnamese states were portrayed as pawns manipulated by outside invaders. Whereas the RVN was a puppet of US imperialism, the DRV was controlled by the world communist powers, especially the Chinese, the ancient national enemy of the Vietnamese people. Thus, the Vietnamese nation was deprived of a truly representative government, embodying the sovereign will of the people and its 2,000-year history of anti-colonial struggle. The SSPL, therefore, regarded the Republic as well as the Communist Party as proxies of the world imperialist powers, calling for the country to be reunited under a legitimate sovereign authority, free of all foreign influence.[10]

Working together with the RVN's Strategic Technical Directorate (*Nha Kỹ thuật*), US personnel in the program attempted to implant the idea of the SSPL through the use of modern mass media. Leaflets and

The unimagined community

posters for the phony organization, printed in color, were produced at a propaganda production studio located in Sài Gòn, which employed numerous Vietnamese artists, painters and translators.[11]

In one of the leaflets, Lê Lợi is depicted in front of a large peasant army, exhorting his followers to promote the "indomitable will" (*ý chí bất khuất*) of the Vietnamese people by "destroying the Communists and saving the country" (*diệt Cộng cứu nước*). The Communist Party is condemned for confiscating the property of the peasantry, and for fixing the prices in its state-owned stores, further exploiting the people.

In addition, SSPL radio stations were established in Huế and Thủ Đức, transmitting hours of programming by the "Voice of the Sacred Sword," broadcast supposedly from a clandestine base in Hà Tĩnh. The content of the radio programs consisted of phony communications and orders to local committees, instructions to the general population on techniques for resisting the government, reports on enemy casualties, and lurid accounts of corruption and scandal in the Communist Party. The stations also played patriotic music, including an SSPL marching song titled "Let Us Rise up Ardently and Liberate our Nation," which was composed as part of the psywar campaign.[12] Like the mock news reports in Orson Welles's *War of the Worlds* broadcast, moreover, the programming was periodically interrupted for realistic effect. Radio operations were shut down temporarily, to allow broadcasters, supposedly, to evade detection by communist patrols. In order to expand the audience for SSPL propaganda, moreover, thousands of fixed-frequency radios, bearing the insignia of the organization (an image of the sacred sword of Lê Lợi), were distributed through covert air operations over North Vietnamese territory.[13]

The leaflets and broadcasts, however, were only a preliminary stage in the program of implanting the idea of an anti-communist organization in the North. The next phase of the psywar campaign involved the abduction of North Vietnamese peasants from coastal villages beyond the demilitarized zone.[14] The detainees were brought to an island off the coast of Đà Nẵng, where a mock SSPL base, supposedly located in one of the liberated zones controlled by the Front, had been built in the style of a North Vietnamese fishing village. On the island, the prisoners were interrogated for intelligence about the regime, and conditions within the DRV, intelligence that was incorporated as content in the SSPL leaflets and radio broadcasts.

Prisoners who expressed dissatisfaction with the Communist Party were assigned to a separate part of the island and subjected to a program of indoctrination, modeled after the Maoist technique of self-criticism, employed by the National Liberation Front. The indoctrination, consisting of lessons on the ideology and history of the SSPL, was conducted by South Vietnamese agents of the Strategic Technical Directorate posing

4.1 Lê Lợi on Sacred Sword Patriotic League propaganda flyer (Joint United States Public Affairs Office).

as members of an underground cell. After several weeks of indoctrination, the prisoners were returned to the North to serve as sleeper agents, charged with establishing new SSPL cells to transform the fictional organization into a reality.[15]

In the end, however, the SSPL, like other US and RVN intelligence programs, would fail to produce any substantial results. This failure was in large part a reflection of a fundamental disagreement between RVN leaders and policymakers in Washington. Like the counterinsurgency strategy employed in the South, programs such as SSPL were viewed by the RVN government as a means of producing a politically mobilized and economically autonomous national people. Republican leaders, in other words, considered such programs to be an extension of a second Southward Advance toward modernity, a form of popular mobilization that would lead, through the clandestine creation of new social structures, to a "reoccupation of the North."[16]

This perspective was consistent with the original aim of the program, which John F. Kennedy defined in 1961 as the creation of "networks of resistance" in the North, applying the same strategy of social revolution employed by the insurgency in the South. The program, then, was originally devised as part of an "integrated" conception of counterinsurgency, in which unconventional warfare was combined with social and economic development.[17] After Kennedy's assassination, however, this "integrated view of ... covert warfare," which "would become the operational framework for ... containment strategies everywhere in the world," was abandoned by Washington policymakers.[18] In the Vietnam War, the worldwide operational framework for counterinsurgency established by Kennedy was largely displaced after 1963 in favor of what Hannah Arendt referred to as "image-making as global policy."[19] Thus, for McNamara, the aim of programs like the SSPL was not to establish "networks of resistance" in the North, but rather to develop a purely "notional (fictitious) Vietnamese national liberation movement."[20] Just as the war in general, then, was conceived as a public relations campaign to "convince the enemy that he could not win," so the use of psywar was mostly confined to the spectacular goal of producing the impression of an alternative to the communist state in the North. As one intelligence officer emphasized, "special psychological operations" were "not an attempt by the United States or RVN to invade or conquer the DRV, but to serve notice upon the DRV that the United States and RVN are prepared, if necessary."[21]

Such a strategy, according to William Colby, CIA chief in Sài Gòn, would be sufficient to exploit the weakness inherent in such

Psychological warfare

non-democratic regimes as the DRV, which, lacking popular support expressed through elections, were prone to paranoia and violent overreaction against perceived internal threats.[22] For many observers, this tendency was confirmed by the Party's excessive response in the Nhân Văn-Giai Phẩm Affair in the late 1950s, and its brutal repression of Northern writers and artists for criticizing its cultural policies. Based on internal repression, such a communist regime, so the policymakers assumed, was inherently unstable. As a sovereignty without support from the people, the regime, because of its lack of democracy, would inevitably engender political opposition to its authoritarian rule.

Yet, despite this assumption, US officials believed at the time that an attempt to establish a real network of resistance in the North would be counterproductive. By destabilizing the government, such an action could potentially compel the Communist Party to escalate its war in the South, or worse, provoke Chinese intervention, leading to either a nuclear confrontation or a repetition of the stalemate in Korea. Thus, while Henry Cabot Lodge called for covert operations against the North, aimed at diminishing its ability to support the insurgency, he also insisted that such actions should not be used to overthrow the regime. For Lodge, the goal, then, was not to depose Hồ Chí Minh, since his "successor would undoubtedly be worse."[23] Rather, American policymakers believed that such programs as the SSPL should be intended primarily as a spectacular form of distraction, used to persuade the enemy to give up its war in the South, instead of creating a real opposition to the DRV in the North. This policy imposed "an almost crippling limitation" on the SSPL and similar programs.[24]

In their campaign to create the impression of an alternative to the DRV, US officials, moreover, assuming that the communist state was inherently unstable because of its lack of liberal democracy, emphasized the advantages of free-market capitalism and freedom of expression.[25] SSPL leaflets depicted the shortage of food and supplies in communist countries, comparing this self-imposed poverty to the abundance of consumer commodities enjoyed in the free capitalist world.

This sort of propaganda, however, embodied an economic liberalism and a liberal ideal of democracy that was directly opposed to the "national discipline" early RVN leaders considered a necessary condition for creating a viable alternative to the communist state. As such, the purely spectacular goal, prescribed by US officials, of producing the image of a democratic alternative to the Communist Party, was indicative of a more fundamental ideological disagreement between early RVN leaders and Washington policymakers.

The media and the collapse of the early republic

"But even if you're not involved in corruption," Karnow said, "people believe you are, and that in itself is a political reality." To this Nhu answered, "I don't care what the people think."[26]

For the Ngos, of course, the absurdly simplistic prescription of using free-market capitalism and liberal democracy to establish a politically and economically autonomous state, which they repudiated as a fraudulent "liberal model ... of development,"[27] would only perpetuate economic dependency and undermine political unity. For the Americans, on the other hand, Diệm's attempt to reproduce the people's war strategy in the Strategic Hamlet Campaign was compromised by his use of the same political and economic forms of repression employed by the communist state. From the perspective of its American ally, therefore, the diemocracy of the early Republic was marked by the same lack of democracy that threatened to destabilize the regime in the North.

Contrary to the criticism of US officials, however, these dictatorial measures had proven to be largely successful in the war against the insurgency by 1963: "Military operations are more effective; rural economic progress is manifest; US/Vietnamese coordination is heartening."[28]

> The enemy ... actively consolidated and strengthened the ... administrative apparatus from the central to the hamlet levels ... and truly and efficiently destroyed our Party. By relying on force the U.S.-Diem regime was ... able to stabilise the situation and increase the prestige of the counterrevolutionaries ... Party bases, although not completely destroyed, were significantly weakened and in some areas quite seriously; the prestige of the masses and of the revolution was lessened.

Yet despite the increasing success of the program, American and international media coverage of the widespread repression would serve to turn public opinion unanimously against the South Vietnamese government.[29] Owing to the media exposure, the authoritarian methods that had allowed the regime to reestablish stability and prevail against the insurgency created a spectacle that undermined the image of the RVN government as a stable democracy. The result was a "crisis [that] ... occurred while the anti-communist war was on the road toward overall victory because of the Strategic Hamlet Program."[30] As in the case of the

Psychological warfare

4.2 Thích Quảng Đức's self-immolation (AP Photo/Malcolm Browne).

Tết Offensive in 1968, American media coverage of the conflict would serve to transform defeat into victory for the communist forces, reversing the gains achieved through the Strategic Hamlet Campaign by creating a spectacular crisis.

This crisis would culminate in the Buddhist protests in 1963, following the international outcry provoked by the photographs of Thích Quảng Đức's self-immolation – "*ce spectacle unique au XXème siècle,*" as Nhu described it – which quickly spread through the wire services and appeared on front pages all over the world.[31]

The newspapers repeated the misleading assertion that Buddhists made up the overwhelming majority of the population, when in fact most Vietnamese practiced a syncretic religion, combining ancestor worship with Buddhism and other beliefs.[32] Accompanied by the inaccurate claim, the powerful images of the ritual act of self-sacrifice, staged with "a clear intention of courting the Western press," confirmed the impression that Diệm was an illegitimate ruler, adamantly opposed by his own population.[33]

As a president without popular support, one who could only maintain his position through the use of coercion, Diệm, as he was presented in the international press, appeared to be completely incapable of uniting the South Vietnamese people in its war against the insurgency. As a *New*

York Times editorial demanded, therefore, "It is time that Mr. Diem realised that he cannot discriminate against a majority of the people of South Vietnam and win his war against the Communists. If he cannot genuinely represent a majority then he is not the man to be President."[34]

This portrait of Diệm simultaneously served to discredit the image of the American government: "[D]on't you realize that Diem has tarnished our image everywhere in the world?"[35] In the international media, the USA, as a result of the crisis, appeared increasingly like an imperialist power trying to "bolster a regime universally regarded as unjust, undemocratic, and unstable."[36] In a desperate attempt to alter this public perception, US officials demanded immediate reforms from the Diệm regime for the purpose of restoring its image as a liberal democracy (an image to which its leaders had never aspired). These reforms, which included the lifting of censorship laws, the inclusion of oppositional figures in the RVN government and economic liberalization,[37] were considered absolutely essential for ensuring political and economic stability in the South.[38]

Assured, however, by his own secret intelligence sources that the crisis was only apparent, and convinced that the ongoing success of the war and rural development would rally popular support while bringing the USA around to his policies, Diệm refused to concede. In the midst of the spectacular breakdown of order, televised for an international audience, Diệm's uncompromising resolve, based upon information obtained through the regime's extensive surveillance apparatus, seemed like "delusional optimism."[39] Focused on the reality of the war, and the actual political situation on the ground, while ignoring the way it was portrayed in the press, Diệm appeared "unbelievably stubborn," in Lodge's terms, completely "cut off from the present."[40]

Contrary to Edward Lansdale, Diệm's inability to recognize the severity of the situation was not the result of misinformation derived from "self-serving" government spies, which made him a "captive of his own intelligence." If Diệm had arrived at the "wrong view" of the situation, at an inaccurate reading of "the feelings of the people," it was not because he was detached from reality, seeing things only through a "long pipeline of information" containing phony intelligence. Diệm's ignorance of the true state of affairs, in other words, was not because he had not "eyeballed these things himself."[41] As Marguerite Higgins describes, the protests "had nothing whatsoever to do with the reality of life as experienced by the overwhelming majority of people in the countryside," where the Strategic Hamlets had largely succeeded in restoring stability: "I went to a string of eleven different strategic hamlets before I found anyone who would even heard of the fiery death of Thich Quang Duc."[42]

This spectacle, then, was largely confined to the cities, while in the countryside, "most people ... did not have any notion of what was going on in Saigon."[43] For the majority of South Vietnamese, "Thich Quang Duc's fiery suicide" did not "produce the same instant horrific effect in ... as it had in an advanced, televised, Western nation like America."[44] After the media coverage of the Buddhist Affair, the "facts," as Roger Hilsman says, "became irrelevant."[45] "Seldom has any drama had such weird, confusing, and spectacular ingredients," according to Higgins.[46]

Diệm, then, was not detached from reality. Rather, he was insufficiently wary of how the reality *appeared* in the press. Stubbornly fixated upon the reality of the war in the countryside, he had become completely cut off from the image of the war in the media. Thus, Diệm's inability to grasp the true state of affairs, to perceive the gravity of the political situation, was not the result of an ineffective network of surveillance, but of his inability to understand the power of the international press as it had developed in the Society of the Spectacle.[47]

This inability to grasp the importance of preserving the image of democracy (of protecting what Lodge referred to as the "liberal image" of the nation in the American media) was directly opposed to the global policy of "image-making," pursued by the American government.[48] This policy, according to Arendt, defined a US imperialism whose goal had become the image itself, "to win hearts and minds," rather than achieving world domination.[49] For policymakers in Washington, this image was not simply a form of deception used to disguise an underlying reality, but rather a condition for obtaining public approval on every important political matter. The image, in other words, as Diệm would discover, was a deception that policymakers were compelled to preserve, regardless of the reality. This condition, as Lodge hopelessly tried to explain to the stubborn South Vietnamese leader, was precisely what distinguished the sovereign authority of the American president from the despotism or "diemocracy" of which his client was accused by the media. Unlike Diệm's authoritarian rule, the American presidency, as Lodge explained in a rudimentary lecture on the merits of liberal democracy in the Society of the Spectacle, was a truly popular sovereignty because it was subordinated to public opinion:

> The American President, unlike some Chiefs of State, does not have unrestricted power. While his word is absolutely good and can never be

questioned, the American President, nevertheless, cannot undertake future commitments which would not be supported by public opinion, and this public opinion is influenced by the press ...[50]

By undermining the image of a stable democracy, in a spectacle that attracted an international audience, Diệm's anti-democratic repression (which, in reality, had succeeded in restoring stability) threatened to jeopardize the entire American mission. As Lodge explained in a government telegram, Diệm's refusal to satisfy American public opinion had made him an obstacle to American goals in Vietnam:

> No long range foreign policy could be carried out by the U.S. Government without the support of ... public opinion [and the] public opinion in the U.S. was much distressed by the treatment of the Buddhists ... These have greatly complicated the job of the Executive branch of the U.S. Government in aiding Vietnam.[51]

Diệm's intransigence, his refusal to conform to the imperial policy of image-making, then, would mark the South Vietnamese leader as the greatest "barrier of US policy in Vietnam."[52] For "the Americans," as Catton describes, "the emerging problem in South Vietnam" was not just the insurgency, but "Diem's ... self-defeating brand of authoritarianism, which reduced the regime's effectiveness as well as the prospects for achieving long-term stability."[53] Thus, according to Văn Nguyên Dương, the "coup to eliminate these political barriers was inevitable." For the sake of restoring the image of democratic stability, Lodge, acting as a "new type of neocolonial governor in the land,"[54] who *"souhaite lancer Viet-Nam vers une modernité Américain,"*[55] collaborated with South Vietnamese generals to remove Diệm from power.[56] Thus, the spectacular "drama" of the Buddhist affair was the "cause and consequence of the momentous and controversial US decision to flash the green light that would topple an ally in the middle of a war with a common enemy."[57]

Following a siege on the Presidential Palace on November 2, 1963, Diệm and Nhu were arrested by the conspirators. Although US officials assumed that the two would be sent into exile, their assassination, as many observers maintained, was inevitable. Having deposed a foreign president portrayed in the American media as an obstinate tyrant, unaware that the majority of his own people opposed him, the generals, paradoxically, were compelled to assassinate Diệm precisely because he had too much support from the people. And having prevailed in the coup against an ineffective regime, misinformed by its own secret intel-

Psychological warfare

ligence, the generals were forced to execute Nhu because his network of surveillance had proven to be far too effective:[58] "We had no alternative," explained Dương Văn Minh, one of the generals involved in the coup, who would later serve as the last South Vietnamese president:

> They had to be killed. Diệm could not be allowed to live because he was too much respected among simple, gullible people in the countryside ... We had to kill Nhu because he was so widely feared – and he had created organizations that were arms of his personal power.[59]

The inexorable logic that led to Diệm and Nhu's assassination was the same as the one that informed the US approach to psychological warfare. In the latter, the aim of establishing an actual resistance organization in the North was subordinated to the spectacular goal of creating the image of a democratic alternative to the repressive communist state. In accordance with the same imperial policy of image-making, Diệm's authoritarian rule, which had largely succeeded in restoring stability, was overthrown in order to save the image of a stable democracy.[60] In Vietnam, then, the immediate aim of this policy was not to defeat the North Vietnamese government while establishing a stable regime in the South. Rather, the goal was to produce the public impression of a viable Republican state, while persuading the Communist Party to give up the war. "While in the South the overriding goal," as Frank Ninkovich points out, "was to create morale, in the North it was to destroy it." As Lodge reminded the president, "We do not need to define 'victory' and then go ahead and achieve it 100 percent. If it becomes generally believed that we are going to win ... all else will be a mopping up."[61]

Strictly adhering to this principle of imperial image-making, Lodge, who helped to remove the South Vietnamese leader, eliminating an American ally for refusing the sovereignty of US public opinion, was opposed to the use of American power to depose Hồ Chí Minh. Instead, he prescribed covert operations in a limited war aimed not at defeating the Communist Party, but of persuading its leadership that victory was impossible: "What we are interested in ... is not destroying Ho Chi Minh ... but getting him to change his behavior." Insofar as the goal was to achieve the image itself, destroying the North Vietnamese leader and the communist state would be far too extreme a measure, not only because millions of lives would be lost, but because the image would be deprived of an audience. If "you lay the whole country to waste," as Lodge pointed out with impeccable logic, "there will be nobody left in North Vietnam on whom to put pressure."[62] On the other hand, Diệm, by restoring stability through the use of repression, had made it impossible to persuade the American public that the war in Vietnam could be won, provoking a spectacular crisis that would lead to his downfall. "If this country is lost," as Diệm correctly surmised, "it will be because of the American press" (*Nếu xứ này mất thì là tại báo chí Mỹ*).⁶³

In the end, however, the attempt by the American government to resolve this spectacular crisis, to reestablish the image of a stable democracy by deposing an authoritarian president, would result in a *real* crisis of sovereignty.⁶⁴ In the coup, as Văn Nguyên Dưỡng described, the "United States had used its power to transform South Vietnam from an efficacious anti-communist government into an ineffective coalition that would not help the United States win the war."⁶⁵ "Vietnam," as Madame Nhu lamented in a letter to Lyndon Johnson, "was at the threshold of victory." The coup, which would completely reverse the country's political fortunes, had not been the expression of popular opposition to Diệm and his dictatorial rule, but had been instigated by a treacherous ally in order to appease American public opinion:⁶⁶ The "leaders of the legal government ... were not overridden by any superiority, they were simply knifed in the back, not by an enemy ... but by the ally and friend whom they were wrong to have trusted."⁶⁷

As a result of the democratic inclusion of oppositional figures – the incompetent generals who took part in the coup – the Republic was reduced to a sovereignless state, a "snake with no head" (*rắn không đầu*). In a telephone conversation with Eugene McCarthy, Lyndon Johnson complained about the faulty intelligence that had led the American government to encourage the coup that created this disastrous state of affairs: "they [said that] Diem ... was corrupt and he ought to be killed. So we killed him. We ... got a goddam bunch of thugs and we ... assassinated him. Now, we've really had no political stability since then."⁶⁸

Without Diệm's despotic authority, the gains achieved through the Strategic Hamlet Campaign were quickly reversed in the countryside:

> The program stalled completely once its driving force was removed. Its administrative machinery ground to a halt, and its security effectiveness fell sharply as both local and military forces lost their ... incentives to risk themselves to protect the hamlet population.⁶⁹

As Albert Fraleigh, a senior pacification advisor, observed: "There seemed to be no new initiatives or programs, and no one seemed to be leading." This "aimless drift" resulted in the "growing erosion of popular confidence."⁷⁰ As a result, the "balance of forces," according to a communist assessment, "changed very rapidly in our favor ... The bulk of the enemy's armed forces and paramilitary forces at the village and hamlet level have disintegrated." By early 1965, just over a year after the coup, the "strategic hamlets ... the 'backbone of the special war,' have been destroyed, and most of the people and land in the rural countryside are in our liberated zones."[71]

Escalation, attrition and urbanization

The crisis, precipitated by a coup aimed at restoring stability by satisfying public opinion, imposed the need for decisive and immediate action by the American government in order to save the South Vietnamese state, which it had completely destabilized for the sake of protecting its image. Like the coup that created the crisis, however, this action was also constrained by public opinion, which was influenced by the American media. With the election looming in 1964, Johnson, wary that a resolution on the war could ruin his chances of winning the White House, ordered a bombing campaign in the North as a spectacular means of boosting morale in the South, while postponing an official decision. Thus, the crisis of sovereignty in the South, which the coup had created, would be solved by a form of sovereign inaction on the part of the American government. The bombings, aimed at merely persuading the North to withdraw its support for the Southern insurgency, would serve as a means of containing the crisis without adversely affecting public opinion during the presidential campaign.[72]

But because the air bases employed in the bombing campaign required American troops to ensure their security, this sovereign inaction would lead to a series of equally impromptu and tentative decisions, increasing US involvement in the undeclared war.[73] With the aim of establishing a military presence that could be used "either to escalate the war ... or to protect an American withdrawal," Johnson, "once again avoid[ing] any hard decisions," ordered the first combat troops to Vietnam to defend the airfield in Đà Nẵng.[74] As the poet Phan Nhật Nam described, this clear act of indecision, carried out without the consent of Republican leaders by an American president whose sovereignty was subordinated to public opinion, would exacerbate the crisis of sovereignty in the South:

> Our sovereignty [chính quyền] was lost when hundreds of thousands of American soldiers came to Cam Ranh and Chu Lai without asking permission from the Vietnamese government ... What is left of our sovereignty?

Absolutely nothing, not even one thing was left for us to be proud to be Vietnamese.[75]

As the American commitment increased in a series of ad hoc troop escalations, the USA, disregarding the sovereignty of the dysfunctional state it had helped to destabilize, would assume the leading role in a war that had begun to resemble a neocolonial enterprise. Having undermined the success of the Strategic Hamlet Campaign, policymakers in Washington would rely increasingly on the "deadly combination" of information and image-making in order to persuade the enemy to give up the war.[76] Instead of establishing a system of national discipline, securing the countryside through the creation of new economic and political structures, the USA would wage a deterritorialized war of attrition based on the metrics devised by the problem-solvers.[77] Detached, however, from the goal of producing "organized solidarity," this approach to the war would amount to what Arendt described as a spectacular form of coercion devoid of real political power (see Chapter 7).[78] In the war of attrition, an "enormous superiority in the means of violence" was employed in the absence of a "superior organization of power." As Lansdale would later acknowledge, it was precisely the emphasis on organization, rather than on the means of coercion, that made the communist forces effective against a superior American army: "Our side was always ... after defeating the enemy forces with military [might] ... [T]he Vietnamese communists were trying to gain control over the people where we were trying to destroy an enemy. They were political, we were military."[79]

After 1964, the use of superior violence, combined with the absence of an effective program for producing a "superior organization of power," would result in the mass displacement of peasants into the cities. "The intensified violence caused the pacification program to degenerate into the depopulation of the countryside. By early 1965, when the first U.S. combat units begin arriving, pacification was turning more into an effort 'increasingly devoted to refugee centers and relief.'"[80] Instead of building the institutional conditions for the creation of a new national people, the deterritorialized war of attrition, aimed at simply destroying the enemy, would lead to large-scale rural depopulation. Between 1962 and 1970, the urban population more than doubled from 20 percent to 43 percent. By 1972, 12 million out of a total population of 18 million had been reduced to the status of refugees.[81] Driven by the intensified violence into the cities, the South Vietnamese people, who Diệm had attempted to mobilize in a march toward political and economic modernity, would become a displaced population, requiring increasing amounts of American aid.

In the cities, this process of war-induced rapid urbanization, together with the expanded American presence, would lead to the creation of a service-oriented economy that "primarily tended to the varied needs of Americans." This dependent economy constituted a "significant transformation in Vietnamese social structure."[82] In traditional sayings, this structure was characterized as that of a society based on the autonomy of the village: "First comes the scholar, then the peasant; when rice has run out and people run back and forth, first comes the peasant, then the scholars" (*Nhất sĩ nhì nông, hết gạo chạy rông, nhất nông nhì sĩ*). This saying was used to qualify another common expression that defined the traditional Confucian hierarchy of occupations: "First the scholar, second the peasant, third the artisan, fourth the merchant" (*Nhất Sĩ Nhì Nông Tam Công Tứ Thương*).[83] The meaning of the first saying, therefore, is that, despite the priority traditionally according to scholar-officials, these scholars, nevertheless, were dependent upon the peasantry. On the other hand, the peasants could do just as well without the scholar-officials who ruled on behalf of the emperor.

In contrast to this traditional structure of society, based upon the autonomy of the peasantry, the service economy that emerged during the war was defined by new occupations, ranked according to their ability to appropriate American money by illicit means: prostitutes, religious charlatans and corrupt military leaders. "The presence of Americans in the South," as the composer Phạm Duy described, "made the society so corrupt ... Let me mention the reaction of everyday people that was expressed in the saying: 'First the prostitutes, second the Catholic priests, third the [fake] bonzes, fourth the generals'" (*Nhất đĩ Nhì cha Ba sư Bốn tướng*).[84]

Thus, with the collapse of the early Republic, the project of establishing a South Vietnamese socialism, based on a modernized peasant autonomy, would be supplanted by the emergence of a corrupt urban consumer society, completely dependent on American aid.

Notes

1 Memorandum for the Chairman, U.S. Joint Chiefs of Staff – Continued CIA Participation in Operation Plan 34A with Related Documents, Information of Visits to Vietnam and Unconventional Warfare. VCA. 1320105006 December 21, 1964. Box 01, Folder 05. David Lifton Collection.

2 Robert M. Gillespie, *Black Ops, Vietnam: The Operation History of MACVSOG* (Annapolis: Naval Institute Press, 2011), 7.
3 Lâm Lễ Trinh, "Mặt trận Gươm Thiêng Ái Quốc và Thiên Đàng Đảo" [The Sacred Sword Patriotic Front and Paradise Island]." *Nhật Báo Văn Hóa* online. March 2, 2016. https://www.nhatbaovanhoa.com/p186a3657/8/ls-lam-le-trinh-guom-thieng-ai-quoc-va-thien-dang-dao. Last accessed July 21, 2019.
4 Robert W. Chandler, *War of Ideas: the U.S. Propaganda Campaign in Vietnam* (Boulder, CO: Westview Press, 1981), 7.
5 Cecil B. Currey, *Victory at Any Cost: The Genius of Viet Nam's General Vo Nguyen Giap* (Washington DC: Potomac Books, 1997).
6 Kenneth Conboy and Dale Andrade, *How America Lost the Secret War in North Vietnam* (Lawrence: University Press of Kansas, 2000), ix.
7 MACSOG Documentary Study.
8 See the discussion of Lê Lợi in Annex, MACSOG Documentation Study – Pschological Operations, 10 July 1970, Box 05, Folder 04, Dale W. Andrade Collection, VCA.
9 Ibid.
10 MACSOG Documentary Study.
11 Ibid.
12 Ibid.
13 Ibid.
14 "Psywar Vulnerabilities in Nghe An Province." VCA. 2320401001 January 1972. Box 04, Folder 01. Douglas Pike Collection: Unit 06 – Democratic Republic of Vietnam.
15 Command History 1967, U.S. MACV Studies and Observations Group (SOG) – Annex G, G-III-3-2. VCA. 24990602001 September 1968. Box 06, Folder 02. Dale W. Andrade Collection.
16 "Indication of Planning for the Reoccupation of North Vietnam," November 20, 1962, Box 197, NSF, JFKL. 12.
17 "Bert Fraleigh, Draft – The Story of America's Counterinsurgency Efforts in Vietnam in the Early 1960s," 2. VCA. 23970130040 January 1966. Box 01, Folder 30. Rufus Phillips Collection.
18 Schwab, *Defending the Free World*, 42.
19 Arendt, Hannah. "Lying in Politics," in *Crisis of the Republic* (New York: Harcourt Brace, 1972), 39.
20 Gillespie, *Black Ops, Vietnam*, 7.
21 MACSOG Documentation Study.
22 Gillespie, *Black Ops, Vietnam*, 104.
23 Message From the Ambassador in Vietnam (Lodge) to the President, Saigon, May 15, 1964.
24 John H. Plaster, *The Secret Wars of America's Commandos in Vietnam* (New York: Simon & Schuster, 1997), 118. See also Annex, MACSOG Documentation Study, and "Article, [Vietnam Magazine] – Sneaky Petes: Secret operations

Psychological warfare

In Indochina were MACV-SOG's Specialty, but turning the job over to the South Vietnamese proved to be its hardest task of all." VCA. 3671203005 No Date. Box 12, Folder 03. George J. Veith Collection.
25 Collection: DRV Commentaries on U.S./GVN Psychological Operations, 1. VCA. 2171410079 July–December 1972. Box 14, Folder 10. Douglas Pike Collection: Unit 03 – Insurgency Warfare.
26 Halberstam, *The Making of a Quagmire*, 25.
27 Press interviews with President Ngo Dinh Diệm, 38.
28 Report by the Joint Chiefs of Staff's Special Assistant for Counterinsurgency and Special Activities (Krulak).
29 Booklet, Ed Moffitt – The Vietnam War 1954–1975, America's Defeat in Vietnam was by Choice! – re: Background Information and Media Involvement. VCA. 20740103001 October 2013. Box 01, Folder 03. Ed Moffitt Collection. See also Hammer, *A Death in November*, 252–8.
30 Nguyễn Văn Châu, *Ngô Đình Diệm và nỗ lực hòa bình dang dở*, 217.
31 Willemetz, *La République du Viêt-Nam*, 66.
32 L. M. Skow and G. Dionisopoulos, "A struggle to contextualize photographic images: American print media and the 'Burning Monk,'" *Communication Quarterly*, 45 (Fall 1997), 393–409. See also A Short History of Buddhism in Vietnam. VCA. 0720601004 July 1963. Box 06, Folder 01. John Donnell Collection; The Religions of Vietnam. United States Military Assistance Command Vietnam. Guam, 1970, 1. The Religions of Vietnam. VCA. January 1, 1970. Folder 02, Box 01. Jackson Bosley Collection. According to one CIA report: "There is no evidence that the Diem regime has curbed freedom of religion or that it carried out repressions against Buddhists prior to the 8 May outburst." Report, Republic of Vietnam – The Nature of the Buddhist Conflict in South Vietnam – CIA Research Reports. VCA. September 27, 1963. Folder 0300, Box 0003.
33 Report by the Joint Chiefs of Staffs Special Assistant for Counter-insurgency and Special Activities (Krulak) (1963), *FRUS, 1961–1963, Volume III, Vietnam*, January–August 1963. See also Dennis J. Duncanson, *Government and Revolution in Vietnam* (New York: Oxford University Press, 1968), 330.
34 "Diem and the Buddhists" (editorial), *New York Times* (June 17, 1963), 24.
35 Higgins, *Our Vietnam Nightmare*, 186.
36 Quoted in Richard Reeves, *President Kennedy: Profile of Power* (New York: Simon & Schuster, 1994), 560.
37 Walter C. Ladwig III, *The Forgotten Front: Patron-Client Relationships in Counter Insurgency* (Cambridge: Cambridge University Press, 2017), 174.
38 Catton, *Diem's Final Failure*, 23.
39 Jessica M. Chapman, "Reviewed work: *Misalliance: Ngo Dinh Diem, the United States, and the Fate of South Vietnam* by Edward G. Miller," *The Review of Politics*, 76:1 (2014), 157.

40 Quoted in ibid.
41 "Vietnam: A Television History; America's Mandarin (1954–1963)"; interview with Edward Geary Lansdale, 1979 [Part 1 of 5]." January 31, 1979. WGBH Media Library & Archives. http://openvault.wgbh.org/catalog/V_76F F42FB387043579AAE7F39B43D2D1C. Last accessed July 22, 2019.
42 Higgins, *Our Vietnam Nightmare*, 39–40.
43 Ibid., 5.
44 Ibid., 37.
45 Ibid., 186.
46 Ibid., 39–40.
47 See General Cao Van Vien. Folder 20, Box 17 Indochina Monographs, U.S. Army Center of Military History – Leadership. VCA. January 1, 1981. Folder 20, Box 17. Garnett Bell Collection.
48 Higgins, *Our Vietnam Nightmare*, 167.
49 Arendt, "Lying in Politics," 18.
50 Quoted in Anne E. Blair, *Lodge in Vietnam: A Patriot Abroad* (New Haven, CT: Yale University Press, 1995), 21.
51 Telegram from the Embassy in Vietnam to the Department of State, Saigon, August 27, 1963.
52 Văn Nguyên Dương, *The Tragedy of the Vietnam War: A South Vietnamese Officer's Analysis* (London: McFarland & Company, 2008), 86.
53 Catton, *Diem's Final Failure*, 22.
54 Ibid.
55 Willemetz, *La République du Viêt-Nam*, 52.
56 Lương Khải Minh [Trần Kim Tuyến] and Cao Vị Hoàng [Cao Thế Dung], *Làm thế nào để giết một tổng thống* [How to Kill a President] (Sài Gòn: Đinh Minh Ngọc, 1970), 14–21, 692.
57 Higgins, *Our Vietnam Nightmare*, 5–6.
58 On Nhu's surveillance network, see Harvey Henry Smith, *Area Handbook for South Vietnam* (Washington, DC: US Government Printing Office, 1967), 220; and Robert Scigliano, *South Vietnam: Nation Under Stress* (Boston, MA: Houghton-Mifflin Company, 1964), 187.
59 Quoted in Jones, *Death of a Generation*, 435. According to Bert Fraleigh, 1962 to 1963 was "a very, very effective period … then came the coup – the overthrow of Diệm … [That] destroy[ed] security in central Vietnam because Diệm's brother … had a tremendous apparatus stretching down to every hamlet … [which] prevented the VC infrastructure from really getting started … When Diem fell, the force melted overnight and left a vacuum." Fraleigh Interview – Mr. Bert Fraleigh, 23. VCA. 23970216021 February 3, 1967. Box 02, Folder 16. Rufus Phillips Collection.
60 This discrepancy between the image and the reality of the war was recorded in Kennedy's personal memo to himself on the coup in Sài Gòn: "Harkins continued to oppose the coup on the grounds that the military effort was

Psychological warfare

doing well. There was a sharp split between [the political climate in] Saigon and the rest of the country. Politically the situation is deteriorating. Militarily it had not had this effect ... I was shocked by the death of Diem and Nhu. I'd met Diệm ... many years ago. He was a extraordinary character, and while he became increasingly difficult in the last months, nevertheless, over a ten-year period he held his country together to maintain its independence under very adverse conditions." Despite "Diem's bad press in the United States," therefore, Kennedy believed that, "it was essential that we do not permit [journalists like] Halberstam unduly to influence our actions." "When we move to eliminate this Government, it should not be as a result of *New York Times* pressure." Quoted in Winters, *The Year of the Hare*, 62–3.

61 Frank Ninkovich, *Modernity and Power: A History of the Domino Theory in the Twentieth Century* (Chicago: University of Chicago Press, 1994), 299.
62 Message from the Ambassador in Vietnam (Lodge) to the President, Saigon, May 15, 1964.
63 Minh Võ, *Ngô Đình Diệm và chính nghĩa dân tộc*, 127.
64 Zwick et al., *U.S. Economic Assistance in Vietnam*, 2.
65 Văn Nguyên Dưỡng, *The Tragedy of the Vietnam War*, 86.
66 "Papers of John F. Kennedy. Presidential Papers." National Security Files. Meetings and Memoranda. Meetings on Vietnam: General, September 1963," Papers of John F. Kennedy. Presidential Papers. National Security Files. Series 06. Meetings and Memoranda.
67 "Letter to Madame Nhu from Lyndon B. Johnson." VCA. 2361213070 September 20, 1963. Box 12, Folder 13. Douglas Pike Collection: Unit 08 – Biography.
68 Tape WH6601-11-9541, Lyndon B. Johnson Library.
69 Paper – The Political Factor in Pacification: A Vietnam Case Study [Draft], 11–12. VCA. 21470122001 No Date. Box 01, Folder 22. Vincent Puritano Collection.
70 Fraleigh, "Counterinsurgency in Vietnam," 112–13.
71 *Một số văn kiện của Đảng về chống Mỹ, cứu nước*, Tập 1 [Party Documents on the Anti-American [War] of National Salvation, Vol. 1] (Hà Nội: Nhà xuất bản Sự thật, 1985), 212, 216.
72 Herbert Y. Schandler, *Lyndon Johnson and Vietnam: The Unmaking of a President* (Princeton, NJ: Princeton University Press, 1977), 5–11. On the other hand, Fredrik Logevall, downplaying the role of advisors and the structural factors in foreign policymaking during the "long 1964," emphasizes Johnson's personal culpability as commander-in-chief in "choosing war": Logevall, *Choosing War*. Similarly, John Stoessinger contends that the decision to escalate was guided by Johnson's "enormous ego and machismo": John Stoessinger, *Why Nations Go to War*, 4th ed. (New York: St. Martin's Press, 1985), 99. In contrast, Larry Berman and Brian VanDeMark connect Johnson's decision to his domestic political agenda, and his desire to win

The unimagined community

congressional support for his Great Society and civil rights legislation: Larry Berman, *Planning a Tragedy: The Americanization of the War in Vietnam* (New York: W. W. Norton, 1982); and Brian VanDeMark, *Into the Quagmire: Lyndon Johnson and the Escalation of the Vietnam War* (New York, Oxford: Oxford University Press, 1995). For a similar view, see Jeffrey W. Helsing, *Johnson's War/Johnson's Great Society: The Guns and Butter Trap* (Westport, CT: Praeger, 2000).

73 Wayne Thompson, *To Hanoi and Back: The United States Air Force and North Vietnam, 1966–1973* (Washington DC: Smithsonian Institution Press, 2000), 20–1.
74 Allen Reed Millett, *Semper Fidelis: The History of the United States Marine Corps* (New York: Macmillan, 1980), 564. See also VanDeMark, *Into the Quagmire*, 94.
75 Quoted in Nguyễn Nguyệt Cầm, "Z.28 and the Appeal of Spy Fiction in Southern Vietnam, 1954–1975" (Master's thesis, University of California, Berkeley, 2002), 40.
76 Arendt, *On Revolution*, 39.
77 Gregory A. Daddis, *No Sure Victory: Measuring U.S. Army Effectiveness and Progress in the Vietnam War* (New York: Oxford University Press, 2011).
78 Arendt, "Lying in Politics," 149–50.
79 "Vietnam: A Television History." Interview with Edward Lansdale.
80 Beverly Deepe Keever, *Death Zones and Darling Spies: Seven Years of Vietnam War Reporting* (Lincoln: University of Nebraska Press, 2013), 54.
81 Nguyễn Đức Nhuận, *Désurbanisation et développement régional au Viet-Nam (1954–1977): Etude préliminaire sur la politique d'industrialisation et de répartition de la population au Viet-Nam* (Paris: Centre de Sociologie Urbaine, 1978), 16, 19.
82 Neil L. Jamieson, *Understanding Vietnam* (Berkeley and Los Angeles: University of California Press, 1995), 294.
83 Phạm Duy, *Hồi K. Phạm Duy* [Memoir of Phạm Duy] (Midway City, CA: P.D.C. Musical Productions, 1991), 34.
84 Ibid., 390–1.

5

Mass culture in the later Republic

> What ... is done against Vietnam will be felt in America too. It is not enough to try to kill or subdue the ... leaders of a country ... because one wants to transform [it] ... into a satellite. To kill or subdue is easy, but what happens afterwards? ... [N]obody can rule Vietnam with just money and puppets. ... In spite of all the distortion ... directed by that international Communist propaganda network ... Ngo only wanted to give to Vietnam its own identity, which cannot be the same as the one wanted by ... Americans. ... And all those ... the Americans intend to ... tutor ... how long will they hold power?
>
> Madame Nhu

US neocolonialism: Invading the national culture

In *South Vietnamese Literature* (*Văn Học Miền Nam*), one of the few studies on the subject of fiction from the non-communist South, the writer Võ Phiến presents a portrait of what he describes as "a whole generation of literature ... [embodying] the joys, sadness, laughter and tears of 20 million of our people over a period of 20 years that no one has examined or tried to understand."[1] Many of the works from the period from 1954 to 1975 were confiscated and destroyed after the fall of Sài Gòn.[2] This act of repression, according to the scholar Nguyễn Văn Lục, was part of a coordinated campaign to "wipe away all of South Vietnamese literature," one that was carefully planned by the Communist Party well before the end of the war: "And so, immediately before the invasion ... Northern journals like *Học Tập, Văn Học, Văn Nghệ* ... published over 200 articles in accordance with this policy."[3] The physical destruction of this literature was accompanied by its erasure from the official histories of the period, published in the Democratic Republic of Vietnam. In Phạm Văn Sĩ's *Literature of Liberated South Vietnam*, for example, the discussion of fiction from the non-communist South is limited to an appendix on the "arts of the occupied zone" (*văn nghệ vùng tạm chiếm*).[4]

During the war, these arts were regarded as dangerous "cultural poisons," "propagating the philosophy of existentialism, or spreading corruption and pornography or proselytizing anti-communism."[5] Together with the foreign popular works, imported into the South, this literature was condemned as the "decadent product[s]" of a neocolonial "civilization of consumption," used to enslave the South Vietnamese people.[6] During the war, according to communist critics, the Americans had deliberately promoted "reactionary ... cultural products of the 'free world' as never before for maximum impact on the mode of thinking, the psychology and life-style of the people in the South."[7] As the violence of the war of attrition continued to escalate in the countryside, peasants, forced to flee into the cities, became caught within "the encirclement of the enemy's morale-affecting apparatus."[8] This apparatus was supplied by the Commodity Import Program, a "scheme ... designed to make the people stuck in the 'U.S. Aid' machinery."[9] The flow of consumer commodities was further expanded with the establishment of a system of post-exchange (PX) offices to serve American military personnel, whose numbers increased dramatically after the crisis created by the collapse of the early Republic. The PXs would quickly become a primary source of supply for the booming black market in cities such as Sài Gòn and Đà nẵng.[10]

According to the economist Nguyễn Xuân Lai, this flood of consumer commodities:

> engendered among the population a tendency to consume foreign manufactured goods. Even among the laboring classes, people are inclined to hanker after refrigerators, air-conditioners, television sets, washing-machines, electric or gas stoves ... motor-scooters, Lambretta, Honda and Suzuki motor-cycles, powerful American cars and elegant Mercedes. They took a liking for synthetic fabrics, got accustomed to smoking Luckies, drinking Scotch and chewing gum. Little by little, the "American way of life" penetrates into daily life ...[11]

Thanks to American aid, the South would become "the easiest place in the world to acquire some of the external attributes of prosperity."[12] Sài Gòn was "roaring with thousands of vehicles, filled ... with American,

Mass culture in the later Republic

5.1 Sài Gòn traffic, Hàm Nghi Street (John Beck).

Japanese, and French goods."[13] In "downtown ... modishly dressed youths stroll past shop windows filled with expensive stereo tape decks, amplifiers, record players, television sets and radios."[14]

Although this prosperity, according to Nguyễn Khắc Viện, was only "fictitious" ("everything [coming] ... from abroad by a sort of miracle which might never happen again"),[15] the foreign commodities that the program provided were real: "the buildings, the cars, the goods, none of these things are artificial."[16] And despite the widespread corruption surrounding the aid, this fictional wealth extended to even the most marginal members of the expanded wartime population in the cities. Refrigerators and televisions could be found "even in infested squatter-areas, where a dense population lives ... along canals filled with rubbish and waste."[17] As a result of American aid, "life in Saigon," as Nguyễn Đức Cường described, "gave ... the impression of an artificial society [funded by] ... US tax payer money. It conjured up the image of a society enjoying the good life, while ... letting the farmers deal with the guerillas in the countryside."[18]

Driven en masse into the cities, the peasants were reduced to a "captive population" of neocolonial subjects, compelled to consume American products to the point of exhaustion:

The unimagined community

The waves of commodities in this horrible ocean come in great numbers and exert a pull, and people are attracted by and play with them until they are exhausted and sink. Here, commodities are really cruel; they kill people without trembling and no one can avoid their claws and teeth.[19]

The waves of consumer commodities also included a new popular culture, providing urban South Vietnamese with a variety of mindless amusement while the war of attrition raged in the countryside:

Under the direction of the U.S. psywar agency, the temporarily controlled areas of South Viet-Nam have been flooded with obscene books and newspapers, U.S. "western" films, Chinese "knight-errant" films from Hong Kong, pictures of diehard U.S. mercenary troops and puppet and satellite soldiers revered as heroes, existentialist novels, dramatic poems.[20]

For the Communist Party, these new cultural commodities were emblematic of the neocolonial consumer society, used to distract the South Vietnamese people from the reality of the war: "The wicked aim of the US-Puppet regime was to embellish the image of the cities and obscure the image of the countryside which was then being destroyed ... Their aim was to make people forget rural desolation and to embellish artificial urban prosperity to attract youth to the frenzied rootless life of neo-colonialism."[21] Mass culture, then, served as one of the "methods of cultural enslavement used by the U.S. imperialists in their aggression in South Viet-Nam."[22]

This form of cultural imperialism, however, was different from that of the mission to civilize. Whereas the French had imposed their civilization on the indigenous urban elite in order to erase the national culture, the Americans sought to enslave the Vietnamese masses by promoting a completely uncivilized form of mass-produced culture, a culture devoid of culture itself. In the "rotten society" created by the Americans and their puppet regime in the South, "culture is made of whiskey, Salem cigarettes, twist music, miniskirts, and western films."[23] In contrast to French civilization, therefore, this neocolonial culture was characterized, paradoxically, by its anti-cultural character: "America's cultural measures, while similar in some ways [to those of the French], were also anti-cultural [phi văn hoá]. ... Crudity [thô bạo] was the hallmark of U.S. cultural policies."[24]

Employing psychological techniques derived from modern advertising, the products introduced as part of this anti-cultural policy appealed to the irrational instincts of its captive consumers.[25] Its aim was not to elevate the colonial subject to the level of a European humanity, but to dehumanize the South Vietnamese people. "In neo-colonial society, human values are reversed and discredited."[26] The decadent products of US neocolonialism served to "animalize [individuals] with regard to their souls and [their] way of life."[27] The project of American cultural imperialism, then, was to reduce the colonial population to the status of "animals (động vật) and dimwits (u mê) ... half intoxicated, half-conscious."[28]

Because of its crudity, however, the anti-cultural policy imposed under US neocolonialism would have a far more destructive effect than the French civilizing mission: "Ten years in the incubator of U.S. culture can be much more harmful than 100 years of French colonialism."[29] Whereas French colonialism had preached a hypocritical Enlightenment humanism that was denied to the colonial subject, the aim of American neocolonialism was to completely dissolve the latter's humanity. Communist critics, therefore, as Philip Taylor describes, denounced the "anti-modernity of ... the neo-colonial system," which "permeated the population of the South ... stifling their consciousness ... and ultimately effacing their humanity."[30] As a result of the dehumanization produced by the anti-modernity of American cultural policies, South Vietnamese were deprived of their collective sense of identity as a national people. The "American consumer lifestyle, based on American aid" (lối sống tiêu dùng Mĩ, thông qua viện trợ Mĩ), was condemned, therefore, as a cultural weapon in a "war without guns" (chiến tranh không có súng đạn), used to "sabotage national consciousness" (phá hoại ý thức dân tộc).[31] By destroying the national culture, the American "cultural invasion" (ngoại xâm văn hoá) had removed the very will to resistance that the Vietnamese had inherited from their 2,000-year history of resistance to foreign invaders, a history which, as one communist critic observed, was "one of the important factors serving as a foundation of consolidated strength of our people."[32]

Deprived of their national history by the "rootless life of neocolonialism," the South Vietnamese were reduced to what Fanon referred to as "individuals without an anchorage, without borders ... stateless, rootless, a body of angels."[33] The result was a kind of non-community of a nation that could no longer imagine its own national history: "20 years of domination [has] left behind a debauched and lewd society full of beggars, cowboys and prostitutes; a dependent, unproductive economy; and an enslaving, uprooted, depraved and reactionary culture."[34] Owing to the anti-modernity of US neocolonialism, a displaced population,

The unimagined community

devoid of a national culture, was unable to imagine itself as a nation in the midst of a war for the nation's survival. If print media, then, during the colonial era had served as an instrument of surveillance and discipline that constituted the "soul" of the Vietnamese people, mass culture under US neocolonialism was condemned as a means of destroying the national culture itself.

For the Communist Party, this anti-cultural strategy was far more effective, particularly in its use of mass communications technology, than the psychological warfare campaign carried out in the North: "The use of mass media – the radio, TV, newspapers, posters, and films – was intensive in the effort to force upon millions of people a set of notions and attitudes which were calculated to turn them against communism."[35] While such programs as the Sacred Sword Patriotic League employed modern mass media to project the illusion of a nationalist movement opposed to the Communist Party, the commercialized culture of US neocolonialism was designed to dissolve national consciousness itself. Neocolonial culture, then, was "essentially a kind of antithesis of culture, a tool of aggression in the hands of U.S. imperialism … even more dangerous than the U.S. schemes in the military, political and economic fields."[36]

As communist writers lamented, peasants who were "caught up in the urban maelstrom" of a consumer society, contaminated by "prostitution … 'addiction' to foreign films, romance novels … pornography, and … drug[s]," became "lost to the revolution."[37] In the cities, the American intervention had created what Gabriel Kolko described as a "transitional youth culture [that] cut[s] through a class culture," a displaced population, stripped of tradition, "family cohesion" and "connection to community," devoid of both class and national consciousness.[38] "Under the yoke of neo-colonial rule, American aid," according to the historian Trần Ngọc Dinh, "made many people, especially the youth lose all character, thought, sentiment, sense of purpose."[39] To "a great extent," this "transitional youth culture," as Kolko described, "broke the solidarity of the masses with the Revolution," which "simply could not reach this lumpen constituency."[40]

Having failed in its use of superior means of coercion to crush the indomitable will of the Vietnamese people, rooted in an ancient tradition of resisting foreign invaders (*truyền thống chống ngoại xâm*), the Americans attempted to "invade the national culture" (*ngoại xâm văn hoá*) itself in order to undermine the will to resist. As a result of the rise of mass culture, the 2,000-year national culture (which had been invented

Mass culture in the later Republic

during the colonial era as the effect of a technique of surveillance) was destroyed by the "decadent cultural products of American neo-colonialism." Instead of providing a medium for imagining the nation, the products of US neocolonialism created a kind of *unimagined community*. Dependent on American aid and deprived of their own national culture, South Vietnamese became increasingly indifferent to the revolutionary appeals of the Party.

A regime of freedom

According to Võ Phiến, this account of South Vietnamese culture was largely a product of communist propaganda. For the "Communist state," "the newspapers and books that appeared … in Vietnam … south of the seventeenth parallel … were not cultural works. All of them were products manufactured by the CIA. The CIA controlled the puppet regime, the puppet regime controlled the pen-lackeys [*bồi bút*], ordering them to write … all for the purpose of poisoning the masses and harming the people."[41]

For Võ Phiến, this characterization of South Vietnamese literature was, in reality, a reflection of the authoritarian system of cultural production imposed in the North. Having known only a communist system in which culture, "under the command of the state, aimed only at serving politics," North Vietnamese cadres, as the composer Phạm Duy observed, could not conceive of a culture that, "in private hands, had become a commercial product (*produit commercial*) within a consumer society (*société de consommation*)."[42] Thus, during his reeducation, the Southern writer Hà Thúc Sinh was condemned as a CIA asset, based on the irrefutable evidence that he could not have written so many works without the support of US imperialism: "There can be no doubt that you are part of the CIA machine … In the socialist North, even leading writers wait three years to publish a book. What did you have to do to get the puppet regime to allow you, at the mere age of 30, to print so many?"[43]

"[U]nlike their northern partners," however, artists in the South, according to Boitran Huynh-Beattie, "were not constrained by the agenda of psychological warfare. Saigonese artists could survive in a market driven environment."[44] At the end of the war, the Northern officials, in fact, were concerned that the sight of this market-driven environment could serve to unmask the authoritarian character of the Communist Party and its control of all information and culture. Thus, as the writer Bảo Ninh describes in *Sorrow of War*, soldiers traveling South on the

"Unification Train" in 1975 were bombarded with propaganda, warning of the dangers of neocolonial culture: "At every station the loudspeakers blared, blasting the ears of the ... troops [with] ... an endless stream of the most ironic of teachings, urging them to ... beware of the 'bullets coated with sugar' [đạn bọc lường] in ... the luxurious society of the South."⁴⁵

For the novelist Dương Thu Hương, the sight of this luxurious society and its diverse cultural products was an overwhelming experience, causing her to question her role in the war. When the "victorious army entered Sài Gòn in 1975 ... I cried because I saw that my youth had been wasted":

> I was ... overcome by ... all of the works that South Vietnamese authors had been allowed to publish under a regime of freedom, all these writers I had never known, writers whose works were in book stores, [sold] even on sidewalks ... [The city] was filled with media, televisions, radios and cassettes. For Northerners, such media were the stuff of dreams. ... [I]n the North, all the newspapers and books were controlled by the state. ... The entire population was allowed to listen ... only to one voice. It was in going to the South that I understood that the regime in the North was ... barbaric, because it blinded people's eyes ... [T]he South ... was a civilized regime.⁴⁶

For Dương Thu Hương, then, the media that proliferated during the war was not an instrument of cultural enslavement. On the contrary, it was evidence of a "regime of freedom" that exposed the oppression of the cultural policies of the Communist Party.⁴⁷ If these policies, moreover, had helped to mobilize the North Vietnamese in the war against the Americans, they had notably failed to produce any lasting artistic achievements. "[C]ultural cadres" in the North, "writers, artists, composers, and filmmakers of that era later looked back on their wartime output with embarrassment."⁴⁸

In the South, on the other hand, the Vietnamese, according to Võ Phiến, had fought to defend a regime that promoted political freedom and artistic autonomy. Millions "died out of the desire to be a soldier as well as a poet, without working for the CIA or the secret police."⁴⁹ During the conflict, this devotion to liberty, in the midst of the horrors of wars, produced what Võ Phiến describes as a remarkable body of literary art, which would be swept away by the repression imposed at the end of the war.

Mass culture in the later Republic

The decline of culture in South Vietnam

But if the literature from 1954 to 1975 was defamed by the Communist Party as an American plot to enslave the South Vietnamese people, the account that Võ Phiến provides of this period leaves doubt as to the lasting quality of its literary achievements. As Võ Phiến points out, this literary period was characterized paradoxically by a growing lack of interest in literature itself, and by the diminished prestige and importance of high culture in general. It was a period when "we as a people finally lost our tradition of respect for the arts,"[50] when "culture," as the scholar Nguyễn Hiến Lê lamented, could "only hang around at the periphery, playing a … very, very minor role."[51] In the augural issue of *Contemporary Culture* (*Văn Hóa Ngày Nay*), published in 1958, the novelist Nhất Linh, the most influential writer of the prewar generation, described the period as one in which the "cultural life [of the country] exists in a state of inertia, unable to find a direction." Artists at the time were "tormented by the question of why the people expressed such … a weary attitude towards … cultural activities."[52] Thus, the lost literary period from 1954 to 1975 was one that was defined by its non-literary and anti-cultural character.

The decline of literature in the South was exemplified in the attitude of indifference towards luminaries such as Nhất Linh and Tam Lang, "men of letters" (*danh sĩ*) who, during the colonial era, had played a principal role in developing a modern Vietnamese vernacular literature and journalism, and whose works remain among the most well known and admired in Vietnamese fiction.[53] These luminaries, however, were not displaced by the emergence of new cultural movements, in spite of what Võ Phiến describes as a "yearning for the new" among Vietnamese readers, who demanded a new "direction" in culture.[54] During the period, journals such as *Creation* (*Sáng Tạo*), edited by Mai Thảo, called for a definitive break with the precedents established by prewar Vietnamese writers, and for the invention of "new art concepts" that would lead to an "inevitable dialectical revolution of literature" (*cuộc cách mạng tất yếu và biện chứng của văn chương*).[55] Instead of founding a new literary tradition, however, the new art concepts, developed by writers affiliated to *Creation*, would fail in large part to inspire the public, which had become increasingly wary of culture and art.[56] Therefore, if movements such as Nhất Linh's Self-Strength Literary Group (*Tự Lực Văn Đoàn*) could be considered among the country's first avant-garde, they were also the last: "[I]n the South after 1954, there was no literary association like the prewar *Tự Lực Văn Đoàn* … There were no organized groups with any longevity, no groups with trend-setting influences, no literary manifestos and the like."⁵⁷ During the postwar period, therefore, the old "famed men of letters disappeared," but without being supplanted by a new generation that was equal in stature and cultural influence.⁵⁸ The lost literary period in the South was one that was apparently "without any worthy achievements, without any representative writers who could speak with a representative voice for the era, without any of the refined talents of the prewar period."⁵⁹

The people and national media

The absence of movements such as the Self-Strength Literary Group also implied an end to the political project of creating a national culture. During the colonial era (as I examine in Chapter 1), Vietnamese intellectuals believed that the spread of modern print media would provide the condition for the emergence of a new "national people" (dân tộc): "Many came to equate national power with an alert, informed, literate citizenry."⁶⁰ In the 1920s and 1930s, the literary form of the novel, written in the vernacular script, would become an important medium for the promotion of national consciousness. "By 1940," according to David Marr, "there was hardly anyone who had not come to empathize with the plight of the poor and downtrodden as seen through quốc ngữ fiction."⁶¹

After 1954, the project of imprinting the nation in the minds of the Vietnamese people was pursued by the two Vietnamese states that emerged in the wake of the Geneva Accords. "In 1954, the DRV [Democratic Republic of Vietnam] … wished to revive the 1930s tradition of publishing." "Communist Party leaders … insisted that all cultural activity serve the interests of the nation and the people." Creating a national culture in the service of the people, however, would require "dictatorial control over cultural output, especially the print media," as a means of mobilizing the masses in accordance with the policies of the Communist Party.⁶² By 1960, publishing in the North was completely nationalized, with the production of all printed material placed under the authority of the Ministry of Culture, which distributed supplies and equipment.⁶³ The number of periodicals was reduced to two daily newspapers, Nhân Dân (The People) and Quân Đội Nhân Dân (People's Army). Following the Soviet model, moreover, editors were instructed on the Party's official positions by an Ideology Commission, which approved all appointments to the editorial board. All content material was reviewed by party committees, which were assigned to each publishing unit.⁶⁴

Mass culture in the later Republic

In the South, similarly, the creation of a national culture was a political priority for the early Republican government. During "Ngô Đình Diệm's first years," the "construction of the state," according to Phạm Duy, was accompanied by significant support for cultural activities. National schools of fine arts and music were established in Sài Gòn and other large cities. A Cultural Affairs Division (*Văn Hóa Vụ*) was founded within the elite Military Academy in Đà Lạt, providing instruction in law, literature, history and psychology. The government, moreover, placed "significant emphasis on ... mass media" (*thông tin đại chúng*), creating a National Radio Service and a Center for Cinema (*Trung tâm Quốc gia Điện ảnh*), as a branch of the Republic of Vietnam Information Service.[65]

As in the North, moreover, much of the media, under the "dictatorial rule of anti-communist President Ngo Dinh Diem," was directly controlled by the state.[66] Thus, from "1954 to 1963 ... the government closed down newspapers that dared to ... question current policies, until only a couple of docile mouthpieces remained,"[67] one of which was run by the Republic's director of psychological warfare.[68] As a result, "not a single newspaper could escape the orbit of the Ngô Đình Diệm regime" (*chẳng có một tờ báo nào thoát được ra ngoài quỹ đạo của chế độ Ngô Đình Diệm*).[69]

In comparison with the North, however, the control of culture was applied in the early Republic in a far more limited fashion. Even though "the Diệm government was never ... a government that really respected freedom and democracy, artists, nevertheless," as Phạm Duy explained, "were rarely suppressed, except in the case of writers and journalists ... directly opposed to the government. In contrast to the North, the purely literary artist [*người làm văn học nghệ thuật thuần túy*] in the South was relatively free to compose what they wanted." If the South, then, "was not exactly a paradise for artists searching for freedom," "it was nevertheless an environment in which free spirits could thrive" (*cũng là nơi đất lành cho chim đậu*) owing to the "laxity of cultural policies [*sự quá lỏng lẻo trong chính sách văn hoá*] ... under the Ngô Đình Diệm government."[70]

Yet, in spite of the efforts by the early Republic to promote culture and art, the latter would play only a "very, very minor role" in South Vietnamese society. The period of the war, as Võ Phiến observes, was marked by a decline in the consumption of literature: "Vietnam, of course, is a civilized country [*nước văn hiến*], but this cultural character has come with a difficulty [*có phần éo le*]: there are more and more writers every day and always fewer and fewer readers [of literature]."⁷¹ "[T]here has been no noticeable increase in the readership of the South after 1954."⁷²

During the war, then, the literary scene in Sài Gòn, with its diminished readership and its marginal social and cultural influence, was not defined by the predominance of a national movement similar to the Self-Strength Literary Group, articulating a unified vision of the larger historical vocation of culture and literature. Instead, it was marked by the proliferation of literary fashions and trends, embodying discordant and incompatible conceptions of aesthetics and politics. And rather than realizing a completely secularized modern national literature, the works produced during the lost literary period between 1945 and 1975 were characterized by a mixture of the sacred and the profane. While writers like Dương Nghiễm Mậu and Nhã Ca produced works in the 1950s that were classified as part of a daring new literature of nihilism and decadence,⁷³ proclaiming the end of "things like God, homeland, duty, love, family etc.,"⁷⁴ Buddhist monks such as Nhất Hạnh and Phạm Công Thuận, together with Catholic priests such as Thanh Lãng and Trần Thái Đỉnh, "invaded the literary and newspaper world [làng văn làng báo] in large numbers." "[T]he time when 'God is dead' is heard everywhere ... was also a time of tremendous religious revival and widespread religious fervor." A lucrative market emerged for religious writings – including works on the Cao Đài and Hòa Hảo religious sects – as well as texts on European and Eastern philosophy ("Books of philosophy, or even of a philosophical flavor, were moneymakers").⁷⁵ And although the literature of the 1950s and early 1960s was, in general, more overtly political than its counterpart in the prewar period, its politics tended toward no particular political doctrine. The Sartrean notion of *littérature engagée* (*văn chương dấn thân*), as Võ Phiến describes, "became a fashionable term." Its "emphasis," however, "might be religious, political, social or psychological, depending on the individual artist and his circumstances":

> There were the extreme *engagé*s, like Vũ Hạnh, Lữ Phương, Lý Chánh Trung, Thế Nguyên ... and then the moderate *engagé*s like Thế Uyên, Nguyễn Văn Xuân etc. ... Buddhist *engagé*s like Nhất Hạnh, as well as Catholic *engagé*s like Nguyễn Ngọc Lan. There were *engagé*s who advocated communism and resisted the war of resistance against communism (Nguyễn Văn Trung, Nhất Hạnh, Vũ Hạnh ...), and there were "*engagé*s" who condemned communism ...⁷⁶

Mass culture in the later Republic

After the escalation of the war in Vietnam in the 1960s, however, this literature of engagement was quickly eclipsed by an increasing apolitical fiction that explored "notions like nothingness and illusion." In the short story "Spirit in the Tower of the Tortoise" (*Thần Tháp Rùa*), Vũ Khắc Khoan captures the confusion of the literary scene in the South in his satirical portrait of a typical Saigonese socialite intellectual:

> [W]henever someone mentioned current events, or compared different ideologies ... [Đỗ] would throw himself into the argument, debating for hours on end without getting tired. ... He would expound on the wisdom of Buddhism and demand [that his listeners] give up their Christian beliefs. Or else he would praise the insights of Pascal and demolish atheist arguments. ... [H]e would advocate the class struggle while exposing capitalist machinations, and then [move on to] defend individual freedom against collective dictatorship. If anyone dared to suggest that art was intrinsically valuable he would raise his voice and explain [the doctrine that art should serve] humanity. But if anyone tried to bring literature down to the level of "useful things," Đỗ would ... proceed to remind his listeners of Kant's conception of art.[77]

The rise of popular culture

In the South, the decline of culture coincided with what Võ Phiến describes as the development of a "phenomenon unique to our time, a time of vast communication and enormous consumption, namely, literature as a consumer's product."[78] This product was part of a range of new "cultural commodities [*món hàng văn hóa*] aimed at the masses of a poor, developing country."[79] The lost literary period of war, then, was defined by the emergence of a new *paralittérature*, a "non-literary" (*phi văn chương*) "pseudo-literature" that would become an increasingly prevalent part of everyday life in the cities.[80]

Contrary to the communist account of South Vietnamese culture, the proliferation of these cultural commodities was not the result of an American plot to enslave the Vietnamese masses. Rather, it emerged as an unintended effect of the "freedom" established by the new RVN government after the overthrow of Ngô Đình Diệm's repressive regime. The coup, which the US supported in order to save the image of the South Vietnamese state as a liberal democracy, precipitated a crisis that led to a dramatic increase in the American military presence, from 16,300 in 1963 to over 553,000 by 1969. Following Diệm's assassination, "foreign troops," as Phạm Duy described, "poured into Vietnam, too many, too quickly, carrying countless products of Western society." "[E]veryone was afraid of being invaded culturally [*bị ngoại xâm văn hoá*]. People did not like communism, but nor did they like American culture."[81] A "half-million American soldiers," wrote the Information Minister Tôn Thất Thiện, who had been sent to save Vietnam, were simultaneously "suffocating it with their fantastic wealth, their gadgetry ... and their destructive innocence."[82]

At the same time, the new dysfunctional government, in an attempt to project the image of a stable democracy, enacted reforms promoting the institutions of liberal democracy and free-market capitalism, lifting the censorship laws and state regulations on free enterprise imposed under Diệm.[83] These policies, however, did not imply a genuine commitment to the ideal of democracy (an ideal for which millions, according to Võ Phiến, would die in the South). Although the reforms were intended, in part, to appease the Americans ("who use the press as a barometer of freedom"),[84] they also reflected the "absence of alternative philosophies" among the new political leadership,[85] who had "narrow minds and visions."[86] Lacking any larger political vision for the country, the "talented men" who took part in the coup replaced the doctrine of Personalism with a largely negative conception of freedom, as the absence of state regulation over the economy and the media.

After the coup, the Americans, according to a State Department report, had "no way of providing either mass or elite political organizations ... themselves, and the Vietnamese were unable to do so." And so, as a "reaction by both Americans and Vietnamese to the more oppressive aspects of the Strategic Hamlets," the latter adopted the "under-politicized," "pragmatic ... approach of using economic and social benefits as the primary means of inducing popular political support." In contrast to the early Republican program of establishing political and economic autonomy in the South, this "under-politicized" political strategy was "closely geared to the resources the U.S. was best able to supply – the material ones."[87] After 1963, then, the Southward Advance toward economic modernity through centralized planning and national discipline would give way to a "period of business freedom" (*thời kỳ tự do kinh doanh*). While the rural areas increasingly fell to the communists, after the Strategic Hamlet Campaign was dissolved, "the private sector" in the cities "invested only in areas with quick profits."[88]

Unable to maintain control of the countryside, the new government, moreover, would abandon the project of imprinting the national culture on the South Vietnamese people through the mass dissemination

Mass culture in the later Republic

of media. During Diệm's administration, print media, distributed by the RVN Information Service, "went deep into the rural areas." Books "reached as far as the reading rooms of the district offices," while "newspapers could go … all the way down to the hamlets."[89] This "happy situation," however, "would not last for long." With the collapse of the early Republic, "the situation became so confused," and because "the authorities were busy dealing with [other] urgent concerns, the issue of culture was [simply] ignored" (*vấn đề khẩn bách nên chuyện văn hóa bị bỏ qua*).[90] After 1963, government "newspapers and books only made it as far as the provincial capital." For individual booksellers, moreover, "there was little demand and hardly any profit to be made" in the countryside. "Once in a while, you might encounter a bookstore in a district capital selling cheap Kung-Fu novels. That was the extent of the goodwill of private distributors." Because the Republican government, then, was too preoccupied with its own internal problems to promote the national culture, and because the free market for media, as it emerged in the era of economic liberalization, was interested only in profit, the flow of reading material to the villages had to be cut off.[91] "Since the government didn't care, and the private [distributors] weren't interested, the issue of distributing newspapers and books to the rural population had arrived at an impasse."[92]

Meanwhile, in the cities, the policy of liberalization, and the indifference on the part of the new South Vietnamese state to the question of culture (the fact that "officials at the time would rather leave books alone"),[93] would lead to a period of unprecedented freedom in public expression. "South Vietnamese culture during this period," according to an RVN intelligence report, was defined by "a certain libertarianism verging on permissiveness," a permissiveness that at times was "detrimental to the cause of the RVN war effort."[94] To demonstrate its commitment to liberal democracy, the later Republican regimes removed restrictions on the content and distribution of media.[95] The result was a dramatic increase in the number of newspapers, circulating in the cities in what one writer described as the "relatively freewheeling days of the old South Vietnamese press."[96] "Following Diệm's demise, scores of newspapers hit the streets again … often attacking each other vigorously."[97] "In the midst of war, newspapers and periodicals flourished in Saigon and elsewhere." By 1970, there were thirty-four Vietnamese-language newspapers in circulation, as well as twelve in Chinese, three in English and one in French.[98] According to Arthur Dommen, an American journalist in the South during the war, this "genuine expression of pluralism" was not the result of an elaborate American plot: "The impulse did not come from the American Embassy or the [United States Information Agency]," but from the free market for media that emerged in the wake of the coup.[99]

In the 1960s, intellectuals on the left such as Thích Nhất Hạnh and Nguyễn Văn Trung published books that were openly critical of both the Southern regime and US imperialism. Popular plays such as *Durian Leaves* (*Lá Sầu Riêng*), which aired on South Vietnamese television, explored explicitly communist themes, such as class exploitation in the countryside. In the South, political demonstrations, which would continue until the end of the war, were staged with the official sanction of the South Vietnamese state. The songwriter Trịnh Công Sơn (who was dubbed the "Bob Dylan of Vietnam" by Joan Baez) would become one of the most popular and influential artists of the period for his anti-war songs, songs that were banned in the North by the Communist Party because their poignancy reportedly demoralized listeners.[100] For the Marxist philosopher Trần Đức Thảo, these songs were powerful poetic expressions of political protest that epitomized the difference between the cultural policies in the North and the South:

> [O]ne thing about Sài Gòn ... that shocked me extremely ... were the songs of a young musician from the South, or, in more [politically] correct terms, the "American-Puppet" [regime] ... The lyrics ... touched me so much that I could not hold back my tears. ... I could not understand how authorities in the South could give [Trịnh Công Sơn] the freedom to compose songs that caused people to lose the will to fight ... A regime that gave artists the freedom to sing of such feelings could not be a bad regime. ... [T]he South had a clear degree of democracy. Intellectuals as well as ordinary people ... could openly talk about politics, and criticize the leadership ... In the North, it was not this way. The North was a furnace of dogma ... It is easy to understand that there could have been no room for a Trịnh Công Sơn.[101]

Culture for passing the time

But if the freedom that defined the Republic, a freedom that "at times even caused problems for the government,"[102] served to encourage democratic debate in the South,[103] it would also produce what Võ Phiến describes as an important but unintended transformation in culture. In the cities, the liberalization of media laws and the creation of an economic environment that encouraged "quick profits" would result in a dramatic increase in the flow of foreign cultural goods. In the 1960s, translations

5.2 Bookstall on Tự Do Street, Sài Gòn, April 1969 (Brian Wickham).

of European and American writers – Françoise Sagan, Henry Miller, J. D. Salinger, Saul Bellow and Hermann Hesse – would dominate the market for literature, competing with the titles by Vietnamese authors in the bookstores and street stalls in Sài Gòn.[104]

While readers in the South would become increasingly more interested in literary trends outside the country than in the development of their own national culture, writers preferred to explore "foreign sentiments inspired by the West rather than live in the reality of Vietnam. They raise the problems that usually obsess bookworms rather than the ones that obsess and test the conscience of Vietnamese today."[105] Between 1964 and 1975, *Literature* (*Văn*), one of the most influential reviews during the war, devoted nearly a third of its issues to foreign authors and poets. This was the first time that "a Vietnamese literary publication had given so much attention and priority to non-Vietnamese writers and writings."[106] The lost period of Vietnamese literature, then, was one in which Vietnamese readers and writers had become less and less interested in their own national literature.

The unimagined community

Because this period was defined by the decline of high culture, and because mass "entertainment was the distinguishing feature of this phase" (*tiêu khiển là một đặc điểm của giai đoạn này*),[107] the majority of works in translation were of a popular variety: Mario Puzo's *The Godfather*, Gérard de Villiers's SAS (*Son Altesse Sérénissime*) espionage series, and popular romances such as Eric Segal's *Love Story*. These "books of entertainment [*sách tiêu khiển*] … flooded Sài Gòn all at once … causing many people to panic." "The concern," according to Võ Phiến, "was legitimate." "[M]any, too many were addicted to … Kung-Fu novels." Vietnamese writers and poets warned that "foreign culture would completely eat up the culture of our own people" (*sợ văn hóa ngoại quốc ăn gỏi mất văn hóa dân tộc*).[108]

In the cities, therefore, the same policy of liberalization that promoted democratic debate and artistic expression would also create the conditions for the "cultural invasion," condemned by the Communist Party as an American plot to destroy the national culture. This invasion, however, was not the result of a deliberate strategy. Although mass media was employed in the cities for the purpose of psychological warfare, the aim of the latter was not to assimilate the Vietnamese into American culture.[109] On the contrary, US "advisors … are constantly cautious not to enforce American culture on the Vietnamese."[110] As a means of containing the "tremendous impact of American culture," moreover, US officials encouraged the development of a modern South Vietnamese media based on the national culture.

In his report on a program to establish a television network in the South (the *Truyền hình Việt Nam*), Loren Stone, for example, advised his Vietnamese counterparts to "not look to American packaged programs for their Television operation, as do so many television stations in the Asian area, but to develop programs growing out of their own historical and cultural background."[111] According to Stone, the spread of American popular culture would be inconsistent with the "principal reason for [the] US … wanting to help [the] GVN develop a Television capability," which was "to try to create among the Vietnamese a sense of Vietnamese nationalism. They must identify themselves as part of a nation that has a history, as well as a future."

This national culture, however, as Stone recommended, should not be imposed through the media, as the propaganda of the Communist Party was, as this would be contrary to the policy of freedom. For the sake of democracy, then, programs that promoted the national culture would have to compete with mass entertainment, which was preferred by the

Mass culture in the later Republic

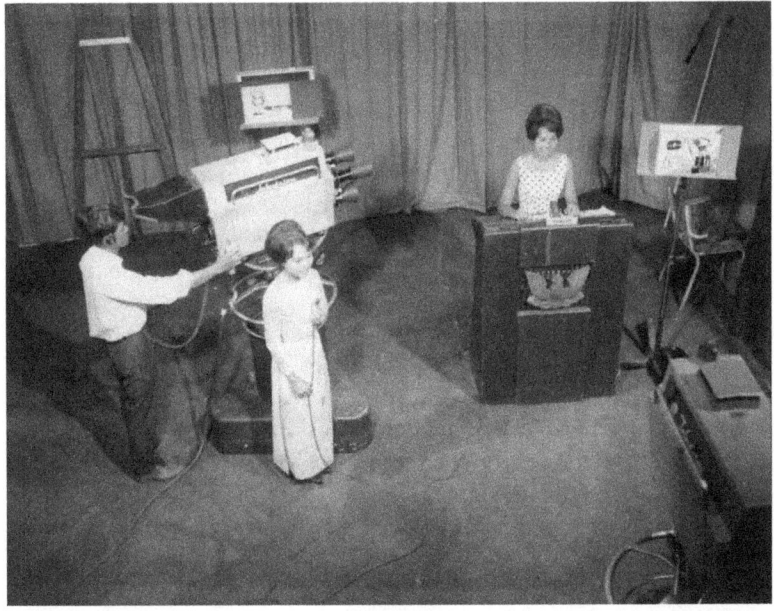

5.3 Taping of the daily news on RVN TV, January 1967 (Đài Truyền Hình Việt Nam Cộng Hòa).

South Vietnamese audience: "It is generally recognized in the United States that 'culture' or 'education' cannot be enforced via Television on a viewing public ... interested in release and entertainment. The general popularity of kitsch is the same in Vietnam."[112]

Stone, therefore, proposed a "middle ground posture": "Vietnamese ... will bring their own history and culture to the mass Vietnamese audience while permitting at the same time the appearance of ... American ... features."[113] While programs on culture and history would serve to inspire a sense of Vietnamese nationalism, the inclusion of kitsch would help to develop the industry in a commercial direction, "encourag[ing] GVN Television to move toward ... support from advertising."[114]

This middle ground, however, would become increasingly difficult to maintain, owing to both the popularity of kitsch in the South and the fact that "nationalism," as one newspaper editor lamented, "did not sell."[115] In the cities, the foreign cultural works that served to diminish the role of Vietnamese literature would also inform the development of a new South Vietnamese popular culture. Like the foreign invasion of mass entertainment, this development was directly tied to the lifting of censorship laws in the South by the generals who carried out the coup against Diệm. In the Southern publishing industry, the immediate consequence of the collapse of the early Republic was the spread of serialized fiction: "After November 1st, 1963, the government wanted to spell out its 'revolutionary' policy by expanding freedom. This freedom ... had [a] ... literary implication: the development of a tendency toward popularization [xu hướng bình dân] and a new form of the novel," the *feuilleton* (*phơi-dơ-tông*).[116]

Thus, in acceding to US demands for democratic reform, the conspirators, "who caused the events of November ... 1963," and who "never thought they would make a significant change in the cultural activities in the South" (*thay đổi khá quan trọng trong sinh hoạt văn nghệ ở Miền Nam*), precipitated the rise of a new form of popular fiction. By simply ignoring the issue of national culture, the South Vietnamese leaders had inadvertently helped to create a new kind of mass culture, the *feuilleton* as an "entertainment commodity for passing the time" (*thứ hàng tiêu khiển để xài nhất thời*).[117]

According to the writer Lê Văn Nghĩa, the *feuilleton* section played an "important role in the formation of a newspaper. In publishing a paper, the owners and managers had to immediately consider serial writers [*tác giả viết truyện dài kỳ*] in order to guarantee readers. ... Saigonese newspapers lived or died by these stories."[118] The "newspaper with the largest circulation during this period was always the one that carried the newest and longest installment of the most appealing knight-errantry story to-date."[119] If the increase in the number of newspapers, then, resulting from the liberalization of media laws, expanded democratic debate, the papers were dependent upon their *feuilleton* sections, which largely determined their sales, as well as the reach they afforded to advertisers. Freed from the sponsorship and control of the state, the expanded media industry would come to rely increasingly on advertising for its very existence. As a result, the need for serial writers would outweigh the demand for journalists reporting news on the war, which became an increasingly unprofitable enterprise: "For Vietnamese," as one Saigon editor complained, "the war has gone on too long. Nobody wants to read about it."

Consequently, "Vietnamese newspapers," which paid extravagant sums to their *feuilleton* writers, employed few "stringers working for them outside of metropolitan Saigon."[120] While newspapers, then, in

Mass culture in the later Republic

the South operated largely without regulation, allowing the "press to run the ... gamut from pro ... to anti-government and anti-U.S. ... in tone," much of the content, precisely because of this freedom, was "given over to ... serialized fiction, horoscopes, and other regularly featured nonnews items that ... enjoy great popularity among readers of the vernacular press." Under a regime of freedom, therefore, the press, rather than simply reporting the facts, would primarily serve as a tool for product promotion through popular fiction: "Saigon's papers ... are short of serious news of any kind, their chief stock in trade being translations of Chinese novels and gaudy sex and crime stories."[121]

This tendency, as one study observed, undermined the effectiveness of government cultural programs and psychological warfare campaigns. Official programs, aimed at creating a sense of Vietnamese nationalism, suffered from a "competitive disadvantage," owing to their "avoidance of non-news and fictional items such as horoscopes and serialized stories [that] ... the commercial press appears to find ... useful to gain and hold readership."[122]

After the coup, increased competition in the burgeoning newspaper industry would result in a dramatic reduction in the price of print media. "Compared to the cost of food for the body, [the cost of food] for the mind," as Võ Phiến writes, "decreased by almost 100 times. Books and newspapers became so incredibly inexpensive."[123] With the advent of newspaper and book rentals during the 1960s, they would become available to even the poorest segments of the urban South Vietnamese population.[124] At the same time, the mass appeal of the serialized fiction published in the daily newspapers would serve to further extend the reach of their advertising.

In the 1960s, the "tendency toward popularization" would dramatically increase the demand for the intellectual labor of individuals engaged in disparate areas of cultural work: "[T]he need for more writers ... was great. Full-time professional writers, even with help from part-time writers, could not keep up with demand. The daily newspapers approached other kinds of writers: novelists, poets, essayists, researchers."[125] While "few writers of any renown" during the earlier part of the war "would deign to write for the large popular dailies,"[126] by the mid-1960s "few ... could resist the lure of the *feuilletons* [phơi-dơ-tông],"[127] including many of the most important literary artists of the period, such as Mai Thảo, Nhã Ca, Nguyễn Đình Toàn and Dương Nghiễm Mậu.[128] While an earlier generation of South Vietnamese artists had aspired to the ideal of culture associated by the Self-Strength Literary Group, in the late 1960s "everyone dreamed of becoming another Kim Dung" (*mơ tưởng trở thành một* Kim Dung), the most successful martial arts writer of the twentieth century.[129]

In the 1960s, therefore, artists and intellectuals who had previously participated in the project of creating a new national culture were recruited en masse to participate in the production of popular fiction. If "millions," then, in the South, "died for the desire to be an officer and a poet, without working for the CIA," poets, living under a "regime of freedom," would be compelled by the market to produce popular works that "would be difficult to call literature." In the South, *feuilleton* writing, as Võ Phiến describes, would provide the primary source of income for Vietnamese who "lived by the pen." While in 1965 authors typically received a royalty of 10,000 *đồng* for new novels (a mere third of the annual income of the lowest government clerk), the average monthly salary for *feuilleton* writers was 15,000 *đồng* per newspaper.[130] Ngọc Sơn, one of the most popular *feuilletonistes* of the period, negotiated a salary of 50,000 *đồng* from the owners of the dailies *Tiếng Chuông* and *Sài Gòn Mới*, in addition to a 100,000 *đồng* retainer for the exclusive right to the use of his pseudonym, Phi Long.[131]

This account of the "tendency toward popularization" in South Vietnamese literature corresponds to Walter Benjamin's analysis of the rise of serialized fiction in France. In this period, the "high payments for the *feuilletons* were grounded in ... the decrease in the cost of newspaper subscriptions," which coincided with an "increase in advertising, and the growing importance of the *feuilleton* section." In France, these conditions led to what Benjamin refers to as "the assimilation of [the] man of letters to the society in which he lived."[132] Poets, who had previously enjoyed a degree of autonomy with respect to the market, were reduced, like the rest of society, to the status of wage laborers: "the man of letters ... goes to the marketplace as a *flâneur* ... to find a buyer."[133] Paid by the word or the page for his "everyday literary merchandise," the poet, employed as a *feuilletoniste*, would learn to "behave as if he had learned from Marx that the value of a commodity is determined by the work-time needed from society to produce it."[134] As a result, the leisure required for the creation of culture would be remunerated as wage labor, while culture became a commodity whose value is measured according to labor time: The *feuilleton* writer "spent his hours of idleness ... as part of his working hours," since his "protracted hours of idleness ... were necessary for the realization of his own labor power."[135]

Mass culture in the later Republic

But as a producer of cultural merchandise, the *feuilleton* writer would be subject to the demands of a market that catered to what Baudelaire called the *hypocrite lecteur*. Hired to work for dailies, the man of letters was forced to write for "the least rewarding type of audience," readers whose "willpower and ability to concentrate are not their strong points. What they prefer is sensual pleasure ... which kills interest and receptiveness."[136] In the 1960s, this hypocritical reader became the subject of a joke that circulated in the publishing world in Sài Gòn. Authors "put the blame for [their] inferior writing squarely on the readers who ... were too lazy to read" (*độc giả lười đọc*).[137] Absorbed into the burgeoning newspaper business, "esteemed and respected" producers of culture were obliged to meet the demands of an uncultured audience, readers who "expressed such ... a weary attitude toward ... cultural activities."[138] Instead of educating the people through the creation of high works of culture, during the war writers "had to mix with the masses" (*phải hòa mình vào quần chúng*), whose will was expressed by the dailies: "The dailies were the masses, the great masses of the people" (*Nhật trình là quần chúng, là quảng đại quần chúng*).[139] "Once you accepted to write for the dailies, [you had] to 'come down into the streets'" (*xuống đường*).[140] As a result, artists were forced to "turn tricks" (*đi khách*) for their readers, prostituting their artistic ability for the production of popular culture, cultural commodities belonging to what Mai Thảo described as the "street civilization" (*văn minh phường phố*) of the South Vietnamese people.[141] In the 1960s, then, poets and writers would be paid to produce "everyday literary merchandise," writing for a mass audience that was too lazy to appreciate art.[142] Thus, "famed men of letters" (*danh sĩ*), who had previously "occupied a lofty place in society," "became much closer to society and their fellow man than in earlier times."[143]

Although South Vietnamese artists, therefore, were free in large part from the control and censorship of the government, they were subordinated to another kind of compulsion. Reduced to the status of workers paid by the private owners of the means of mass reproduction, writers became subject to a time discipline imposed by the free market for media that had emerged in the South. This compulsion not only deprived them of the "peace and leisure" required for the creation of art,[144] it also forced them to create works "that would be difficult to call literature" and compose them at an unprecedented rate of productivity: "It was a difficult situation: although you couldn't be sure it was literature, you had to go on writing it, then publishing it."[145] According to Võ Phiến, writers in the South identified this force of necessity with the compulsion of time itself:

> Agreeing to write for the dailies meant being forced into a trap: once you got "stuck," you were pulled along, unable to stop. But as a consequence, the creative energy of novelists increased dramatically during this period. Writing for several newspapers at a time, continuously for several years, writers would end up with dozens of published works. Without "time" [thời thế] pushing [writers to work], how would they have been so productive?[146]

Between 1952 and 1975, for example, Bà Tùng Long, the most highly paid *feuilletoniste* of the period, produced a hundred novels, dozens of children's books and over a thousand short stories, an immense body of work that was notorious for its atrocious style and implausible plotlines.[147] In the South, then, writers were forced by an impersonal compulsion of "time" to create cultural products on which time was frivolously wasted. The increased productivity, engendered by the time discipline imposed by the free market for media, served to promote an entirely unproductive use of leisure or non-laboring time among the South Vietnamese masses, "passing the time" (*xài nhất thời*) in the midst of an extended state of emergency.

In "The era of consumption and the profession of writing" (*Kỉ nguyên tiêu thụ và nghề viết văn*), a text published shortly before the fall of Sài Gòn, Nguyễn Hiến Lê suggests that this time discipline was a byproduct of American aid. In South Vietnam, the American presence created a "civilization of consumption" (*văn minh tiêu thụ*) accompanied by economic underdevelopment. As a result, the country was able to enter the postindustrial "*ère d'abondance*" in spite of its preindustrial stage of development: "Production was weak, but consumption was strong. Without producing, urban residents could consume as much as… Americans. In terms of consumption, we leaped ahead … to … the postindustrial stage (*giai đoạn hậu kỹ nghệ*)."[148]

In the advanced societies, this post-industrial stage of development was defined by the fact that "people produce everything very quickly and in large quantity, so that trying to produce is easy. It is finding new ways to consume that is difficult."[149] In an era of abundance in which work has been made obsolete by the progress of technology and production,[150] consumption, paradoxically, becomes a necessity for the reproduction of capitalism. In order to preserve the relation between wage labor and capital, "people must think of ways to increase consumption, so that the factory does not have to close and laborers are not unemployed."[151] As a

Mass culture in the later Republic

result of the problem produced by abundance, the "advertising industry appears" as a means of promoting consumption.[152] In the postindustrial era, therefore, consumption becomes a necessary condition for the production of goods, goods that must be consumed, in spite of the fact that they satisfy artificial desires that are invented by advertising.

During the war, this industry was devoted to selling new "entertainment commodities for passing the time."[153] The frivolous consumption of free time, however, was not simply a means of manipulating the masses. Rather, this "waste" (lãng phí), as Nguyễn Hiến Lê explains, was a necessity for the survival of the nation and continuing technological progress (a progress which created this form of necessity by making production so easy that labor was rendered unnecessary). "Waste," then, "is a virtue."[154] It "is a duty to the nation, to the community ... We must waste so that workers can work, so that sellers can sell, so that the community can live, so that the national economy can prosper, so that technology can progress."[155]

The era of abundance, therefore, is defined paradoxically by the need for unnecessary forms of consumption, "waste" which, through the intervention of advertising, creates the demand for production and labor, so that the "community" can continue. Because consumption, in the postindustrial era, is the underlying condition for wage labor and capital, waste is a virtue that is born of necessity. To frame the problem in Personalist terms, man, then, under postindustrial capitalism, is in the service of a sovereign economy in which consumers are forced to squander their free time, so that workers can engage in production by selling their labor as merchandise.

In that sense, the principle of this post-industrial society is directly opposed to that of the Personalist form of community envisioned by the early South Vietnamese leaders, a community for which the "goal of production must be the satisfaction of needs."[156] In the "era of consumption," on the other hand, the community depends on what Guy Debord described as the "distorted principle" of the Society of the Spectacle: "to each according to their false needs."[157] "Because there is so much production, new ways to consume must be found. The advertising industry appears. It creates additional needs for people."[158]

In the South during the war, this principle, as Nguyễn Hiến Lê describes, was one that was also applied to the objects of culture: "Just like in industry... creators of culture produce so that readers can consume," while "readers have to quickly consume so that creators of culture can produce and not be unemployed."[159]

As Mai Thảo described, this compulsion of time on the production of culture required Vietnamese artists to develop a new "way of writing" (*bút pháp mới*). The "phenomenon of the long story written in episodes, published periodically on the pages of newspapers ... pushed ... the pens of professional writers today toward the discovery of new stylistic approaches" (*một văn thể mới*). In contrast, however, to the "new art concepts" that Mai Thảo, as the editor of the journal *Creation*, had previously proposed as the basis for a "dialectical revolution" in Vietnamese literature, these new stylistic approaches were defined precisely by the absence of style and art: "[F]or the dailies, a story line could not ... be too dense and subtle, and the writing itself had to be plain and direct."[160]

In order to appeal to a *hypocrite lecteur* who lacked the "ability to concentrate," required for the reception of art, Vietnamese writers would turn to another medium as the model for developing a new popular prose. This, which included television and film, as Phạm Duy points out, became widely available as a result of the war: "When the Americans brought their money and guns to Việt Nam, they also brought ... new technologies [to] ... an agricultural society," which had previously possessed "a predominantly oral tradition of popular art." Although these technologies had the "ability to aid the development of art" (*khả năng giúp ích cho việc phát triển nghệ thuật*), in the South, they would also serve to reinforce habits in the reading public that undermined its capacity for aesthetic experience.[161] As Mai Thảo observed, the preference for sensual pleasure among South Vietnamese readers, encouraged by the consumption of television and film, would give rise to a new mode of writing in serialized fiction:

> Hundreds of thousands of martial arts movies excited the senses [*hâm nóng cảm giác*], dulled every thought [*làm ngỡ ngàng mọi tưởng trước*], exasperating all of these shortcomings, and transported this chaos [*bộn bề*] into the novel published in our newspapers today ... [Stories today must follow] the direction of cinema ... [We must] coordinate the way that we write with the way movies are made. In summary, this is the technique of the detective movie, breathless, sensual, always creating a tension ...[162]

This description closely corresponds to Benjamin's account of serialized fiction: "Literature submits to montage in the feuilleton."[163] Like popular cinema, the new stylistic approach adopted by South Vietnamese writers would allow for what Benjamin referred to as a mode of *"reception in distraction,"* appropriate for readers "too lazy to read," lacking the "ability to concentrate," and preferring "sensual pleasure."¹⁶⁴ As a result of its serialization, "[l]iterature submits to montage in the feuilleton." According to Benjamin, this distracted form of reception is opposed to the "contemplative immersion" required for the appreciation of artworks, artworks the experience of which presupposes the ability on the part of the reader to concentrate and recall intricate organization or structure.¹⁶⁵ In mass culture, this aesthetic experience is replaced by what Theodor Adorno described as a pleasure devoid of all concentration or effort. In the culture industry, the reduction of artistic creation to a rationalized process of labor – a process that deprives the artwork of its artistic organization and style – produces a form of leisure that is devoid of all traces of work, a "workless time [that] must not resemble work in any way whatsoever."¹⁶⁶ In the distracted reception that characterizes mass entertainment, "active contribution" in the experience of culture or art "is denied to the subject by industry."¹⁶⁷ The application of industrial technique to the production of art, therefore, gives rise to a completely deinstrumentalized leisure, a "free time" that emerges, paradoxically, as the exact mirror opposite (or "afterimage") of the total instrumentalization of labor within capitalism.

During the war, this mindless form of amusement would become a distinguishing feature of the society that emerged in the South, one that was explicitly thematized in the poetry of the period – poetry that most of the public was too lazy to read.¹⁶⁸ In Nguyễn Đức Sơn's "*Một mình nằm thở đủ kiểu trên bờ biển*" (Lying Alone Breathing in Every Way on the Beach), for example, this vacuous and effortless experience of pleasure, in which one "forgets all torments and worries," is referred to as *sướng*: "First I blew out a sigh/and it was as though every worry and torment went with it/after a pause I blew out a sigh/and every illusion blew away into the empty space/exhilarated [*sướng*], I breathed heavily."¹⁶⁹

According to Võ Phiến, this "vulgar" (*sỗ sang*) and "unaesthetic" (*chướng*) expression "was never a part of the language of poetry, either modern or ancient."¹⁷⁰ Unlike the aesthetic enjoyment afforded by past works of art, which could be "appreciated again and again, the way our forefathers did," this vulgar pleasure is one that, like popular culture, is quickly consumed and forgotten: "Today the masses need more, read more, consume more, but once they've finished using something, they throw it away and forget about it, and immediately look for something new."¹⁷¹ As Nguyễn Hiến Lê emphasized, this wasteful form of gratification was entirely separate from the way that literary works had once been appreciated: "[L]iterature in this era of consumption is produced for consumption [*tiêu thụ*], like Coca-Cola and nylon, not for enjoyment [*thưởng thức*]."¹⁷²

Thus, subordinated to the discipline of time imposed by the market for media, South Vietnamese writers were compelled to produce "entertainment for passing the time," embodying a "workless leisure" that could be consumed in a continual cycle of mindless amusement.

In communist sources, this compulsion, born of the "regime of freedom" that prevailed in the South, is identified as the deliberate product of an American neocolonial policy. This policy was implemented by "cultural mercenaries" who created products that "appealed to man's base instincts [and] ... instigated a rat race inspired by pleasure":[173]

> In neo-colonial society ... people live at a hysterical tempo, art aims only at giving them transient pleasure as they follow, for instance, the intricacies of a hopeless love affair, or watch a scene of swordsmanship or some act of robbery and murder in a far-off land.[174]

During the 1960s, the unaesthetic experience of "transient pleasure" would become increasingly pervasive as a result of the spread of media such as the cinema, which served as a model for the reduction of art into popular culture, providing distraction for the Vietnamese masses. In the South, then, cinema would betray its promise as the *"septième art,"* synthesizing all the others (architecture, sculpture, painting, music and poetry) to become a supreme "art of the masses."[175] While film – along with the other new forms of "technological reproduction" (*phương tiện kỹ thuật*), which were "widely disseminated ... when the Americans poured into Vietnam," helped to "spread works of art to the masses with a new and powerful momentum, at the same time, it lowered standards."[176] Instead of providing the people with culture, these new forms of media were used to repackage elite forms of high art for commercial consumption. Poets became overnight celebrities by adapting their works to popular musical styles, which were performed by attractive young female singers on television or radio.[177] Authors were rated according to the number of works that had been made into movies.[178] Rather than encouraging a genuine appreciation of art, this mass reproduction of culture merely produced the "appearance of respect for the written word, for a 'literature' that was not really literature."[179]

In the South, the technological media would also be used as a means of manipulating the masses, as an instrument of "advertising" or "publicity" (*quảng cáo*) that increased the commercial value of cultural products that were devoid of artistic merit:

Put to music or made into a movie, poetry and fiction [were able to] expand their audiences multifold ... Music and film gave poetry and fiction a tremendous publicity. And publicity became an important aspect of the cultural activities of this post-1963 phase. It had been known to create the value [giá trị] of a piece of writing, or at least a curiosity and demand on the part of the masses.[180]

This form of mass manipulation would become a distinguishing characteristic of South Vietnamese culture. According to Võ Phiến, "publishers and distributors ... began to apply new techniques to their ventures, just as their colleagues had done before them in other businesses, and with equal success. Publicity was a very effective tool, one that could not be ignored." Publishers became adept at using "the fear of seeming ... old-fashioned [to] propel people to the bookshops to buy ... books ... and to the theaters ... to see ... movies."[181]

During the war, then, media in the South was not employed primarily for the purpose of creating an "imagined community," but for persuading the South Vietnamese people to purchase mass entertainment and other commodities. This entertainment, however, was intended almost entirely for the urban South Vietnamese market. As the violence increased in the countryside, "all artistic life and activities were concentrated in the cities: the rural areas were left to fend for themselves." As a result, the "rural population became separated from [the country's] overall cultural activities." Consequently, "there was no rural readership in the period of '54–'75."[182] Cut off from the countryside by the war of attrition, South Vietnamese writers were compelled, by the discipline of the market, to produce popular culture for an imagined community that was largely confined to the cities.[183] Writing for dailies that paid more for the tales that appeared in their *feuilleton* sections than reports on the war in the countryside, Vietnamese authors sought to appeal to an audience that was almost exclusively urban. As a result, "little by little," the peasantry "disappeared from the new writings." While writers in the colonial era had identified the peasantry with the Vietnamese people as such, during the war, "hardly anyone in the generation of young authors even so much as mentioned them."

Thus, instead of imprinting the nation on the minds of the South Vietnamese masses, the regime of media freedom that prevailed in the 1960s would serve, as Võ Phiến describes, to psychologically reinforce the divide between the rural and urban population. The countryside "became indifferent to the culture of the cities and the towns" while the "peasantry, their lives, and activities … became pale, distant memories in the minds of city authors and writers."[184] Contrary to communist critics, however, this separation was not the "wicked aim of the US-Puppet regime," seeking to "obscure the image of the countryside which was then being destroyed," by enslaving the masses by means of the decadent products of US neocolonialism.[185] Rather, it was a result of the policy of liberalization that prevailed under the Republican government. Freed from the control of the state, the market that imposed a compulsion of "time" upon Vietnamese writers, creating cultural products for "passing the time," would also give rise to an uneven distribution of media, separating the cities from the rest of the country.

After the war, this unimagined community, created by a liberal regime of media freedom, would be suppressed by the Communist Party, replaced by state propaganda and an officially sanctioned national culture:

> Within twelve months more than 3,000,000 books were printed in Ho Chi Minh City, and some 170,000 books and 450,000 pictures (mostly of Ho Chi Minh) were sent down from Hanoi. The writings of Ho Chi Minh himself received the highest priority. Works by Marx, Lenin, and Engels were also featured, along with books presenting the achievements of the Vietnamese Communist party.[186]

Notes

1 Võ Phiến, *Hai mươi năm Văn Học Miền Nam: Tổng Quan* [Twenty Years of Literature in South Vietnam, 1945–1975: Overview] (Nhà Xuất Bản Văn Nghệ: Westminster, 1986), 19. "Sovereignty, Surveillance, and Spectacle in South Vietnamese Spy Fiction" was originally published in *positions*, 26:1, 111–50 (Copyright 2018, Duke University Press. All rights reserved. Republished by permission).

2 The Official Policy of Repression in the Socialist Republic of Vietnam. VCA. 2322305001 January 1, 1982. Box 23, Folder 05. Douglas Pike Collection: Unit 06 – Democratic Republic of Vietnam.

3 Nguyễn Văn Lục, "Đọc Và Nhận định *Cuộc Xâm Lăng Về Văn Hóa Và Tư Tưởng Của Đế Quốc Mỹ*" [American Imperialism's Invasion of Culture and Thought by Lữ Phương] http://www.quehuongta.com/index.php/41-vn-hc-a-ngh-thut/cau-chuyn-vn-hc/139-c-va-nhn-nh-cuc-xam-lng-v-vn-hoa-va-t-tng-ca-quc-m-i-nguyn-vn-lc. Last accessed May 11, 2016.

4 Phạm Văn Sĩ, *Văn học giải phóng miền Nam* [Literature of the Liberated South] (Hà Nội: Nhà xuất bản Đại học và Trung học chuyên nghiệp, 1975).

Mass culture in the later Republic

5 Võ Phiến, *Hai mươi năm Văn Học Miền Nam*, 22.
6 Principal Reports from Communist Press Sources, 4. VCA. 2321830001 March 22, 1971. Box 18, Folder 30. Douglas Pike Collection: Unit 06 – Democratic Republic of Vietnam.
7 Hà Xuân Trường, "Cuộc đấu tranh chống ảnh hưởng của văn hóa nghệ thuật tư sản" [The Struggle against the Influence of Bourgeois Culture and Art]. *Nghiên Cứu Nghệ Thuật* (1) (Hà Nội: Viện Nghệ Thuật), 1977.
8 Thạch Phương and Trần Hữu Tá, *"Những nọc độc văn nghệ thực dân"* [Neocolonial Poisons in the South] *Tạp chí Cộng Sản* (8) 1977, 54.
9 Principal Reports from Communist Press Sources, 4.
10 Black Market Makes Ho Chi Minh City Run. VCA. 0720125061 August 9, 1979. Box 01, Folder 25. John Donnell Collection. See also Fact Sheets, Office of Information: Command Information Division – re: Elections1971, Black Market, Alcohol, Drug Abuse, and First Aid – Record of MACV Part 1. VCA. F015800090718 September 15, 1971. Box 0009, Folder 0718. Vietnam Archive Collection.
11 Nguyễn Xuân Lai, "Economic Gears and Levers," 163.
12 Kolko, *Anatomy of a War*, 204.
13 Nguyễn Khắc Viện, *Southern Vietnam, 1975–1985* (Hanoi: Foreign Languages Publishing House, 1985), 22.
14 Vietnam Feature Service, TCB-059 – Third renaissance ... Culture in Vietnam, 5. VCA. 2321827010 1969. Box 18, Folder 27. Douglas Pike Collection: Unit 06.
15 Nguyễn Khắc Viện, *Southern Vietnam*, 32.
16 Ibid., 22.
17 Ibid., 32.
18 Nguyễn Đức Cường, "Building a Market Economy in Wartime," in *Voices from the Second Republic of South Vietnam (1967–1975)*, ed. K. W. Taylor (Ithaca, NY: Southeast Asia Program Publications), 95.
19 Hoang Nhu Ma, "The strangle of neocolonialism is being broken in South Vietnam," *Độc Lập* (October 20, 1976), 1, 6, 19–24.
20 Principal Reports from Communist Press Sources. VCA. 2321830001 March 22, 1971. Box 18, Folder 30. Douglas Pike Collection: Unit 06 – Democratic Republic of Vietnam.
21 Cửu Long Giang, "Âm nhạc phản động" [Reactionary Music], *Nghiên Cứu Nghệ Thuật*, 10 (1976), 44.
22 Saigon Savant condemns cultural "Enslavement" by U.S. says LPA. VCA. 2321828001 November 1970. Box 18, Folder 28. Douglas Pike Collection: Unit 06 – Democratic Republic of Vietnam.
23 Principal Reports from Communist Press Sources, 6.
24 Trần Quang, "Vài suy nghĩ về tàn dư văn hóa thực dân mới ở Miền Nam hiện nay" [Reflection on the remnants of neo-colonial culture in contemporary South Vietnam], *Văn hóa Nghệ thuật*, 1 (1976), 12.

25 Mạc Đường, "A number of theoretical bases of U.S. psychological warfare," *Nhân Dân* (November 25, 1973). VCA. 2171413009. Box 14, Folder 13. Douglas Pike Collection: Unit 03 – Insurgency Warfare.
26 Nguyễn Vĩnh Long, "Changes in Saigon's stage and cinema," *Vietnamese Studies*, 52 (1978), 125.
27 Thạch Phương and Trần Hữu Tài, "Những nọc độc văn nghệ thực dân," 48.
28 Tran Quang, "Vài Suy Nghĩ về tàn tích văn hóa thực dân mới ở miền Nam hien nay' [Several reflections on the vestiges of neo-colonial culture in the South today], *Văn hoá nghệ thuật*, 1 (1976), 12.
29 Huỳnh Minh Siêng, Vietnamese Culture Defeats Culture of U.S. Imperialists. VCA. 2320718050 September 1974. Box 07, Folder 18. Douglas Pike Collection: Unit 06 – Democratic Republic of Vietnam.
30 Philip Taylor, *Fragments of the Present: Searching for Modernity in Vietnam's South* (Honolulu: University of Hawaii Press, 2001), 32.
31 Lữ Phương, *Cuộc xâm lăng về văn hóa và tư tưởng của đế quốc Mỹ tại miền Nam Việt Nam* [The American Empire's Invasion of Culture and Ideas in South Vietnam] (Hà Nội: Nhà xuất bản Văn Hóa, 1985), 165.
32 Huỳnh Minh Siêng, "Vietnamese culture defeats culture of US imperialism," *Học Tập*, 9 (September 1974), 68–74.
33 Fanon, *The Wretched of the Earth*, 155.
34 Youth Student Union Urges Action Against Depraved Culture – South Vietnam. VCA. 2321839002 May 27, 1975. Box 18, Folder 39. Douglas Pike Collection: Unit 06 – Democratic Republic of Vietnam. On the RVN's economic dependency and "addiction" to American aid, see Guy Gran, "Vietnam: The Human Costs of the American Aid Programs – An Alternate FY 75 Foreign Aid Proposal," Indochina Resource Center, May 1975, Douglas Pike Collection: Unit 03 – Antiwar Activities, VCA.
35 "Interview with Nguyễn Khắc Viện," *Viet Nam Courier* (April 1976).
36 Vietnam News Agency, Hanoi (January 14, 1978), Foreign Broadcasting Information Service (January 16, 1978).
37 Taylor, *Fragments of the Present*, 30.
38 Kolko, *Anatomy of a War*, 202–3. See also Mạc Đường, "A number of theoretical bases of U.S. psychological warfare."
39 Trần Ngọc Dinh, "'Viện trợ' Mỹ: Nhân tố quyết định sự tồn tại của chế độ Nguỵ quyền Sài Gòn" [American Aid: The Determining Factor in the Existence of the Saigon Puppet Regime], in *Nghiên Cứu Lịch Sử*, 177 (1978), 51.
40 Kolko, *Anatomy of a War*, 203.
41 Võ Phiến, *Hai mươi năm Văn Học Miền Nam*, 15.
42 Phạm Duy, *Hồi Ký*, 189–90.
43 Quoted in Võ Phiến, *Hai mươi năm Văn Học Miền Nam*, 46.
44 Boitran Huynh-Beattie, "Saigon Art During the War," in *Cultures at War: The Cold War and Cultural Expression in Southeast Asia* (Ithaca, NY: Southeast Asia Program Publications, 2010), 87.

45 Bảo Ninh, *Nỗi buồn chiến tranh: tiểu thuyết* (Hà Nội: Nhà xuất bản Trẻ, 2011), 283.
46 Đinh Quang Anh Thái, "Dương Thu Hương: '30 tháng Tư 75, nền văn minh đã thua chế độ man rợ'" [Dương Thu Hương: April 30th '75, Civilization Loses to a Barbaric Regime], *Người Việt* (April 12, 2012).
47 For a discussion of cultural policies in the North, see Kim Ngoc Bao Ninh, *A World Transformed: The Politics of Culture in Revolutionary Vietnam, 1945–1965* (Ann Arbor: University of Michigan Press, 2002), 252.
48 David G. Marr, "A Passion for Modernity: Intellectuals and the Media," in *Postwar Vietnamese Society: An Overview of Transformational Dynamics*, ed. Hy V. Luong. Institute of Southeast Asian Studies (Singapore, Lanham, Boulder, New York and Oxford: Rowman & Littlefield Publishers Inc., 2003), 274.
49 Võ Phiến, *Hai mươi năm Văn Học Miền Nam*, 34.
50 Ibid., 50.
51 Nguyễn Hiến Lê, "Tình hình xuất bản trong năm 1964" [The situation of publishing in the year 1964], *Tin Sách*, no. 35, 5–1965.
52 Nhất Linh, "Văn hóa ngày nay với văn hóa việt nam" [Contemporary Culture and Vietnamese Culture], *Văn Hóa Ngày Nay* [Contemporary Culture], 17-6-1958, 17.
53 Bà Tùng Long, *Hồi Ký Bà Tùng Long* [Autobiography of Bà Tùng Long] (Hà Nội: Nhà Xuất Bản Hội Nhà Văn, 2014), 146.
54 V. Phiến, *Hai mươi năm Văn Học Miền Nam*, 184.
55 "In a new reality in which there exists so much material and energy, art and literature obviously cannot return to the realism of Nguyễn Công Hoan, the romanticism of Thanh Châu … or the Tự Lực themes." Mai Thảo, "Đứng Về Phía Những Cái Mới" [Standing in the direction of the new], in *Tuyển truyện Sáng Tạo Kỳ* [Stories of the Creativity Group] (Fort Smith, AR: Sống Mới, 1982?), 8–13.
56 Nguyễn Hiến Lê, *Hồi Ký Nguyễn Hiến Lê*, 564.
57 Võ Phiến, *Hai mươi năm Văn Học Miền Nam*, 30.
58 Nguyễn Hiến Lê, *Hồi Ký Nguyễn Hiến Lê* [Memoir of Nguyễn Hiến Lê] (Thành phố Hồ Chí Minh: Nhà xuất bản tổng hợp thành phố Hồ Chí Minh, 2012), 562–3.
59 Võ Phiến, "Nhìn lại 15 năm văn nghệ miền nam" [Looking back on 15 years of South Vietnamese arts and culture], *tạp chí Bách Khoa* (361–2), January 15, 1972, 40.
60 David Marr, *Vietnamese Tradition*, 149.
61 Ibid., 352.
62 Ibid., 2.
63 Marr, "A Passion for Modernity," 272.

The unimagined community

64 On periodicals in the North, see Report, USIA Research and Reference Service – North Vietnam's Propaganda Apparatus. VCA. 20580504016 August 1965. Box 05, Folder 04. Fred Walker Collection.
65 Phạm Duy, *Hồi Ký*, 56. See also Duyên Anh, *Nhìn lại những bến bờ: hồi ký văn nghệ* Looking Back at the Shore: A Memoir of Art] (Los Alamitos, CA: Xuân Thu, 1988), 271. On US support for media in the RVN, see Booklet, Agency for International Development – USOM Vietnam Operational Report, 55–62. VCA. 21470210001 1963 to 1964. Box 02, Folder 10. Vincent Puritano Collection.
66 See Nguyễn Việt Chước, *Lược Sử Báo Chí Việt Nam* [A Brief History of the Vietnamese Press] (Sài Gòn: Nam Sơn, 1974), 64.
67 David Marr, *Mass Media in Vietnam* (Canberra: Department of Political and Social Change, Research School of Pacific and Asian Studies, Australian National University, 1998), 3.
68 Vũ Bằng, *Bốn mươi năm nói láo* [Forty Years of Lying] (Sài Gòn: Cơ sở Xuất Bản Sống Mới, 1969), 218.
69 Ibid., 221.
70 Phạm Duy, *Hồi Ký*, 96.
71 Võ Phiến, *Hai mươi năm Văn Học Miền Nam*, 73.
72 Ibid., 75.
73 See Mai Thảo, "Con đường Dương Nghiễm Mậu" [The Path of Duong Nghiem Mau], in *Chân dung mười lăm nhà văn nhà thơ Việt Nam* [Portrait of 15 Vietnamese Writers] (Westminster, CA: Văn Khoa, 1985), 89.
74 Dương Nghiễm Mậu, "Rượu Chưa Đủ," in *Tuyển truyện Sáng Tạo*, ed. Mai Thảo (Fort Smith, AR: Sống Mới, [1982?]), 41.
75 Võ Phiến, *Hai mươi năm Văn Học Miền Nam*, 119–20.
76 Ibid., 109.
77 Vũ Khắc Khoan, *Thần Tháp Rùa: truyện* (Sài Gòn: Ngày Nay, 1964), 14.
78 Võ Phiến, *Hai mươi năm Văn Học Miền Nam*, 225.
79 Ibid., 226.
80 Ibid., 230.
81 Phạm Duy, *Hồi Ký*, 276.
82 Cited in Bernard Weinraub, "US Impact on Vietnam Called 'Devastating,'" *New York Times*, June 10, 1968.
83 Nguyễn Đức Cường, "Building a Market Economy during Wartime," 94.
84 Arthur J. Dommen, Kahin's intervention: Turning wartime propaganda into peacetime myths, 17. VCA. 2360803011 January 1990. Box 08, Folder 03. Douglas Pike Collection: Unit 08 – Biography.
85 Paper – The Political Factor in Pacification: A Vietnam Case Study [Draft], 16. VCA. 21470122001 No Date. Box 01, Folder 22. Vincent Puritano Collection.
86 Vinh The Lam, *Republic of Vietnam 1963–1967: Years of Political Chaos* (Hamilton, ON: Hoai Viet, 2010), 6.

87 The Political Factor in Pacification.
88 Nguyễn Huy, *Hiện Tình Kinh Tế Việt Nam* (quyển 1) [The Economic Situation in Vietnam] (Sài Gòn: nhà xuất bản Lửa Thiêng, 1972), 12-13.
89 Võ Phiến, *Hai mươi năm Văn Học Miền Nam*, 79-80.
90 Ibid., 200.
91 Ibid., 79-80.
92 Ibid., 72.
93 Ibid., 120.
94 Indochina Monographs – Intelligence. VCA. 1070821001 January 1, 1982. Box 08, Folder 21. Glenn Helm Collection, 27.
95 PSYOPS Quick Response Team, Summary Report # 4, sponsored by the Advanced Research Projects Agency of the U.S. Department of Defense – "History of the Viet-Nam Ngay Nay" – includes results of readership survey, 12. VCA. 2322024001 October 27, 1970. Box 20, Folder 24. Douglas Pike Collection: Unit 06 – Democratic Republic of Vietnam.
96 Nguyen Ho, Erasing Vietnam's Past, 18. VCA. 2322205059 November 1, 1978. Box 22, Folder 05. Douglas Pike Collection: Unit 06 – Democratic Republic of Vietnam.
97 Marr, *Mass Media in Vietnam*, 3. In 1963, there were only forty-four daily newspapers in Sài Gòn (*Đoàn Thêm, 1945-1964 Việc từng ngày - Hai Mươi Năm Qua* [1945-1964 Everyday Affairs – Twenty Years Ago] (Saigon: Phạm Quang Khải, 1968-71), 373) By the end of the war, there were over 1,000 printing establishments and 150 publishing houses (Nguyễn Khắc Ngữ, *Những ngày cuối cùng của Việt Nam Cộng* [The Final Days of the Republic of Vietnam] (Montreal: Nhóm Nghiên-cứu Sử-địa, 1979), 79).
98 "History of the Viet-Nam Ngay Nay," 12.
99 Dommen, Kahin's intervention, 16.
100 On Trịnh Công Sơn, see John C. Schafer, "The Trịnh Công Sơn Phenomenon," *The Journal of Asian Studies*, 66:3 (2007), 597-643.
101 Trần Đức Thảo, *Những lời trăn trối* [Some Final Testaments] (Tổ hợp Xuất bản Miền Đông Hoa Kỳ, 2014), 211.
102 Quoted in Võ Phiến, *Hai mươi năm Văn Học Miền Nam*, 71.
103 See Joseph Treaster, "South Vietnamese Revisiting Outmoded Press Laws," in *Political Censorship*, ed. Robert Goldstein (Chicago: Fitzroy Dearborn, 2001), 266-7.
104 The Official Policy of Repression in the Socialist Republic of Vietnam, 5.
105 Quoted in The Urban Intelligentsia in South Vietnam Fight American Neocolonialism. VCA. 2311102013 July 1970. Box 11, Folder 02. Douglas Pike Collection: Unit 05 – National Liberation Front.
106 Võ Phiến, *Hai mươi năm Văn Học Miền Nam*, 240-1.
107 Ibid., 80.
108 Ibid., 241-2.

109 For an overview of US psychological warfare programs involving media, including radio, television and print, see Report, JUSPAO Support – Talking Paper: Psychological Operations in Vietnam. VCA. 20580214002 1968. Box 02, Folder 14. Fred Walker Collection and Book, Joint United States Public Affairs Office – JUSPAO Vietnam General Briefing Book. VCA. 20580214005 November 1966. Box 02, Folder 14. Fred Walker Collection.
110 Loren Stone, Report, NBC International – Television in Vietnam, 32. VCA. 20580309001. 1 April 1967 Box 03, Folder 09. Fred Walker Collection.
111 Ibid., 30.
112 Ibid., 31–2.
113 Ibid., 34.
114 Ibid., 22.
115 Nghiêm Xuân Thiện, "*Vấn đề Phát hành báo chí ở Việt Nam*" [The Problem of Newspaper Distribution in Vietnam], *Thời Luận*, July 29, 1955.
116 Võ Phiến, *Hai mươi năm Văn Học Miền Nam*, 221. For an overview of the changes in RVN cultural policy concerning literature, written from a North Vietnamese perspective, see Nguyen Duc Dan, "The Ideological Struggle in Literature Continues in Temporarily Occupied Areas in South," *Van Nghe* (Hanoi, January 8, 1971), 10. Folder 08, Box 04. Douglas Pike Collection: Unit 05: National Liberation Front.
117 Võ Phiến, *Hai mươi năm Văn Học Miền Nam*, 223.
118 Lê Nghĩa Văn, "Về 'Truyện Dài Kỳ', Một Chuyên Mục Nhật Báo Trước 1975" [On the serialized story: a daily newspaper column before 1975], Trieuxuan. info, November 21, 2015, trieuxuan.info/print.php?id=13449&catid=7. Last accessed July 29, 2019.
119 Indochina Monographs – Intelligence. VCA. 1070821001 January 1, 1982. Box 08, Folder 21. Glenn Helm Collection, 27.
120 "History of the Viet-Nam Ngay Nay," 11.
121 License Vs Liberty. VCA. 2322023035 February 1967. Box 20, Folder 23. Douglas Pike Collection: Unit 06 – Democratic Republic of Vietnam.
122 History of the Viet-Nam Ngay Nay, 14.
123 Võ Phiến, *Hai mươi năm Văn Học Miền Nam*, 88–9.
124 "History of the Viet-Nam Ngay Nay," 13.
125 Võ Phiến, *Hai mươi năm Văn Học Miền Nam*, 221–2.
126 Ibid., 48.
127 Ibid.
128 Lê Văn Nghĩa, "Về truyện dài kỳ trước 75."
129 Trần Nhật Vy "Feuilleton – Hàng độc của báo chí quốc ngữ thời xưa" [Feuilleton – quốc ngữ print products of the past], *Tuổi Trẻ Online*, October 31, 2016. https://tuoitre.vn/feuillton-hang-doc-cua-bao-chi-quoc-ngu-thoi-xua-1209955.htm. Last accessed July 28, 2019.
130 Võ Phiến, *Hai mươi năm Văn Học Miền Nam*, 48–9.
131 Ibid., 78.

132 Walter Benjamin, "The Paris of the Second Empire in Baudelaire," in *Walter Benjamin: Selected Writings*, vol. 4: *1938–1940*, ed. Michael W. Jennings (Cambridge, MA: Belknap Press of Harvard University Press, 2003), 14.
133 Ibid., 17.
134 Ibid., 14.
135 Ibid.
136 Benjamin, "On Some Motifs in Baudelaire," in *Selected Writings*, vol. 4: *1938–1940*, ed. Michael W. Jennings (Cambridge, MA: Belknap Press of Harvard University Press, 2003), 313.
137 Võ Phiến, *Hai mươi năm Văn Học Miền Nam*, 76. According to Nhất Linh, "the role of the reader is very important, even more important than that of the writer." "The level of a nation's culture does not depend on its writers, but rather its readers." Nhất Linh, *Viết và đọc tiểu thuyết* (Sài Gòn: Nhà xuất bản Đời Nay, 1969), 101.
138 Nhất Linh, "Văn hóa ngày nay với văn hóa việt nam," 17.
139 Võ Phiến, *Hai mươi năm Văn Học Miền Nam*, 223.
140 Ibid., 222.
141 Mai Thảo, "Lời tựa" (Preface), *Chú Tư Cầu* [Cầu, The Eighth Uncle], by Lê Xuyên (cơ sở xuất bản Đại Nam, Glendale, CA), 7.
142 Benjamin, "The Paris of the Second Empire," 14.
143 Võ Phiến, *Hai mươi năm Văn Học Miền Nam*, 42.
144 "I keep thinking that if writers had been able each day to sit down and write and write at their leisure, revising and revising just a few books, then the results would have been better … [Instead they] had to perform the back-breaking work of writing ten or more *feuilletons* every day, for years on end," ibid., 76.
145 Ibid., 225.
146 Ibid., 222.
147 Bà Tùng Long, 111.
148 Nguyễn Hiến Lê, "Xã Hội Việt Nam Trong Thời Mĩ" [Vietnamese society during the American period], Bút sen, http://butsen.net/thuvien/hoi-ky-nguyen-hien-le. Last accessed July 29, 2019.
149 Ibid.
150 Nguyễn Hiến Lê, "Kỉ nguyên tiêu thụ và nghề viết văn" [The era of consumption and the profession of writing], *Mười Câu Chuyện Văn Chương* [Ten literary tales] (California: Văn Nghệ xuất bản, 1986), 155.
151 Ibid., 149.
152 Ibid., 148.
153 Võ Phiến, *Hai mươi năm Văn Học Miền Nam*, 223.
154 Ibid., 149.
155 Nguyễn Hiến Lê, "Xã Hội Việt Nam Trong Thời Mĩ."
156 *Đảng cương Cần lao Nhân vị Cách mạng Đảng* [Principles of the Cần Lao Personalist Revolutionary Party].

The unimagined community

157 Guy Debord, "The Decline and Fall of the Spectacle-Commodity Economy," in *The Situationist International Anthology*, trans. and ed. Ken Knabb (Berkeley: Bureau of Public Secrets, 2007), 187.
158 Nguyễn Hiến Lê, "Kỉ nguyên tiêu thụ và nghề viết văn," 148.
159 Ibid., 153–4.
160 Quoted in Võ Phiến, *Hai mươi năm Văn Học Miền Nam*, 222.
161 Phạm Duy, *Hồi Ký*, 173–4.
162 Mai Thảo, "Lời tựa" (Preface), 6.
163 Walter Benjamin, *The Arcades Project*, trans. Howard Eiland and Kevin McLaughlin (Cambridge, MA: Belknap Press of Harvard University Press, 1999), 13.
164 Walter Benjamin, "Work of Art in the Age of Reproducibility," in *Walter Benjamin: Selected Writings*, vol. 4: *1938–1940*, ed. Michael W. Jennings (Cambridge, MA: Harvard University Press), 269.
165 Ibid., 266.
166 Theodor W. Adorno, *The Culture Industry: Selected Essays on Mass Culture* (London: Routledge, 1991), 189.
167 Max Horkheimer and Theodor W. Adorno, *Dialectic of Enlightenment: Philosophical Fragments*, ed. Gunzelin Schmid Noerr (Stanford, CA: Stanford University Press, 2002), 98.
168 Võ Phiến, "Nhìn lại 15 năm văn nghệ miền nam," 41.
169 Nguyễn Đức Sơn, "Một mình nằm thở đủ kiểu trên bờ biển." Góc Nhìn: bài vở, tranh ảnh, ca khúc biểu dương văn hóa Việt Nam [Perspective: documents, pictures, songs in praise of Vietnamese Culture]. http://www.gocnhin.net/cgi-bin/viewitem.pl?2913. Last accessed October 27, 2018.
170 Võ Phiến, *Hai mươi năm Văn Học Miền Nam*, 235.
171 Ibid., 226.
172 Nguyễn Hiến Lê, "Mười Câu Chuyện Văn Chương," 151.
173 Interview with Culture Minister Nguyen Van Hieu. VCA. 2361006019. May 31, 1985. Box 10, Folder 06. Douglas Pike Collection: Unit 08 – Biography.
174 Nguyễn Vĩnh Long, "Changes in Saigon's stage and cinema," 125. In a futile attempt to reach the South Vietnamese masses, enslaved by this neocolonial culture, Communist cells in the cities inserted propaganda materials between the covers of *wuxia* novels by Kim Dung. (See Indochina Monographs – Intelligence. VCA. 1070821001. January 1, 1982. Box 08, Folder 21. Glenn Helm Collection.)
175 Phạm Duy, *Hồi Ký*, 172.
176 Võ Phiến, *Hai mươi năm Văn Học Miền Nam*, 228.
177 Ibid., 227. See also Trần Cùng Sơn, *Một thoáng 26 năm* [A brief 26 years] (San José, CA: Hương Quê, 2011), 414.
178 Ibid., 229.
179 Ibid., 230.
180 Ibid.

181 Ibid., 229.
182 Ibid., 80–4.
183 "History of the Viet-Nam Ngay Nay," 2.
184 Võ Phiến, *Hai mươi năm Văn Học Miền Nam*, 269. Two notable exceptions to this trend were the writers Sơn Nam and Lê Xuyên whose works depicted rural life in the South.
185 Cửu Long Giang, "Âm nhạc phản động" [Reactionary Music], *Nghiên Cứu Nghệ Thuật*, 10, 44.
186 Neil L. Jamieson, *Understanding Vietnam* (Berkeley and Los Angeles: University of California Press, 1993), 362.

6

Surveillance and spectacle in Bùi Anh Tuấn's Z.28 novels

Introduction

This chapter develops a reading of one of the most successful examples of South Vietnamese popular culture: Bùi Anh Tuấn's Ian Fleming-inspired Z.28 novels. Between 1965 and 1974, over 5 million copies of the stories were sold,[1] at a time when the average first edition run for a novel was only 2,000 copies.[2] The novels belonged to what the South Vietnamese writer and critic Võ Phiến describes as a new "entertainment culture," or "culture for passing the time" (*văn hóa tiêu khiển*).[3] In contrast to traditional forms of cultivated amusement and leisure, associated in the colonial era with figures such as the *phong lưu* or the gentleman, this culture for passing the time was identified with the new forms of recreation and play (*ăn chơi*) that appeared as part of the consumer society that emerged in the 1960s and 1970s.[4] These new varieties of commercialized leisure, moreover, were bound up with the persuasive power of advertising (*quảng cáo*), a power that observers described as a paradoxical form of compulsion exercised through the promise of mindless amusement and pleasure, rather than discipline or physical forms of coercion.[5]

In the Z.28 series, the model of advertising provides the primary resource for much of the novels' appeal, featuring narratives of surveillance composed of passages that often read like commercials for name-brand commodities. In that sense, the novels can be understood as a sort of universal endorsement for the "neocolonial" culture that emerged in the South. But if the success of the celebrity superspy in the Z.28 series was due in large part to the latter's appeal as a figure of vicarious consumption for readers, the spy was also a symbol for the South Vietnamese state and

Surveillance and spectacle

its precarious position within the broader political context of the Cold War. The novels' apparently frivolous tales of high mass consumption, set in a world reduced to an advertised image, also involve a reflection on the place of the nation within the geopolitics of the period.

In *Specter over Red Square* (*Bóng Ma Trên Công Trường Đỏ*) – one of the most popular novels in the Z.28 series – the Cold War is depicted as a conflict in which espionage and surveillance serve as a means of perpetuating the spectacle of an atomic catastrophe. At the same time, the purely spectacular threat of a potential nuclear exchange, secured through surveillance, is described in the series as a means of maintaining the balance of terror. The series, then, is set in a fictional Cold War universe in which the combined security apparatus of the USA, the USSR and the Republic of Vietnam (RVN) are deployed in order to prevent other nations from using atomic weapons in actual warfare, thereby preserving their purely spectacular use for the purpose of nuclear deterrence. Conversely, deterrence appears as a spectacle orchestrated by the USA and the USSR in order to justify the surveillance that serves to maintain the appearance of a potential nuclear catastrophe. Surveillance, then, provides support for spectacle as well as vice versa.

This characterization of the Cold War in South Vietnamese popular fiction is consistent with Western accounts of the role of nuclear deterrence. Drawing upon the critiques of surveillance and spectacle developed in the works of Guy Debord and Michel Foucault, Jean Baudrillard argued, for example, that the virtual threat of a global nuclear exchange provided the pretext for the establishment of a universal security apparatus operated primarily by the two nuclear powers.[6] A similar analysis of the Cold War appears in Carl Schmitt's *Theory of the Partisan*, a text that was written in part as a reflection on the anti-colonial wars in Vietnam and Algeria. These two unconventional (but non-nuclear) confrontations were waged not as actual wars, but as police interventions or security measures that occurred in the framework of an emerging balance of terror. In the text, Schmitt describes this balance of terror as an instrument used by the USA and the Soviet Union to impose a virtual state of emergency on the rest of the world.

Reading the Z.28 novels in dialogue with this account of the partisan war in the context of nuclear deterrence, I argue that the novels' depiction of the South Vietnamese state calls attention to a key implication of Schmitt's characterization of the Cold War in relation to his theory of sovereignty and his concept of the political. In the novels, the RVN, as embodied in the figure of the Vietnamese superspy, appears as a state that is unable to assert its political sovereignty owing to its dependence on American military and financial assistance. Constrained, moreover, by the virtual threat of a global nuclear exchange to fighting a limited war with the North (which excluded the possibility of real political enmity), the republic was deprived by its American ally of the sovereign political right to decide upon the state of emergency. Insofar as the decision on the "extreme case of war" (as Schmitt argues in earlier writings) constitutes the condition of the political as such, this situation is one in which politics itself is precluded by the policy of nuclear deterrence employed by the two superpowers for the purpose of imposing a virtual state of emergency.

In the novels, this virtual state of affairs collapses the properly political distinction between friend and enemy. As a superpower patron whose economic assistance appeared to undermine the political sovereignty of the RVN, the American government is portrayed as both an ally and an object of political enmity. In the Z.28 novels, this ambivalent friend is opposed by its South Vietnamese partner not through overt forms of resistance, but rather through the act of consuming American aid in the form of brand-named commodities and by overindulging in the new forms of commodified leisure and play associated with the modern consumer society that American aid had helped to establish. In the novels, therefore, the celebration of consumerism implies both an endorsement of the "neocolonial" culture that emerged in the South and a repudiation of the imperialism or dependence on American aid that this culture embodied. The novels, then, owe their appeal to an obsession with commodity culture that served simultaneously as advertising for the consumer society of which the novels themselves were a part and as an ambivalent figure of enmity or antagonism toward the republic's primary sponsor. In the novels, therefore, the American government appears as an ambivalent partner that undermines South Vietnamese sovereignty through the very support it provided to its political ally, as well as by imposing a policy of deterrence that, from the republic's perspective, restricted its sovereign right of decision in the extreme case of war.

This depiction of the ambiguous position of the South Vietnamese state recalls the "theory of 'sovereign indecision'" that appears in Walter Benjamin's "exoteric" exchange with Schmitt.[7] This theory was one that Benjamin would pursue in his work on mass reproduction, a phenomenon that, according to Benjamin, created the conditions not only for the development of mass culture and media, but also for the rise of the cult of the Führer, with its spectacular aestheticization of politics and political sovereignty.⁸ In works such as the reproducibility essay, therefore, Benjamin appears to engage in a broader reflection on the relationship between modern political power and the apparently depoliticizing effects of mass culture and media. These works, then, suggest a connection within Benjamin's writing between his critique of the state of exception as the extrajuridical domain of political power and sovereignty,⁹ and the concept of the "state of distraction," as the historically appropriate mode of collective reception for popular works of mass reproduction.¹⁰

As a conflict "accompanied by a large scale dissemination of novels, films, magazines," an extended state of emergency that coincided with the spread of mass culture and media, the war in Vietnam in the South provides a particularly compelling occasion to revisit, and to revise in a non-Western setting, Benjamin's fragmentary reflections on the relationship between the political and popular culture.¹¹ These reflections appear particularly appropriate to the purposes of this book, given Benjamin's interests in many of the Western forms of *paralittérature* – including the detective story and the *feuilleton* – which writers like Bùi Anh Tuấn would attempt to adapt to the Vietnamese context both before and during the war. In this chapter, therefore, Benjamin's writings will provide a key critical resource in developing a more nuanced assessment of South Vietnamese popular works from the period, works such as the Z.28 novels that have been largely dismissed in the Vietnamese scholarship produced since the war as imperialist propaganda, "spreading corruption and pornography or proselytizing anti-communism."¹²

Bùi Anh Tuấn

Bùi Anh Tuấn's career is exemplary of his generation of writers, both in terms of his commitment to liberal democracy and the constraints that this free market for media imposed on his work. During the 1950s and 1960s, he worked as a columnist, radio editor, war correspondent and *feuilleton* writer for numerous periodicals in the South, including *The People* (*Dân Chúng*), *Political Commitment* (*Chính luận*) and the newspaper *Action* (*Hành Động*), which he ran single-handedly.¹³ During the Buddhist-led protests against the regime of Ngô Đình Diệm, Bùi Anh Tuấn, circumventing state censorship laws, published articles in foreign newspapers attacking the government. These articles resulted in several "close calls with the Saigon secret police." In the following year, Bùi Anh Tuấn's criticism of official corruption and state censorship in *Action* led to the closure of his one-man newspaper, and his "imprison[ment] without trial by the very generals who overthrew President Diệm."[14]

After the closure of *Action*, Bùi Anh Tuấn established a publishing house of the same name, and following the liberalization of media laws shifted his attention from political journalism to spy novels and crime fiction, producing commodities for a developing market for "entertainment culture" or "culture for passing the time," which expanded dramatically after the assassination of Diệm. What began as a hobby would now become the mainstay of Bùi Anh Tuấn's work as a writer. After 1963, his efforts would be primarily devoted not to informing the South Vietnamese public on the current political climate, but to "entertain[ing] the readers" and "help[ing] them forget the anxiety of everyday life" during the war.[15]

Although spy fiction in the South was never as popular a form of *paralittérature* as martial arts novels, its "influence upon our 'literature for passing the time,'" as Võ Phiến explains, "cannot be overlooked: stories about this spy or that spy, Dr. No or Dr. Mo, terrifying accounts of life under the Nazis, Mafia activities ... any Western detective or spy novel was snapped up as soon as it was translated."[16] The first edition of Bùi Anh Tuấn's first spy novel, *Case of the Stolen Atomic Documents* (*Một Cụ Đánh Cắp Tài Liệu Nguyên Tử*), written under the pen-name Người Thứ Tám, was published in 1965. The first edition sold out in three weeks, establishing him as the "no. 1 spy fiction writer in Vietnam" (at least according to the publicity on the back cover of his novels).[17] As we have seen, according to Nguyễn Nguyệt Cầm, over 5 million copies of Bùi Anh Tuấn's novels were sold between 1965 and 1974,[18] and "hundreds of thousands of readers devoured serialized versions of [the novels] in daily newspapers prior to publication."[19] His total output during these years amounted to over sixty novels and seventeen works of non-fiction, making him the "most productive writer in 20th century Vietnamese history."[20] In that sense, Bùi Anh Tuấn's career exemplifies what Võ Phiến described as the "difficult situation" that Southern writers confronted – writers who were compelled by "time" to produce cultural commodities on which time is frivolously wasted, giving "birth to [a] phenomenon unique to our time, a time of vast communication, and enormous consumption, namely, literature as a consumer's product."

Surveillance and spectacle

The Cold War balance of surveillance and spectacle

The Z.28 novels are set in the Cold War universe of Ian Fleming's Bond series, a fictional universe into which the Vietnamese Secret Affairs Bureau (*Sở mật vụ*) is inserted as another institutional player alongside the various Western intelligence agencies and international criminal organizations that appear in the Bond novels (SMERSH, MI-5, GRU and SPECTRE). Many of the stories take place in the "pleasure periphery," the "tourist belt surrounding the industrialized world ... dependent upon the neo-colonialism of the tourist industry," luxury resorts as well as red light districts in cities such as Bombay, Saigon and Bangkok.[21] In the novel *Golden Regret in India* (*Hận Vàng Ấn Độ*), Bangkok is described as a "center of carnal forms of relaxation serving American military personnel" (*trung tâm giải trí xác thịt của quân nhân Mỹ*).[22] These cities are situated within a larger imaginary Cold War geopolitical space, a fictional and ideological world system organized around the two poles of "free nations" (*quốc gia tự do*) and "communist dictatorships" (*chế độ độc tài cộng sản*).

In *Specter over Red Square* (*Bóng Ma Trên Công Trường Đỏ*), Bùi Anh Tuấn provides a glimpse into the misery of everyday life under a communist regime:

> He [Văn Bình] was walking down the main thoroughfare of the Soviet capital, where the Museum of History and Lenin Museum are located ... During the day, there are usually visitors ... going into the GUM department store to stare at the goods, or paying 3 rubles for a ticket to look at the outside of the Kremlin, the central offices of the Soviet authorities, or visiting Lenin's mausoleum, founder of the Communist Party and the Soviet state. Previously, Stalin's body was placed beside Lenin's, but it has since been carried off somewhere. This is life behind the iron curtain: no one dares to think of tomorrow, because no one knows what tomorrow will bring.[23]

In this passage, Moscow is described as a tourist and consumer nightmare, a dreary city whose only attractions are a state-owned supermarket, the administrative headquarters of a totalitarian bureaucracy and the tomb of a former dictator. During his stay in Moscow, Văn Bình encounters uncooperative waitresses, busboys and hotel staff who serve bad food and provide even poorer hospitality services, which always include complementary wire-tapping and undercover KGB escorts. As the character Guy, a US embassy official in *Specter*, explains to Văn Bình, the general lack of motivation among service workers in the Soviet

Union is the result of state ownership of restaurants and hotels: "In the West, restaurants and hotels have to please their guests to survive. Here, the state is the sole proprietor, and it doesn't need to make a profit and worry about losses. If you enter a store and you can't wait for service, you're always welcome to leave."[24]

As these descriptions of Moscow suggest, free nations and communist dictatorships are not primarily depicted in the novel as embodiments of opposing political ideologies, nor as antagonistic forms of social organization. Communism, for example, does not mean collective ownership over the means of production, but rather something like total state monopoly over consumer goods and services, a system of hierarchical consumption, a society in which fine food, expensive aged liquors, luxury sports cars, designer clothing and beautiful women are the exclusive prerogative of a bureaucratic elite and the latter's trusted agents and bodyguards.

Meanwhile, those excluded from membership in the bureaucratic elite "cannot even dream" of affording such consumer pleasures, whose price is "higher than anyone can imagine." In the Soviet Union of the Z.28 novels, ordinary people are condemned to shop at poorly stocked state supermarkets, which, as Văn Bình explains, means "that you have to stand in long lines, waiting forever for ration tickets." "Since the bloody dictator Stalin died," he adds, "the lines have become somewhat shorter, and the goods more plentiful. But naturally the quality is just as bad as before."[25]

Communism, then, is characterized by the suppression of consumer choice, as well as by the subordination of the latter to state political objectives. Freedom, conversely, is equated with consumer sovereignty, which is why for Văn Bình the fact that pornography is not made available on American commercial flights represents a fundamental contradiction to the principles of democracy: "Western airlines usually carry all sorts of reading material, except the kind that men tend to enjoy the most, erotic reading material. Văn Bình never really understood how America could be a free country [*nước tự do*] and yet prohibit Playboy magazines on airplanes. It's true that Playboy contains mainly pictures of naked women, but these, nevertheless, are aesthetically pleasing images."[26]

The "realism" of such passages – and of the novels' detailed descriptions of historical monuments, restaurants and hotels in both the free world and Soviet bloc – have been attributed by readers to the author's imaginative reworking of content taken from travel brochures and tourist guides.[27] As this realism would seem to suggest, communism

Surveillance and spectacle

and democracy are portrayed in the novels as two particular regimes of consumption, different systems for the distribution of consumer goods, or, to borrow an expression from Guy Debord, variations on the form of the commodity-spectacle, "concentrated" and "diffused."[28] The consumer product, or more precisely the advertising image or spectacle, is presupposed as something like the elementary cell or fundamental building block of this imaginary Cold War universe, the basic descriptive unit or textual category around which the narrative is organized. To use Debord's reformulation of the opening lines to *Capital*, "Life is presented as an immense accumulation of *spectacles*."[29]

During the war in Vietnam, such spectacles became a ubiquitous feature of urban life in the South:

> In the West, the role of advertising commodities [*quảng cáo cho món hàng*] has long been significant, but we had to wait until … the '60s before this became an important event [in Vietnam]. In the past, one had to use ads in order to sell, yet the ads … were discreet. Later, starting in the West … publishers and distributors employed techniques of business administration and communications technology … And they were right. Advertising had an enormous effect. In the end, no one could resist it. … People in the [Vietnamese] cities were easily manipulated by advertising.[30]

This new urban environment is reflected, of course, in popular works from the period such as the Z.28 series. In the novels, the object world is rendered by means of the language of tourist guides and advertising more generally (tailored, of course, to suit urban Southern Vietnamese tastes and sensibilities), a language that is used indiscriminately to depict everything from wine and women to cigarettes: "Văn Bình removed a fresh cigarette and offered it to the [Russian] agent. Soviet cigarettes make your mouth dry, so the agent was thrilled to have one of Văn Bình's sweet-smelling Salem menthols. He tapped the end of the cigarette gently on the side of his glass."[31] "When central European women make love … it's like a hurricane … Of course, Hungarian women are the most famous for lovemaking, not only in Europe, but all over the world."[32]

As the reference to Salem brand cigarettes indicates, advertising does not serve merely as an implicit model for Bùi Anh Tuấn's descriptive prose, as, for example, in the case of the various invented or fictional brand names that appear in many of the novels: Eram-brand running shoes in *Golden Regret* and the Maxman advertising company in *Specter*. Rather, the novels contain what appear to be real advertisements, or rather fictional advertisements for real luxury and consumer products, embedded in passages that read as though they could have been lifted directly from actual ads and promotional material:

> The Rolls [Royce] company produces 2000 cars every year in only 4 or 5 different models. The cheapest is 10 times as expensive as a French [Citroen] DS, and the most expensive is 15 times the price. Although Văn Bình was by no means short on funds, he couldn't even imagine owning a Phantom VI, though he liked them immensely. Despite its size – 1.8 meters in height and 6 meters long, longer than most U.S. luxury cars – it was as fast as a missile, ran very smoothly, [was] soothing to the ears, and the seating was incredibly comfortable.
> "This is a beautiful car," Văn Bình exclaimed.
> Bani laughed. "Yes, but it's old. This year's Phantom VI model comes with a special refrigerator, telephone and television ... My bad back often keeps me awake at night. I go and sit in the Rolls to ease the pain."[33]

The Cold War and the deterrence of sovereignty

As in the Bond series, however, the ubiquity of commodity-spectacles in the Z.28 novels serves as the pretext for a universal surveillance. In *Specter*, for example, Văn Bình is sent on a secret mission to the USSR, posing as an American advertising executive whom the CIA suspects is involved in a Soviet plot to flood the American market with cheap Russian-made goods in order to "win over the affection of the American people."[34] "Publicity" (*quảng cáo*), then, provides the occasion for an extrajuridical intervention or "international warfare" (*chiến trận quốc tế*) carried out continually by a global security apparatus operating in violation of the norms of international law under the cover of commodity-spectacles. If life, then, appears in the novels as an immense accumulation of spectacles, the spectacle is also portrayed as a disguise for a generalized surveillance in a representation of the geopolitics of the Cold War that recalls Foucault's critique of Debord in *Discipline and Punish*: "Our society is one not of spectacle, but of surveillance; under the surface of images, one invests bodies in depth."[35]

This universal surveillance, however, which occurs under the surface of images, turns out in the end to be a part of a larger conspiracy orchestrated by the two superpowers. In *Specter*, the suspected Soviet plot to employ an American advertising agency to destroy the US economy is later revealed to be only a ploy in a much more elaborate plan: Văn Bình is enlisted by the KGB to thwart a Chinese scheme to trigger World War III by staging a nuclear missile assault on the USA from Albania (Người

Thứ Tám).³⁶ In the novel, therefore, the ultimate object of surveillance by the state is to prevent the deployment of the nuclear apparatus in actual warfare, the goal, in other words, of deterrence.

As Jean Baudrillard and others have argued, the policy of deterrence was not merely intended to avert the possibility of an atomic exchange. Rather, by preserving the *virtual* threat of atomic war, deterrence also provided the "pretext for installing a universal security system," authorizing the unlimited extension of an extrajuridical surveillance that "insinuated itself from the inside into all the cracks of daily life.³⁷ In that sense, the goal of the secret intelligence operation in *Specter* – an operation involving the combined security resources and surveillance capabilities of the USA, the RVN and the USSR – is to perpetuate the image of atomic annihilation by precluding its real possibility. The goal, in other words, is to preserve a spectacle that authorizes the universal surveillance that is used to protect it.

From the perspective of Carl Schmitt's concept of the political, this operation constitutes a paradoxical form of political action. On the one hand, it is a properly political act, defined in Schmitt's terms as an action based upon a sovereign decision as opposed to a legal or juridical judgment that merely applies an existing convention or law.³⁸ Yet the aim of this extrajuridical action is precisely to avert what Schmitt describes as the very "presupposition which … creates a specifically political behavior": the *Ernstfall* or "extreme case" of war that "discloses the possibility which underlies every political idea, namely, the distinction between friend and enemy."³⁹ During the course of the Cold War, the extreme case of a nuclear exchange was quickly precluded as a real possibility by policymakers owing to its enormous destructive potential, a potential that exceeds any political goal it could possibly be used to accomplish.⁴⁰ An implicit consensus emerged among leaders in Moscow and Washington that the only "rational use" of atomic weapons was not preparation for war but increased deterrence as the best guarantee of world peace.⁴¹ This view, as a character in the *Case of the Stolen Atomic Documents* describes, was embraced by scientists in both the USA and the USSR, who "believed the only way to protect world peace is to share atomic secrets with everyone in the world."⁴² Thus, the only way to deter the deployment of nuclear weapons in war is to make them available to everyone in the world, thereby depriving individual states of any political advantage that these weapons could be used to secure.

With the development of atomic weapons, therefore – weapons that had once appeared as the ultimate instrument of national sovereignty –

the USA and Soviet Union were compelled, paradoxically, to relinquish the sovereign right to decide on the extreme case of war.[43] In establishing a state of deterrence, in other words, the two sovereign nations would decide, so to speak, to postpone the decision on the state of exception, a decision on the *Ernstfall* from which "human life," according to Schmitt, "derives its specifically political tension."[44] Thus, with the invention of the ultimate political weapon, the only politics that could be rationally pursued by the two superpowers was to prevent the properly political use of this weapon in war. In this politics, then, the fundamental relationship of political enmity that defined the Cold War – the friend/foe distinction between free nations and communist dictatorships – is set aside in order to preserve the possibility of politics itself.

But since "all politics," as Schmitt argues in the *Concept of the Political*, "is terminate[d] … whenever the possibility of fighting disappears" (that is, when the "possibility of the extreme case … [of] the real war" has been neutralized), the policy of deterrence constitutes a politics that paradoxically outlives the disappearance of its own condition of possibility.[45] No longer oriented toward the "extreme case" of an atomic exchange, politics during the Cold War became what Schmitt describes in the *Theory of the Partisan* as a simulated state of emergency:

> In the shadow of the current atomic equilibrium between the world powers, beneath the glass cover, so to speak, of their vast means of destruction, room for limited and contained war conducted with conventional weapons and even weapons of mass destruction could be de-limited. While the great powers could unite publicly or silently on the matter of degree, it would produce a war in the way of a *dogfight* controlled by these world powers. It would be an apparently harmless play of a precisely controlled irregularity, a sort of "ideal disorder," ideal insofar as it could be manipulated by the great powers.[46]

In *Theory of the Partisan*, then, the sovereign decision on the state of exception – which appears in Schmitt's early writings as the very condition of the political as such – is suspended in the "harmless play of a precisely controlled irregularity." This regulated state of exception was staged by the two fundamental antagonists of the Cold War, political enemies who, in a sort of unified gesture of sovereign inaction, were compelled to withhold a decision upon the properly political distinction between friend and enemy.

Surveillance and spectacle

Surveillance and style

In the fictional Cold War universe of *Specter*, therefore, the generalization of the advertising image corresponds to a normalized state of emergency imposed under the virtual threat of an atomic catastrophe. Văn Bình's intelligence operations take him across a landscape composed of consumer images – walking pin-up models, life-size fashion ads and alcohol commercials – providing cover for an international security apparatus used to perpetuate the very spectacle that authorizes its extralegal activities. His success as an agent of government surveillance depends upon his ability to operate effectively in this environment of commodity-spectacles. For Văn Bình, this means more than simply possessing a mastery of martial arts, firearms and explosives. It requires more than just his uncanny sixth sense (*giác quan thứ sáu*) and his proficiency in dozens of languages. It requires, first and foremost, the ability to embody what Marx called the "economic *fictio juris*" that prevails in bourgeois societies, in which "everyone, as a buyer, possesses an encyclopedic knowledge of commodities."[47] And insofar as the imaginary universe of the Z.28 novels is composed almost entirely of consumer images, this encyclopedic knowledge amounts to a knowledge of the world as such.

Văn Bình's worldliness, then, is based on his understanding of the world of consumer commodities. His extensive knowledge of European fine wines and exotic foreign liqueurs allows him to blend in with the locals and adapt himself to every tourist destination to which his work may take him. His knowledge, then, is not merely a sign of sophistication. It is essential to his work as a secret agent, as a spy operating in an object world of commodity-spectacles in which all the signs, clues and pieces of evidence that will eventually lead to the unraveling of the mystery, to uncovering the plot and to thwarting the international criminal conspiracy are themselves consumer images. In *Specter*, for example, Văn Bình identifies a KGB agent who has been trailing him by the sound of his GUM-brand leather shoes, purchased at a state-run supermarket in Moscow:

> The heavy, deafening sound revealed the identity of the KGB agent in his GUM shoes ... One of the ... goods people always complain about is leather shoes. The shoes are poorly made to begin with, the leather is even poorer in quality, and it becomes soft when the weather is warm and hard as steel when it gets cold. The Soviet Union is cold all year round so the GUM shoes are sheer torture to wear.[48]

The unimagined community

It is primarily this use of the knowledge of consumer goods that distinguishes Văn Bình from the older figure of the detective in Vietnamese fiction, in particular the character of the detective/reporter Lê Phong in the writer Thế Lữ's adaptations of the Sherlock Holmes stories, published in the 1930s. In the following scene from Thế Lữ's *The Treacherous Appointment* (*Đòn Hẹn*), Lê Phong applies his observational skills in analyzing the physiognomy of the criminal mastermind, Lương Bằng:

> His face had an elegant, aristocratic appearance, and he had the gentlemanly air of someone who came from that educated and *phong lưu* class of men. He was well-proportioned, slightly taller than average, fashionably dressed, impeccable and yet unselfconscious. Under the taut collar of his immaculate white shirt, he wore a tidy, expensive-looking white cravat [*ca vát*] matching the handkerchief hanging from the pocket of his suit.[49]

In this passage, Lê Phong confronts an adversary whose intelligence, wit and refinement are equal to his own. The qualities reflected in Lương Bằng's impeccable dress are those of a *phong lưu*. As the colonial-era journalist and scholar Nguyễn Văn Vĩnh explains, the *phong lưu* is a man of leisure who embodies the idea of:

> ease, elegance, taste … good form, independence … jauntiness [and] detachment from all mean interests that excite vulgar men … One will never see a *phong lưu* man … listening breathlessly to stock exchange news … Outward events have no effect on him, yet he knows everything, interests himself in everything and understands everything … [The] *phong lưu* gambles, smokes and drinks. But he gambles without being a gambler … An agitated spirit, preoccupied by the thousands of demands which modern civilization imposes on life, engages itself with difficulty in such pleasures, which are over-refinements of another order.[50]

While the *phong lưu* "has no equivalent in French," what distinguishes this class of men, in Thế Lữ's novel at least, is a specifically French article of clothing: the necktie or *cravate*. According to Balzac, the *cravate* in nineteenth-century France served as an outward sign used to separate the man of private means, "*l'homme qui ne fait rien*," from the ordinary class of "*l'homme qui travaille*."[51] After the French Revolution and the abolition of sumptuary laws – laws that had prescribed for "each class of society … its costume" ("one recognized by his dress the lord, the bourgeois, the artisan") – "all became equal in their rights as well as their toilette, and the difference in the fabric and cut of their clothing could no longer distinguish their [social] conditions." In this "milieu de … [l']uniformité," the *cravate* "was called upon to reestablish all of the

Surveillance and spectacle

nuances" of social station and status. It became an "external sign that distinguished the rank of each individual."[52] For Balzac, the *cravate* was the expression of an innate personal style, one that, like an inherited fortune or title affording a lifestyle of leisure, appears to be naturally attached to the individual who owns it: "*Ce n'est ni par étude ni par travail qu'on arrive à bien; c'est spontanément, c'est d'instinct, d'inspiration que se met la cravat.*"[53]

As an outward marker of class in a society based on the principle of political equality, the *cravate* can be understood as an attempt to restore something resembling a precapitalist form of public display, an aura of authority or innate personal quality embodied in an aristocratic code of behavior, dress, demeanor and rhetoric.[54] Instead of creating a new noble code of conduct, however, the display of this older form of publicity in nineteenth-century France in the form of articles of clothing such as the *cravate* produced the phenomenon of fashion, and the latter's historical function as a means of expressing social distinctions in a postrevolutionary period in which the sartorial codes and signs denoting privilege and rank could no longer be fixed by tradition and law.[55]

As Edward Fuchs has argued, however, the phenomenon of fashion was not simply determined by a "concern for segregating the classes." It was also conditioned by the "private-capitalist mode of production, which in the interests of profit ... must continually multiply the possibilities of turnover."[56] The variations in fashion in nineteenth-century France, in other words, were also the result of the tendency of manufacturers to mass-produce ever-cheaper facsimiles of the fashion worn by the upper classes, threatening the latter with a loss of their signs of public distinction. In that sense, fashion can be characterized as an example of what Walter Benjamin described as compensation for the "obliteration of the individual's traces in the big-city crowd," the dissolution of individual "aura," expressed through appearance or dress, in the context of an urban environment in which the proliferation of commodities rendered the external signs of social distinction increasingly illegible.[57]

As Balzac points out elsewhere in his writings, however, the anonymity of the big city prompted a similarly compensatory response on the part of the postrevolutionary French government, a state that imposed "a civilization which ... will soon have the whole country, down the smallest plot of land, in its registers."[58] Thus, the emergence of a "*milieu de ... [l']uniformité*," in which fashion developed as a means of maintaining social distinction, coincided with the extension of a system of national surveillance, or what Benjamin describes as a "multifarious web of registrations," employed by the state as a "means of compensating for the elimination of traces that takes place when people disappear in the masses of the big cities." "Since the French Revolution, the extensive network of controls had been bringing bourgeois life ever more tightly into its meshes."[59] The disappearance in the cities of individual signs of distinction constitutes, therefore, the condition of both fashion as a modern form of public display or publicity as well as what Foucault referred to as discipline and panoptic surveillance.

For Benjamin, these two compensatory responses to the anonymity of urban existence were combined in the detective story: "The original social content of the detective story focused on the obliteration of the individual's traces in the big-city crowd."[60]

> The detective story came into being when the most decisive of all conquests of a person's incognito [in the application of photography to criminology which "made it possible for the first time to preserve permanent and unmistakable traces of a human being"] had been accomplished. Since that time, there has been no end to the efforts to capture a man in his speech and actions.[61]

The detective, then, is a figure whose skills of observation enable him to register the traces of individuality effaced by the uniformity of the urban milieu. His elegance, refinement and good taste allow him to distinguish the idiosyncrasies of character that would otherwise be lost in the anonymity of manner and dress produced by a private-capitalist mode of production that threatens to reduce the urban population to an illegible uniformity of appearance.

Free time and leisure

To return to the earlier passage from the detective story by Thế Lữ, it is the observation of such individual traces that allows Lê Phong to immediately distinguish Lương Bằng from the ordinary rung of petty criminals and to identify him as a *phong lưu* whose "ease, elegance, taste ... good form [and] independence" separate him from the class of "vulgar men." Lương Bằng's elegant manner and style is the mark of individual character, one that could not be acquired through the purchase of commodity-fashions, whose proliferation, as a result of the market, threatens to render the urban environment illegible, obliterating the traces upon which the detective depends in order to identify the perpetrator of crimes.

Surveillance and spectacle

In Thế Lữ's detective story, then, surveillance serves to distinguish an individuality that can still be uncovered beneath the surface of commodity images. In the Z.28 novels, on the other hand, the individuality detected by means of surveillance is not buried under the appearance of products. Rather, it is a function of the commodity fashions worn by individual characters: "Jack ... wore a silk suit, silk shirt and silk tie [cà-vạt]. Thailand is a country that is famous for producing silk, and yet his silk clothes were from Italy, and obviously more expensive. The outfit alone gave him away as a high-ranking paper-pusher at the CIA regional affairs office."[62]

Unlike Lương Bằng, the character Jack from *Golden Regret* is not a man of private means but a member of the CIA's managerial elite. His expensive silk clothes are not the signs of an inherited fortune and a lifestyle of leisure but of a comfortable desk job that comes with a sizable disposable income. In contrast to Lê Phong, then, Văn Bình's skills of detection do not rely on a sense of personal style cultivated by a *phong lưu* with the leisure required in order to develop his own individual character. Rather, it depends on a brand-name snobbism that allows for the classification of criminals according to their profile as individual consumers. This snobbism, of course, marks Văn Bình as belonging to the same class of privileged employees he is assigned to investigate. His salary as a superspy, along with his "special allowances" from the Bureau of Secret Affairs, enable him to indulge in the same luxury goods and commodified pastimes enjoyed by his opponents in the other intelligence services.

These pastimes, moreover, are not the refined amusements of the *phong lưu*, pursued with a "detachment from all mean interest that excite vulgar men," but rather expensive but uncivilized forms of "play" (*ăn chơi*), such as sex tourism and the consumption of premium American-brand whiskey. In *Golden Regret*, these pastimes are described as a way to "kill time": "To kill time I have to drink wine and play [*chơi bời*]." Văn Bình, then, is not a *phong lưu* but a "playboy" (*kẻ chơi bời*), a more recent expression that connotes not civilized leisure but excessive enjoyment of unrefined amusement and pleasure associated with consumer society.[63]

These kinds of play correspond to what Adorno referred to as "free time," a form of disposable time that, in contrast to leisure, is detached from the ideal of self-cultivation. As Adorno explains, "leisure is the privilege of an unconstrained, comfortable lifestyle," a form of disposable time that is not "shackled" to labor time, in the Marxian sense of the latter as the measure of the value of commodities.[64] "Free time," on the other hand, is a form of time that presupposes the exchange of commodities, and the development of industrial production to the point in which a relative abundance of use-values gives rise to a kind of superfluous time; a time in excess of that necessary for the accumulation of capital but which remains, nevertheless, dependent upon the latter as its presupposition. This time, then, is made available to be organized and converted into the products of what the Frankfurt school referred to as the "culture industry"; in Adorno's words, into the "preoccupations with which [one] becomes mindlessly infatuated merely in order to kill time."[65]

In that sense, the task of surveillance performed by the detective and the spy constitute the expenditure of distinct forms of non-labor time. For Lê Phong, detective work is an activity of leisure, one that he pursues with a detachment that is at once scientific and aristocratic. He is a character who views inexplicable murders and other gruesome crimes as a type of logical puzzle, solvable by means of the skills of detection and deduction he has acquired during his many idle hours. Like his European counterparts, Lê Phong can be described, to borrow Benjamin's well-known formulation, as a *flâneur* with a bourgeois justification for his idleness, a dilettante who applies the powers of deduction that he has cultivated at his leisure to the detection of crime in the service of society, a figure in which "forensic knowledge [is] coupled with the nonchalance of the *flâneur*."[66]

The spy, on the other hand, is a salaried employee of the state, contrary to the misconception held by many fans of the spy fiction genre, as this narration from *Specter* explains: "Readers of popular spy novels tend to believe that Western secret agents make more money than the president of the United States, but the reality is completely different. They earn salaries … just like other officials and authorities. Naturally the pay is better … and includes certain special allowances."[67]

Văn Bình, then, is a sort of glorified civil servant, one with the good fortune of having a salary that provides him with a modest disposable income and official duties that allow him to mix business with pleasure, a job that combines and often blurs the distinction between labor and free time, that allows him to pursue his favorite pastimes of sex, alcohol and martial arts while simultaneously accomplishing his assignments as a professional spy. Indeed, the job is one that requires Văn Bình to indulge in his hobbies as a means of accomplishing his work-related tasks – dining with and making love to a stunning female Russian agent, for example, as a way of extracting information about her superiors at the KGB. Engaging in these free-time activities, in other words, is

Surveillance and spectacle

an essential part of the work of an international superspy, the cost of which is covered by the CIA and the Vietnamese Secret Affairs Bureau: "Văn Bình's extravagant spending, the way he would play and indulge in pleasures like a king [ăn chơi đế vương], none of this came out of his salary. These expenses were covered by the 'extra cash' [những món tiền 'trời ơi đất hỡi'] provided by the Bureau."[68] This extra money, however, is not enough to keep Văn Bình at certain moments from entertaining the temptation of going over to the other side, for the better perks and the higher pay that communist intelligence organizations offer their top agents, as for example in this exchange between Văn Bình and the KGB agent Boris in *Specter*:

> "Now if you're being paid by the mission, you would only be making between 2000 and 3000 dollars. And if you get captured, or taken to court, or killed, you have to take care of it yourself, since the 3000 dollars also includes your danger pay allowance as well as compensation for fatal injuries that may occur. The CIA puts the price of human life at 3000 dollars. So, in your opinion, which organization is more generous, the CIA or the KGB?"
>
> Văn Bình was silent. Boris was right ... The salary ... seemed awfully low considering the possibility of death ... Thousands, tens of thousands of spies all over the world simply accept these absurdly low salaries, including Văn Bình.[69]

In the end, however, all the free time ultimately makes up for the hardships involved in the job, the low pay and the constant work-related injuries, bullet wounds and karate kicks. In that sense, the figure of the spy implies a kind of reversal of the relationship between work and disposable time embodied in the detective. For the latter, work justifies leisure, while in the case of the spy, it is the free time that justifies the job. The profession of an international spy, in other words, is a "lifestyle," a condition combining work and free time that Adorno opposes to the privilege of being able to "follow the path of [one's] own intentions and to fashion one's work accordingly." This lifestyle is an example of what Adorno refers to as the "hobby ideology," an awkward expression that manages, nevertheless, to convey the seemingly innocuous character of the form of social domination that Adorno ascribes to the products of the culture industry, the compulsory character of the "hobby" as a form of "organized freedom": "The naturalness of the question of what hobby you have, harbors the assumption that must have ... a range of different hobbies, in accordance with what the 'leisure industry' can provide. Organized freedom is compulsory."[70]

For many commentators during the war in Vietnam, this compulsory freedom, which Nguyễn Hiến Lê described as a necessity for unnecessary consumption, was a fundamental feature of the "neo-colonial culture" that emerged in South Vietnamese cities.[71] As the economist Nguyễn Xuân Lai observes, for example, "The flood of imported goods … engendered among the population a tendency to consume foreign manufactured goods."[72]

This form of compulsion described in this passage, of course, is not a compulsion applied to the exploitation of labor. Rather, for the population it was purportedly used to "enslave," this compulsion imposes the imperative to consume name-brand goods, creating what communist critics describe as the "illusion" of an urban existence of endless consumption and free time: "[An] artificial glittering exterior of the city … was painted on by the old regime. It must be realized that Ho Chi Minh City cannot be a consumer and commercial city. Ho Chi Minh City must be a producing city."[73]

The principle of this compulsory freedom, therefore, is distinct from that of the forms of coercion that Foucault identified with "discipline," a power that "made it possible to extract time and labor … from bodies," and which tended towards an "ever more detailed internal arrangement" of the time of production.[74] Instead of imposing a "better economy of time and gesture,"[75] this compulsory freedom created a culture for "passing the time" (*tiêu khiển*), consisting of what Adorno described as "preoccupations with which [one] becomes mindlessly infatuated merely in order to kill time." As Nguyễn Vĩnh Long describes, this society was characterized by a compulsion for "transient pleasure" obtained through the consumption of popular culture:

> In neo-colonial society … people live at a hysterical tempo, art aims only at giving them transient pleasure as they follow, for instance, in intricacies of a hopeless love affair, or watch a scene of swordsmanship or some act of robbery and murder in a far-off land.[76]

Domination without discipline: Mass culture and temporal mastery

The domination of free time, therefore, and the compulsion associated with transient pleasure in mass-reproduced culture as it emerged in the twentieth century, is distinct from the domination of discipline, which, in Foucault's account of the latter, was applied in the industrial era for the purpose of producing a more efficient organization of the time.

Surveillance and spectacle

As D. A. Miller famously argues, the historical emergence of discipline is registered in the very formal conventions of the detective story and the nineteenth-century novel more generally.[77] Novelistic narration is characterized by a "temporal mode of mastery," a "'genetic' organization of narrative [that] allows the significant trifle to be elaborated temporally in minute networks of causality that inexorably connect one such trifle to another."[78] The narrative economy of this temporal mastery – in which the apparently insignificant details surrounding a crime are gradually organized into a causal narrative of detection – differs, however, from the temporal organization of the traditional bourgeois work of art. For Adorno, the latter is characterized by a unity of time in which each moment or episode is gradually integrated (by the reader or spectator) into the whole or totality as the artwork is unfolded temporally: in the work of art, the "interconnection of intra-temporal moments becomes so condensed and the relationships between them so comprehensively articulated that the mere passage of time takes on form ... as a powerful configuration of meaningful relationships on the level of conflict before ultimately finding resolution."[79] In the detective story, on the other hand, the resolution to the crime does not establish a total interconnection of all earlier moments. Rather, it connects only those moments that are relevant in some manner to solving the crime. The "detective's final summation," as Miller describes, "offers not a maximal integration of parts into whole, but a minimal one: what is totalized is just – and no more than – what is needed to solve the crime. Everything and everybody else is returned to a bland, mute self-evidence."[80]

Instead of achieving a total interconnection of parts – one in which the meaningless, mechanical passage of time is transformed through a unification of individual moments into a meaningful whole – the tale of detection merely "postulates a world in which everything *might* have a meaningful bearing on the solution to the crime, [but] concludes with an extensive repudiation of meanings that simply 'drop out.'" Rather than totalizing all the signifiers and clues into "a complete and all-encompassing order," the tale of detection in the final summation is "concerned to restrict and localize the province of meaning: to guarantee large areas of irrelevance."[81]

This temporal mode of mastery, characteristic of what Miller refers to as the "mass culture" of the Victorian era, cannot be equated, however, with the form of temporal domination that Adorno attributes to the products of the culture industry. In contrast to the detective story, the domination imposed by mass culture is not effected through the imposition of what Miller describes as a "linear, cumulative time [that] secures duration against the dispersive tendencies," allowing events, objects and characters to be arranged in succession and to be evaluated by the reader or spectator.[82] On the contrary, for Adorno the fundamental "paradox of mass culture" consists in the fact that the domination of time is achieved precisely by dissolving the semblance of narrative and temporal succession. This dissolution of narrative time expresses what Adorno refers to as the "technical control over time [under monopoly capitalism] in which history comes to a standstill":

> This is the paradox of mass culture. The more a-historical and preordained its procedures are, the less temporal relationships become a problem for it and the less it succeeds in transposing these relationships into a dialectical unity of temporal moments, the more craftily it employs static tricks to deceive us into seeing new temporal content in what it does, then the less it has left to oppose to the time beyond itself and all the more fatally does it fall victim to that time.[83]

The products of culture industry, then, are not characterized by maximal or minimal integration of part into a whole but rather by a temporal structure in which "all the moments which succeed one another in time are more or less directly interchangeable … There is no real development, and that what comes later is not one whit richer in experience than what has preceded it."[84] Instead of providing a minimal unity in which the "significant trifle [is] elaborated temporally" (in the form of a final summation that prodigally consigns most of the details of the story to a bland insignificance), the products of the culture industry (in Adorno's description at least) dispense with even a mechanical subordination of parts into a whole, thereby "emancipating" the individual detail: "The temporal moments into which the narrative has disintegrated now even begin to escape from the relationship of temporal succession."[85] In the culture industry, then, the artwork is dissolved into "isolated moments of enjoyment," disconnected "shocks and sensations." The "dialectical unity of temporal moments" that characterized the bourgeois work of art is replaced by an "almost complete interchangeability of time," by a "conflict-less succession of events"[86] devoid of the "coherence of meaning."[87] The unfolding in time of the artwork as an evolving totality is replaced by a "magical repetition," resembling the monotony of industrial production, "in which the selfsame is reproduced through time."[88]

Moreover, in contrast to the classical tale of detection, which, according to Miller, "shows disciplinary power to inhere in the very resistance to

Surveillance and spectacle

it,"[89] the products of the culture industry are characterized by a domination of time that inheres, for Adorno, in a lack of cohesion or a "conflictless succession of events" that "betrays the aspect of resistancelessness."[90] Deprived of any "coherence of meaning" by the disintegration of the narrative into isolated individual episodes, narrative action "becomes all the more subject to abstract time the more resolutely it refuses to wrap up time by means of the dramatic action." If power, as Miller points out, "can scarcely be exercised except on what resists it,"[91] then the domination of the culture industry must be defined paradoxically as power that apparently operates in the absence of the very resistance upon which power depends for its exercise.

Avenging the nation: The image of the prostitute and the people

As in Adorno's account of the temporal organization of mass cultural products, the narratives in the Z.28 novels are composed in large part of "isolated moments of enjoyment," advertising images that are more or less interchangeable in terms of the order of their appearance in the plot. The clues or "trifling details" described in the novels are largely detached from the tale of detection of which they are a part. In the following passage from *Specter*, for example, Văn Bình applies his skills of surveillance to observing a secret delegation of Chinese scientists sent to supervise the construction of a nuclear missile base in Albania:

> 20 minutes passed. The Chinese ... delegation ... shook hands with the welcoming committee ... and then walked to the car. Albania is a socialist country that despises Western capitalism, and yet it's full of Mercédès! And not just the Mercédès 800, which was has a price big enough to make your eyes explode ... Saigon is the capital of making and throwing money away and yet no one has even dared to try the Mercédès 300 (with the exception of course of agent Z.28) ... The Mercédès that welcomed the Chinese delegation was a Pullman 600, [which is] twice the price of a premium 300. [It] weighs 3 tons, has 6 doors, and has a trunk that opens automatically. The seats were raised so that people on both sides of the street could see the officials inside. [It was] ... full of modern devices: a refrigerator with alcohol and ice cubes, a record player, a recorder, a telephone and a microwave radio. Even at a speed of over 200 hundred kilometers an hour, sitting inside was like lying on a foam mattress ... One way or another, Văn Bình would have to purchase this elegant tank and show it off to the folks in Saigon! In the crowded streets of Saigon, [Văn Bình's Pullman] 600 would attract the eyes of all of the girls riding on the back of the motorbikes. He would attach a special pipe to release a fragrant scent ... And of course he'd

attach a small sign to the back [of the car] with his address, so that all of the ... women could write it down in their notebooks and find him.⁹²

The detailed description of the cost and convenience of the luxury car used to escort the delegation from China and the strange commercial-like fantasy it inspires in Văn Bình are not simply "trifling detail[s]," clues whose significance (or irrelevance) will be revealed in a final summation at the end of the novel. The interest that these images are supposed to contain for the reader cannot be equated, therefore, with the satisfaction obtained through the minimal integration of relevant details characteristic of the classic detective story. But nor, of course, can the interest that such descriptions aim to arouse be identified with an aesthetic experience achieved through a total "interconnection of intra-temporal moments." On the contrary, the unfolding narrative or tale of detection appears to serve primarily as a sort of background display for the luxury goods described in the passage. As the price comparisons between the different Mercedes models would seem to suggest, the enjoyment that these "trifling detail[s]" are supposed to produce is the thrill or elation afforded by what Adorno refers to as the "fetish character" of mass culture, in which "exchange value disguise[s] itself as the object of enjoyment" and the consumer is "intoxicated by the act of buying."⁹³

In the fetishism that attaches itself to the products of the culture industry, the satisfaction of needs through the consumption of commodities, and their real useful properties, is replaced by the pleasure produced by "publicity": the pleasure of being observed in the act of enjoying the pure "exchange value" of a commodity from which the "quantum of possible enjoyment has disappeared": "In American conventional speech, having a good time means being present at the enjoyment of others ... The auto religion makes all men brothers in the sacramental moment with the words: 'that is a Rolls Royce.'"⁹⁴ In *Specter*, then, the mass supervision performed by secret intelligence agents inspires dreams of a public celebrity aided by advertisement.

In the Z.28 novels, however, the privileged example of a commodity in which "exchange value disguise[s] itself as the object of enjoyment" is not the automobile but rather the prostitute. Descriptions of women and the solicitation of sex, bordering on pornography, regularly interrupt the narratives of detection in the novels. A particularly explicit example of such a description appears in the following passage from *Specter* in which Văn Bình, disguised as an American tourist, secures the services of an Albanian prostitute through a bellboy acting as a pimp:

Surveillance and spectacle

[Văn Bình:] "Oh, there's so much time left until evening. I can't stand it … Can you call that beautiful woman?" …
[Bellboy:] "I'd very much like to follow your orders, sir, but there's a problem." …
[Văn Bình:] "The problem of money, of course."
[Bellboy:] "Yes, sir. The only reason I dare to accept money from you is that … you're an American."
[Văn Bình:] "50 dollars should cover it. Why so disturbed? Just take it … If you're nice, I'll give you some more." …
[Bellboy:] "It's too difficult. She already has an appointment with the head of the trade delegation from Poland … He's waiting [for her] in his room."
[Văn Bình:] "Bring her to me right now." …
Văn Bình struck him. The bellboy fell down, his head hitting the wall …
"I'll give you five minutes. If she's not here in five minutes, you'll get a beating that's ten times worse." …
[The bellboy] stood up, smiled, and stuffed the 50 dollar bill into his pocket …
Văn Bình climbed into bed. The beds in *Dajti* hotel were anything but comfortable … But from now until evening, he had to find a way to kill time [*giết thời giờ*], to burn a few thousand calories and waste some more of his spending cash [*tiền tẩm quất*].

In the new dictionary of Vietnamese youth, there is a very interesting expression: "avenging the nation" [*trả thù dân tộc*]. Many people are sent abroad, but most of them are either too old, with weak knees and weak hearts, or too young, without enough experience in international warfare, and so the issue of "avenging the nation" is dealt with only in passing [*chỉ thoáng qua ngắn ngủi*] … Fortunately, agent Văn Bình was among the troops who were sent overseas. Not only was he capable of exacting revenge, he shocked and scared people on all the five continents.

The expression "avenging the nation" appeared in Văn Bình's mind. He pulled out a Salem and smoked it, smiling to himself.

He looked at the watch. Exactly six o'clock.[95]

In this passage, the conspiracy plot is interrupted by yet another apparently irrelevant episode or "isolated moment of enjoyment." In this case, the object of enjoyment is not the image of a foreign luxury car but the prospect of sex with an expensive Albanian prostitute. The latter is described as a way to "kill time" (*giết thời giờ*) before the next stage of the mission (a meeting with one of the Chinese scientists sent to install the nuclear missile facility). Although such expenditures of disposable money and time are not directly related to Văn Bình's primary objective, his capacity to kill time, as the passage implies, is precisely what has earned him his reputation "across the five continents" as a celebrity superspy. What distinguishes Văn Bình, then, as an expert in

The unimagined community

"international warfare" is not simply, or primarily, his ability to accomplish his extrajuridical work as an agent of government surveillance. Rather, it lies in the way in which he disposes of the time that transpires *between* his secret assignments, during the lulls in the narrative action when the progress of the conspiracy plot is completely suspended, revealing an empty, mechanical passage of minutes and hours ("He looked at the watch. Exactly six o'clock"), a free time that must be consumed by engaging in expensive and vulgar distractions.

In this case, the time between secret assignments is used by Văn Bình for the specific purpose of "avenging the nation" – or the "ethnicity," "people" or "race" (*dân tộc*) – by purchasing sex with a white prostitute. Unlike other Vietnamese agents who are sent overseas, Văn Bình's experience in international warfare has prepared him to make the most of his free time in "avenging the nation," instead of "getting it over with quickly" in order to resume his intelligence work and return to plot.

According to Nguyễn Nguyệt Cầm, this "image of a Vietnamese man who wins the hearts and bodies of … foreign women … reveals the concern and anxiety of Southern males" during the war in Vietnam.[96] This fantasy was an expression of the widespread sense of resentment and indignation among Vietnamese men in the South toward the "cultural and moral 'depravity'" allegedly produced by the American intervention and, in particular, the spread of prostitution as a result of the presence of American troops. As Neil Jamieson explains: "Vietnamese males felt threatened, humiliated, and outraged by the sight of Vietnamese women with foreign men, especially with Americans, so conspicuous in their affluence and their numbers."[97] In that sense, the phrase "avenging the nation" can be understood as the expression of an ethnic or racial identity based on what Slavoj Žižek has described as the fantasy of a "theft of enjoyment" – a "mythology narrating how other nations deprive [a particular group] of the vital part of enjoyment the possession of which would allow it to live fully."[98]

The particular form of enjoyment whose "theft" is avenged by Văn Bình, however, is not simply the enjoyment of sex with a white woman but rather the pleasure of *purchasing* sex from a woman from another nation or race. As Benjamin has noted, the desire aroused by the prostitute is distinct from the desire for sexual pleasure. In the prostitute, "salability itself can become a sexual stimulus; and this attraction increases wherever an abundant supply of women underscores their character as commodity."[99] The prostitute, in other words, sells not only sexual pleasure but also exchange value or "saleability" itself; the buyer is enticed not only by sex but by the act of buying, intoxicated by the power of exchange value to command even the objects of sexual desire and to purchase another person's consent to their own degradation. Like money (as the embodiment of exchange value), the prostitute becomes, in Marx's words, a "representation of wealth," "which possesses *all* pleasures in potentiality."[100] For this reason, "love for the prostitute," according to Benjamin, constitutes "the apotheosis of empathy with the commodity."[101] In the prostitute, the fictional equivalence of incommensurable forms of labor, which constitutes the basis of exchange value (and therefore of economic exchange), is extended even to sexual pleasure. In that sense, the prostitute "represents the utmost extension attainable by the sphere of the commodity."[102]

The enjoyment, then, whose theft provokes the fantasy of revenge on behalf of the "nation," is the satisfaction that American men were believed to obtain in buying Vietnamese prostitutes, an everyday spectacle in South Vietnamese cities that would become a figure for the republic itself, for the "prostitution" of Vietnamese culture to the Americans. During the war, the image of Saigon as a brothel for American servicemen pervaded print media (in both the South and the North) as well as everyday speech. For example, in the popular expression, *nhất đĩ nhì sư tam cha tứ tướng* ("first the prostitutes, second the fake bonzes, third the Catholic priests, fourth the generals") – which was also a part of the "new dictionary of Vietnamese youth" – South Vietnamese society is depicted as a perversion of the Confucian hierarchy of occupations and moral virtues.[103] In that sense, the fantasy of "avenging the nation" by soliciting sex from a white prostitute also reflects a more general anxiety among South Vietnamese, "fueled by a dependence on American arms and American dollars."[104]

In the Z.28 novels, this dependence is both acknowledged and disavowed by Văn Bình, a "super-talented spy" from a country that is too poor to "afford an effective intelligence network spreading all over the world" and who therefore must "sell his services to the rich."[105] The exorbitant fees paid by US intelligence to solicit these services, however, are never enough to obtain his "humility" or "submission."[106] And while in the novels Văn Bình accepts the material assistance supplied by the CIA, he almost never complies with the instructions on how this assistance is to be used on the missions he is hired to execute. Unlike the popular perception of the Vietnamese prostitute, then, Văn Bình "only sells his services, not his soul."[107]

The unimagined community

Having legitimately earned his wages by selling his indispensable services to the American government, Văn Bình is in a position to avenge the "theft of enjoyment" perpetrated by the Americans by using his disposable income and time to consume commodities whose primary attraction, like that of the sexual services provided by prostitutes, lies in the pleasure of being observed in the act of enjoying exchange value itself. In that sense, such acts of national or racial revenge – to employ the "vocabulary of South Vietnamese youth" – imply what Benjamin described as a "racial community" (*Volksgemeinschaft*) based on an empathetic identification with a representative figure who enjoys exchange value on behalf of the people:

> Basically ... empathy with the commodity is ... empathy with exchange-value itself. And in fact, one can hardly imagine the "consumption" of exchange-value as anything else but an empathy with it ... Empathy with exchange-value can turn even guns into articles of consumption more attractive than butter. If in popular parlance it is said of someone that 'he is loaded; he has five million marks," the "racial community" [*Volksgemeinschaft*] itself likewise feels that it is "loaded" with a few hundred billion; it empathizes with those hundreds of billions.[108]

But if the *dân tộc* in *Specter*, like the fascist *Volksgemeinschaft*, is an imaginary community based on "empathy with exchange-value," it cannot be equated with a sovereign national people, at least in terms of the Schmittian definition of sovereignty. The vengeance that Văn Bình enacts on the *dân tộc*'s behalf is not a political action oriented toward the "extreme case of war." On the contrary, the extrajuridical aim of this "vengeance" is to preserve the spectacle of a virtual state of emergency, one that sustains the appearance of a real political enmity between free nations and communist dictatorships. This unpolitical "vengeance," moreover, is not directed against the official military and political enemies of the RVN. Rather, it is aimed at a figure associated with the republic's principal ally.

During the war, this ally or friend was widely perceived as a threat to South Vietnamese sovereignty, to the emergence of a sovereign South Vietnamese nation united in its enmity against the communist North and prepared for a decision on the "extreme case" of war. This decision, from the perspective of officials in the South Vietnamese state, was obstructed by the American government's overarching concern to avoid the risk of a nuclear exchange with the Soviet Union and China and by the policy of limited war that ruled out the possibility of an invasion of the North by the RVN. Thus the emergence of a sovereign political entity in the South, oriented toward an extreme case of war with the North, was blocked by American policymakers for the sake of saving the institution of sovereignty from destroying itself in an atomic catastrophe. A genuinely sovereign act of "national vengeance" on the part of the republic was therefore precluded by the policy of deterrence, which had been imposed for the purpose of saving sovereignty itself from destroying the world.

The figure of "racial revenge," therefore, is an extremely ambivalent one. It is an assertion of sovereignty against a friend (instead of a foe), seeking to preserve the very possibility of sovereignty by depriving the South Vietnamese people of the ability to engage in a genuine act of national vengeance, an act that would constitute the condition for its emergence as a sovereign political entity.

This vengeance, moreover, is exacted not through an "extreme case of war" with the Americans, but rather through an excessive indulgence in the exchange value used to hire the services of the South Vietnamese. In that sense, "avenging the nation" can be understood as an act of national prostitution (that of a poor Vietnamese spy who "sells his services to the rich") directed against the prostitution to exchange value that both conditioned and undermined the possibility of a South Vietnamese national people or *dân tộc*. As such, the expression "avenging the nation" might also be read as a euphemism for shirking one's national duty, passing off frivolous play and the consumption of free time for the serious work of building and defending a nation, one whose integrity was at once supported and undone by American money and American military policy.

This form of revenge, finally, does not entail resistance to surveillance or discipline, a resistance from which a subject emerges in its opposition to power. In the novels, the reader's attention is drawn not to the tale of detection (which succeeds in the end whether attention is paid to it or not), nor to the gradual accumulation of insignificant trifles that resist detection initially, but only in order to serve as the pretext for a narrative that temporally masters their meaning. Rather, the emphasis is placed on the advertisements that continually suspend the ongoing surveillance, a surveillance that seems to detect only commodity-spectacles. In these "isolated moments of enjoyment," a national people or *dân tộc*, which cannot quite emerge owing to its ambivalent role within "international warfare," makes the most of the in-between moments of a virtual state of emergency.

Notes

1 Nguyễn Nguyệt Cầm, "Z.28 and the Appeal of Spy Fiction in Southern Vietnam, 1954–1975" (MA dissertation, University of California, Berkeley, 2001), v.
2 Võ Phiến, *Hai mươi năm Văn Học Miền Nam: Tổng Quan* [Thirty Years of Literature in South Vietnam, 1945–1975: Overview] (Nhà Xuất Bản Văn Nghệ: Westminster, 1986), 55. The Z.28 novels first appeared in serialized format between 1957 and 1960 in the newspaper *Dân Chúng* [Masses] before they were compiled and published in book format. (Nguyễn Nguyệt Cầm, "Z.28 and the Appeal of Spy Fiction," 5.)
3 Ibid., 286.
4 Vương Hồng Sển, *Phong Lưu cũ mới* [Phong Lưu New and Old] (Saigon: NXB Xuân Thu, 1970).
5 Võ Phiến, *Hai mươi năm Văn Học Miền Nam*, 293, see also Hiền Thu Lương, "Vietnamese Existential Philosophy: A Critical Appraisal" (Ph.D. dissertation, Temple University, 2009), 7.
6 Jean Baudrillard, *Simulacra and Simulation* (Ann Arbor: University of Michigan Press, 1994), 32.
7 Giorgio Agamben, *State of Exception* (Chicago: University of Chicago Press, 2005), 55.
8 Walter Benjamin, "The Work of Art: Second Version," in *The Work of Art in the Age of Its Technological Reproducibility and Other Writings on Media*, ed. Michael W. Jennings, Howard Eiland and Gary Smith (Cambridge, MA: Belknap Press of Harvard University Press, 2008), 41.
9 Walter Benjamin, "On the Concept of History," in *Walter Benjamin, Selected Writings*, vol. 4: *1938–1940*, ed. Michael W. Jennings (Cambridge, MA: Harvard University Press, 2003), 392.
10 Benjamin, "The Work of Art," 40.
11 Bôi Lan, "Letters and Arts in American Times," *Vietnamese Studies*, no. 14, 1967, 45–6.
12 Võ Phiến, *Hai mươi năm Văn Học Miền Nam*, 22. See also Phạm Văn Sĩ, *Văn học giải phóng miền Nam* [Literature of the Liberated South] (Hanoi: Nhà Xuất Bản Đại Học Và Trung Học Chuyên Nghiệp, 1975).
13 Nguyễn Nguyệt Cầm, "Z.28 and the Appeal of Spy Fiction," 3.
14 Bùi Anh Tuấn, *Southeast Asian: Communism on the March. American Council for World Freedom* (Washington DC: American Council for World Freedom, 1978).
15 Người Thứ Tám, *Z.28 Vượt Tuyến* (Z.28 Crosses the Parallel) (Sài Gòn: Nhà Xuất Bản Hành động, 1971), 10.
16 Võ Phiến, *Hai mươi năm Văn Học Miền Nam*, 226.
17 Người Thứ Tám, *Gián Điệp Siêu Hình Quyển Hạ* [The Metaphysical Spy, vol. 2] (Sài Gòn: Nhà Xuất Bản Hành động, 1966).

18 Võ Phiến, *Hai mươi năm Văn Học Miền Nam*, 48.
19 Nguyễn Nguyệt Cầm, "Z.28 and the Appeal of Spy Fiction," v.
20 Ibid., vi.
21 Michael Denning, "Licensed to Look: James Bond and the Heroism of Consumption," in *The James Bond Phenomenon: A Critical Reader*, ed. Christoph Lindner (Manchester: Manchester University Press, 2003), 66.
22 Người Thứ Tám, *Hận Vàng Ấn Độ* [Golden Regret in India] (United States: publisher not identified, 1980?), 16.
23 Người Thứ Tám, *Bóng Ma Trên Công Trường Đỏ* [Specter over Red Square] (Saigon: Nhà Xuất Bản Hành Động, 1969), 40.
24 Ibid., 16.
25 Ibid., 39.
26 Ibid., 189.
27 "Nhiều người mê đọc Z-28 nhưng ít ai biết về tác giả Người Thứ Tám" ["Many People Loved Reading Z.28 but Few Know about the Author Người Thứ Tám"], Người Việt Bốn Phương (June 25, 2012). https://tinyurl.com/yxapo34n. Last accessed July 22, 2019.
28 Guy Debord, *Society of the Spectacle*, trans. Donald Nicholson-Smith (New York: Zone Books, 1995), 41.
29 Ibid., 12.
30 Võ Phiến, *Hai mươi năm Văn Học Miền Nam*, 293.
31 Người Thứ Tám, *Bóng Ma Trên Công Trường Đỏ*, 54.
32 Ibid., 194.
33 Người Thứ Tám, *Hận Vàng Ấn Độ*, 168–9.
34 Người Thứ Tám, *Bóng Ma Trên Công Trường Đỏ*, 18.
35 Foucault, *Discipline and Punish*, 217.
36 Người Thứ Tám, *Bóng Ma Trên Công Trường Đỏ*, 240–3.
37 Baudrillard, *Simulacra and Simulation*, 32.
38 Giorgio Agamben, *Homo Sacer* (Redwood City, CA: Stanford University Press, 1998), 15–16.
39 Carl Schmitt, *Concept of the Political* (Chicago: University of Chicago Press, 2007), 34–6.
40 Nina Tannenwald, *The Nuclear Taboo: The United States and the Non-use of Nuclear Weapons since 1945* (Cambridge: Cambridge University Press, 2007), 109–10.
41 Arendt, "Lying in Politics," 105–6. See also Keith Payne, "The fallacies of Cold War deterrence and a new direction," *Comparative Strategy*, 22:5 (2003), 411–28.
42 Người Thứ Tám, *Một Vụ Đánh Cắp Tài Liệu Nguyên Tử* [The Case of the Stolen Atomic Documents]. Việt Messenger. vietmessenger.com/books/?action=print&title=z28motvudanhcaptailieunguyentu&page=3/. Last accessed March 7, 2019.

43 See Chantal Mouffe, *The Challenge of Carl Schmitt* (New York: Verso, 1999), 17. For Foucault, similarly, this situation implies a "paradox" characteristic of "contemporary political power," one in which the sovereign deployment of atomic weapons would amount to a suppression of sovereign power itself: "Either it is sovereign and uses the atom bomb ... or, at the opposite extreme, you no longer have a sovereign right." Foucault, *Society Must Be Defended*, 253.
44 Schmitt, *Concept of the Political*, 35.
45 Ibid.
46 Carl Schmitt, *Theory of the Partisan* (New York: Telos, 2007), 79.
47 Karl Marx, *Capital: A Critique of Political Economy*, vol. 1, trans. Ben Fowkes (New York: Random House, 1977), 126, n. 5.
48 Người Thứ Tám, *Bóng Ma Trên Công Trường Đỏ*, 39.
49 Thế Lữ, *Đòn hẹn* [The Treacherous Appointment] (Ho Chi Minh City: Nhà Xuất Bản Văn Nghệ, 2000), 34.
50 Quoted in Pierre A. Huard and Maurice Durand, *Connaissance du Việtnam (I)* (Paris: Imprimerie Nationale và Hà Nội, École Française d'Extrême-Orient, 1954), 235–6.
51 Honoré de Balzac, *Œuvres complètes* (Complete Works), vol. 20 (Paris: Michel Lévy Frères, 1869), 478.
52 Ibid., 461–2.
53 Ibid., 463.
54 On premodern forms of publicness or publicity of representation, see Jürgen Habermas, *The Structural Transformation of The Public Sphere: An Inquiry into a Category of Bourgeois Society* (Cambridge: Polity, 1992), 7–8.
55 The preoccupation with fashion in Vietnamese works from the 1920s and 1930s, such as Thế Lữ's detective fiction, reflects the novelty of fashion as a new historical phenomenon that emerged during the colonial period. Immediately after the conquest, French administrators and soldiers displayed their Republican disdain for the elitism of traditional sartorial codes by allowing their Vietnamese "boys" or subordinates (many of whom were drawn from the ranks of the dispossessed and the poor) to wear clothing reserved for scholar gentry. Instead of producing a democratization of manner and dress, this "shoddy populism" led to a "carnival of publically released envy and disrespect, [in which] the 'boy' group might ape the costumes and manners of precolonial Vietnamese bureaucrats." The result was a "pathetic usurpation of the symbols of high status ... a pollution of the old society's privileges and rituals." Woodside, *Community and Revolution in Modern Vietnam*, 11. In the early twentieth century, the adoption of French fashions and styles – which reformist intellectuals such as Phan Chu Trinh and Nguyễn Văn Vĩnh promoted as part of a modernization of Vietnamese culture in accordance with the Republican ideal of universal equality – served as a means of establishing social distinctions among the

indigenous urban elite. This led figures such as Vĩnh to "deplore … social misfits who dressed in Western garb, but who were more interested in social acceptance by the French than in the modernisation of thought that should accompany this sartorial change." Christopher E. Goscha, "'The Modern Barbarian': Nguyễn Văn Vĩnh and the Complexity of Colonial Modernity in Vietnam," *European Journal of East Asian Studies*, 3:1 (2003), 24. By the late colonial era, however, fashion, as a sartorial reflection of modern Republican values and a capitalist industry that perpetuated the appearance of innate social distinction, would become a familiar fixture in Vietnamese cities, thanks in part to the efforts of designers such as Lemur Nguyễn Cát Tường, inventor of the modern *áo dài*. See Ngô Tất Tố, "Xin nhờ Lơmuya cát tường việc này nữa" ["Just One More Favor from Lơmuya"], in Ngô Tất Tố, *Toàn Tập* [Ngô Tất Tố: Collected Works], vol. 4 (Hà Nội: Nhà xuất bản Văn Học, 2000).
56 Quoted in Benjamin, *The Arcades Project*, 77.
57 Benjamin, "The Paris of the Second Empire", 23.
58 Ibid., 26.
59 Quoted in ibid.
60 Ibid.
61 Ibid., 27.
62 Người Thứ Tám, *Hận Vàng Ấn Độ*, 51.
63 Ibid.
64 Adorno, *The Culture Industry*, 188–9.
65 Ibid., 189.
66 Benjamin, "The Paris of the Second Empire," 22.
67 Người Thứ Tám, *Bóng Ma Trên Công Trường Đỏ*, 130.
68 Ibid.
69 Ibid.
70 Adorno, *The Culture Industry*, 190.
71 Nguyễn Hiến Lê, "Kỉ nguyên tiêu thụ và nghề viết văn," 149.
72 Nguyễn Xuân Lai, "Economic Gears and Levers," 163.
73 Quoted in Taylor, *Fragments of the Present*, 37.
74 Foucault, *Discipline and Punish*, 154.
75 Ibid., 153.
76 Nguyễn Vĩnh Long, "Changes in Saigon's stage and cinema."
77 On the development and reception of Vietnamese detective fiction in the colonial era, see Phạm Đình Ân, *Thế Lữ, về tác gia và tác phẩm* [Thế Lữ: on the author and his works] (Hà Nội: Nhà xuất bản Giáo dục, 2006), 39. Although the poet and novelist Thế Lữ is credited as a pioneer of the detective genre in Vietnam, his detective fiction was considered at the time to be too European, particularly in its detailed accounts of the use of modern methods of science in the detection of crime. (See Nam Chi, "Những đóng góp của Thế Lữ vào phong trào Thơ mới" [Thế Lữ's contributions to the

New Poetry Movement], in *Thế Lữ, cuộc đời trong nghệ thuật* [Thế Lữ, a life in art] (Hà Nội: Nhà xuất bản Hội Nhà văn, 1991). The most popular writer of detective fiction during the colonial era was Phạm Cao Củng. Đặng Hồng Nam, "Nhà văn viết truyện trinh thám Phạm Cao Củng đang ở đâu?" [Where is the detective writer Phạm Cao Củng today?]. *Báo Tiền Phong* online, January 15, 2013. https://www.tienphong.vn/van-nghe/127343/Nha-van-viet-truyen-trinh-tham-Pham-Cao-Cung-dang-o-dau.html. Last accessed July 28, 2019.), whose detectives embodied an approach to policing that incorporated more traditional conception of justice, law and penalty.
78 D. A. Miller, *The Novel and the Police* (Berkeley: University of California Press, 1988), 52.
79 Adorno, *The Culture Industry*, 74.
80 Miller, *The Novel and the Police*, 34.
81 Ibid.
82 Ibid., 26.
83 Adorno, *The Culture Industry*, 75.
84 Ibid., 71.
85 Ibid.
86 Ibid., 73–5.
87 Horkheimer and Adorno, *Dialectic of Enlightenment*, 109.
88 Adorno, *The Culture Industry*, 70.
89 Miller, *The Novel and the Police*, 27.
90 Adorno, *The Culture Industry*, 70.
91 Miller, *The Novel and the Police*, 27.
92 Người Thứ Tám, *Bóng Ma Trên Công Trường Đỏ*, 206–8.
93 Adorno, *The Culture Industry*, 40.
94 Ibid., 39.
95 Người Thứ Tám, *Bóng Ma Trên Công Trường Đỏ*, 242–3.
96 Nguyễn Nguyệt Cầm, "Z.28 and the Appeal of Spy Fiction," 45.
97 Neil L. Jamieson, *Understanding Vietnam* (Berkeley and Los Angeles: University of California Press, 1993), 339.
98 Slavoj Žižek, *Tarrying with the Negative* (Durham, NC: Duke University Press, 1993), 204.
99 Benjamin, *The Arcades Project*, 339.
100 Marx, *Capital*, 222.
101 Benjamin, *The Arcades Project*, 375.
102 Ibid., 348.
103 "Many Vietnamese in the capital and cities were very quickly aware of the value of the 'U.S. green dollars' … Under the new living conditions, the society's traditions began to fall. New social classes surfaced, ranking in order from the highest: the prostitutes, the … Buddhist priests, the … Catholic priests, and the generals." "In [the] Vietnamese original … which [was] known everywhere in the country, these 'new social orders' were *nhất đĩ*

nhì sử tam cha tứ tướng ... [T]he number of prostitutes increased considerably with the increased number of GIs in South Vietnam. This was ironic, bizarre, and nauseous, but it was also true. This social phenomenon of South Vietnam might go unmentioned in Western historical books or newspaper articles. However, it was one of the main causes leading to the political deterioration of the South from the spring of 1963." Văn Nguyên Dưỡng. *The Tragedy of the Vietnam War: A South Vietnamese Officer's Analysis* (Jefferson, NC: McFarland, 2008), 74.

104 Jamieson, *Understanding Vietnam*, 341.
105 Người Thứ Tám, *Macao ... Trinh Nữ Giang Hồ* [Macao ... The Underground Virgin] (Saigon: Nhà Xuất Bản Hành Động, 1974), 74.
106 Người Thứ Tám, *Điệp Viên Áo Tím* [The Secret Agent in the Purple Shirt] (Saigon: Nhà Xuất Bản Hành Động), 85–6.
107 Nguyễn Nguyệt Cầm, "Z.28 and the Appeal of Spy Fiction," 37.
108 "Benjamin letter to Adorno, Paris, 9 December 1938," in *Aesthetics and Politics: Debates between Bloch, Lukács, Brecht, Benjamin, Adorno*, ed. Ronald Taylor (London: Verso, 1980), 140.

7

Image-making and US imperialism: Sovereignty, surveillance and spectacle in the Vietnam War

The war in Vietnam is often described as a conflict defined by popular culture and modern mass media, as the first "television war" and the first "Rock 'n' Roll war." These phenomena, mass culture and media, which distinguished the war from earlier conflicts, were the products of what the national security advisor, Walt Whitman Rostow, referred to as a "society of high mass consumption."[1] The war, then, was a conflict waged by the world's first modern consumer society.

By the 1950s, television, which emerged as the most powerful medium of promoting the ever-increasing production of consumer commodities, had also become the primary leisure activity in American households, integrating advertising and everyday life. In accordance with the demands of advertisers, the programming produced for this medium was designed to appeal to the middlebrow tastes of American middle-class workers, who emerged after World War II as a new mass of consumers.[2] The result was what critics of the new consumer society referred to as "mass culture." Following the formula applied in the "standardized production of consumption goods," this culture, as Theodor Adorno argued, "accommodates itself to the regularity of the successful, the doing of what everybody does."[3]

For Guy Debord, this standardized culture was part of a "Society of the Spectacle" that had emerged in the developed capitalist economies after World War II, countries capable of producing an "abundance of commodities." In these economies, the discipline and surveillance of labor established in the era of industrial capitalism was reinforced by the spectacle of mass culture and media. The "worker, suddenly redeemed from the total contempt which is clearly shown him by all the …

Image-making and US imperialism

surveillance of production, finds himself every day, outside of production ... in the guise of a consumer."[4] In "all its ... forms, as information ... advertisement or direct entertainment consumption," the spectacle served as "the omnipresent affirmation of ... [capitalist] production and its corollary consumption ... since it occupies the principal part of the time ... outside of modern production."[5]

The development of this Society of the Spectacle would result in a crisis in liberal democracies, one in which government policy was subordinated to a public opinion that could be manipulated by the new forms of media.[6] Thus, Henry Cabot Lodge, Jr., Ambassador to Sài Gòn in the early 1960s, observed that no "long range foreign policy could be carried out by the U.S. Government without the support of ... public opinion," which was "influenced by the press."[7] As a result of this influence, democratic societies, to borrow another account of the crisis, which had once "exhibit[ed] the politician directly ... before elected representatives," compelled politicians to "present themselves before the ... media."[8]

During the 1960s, the war in Vietnam became an integral part of the Spectacle, pervading everyday life as America's living room war.[9] Television, as General William Westmoreland lamented in 1972, had become "a means of ... involving the American public with the war on an almost hourly basis."[10] As a result, "the powerful imagery provided by modern camera and broadcast technology ... did much to formulate America's reaction to its war in Vietnam."[11]

As a spectacle, then, the war had to be waged for the cameras and promoted together with the commodities sold on TV. And like the standardized culture created for television, the success of the war, so the policymakers believed, would depend upon its appeal to the middlebrow tastes of the new middle classes. Thus, as the election approached in 1968, Lyndon Johnson commanded his aides to "sell our product" and to "get a better story to the American people."[12] These orders were prompted by the media coverage of the Tết Offensive, which helped to transform the event from the greatest defeat in the war for the communist forces to a resounding victory against a superior American military.[13] Despite the overwhelming defeat on the battlefield, the media coverage would lead Walter Cronkite to declare in a special report that the war was unwinnable. "If I've lost Cronkite," Johnson reportedly said in response to the broadcast, "I've lost Middle America."[14]

For Hannah Arendt, it was precisely this aspect of the war that distinguished it from earlier conflicts. The politicians who had "learned their trade from the inventiveness of Madison Avenue" conducted the war as a public relations campaign, using strategies that originated in advertising, as a spectacle for producing a society of high mass consumption: "Public relations is but a variety of advertising; hence it has its origin in the consumer society, with its inordinate appetite for goods to be distributed through a market economy." In the "insane atmosphere of rampant advertising," policymakers came to believe that "half of politics is 'image-making' and the other half the art of making people believe in the imagery."[15]

As a result of the influence of advertising, the ultimate aims of the war were conceived in terms of the production of spectacles intended for domestic consumption as well as for a wider geopolitical viewership. As John T. McNaughton described in a memo to the Secretary of Defense, Robert McNamara, the "relevant audiences" for the war "are the Communists (who must feel strong pressures), the South Vietnamese (whose morale must be buoyed), our allies (who must trust us as 'underwriters') and the US public (which must support our risk-taking with US lives and prestige)."[16] Such accounts of the conflict, according to Arendt, revealed that the "ultimate aim was neither power nor profit." Rather, the aim was primarily to "keep intact an image of omnipotence." "The goal was now the image itself."[17]

For Arendt, it was the importance placed on the image that defined the peculiar form of "imperialism" practiced by the American government. "Image-making as global policy – not world conquest, but victory in the battle 'to win the people's minds' – is indeed something new in the huge arsenal of human follies recorded in history." Instead of pursuing the goal of world domination, US politicians, practicing liberal democracy in the age of mass reproduction, engaged in the imperialistic "pursuit of a mere image of omnipotence."[18]

As a new governmental technique adapted from advertising, this global image-making, however, cannot be equated with mere public deception or lying in politics, a practice that, as Arendt emphasizes, is as old as politics itself. The image of omnipotence is not simply a false representation, staged for the public in order to conceal a truth, preserved by policymakers as an *arcanum imperii* or a classified government secret. The success of a public deception depends on concealing a given reality, whereas in the case of the global policy of image-making, the reality of the war had become a subordinate matter in relation to the overarching priority of producing the image itself. Thus, Johnson's expression of total defeat in response to a purely spectacular victory, which succeeded, apparently, in turning a key demographic against American policy, was not only a concession to popular opinion; it confirmed the autonomous power of the spectacle. The turning point of the imperialist war in Vietnam, then, was marked not by a decisive defeat on the battlefield, but by the failure of the planners, as specialists in the practice of global image-making, to sell the image of omnipotence to its intended audience.

This aspect of the war would appear to conform to Debord's account of the political class, whose "the specialization of power ... is at the root of the spectacle": "The specialization of images of the world evolves into a world of autonomised images where even the deceivers are deceived."[19]

Surveillance and US counterinsurgency

For Arendt, however, the self-deception of American planners was the product not only of the policy of imperial image-making, which politicians appropriated as a new technique of the state from the spectacle of advertising that had colonized everyday life. During the war, this new mode of deception was reinforced by a "second new variety of the art of lying ... less frequently met with in everyday life."[20] The new "folly" of image-making pursued by Washington policymakers was informed by the data produced by a new generation of government technocrats and intelligence experts.[21] Using techniques of surveillance employed in the Taylorist factory, including the collection of empirical evidence and the use of statistical analysis, "problem-solvers" such as Robert McNamara attempted to modernize the political act of decision-making itself.[22] Based on data derived by "translating all factual contents into the language of numbers and percentages," policymaking could be transformed, so the problem-solvers believed, into a process of logical inference.[23] Executive power, including the sovereign right to decide life and death, would be treated as an administrative procedure, rationalizing the work of the war planners, while minimizing the moral burden attached to their extralegal prerogatives: "One sometimes has the impression," Arendt says, "that a computer, rather than 'decision-makers,' had been let loose in Southeast Asia."[24]

In Vietnam, this quantitative approach would be applied in a new kind of colonial counterinsurgency warfare. The problem-solvers in Washington sought to reduce the confusing reality of the conflict on the ground to a "demographics of war," to a collection of calculable figures that could be used to rationalize the executive function. In this new kind of warfare, the "landscape," as Michael Herr described, is:

7.1 IBM computers at the US AID Information Center, 1971 (courtesy of Michigan State University Archives).

converted to terrain, the geography broken down into its more useful components; corps and zones, tactical areas ... vicinities of operation, outposts, positions, objectives, fields of fire. The weather of Vietnam has been translated into conditions, and it's gone very much the same way with the people, the population.[25]

Statistics on the welfare, attrition and pacification of the Vietnamese population, both friendly and hostile, were gathered through government studies, secret informers and surveys dispatched to the provinces. Transferred to punch cards, the data was processed on IBM supercomputers produced for the Pentagon.[26]

This "information panopticon" was used in order to isolate an irregular army hiding in an impenetrable jungle in the midst of an inscrutable people.[27] The partisan war, waged by guerrillas using the land and the peasants as cover so as to reduce a superior enemy to "a giant without eyes," would be met by a system of surveillance based on the quantification of every relevant detail of the environment and the people.[28]

Image-making and US imperialism

While the war was reproduced to the American public as a media spectacle, its reality, reduced to statistics, was recorded for policymakers by means of high-tech surveillance. If the Vietnam War, then, was the most mediatized conflict in history, "the most ... reported, filmed, taped, and ... narrated war,"[29] it was also a war in which data was more widely deployed than in all earlier conflicts: "No previous war deluged military and civilian alike with so much information."[30] The war, then, was defined by both surveillance and spectacle, by modern techniques of mass observation and technologies of mass reproduction, by the panopticon and popular media.

But just as policymakers were deceived by the spectacle, becoming obsessed with the mere image of omnipotence (as opposed to imperialism, defined as colonial conquest), so the problem-solvers were misled by their own top-secret intelligence. The system of information surveillance deployed against the communist partisan war in the countryside produced a "quagmire of quantification," resulting in a completely distorted representation of the war on the ground.[31] As Edward Luttwak observed, "the wholesale substitution of civilian mathematical analysis for military expertise" was based upon the "trained incapacity to understand the most important aspects of military power, which happen to be non-measurable."[32] The reduction of reality to mere information, therefore, constituted what Arendt described a form of self-deception or lying, a state of "defactualization" in which reality itself is disguised by its own numerical representation as a series of quantifiable facts. The problem-solvers used techniques of "translating qualities ... into quantities and numbers with which to calculate outcomes ... which ... never came true ... in order to eliminate ... what they knew to be real."[33]

The war planners, then, were blinded by the very information panopticon that was used to uncover the enemy. Consequently, the intelligence presented to policymakers as a means of rationalizing the sovereign decisions enacted by the executive power was undermined by "information pathologies"[34] and "data anxieties" produced by the demographic-style of colonial warfare.[35] But in that case, the imperial image of omnipotence, which the politicians failed to successfully stage as a spectacle, served to conceal the *arcana imperii* of a colonial war of information surveillance, based on a representation of reality that was already falsified. The politicians, therefore, deploying the new governmental technique of image-making, deceived the American public about the facts of a war whose reality was already defactualized by its reduction to mere information. If the war, then, was defined by surveillance and spectacle,

The unimagined community

by the information and mass communication technologies deployed as the tools of a new imperial statecraft, these new forms of deception would also contribute to its spectacular failure: The "deadly combination of ... the pursuit of a mere image of omnipotence, as distinguished from an aim of world conquest ... with ... an ... irrational confidence in the calculability of reality, became the leitmotif of the decision-making process from the beginning of escalation in 1964."[36]

Sovereignty, information and the image of omnipotence

As Arendt's explanation suggests, the war, as waged by the American government, was the product of a peculiar form of imperialism, defined by two distinct modes of image production that originated in consumer society. Derived from the surveillance employed in the factory, and from the spectacle of advertising used to promote consumer commodities, the techniques of information and image-making were adapted during the war as instruments of governmentality. These instruments, however, would ultimately undermine the imperialism whose power they appeared to extend. Both as tools of the state and the source of its own self-deception, these modes of image production implied an ambivalent form of political sovereignty. Subordinated to the autonomous goal of maintaining the mere appearance of power, this sovereignty was simultaneously subject to a "dictatorship of data," limiting its decision-making powers to the calculation of probable outcomes, which failed to conform to reality.[37] Deceived by its own secret intelligence, which falsified the reality of the war on the ground, this sovereignty was at the same time prevented from winning the war because of the need to preserve the public impression that the war indeed could be won. The imperialism of the American government, then, was that of a sovereignty detached from reality, confined to a "defactualized world" of numerical images produced by its own high-tech surveillance and reduced to impotence by the spectacle of its own global power.

Beginning in 1964, with the escalation of the war, the deadly combination of information and image-making would inform the decision-making process of an imperial power that was too concerned with its image to decide on the question of war in Vietnam. As McGeorge Bundy recalled, the 1964 election "loomed over the political landscape ... blotting out any sense of urgency, initiative, or imagination in the evaluation of America's strategic options in Vietnam." Johnson's "preemptive concern" was to "win the election, not the war." Seeking to avoid the publicity that an official resolution on the conflict could engender, Johnson called upon his advisers to devise a form of decisive action that could allow him, at the same time, to remain undecided, thereby postponing the "Day of Reckoning." In Bundy's words, Johnson wanted "firmness and steadiness in Vietnamese policy, but no large new decisions."[38]

This decisive form of sovereign inaction would result in the strategy of limited warfare, which McNamara proposed as a means of pursuing the conflict without attracting the public attention that would be created by a formal declaration of either war or withdrawal. The strategy relied extensively on the practice of image-making, beginning with the lethal but largely spectacular violence of bombing campaigns and covert operations, aimed not at defeating the enemy but at persuading its audience to give up the war. The objective of the "air attacks in [this] ... limited war," therefore, "was never the destruction of the enemy, but, characteristically, 'to break his will.'"[39]

As Johnson discovered, however, only after the fact, this spectacle could not be successfully staged without the physical presence of thousands of troops on the ground, in order to ensure the security of the bases employed in the bombing campaign. The bombing, then, as a decisive form of sovereign inaction, would lead to a series of ad hoc troop escalations. These escalations, in turn, would result in increased public pressure to quickly prevail in the war, in order to preserve the image of the nation's omnipotence. As Johnson complained at a press conference in 1967, the public demanded a war that resembled the contests portrayed in popular culture:

> Our American people, when we get in a contest of any kind—whether it is in a war, an election, a football game, or whatever it is—want it ... decided quickly; get in or get out. They like that curve to rise like this [indicating a sharp rise] and they like the opposition to go down like this [indicating a sharply declining line]. That is not the kind of war we are fighting in Vietnam.[40]

To meet the ever-growing public demand that the war be quickly decided, the planners developed an equally ad hoc approach on the battlefield. Unable to wage a conventional war of territorial conquest against the North Vietnamese, owing to the nuclear balance of power and wary of the ability of its South Vietnamese ally to consolidate their position, the USA pursued a war of attrition.[41] Deploying its immense modern military machinery, the Americans sought to eradicate enemy soldiers at a faster rate than the insurgency could replace them, in a "necro-political" approach to the conflict resembling production on the assembly line.[42] Using the methods of quantification devised by the problem-solvers, US leaders relied on the metric of "body count" to determine the progress of a "war without fronts," in which victory could not be decided by the conquest of territory.[43] Body count, then, would serve as an absolute measure, revealing exactly the ability of enemy, hidden in the population at large, to wage its war without fronts. Attrition and data, therefore, would be used to develop a deterritorialized strategy in which the depopulation of enemy forces would allow the American military to prevail against the partisan war without the need to establish control over territory.

However, like the bombing campaign initiated by Johnson, the war of attrition was primarily intended as spectacle. The ultimate objective was not "to destroy opponents but to persuade them to break off the conflict short of achieving their goals and without resorting to nuclear war."[44] Detached from the limits imposed by a traditional war of territorial conquest, attrition, therefore, amounted to a purely spectacular violence, deployed by a state that, obsessed with merely appearing omnipotent, was unable to establish a durable basis of power. But since power, according to Arendt, is based on the creation of organized structures, the program of pacification pursued by the American government constituted an immensely destructive but essentially powerless form of coercion or violence:

> Even the most despotic domination ... did not rest on superior means of coercion as such, but on a superior organization of power ... on ... organized solidarity ... [We] have seen in Vietnam how an enormous superiority in the means of violence can become helpless if confronted with an ill-equipped but well-organized opponent who is much more powerful.[45]

For Arendt, moreover, the data informing the use of this spectacular violence provided a completely misleading assessment of the enemy's reaction to this form of persuasion. By reducing the complexities of the conflict to the universal language of numbers, this information, which was supposed to provide an accurate measure of the enemy's fighting capacity, concealed an indomitable will to resist, a will that could never be quantified.

The victory of the spectacle and the defeat of the people's war in the Tết Offensive

During the Tết Offensive, the deadly combination of surveillance and spectacle would produce a credibility gap that would help undermine support for the war. The event, which "marked the turning point between U.S. escalation and withdrawal,"[46] was preceded by a "good news" public relations campaign, in which Johnson and Westmoreland touted US intelligence data in an effort to persuade the American public that progress was being made in the war. According to the intelligence, the war of attrition had finally reached a "crossover-point," in which communist losses had exceeded the enemy's ability to replenish its forces. Following the massive military offensive that began on January 30, however, this optimistic appraisal would seem like a willful deception, concealing the fact that "U.S. intervention ... had produced a negligible effect on the will ... of the Vietcong and North Vietnamese to continue in their struggle to unite Vietnam."[47] And indeed, Westmoreland, under pressure from US policymakers, had deliberately chosen to publicize a lower intelligence estimate of enemy forces in order to support the contention that there was "light at the end of the tunnel."[48]

This selective use of data, however, for the purpose of selling the war to the American people, concealed a more fundamental flaw in US intelligence, the fact that its metrics could never precisely determine the overall size of enemy forces, owing to the problem of quantifying the number of irregular units.[49] These units, therefore, were excluded in Westmoreland's assessment that the conflict had arrived at the crucial crossover-point: "with respect to the self-defense and secret self-defense, we are not fighting those people, they are basically civilians. They don't belong in any representation, numerical representation of the military capability of the enemy."[50] Thus, the surveillance employed in the war of attrition was incapable of producing an accurate count of the strength of the people's war waged by the communist forces.

But in that case, the "credibility gap" was not the result of a discrepancy between the reality of the war and the way it was represented to the American public, since the official account of the war concealed a reality that did not "belong in any ... numerical representation." The public deception, therefore, served to disguise a true state of affairs that was already distorted by the metrics used to measure the progress of the conflict.

Amplified by the media coverage, the Offensive appeared to discredit the data on the war of attrition, which had been presented as part of the public relations campaign to garner support for the war. Evaluating the conflict as a mere collection of data, US policymakers not only appeared to be blind to the incalculable human costs of the conflict, they also seemed to be unable to grasp the indomitable will of the enemy: "Tet would not have had the effect it did had intelligence understood the enemy's will and not become fixated on declining enemy numbers."[51]

Following a familiar convention in the historiography of the war, Arendt attributes this indomitable will to an ancient Vietnamese tradition. What eluded the metric of body count was the unwavering determination for independence that the Vietnamese people had inherited from a 2,000-year history of resistance to foreign aggression: "[N]o one at the top … considered it important that the Vietnamese had been fighting foreign invaders for almost 2,000 years," or that the notion of Vietnam as a "tiny backward nation" … stands in flagrant contradiction to the … old and highly developed culture of the region. What Vietnam lacks is not "culture."[52]

What escaped the high-tech surveillance employed in the American army, therefore, was the unquantifiable element of an ancient national history. In Arendt's analysis, this history constitutes an authentic tradition that exists outside the falsified image, or "world picture," produced by modern techniques of surveillance and spectacle. Ignorant of this ancient anti-colonial history, the United States "had embarked on an imperialist policy, had utterly forgotten its old anticolonial sentiments" and had emerged as a new kind of imperial power, seeking to project its image of omnipotence rather than trying to conquer the world.[53] For Arendt, then, the communist forces were the inheritors of an ancient national culture, relying on "organized solidarity" to oppose an imperialism that was undermined by its own image-making techniques.

This ancient tradition, however, as I argued in Chapter 1, was in fact a modern invention, an image that emerged during the colonial era as a result of the rise of modern mass media. During the Vietnam War, the Communist Party would employ this national culture as a "political weapon" in order to mobilize the Vietnamese masses and cast the conflict as an attempt by new foreign invaders to suppress the indomitable will of the Vietnamese people, which was rooted in ancient tradition. In that sense, the people's war strategy was applied by the Party in order to produce the very "national people" who would fight to defend its immemorial sovereignty in an "anti-American war of national salvation" (chiến tranh chống Mỹ cứu nước).

Image-making and US imperialism

But if this prefatory myth, in Arendt's account of the conflict, is what eluded US intelligence, it would also serve to conceal the enormous military miscalculation that led to the Tết Offensive, transforming a tragic debacle on the part of the communist leadership into a heroic expression of the indomitable will of the Vietnamese people. Like Westmoreland's conclusion of "light at the end of the tunnel," the plan for the communist strategic offensive (which would create the credibility gap in the American media) was based on a "wildly overoptimistic assessment of the situation." In a speech at the Fourteenth Central Committee Plenum on January 1968, Lê Duẩn, the General Secretary of the Central Committee of the Communist Party, defined the situation in the South in the following manner:

> I heard from our Southern brothers that enemy morale is very low [bạc nhược]. They are very afraid. The American 25th Division has been weakened ... [and] will disintegrate if we strike hard ... The puppet troops are very, very weak. I heard that they cry [khóc lóc] when attacked by our troops.[54]

This assessment was based on unreliable intelligence estimates, as well as reports from the American press that appeared to confirm the communist view that the South Vietnamese state was regarded as the "illegitimate puppet of imperialist occupiers" by large segments of its own population.[55] Persuaded by the media representation, Lê Duẩn maintained that a large-scale attack in the cities would foment a general uprising, leading to the collapse of the puppet regime and its army, which would finally force American troops to withdraw.

This projection would be directly refuted in official Vietnamese government studies conducted after the war: "The ... spring '68 Strategic Offensive reveal that reports ... did not ... even closely reflect the realities of the situation. ... This led these authorities to make policy decisions that were in no way in line with the situation." Indeed, Lê Duẩn's appraisal proved to be completely mistaken in every major detail: "The central committee's assessment underestimated the ability of the puppet army and puppet government [and] ... the response of American military forces. The assessment overestimated the capability of ... our political forces in the cities."[56] Thus, whereas the "public relations campaign" by Johnson and Westmoreland, "to bolster support for the war was based upon the crossover delusion," the Party's decision to launch the Strategic Offensive was based upon the delusion of the general uprising. According to Huỳnh Công Thân, the communist general who led the attack on Sài Gòn from the South, "the political part of the offensive," contrary to Lê Duẩn's prediction, "never materialized":

> What were the conditions among the masses and the students in Saigon that led our people to reach the conclusion that millions … were boiling over with revolutionary zeal, and were prepared to sacrifice everything for … independence and freedom? … When we entered Saigon, we found that this assessment was incorrect.[57]

In addition, the irregular units, which had been excluded in Westmoreland's count of the enemy order of battle, would prove to be a woefully ineffective force in the cities. The tactics of partisan warfare that had allowed the insurgency to sustain itself in the countryside against a vastly superior conventional army could not be applied in the urban areas, where the attacks would fail to inspire the general insurrection upon which the success of the strategic offensive depended. Exposed in the cities, the irregular units, which constituted the basis of the communist people's war strategy, something that had eluded the metrics employed in the war of attrition, were almost completely destroyed: "In truth, the Tet Offensive for all practical purposes destroyed the Viet Cong."[58] "Tet was the end of the People's War, and essentially any strategy built on guerilla warfare and a politically-inspired insurgency."[59] For General Võ Nguyên Giáp, then – who had vehemently opposed the Offensive – "Tết was a thoughtless and irresponsible undertaking [*chủ trương thiếu cân nhắc, thiếu trách nhiệm*], foolish fighting [*đánh ẩu*], when the conditions were not yet sufficient."[60]

For Johnson, of course, the spectacle of this "irresponsible undertaking" would produce a credibility gap: the president seemed to be either deceived by his own intelligence sources or was deliberately deceiving the public on the actual state of the war. For Lê Duẩn, on the other hand, the enormous strategic mistake, informed by a completely erroneous assessment of the reality on the ground, would produce a spectacular victory at the cost of almost the entire Southern insurgency. As Võ Nguyên Giáp described, "at the battle of Tet … [y]ou defeated us! We knew it, and we thought you knew it. But … your media … caus[ed] more disruption in America than we could in the battlefield. We were ready to surrender. You had won."[61]

Notes

1. W. W. Rostow, *The Stages of Economic Growth: A Non-Communist Manifesto* (Cambridge: Cambridge University Press, 1990), 88.
2. Christina Klein, *Cold War Orientalism: Asia in the Middlebrow Imagination, 1945–1961* (Berkeley: University of California Press, 2003), 64.
3. Theodor W. Adorno, *The Culture Industry: Selected Essays on Mass Culture* (London: Routledge, 1991), 40.
4. Guy Debord, *Society of the Spectacle*, trans. Ken Knabb (London: Rebel Press, 2004), 21–2.
5. Ibid., 8.
6. M. Crozier, S. Huntington and J. Watanuki, *The Crisis of Democracy: On the Governability of Democracies to the Trilateral Commission* (New York: New York University Press, 1975), 98.
7. Telegram from the Embassy in Vietnam to the Department of State, Saigon, August 27, 1963.
8. Walter Benjamin, *The Work of Art in the Age of Its Technological Reproducibility, and Other Writings on Media* (Cambridge, MA: Harvard University Press, 2008), n. 49.
9. Essay – American news on the Vietnam War and their impact on the American public opinion. VCA. 18450101001 March 2006. Box 01, Folder 01. Andreas Achteresch Collection.
10. William M. Hammond, "The press in Vietnam as agent of defeat: a critical examination," *Reviews in American History*, 17:2 (June 1989), 312.
11. Andrew Wiest, "Introduction," in *Triumph Revisited: Historians Battle for the Vietnam War*, ed. Andrew Wiest and Michael J. Doidge (New York: Routledge, 2010), 6.
12. Quoted in James H. Willbanks, *The Tet Offensive: A Concise History* (New York: Columbia University Press, 2006), 111.
13. Herbert Y. Schandler, *Lyndon Johnson and Vietnam: The Unmaking of a President* (Princeton, NJ: Princeton University Press, 1977), 266–89.
14. Quoted in Willbanks, *The Tet Offensive*, 69. See Historians and the Visual Analysis of the Television News. VCA. 2263009008 June 1, 1978. Box 30, Folder 09. Douglas Pike Collection: Unit 03 – The Press and the War.
15. Arendt, "Lying in Politics," 8.
16. "McNaughton Draft for McNamara on Proposed Course of Action," in *The Pentagon Papers* (New York: Bantam, 1971), 438.
17. Arendt, "Lying in Politics," 17.
18. Ibid., 39.
19. Debord, *Society of the Spectacle*, 7.
20. Arendt, "Lying in Politics," 9.
21. See Ralph E. Strauch, "'Squishy' problems and quantitative methods," *Policy Sciences*, 6 (1975), 175–84. On the Vietnam data problem, see John Prados,

Vietnam: *The History of an Unwinnable War, 1945–1975* (Lawrence: University Press of Kansas, 2009), 461.
22 Alan McKinlay and Ken Starkey, "Managing Foucault: Foucault, Management and Organization Theory," in *Foucault, Management and Organization Theory: From Panoptic on to Technologies of Self*, ed. Alan McKinlay and Ken Starkey (London: Sage Publications, 1998), 7.
23 Arendt, "Lying in Politics," 18.
24 Ibid., 37.
25 Michael Herr, "Hell sucks," *Esquire*, 70 (August 1968), 68.
26 Computers in Vietnam. VCA. 2234308030 September 30, 1968. Box 43, Folder 08. Douglas Pike Collection: Unit 03 – Statistical Data. See also I. G. R. Shaw, "Scorched atmospheres: the violent geographies of the Vietnam War and the rise of drone warfare," *Annals of the Association of American Geographers*, 106:3 (2016), 688–704.
27 *Investigation into Electronic Battlefield Program* (Washington DC: US Government Printing Office, 1971), 12.
28 Quoted in Ben Buley, *The New American Way of War: Military Culture and the Political Utility of Force* (New York: Routledge, 2007), 91. See also Summary, IDHS: Intelligence Data Handling Systems Directorate – Quarterly Digest – Record of MACV Part 1, 9. VCA. F015800200714 March 1970. Box 0020, Folder 0714. Vietnam Archive Collection.
29 John Carlos Rowe, "'Bringing It All Back Home': American Recyclings of the Vietnam War," in *The Violence of Representation*, ed. Nancy Armstrong and Leonard Tennenhouse (London: Routledge, 1989), 197.
30 Donald Fisher Harrison, "Computers, electronic data, and the Vietnam War," *Archivaria*, 26 (1988), 18.
31 Viktor Mayer-Schonberger and Kenneth Cukier, *Big Data: A Revolution That Will Transform How We Live, Work and Think* (New Delhi: John Murray, 2013), 165.
32 Edward Luttwak, *The Pentagon and the Art of War: The Question of Military Reform* (New York: Simon & Schuster, 1985), 269.
33 Arendt, "Lying in Politics," 36.
34 M. Van Crevald, *Command in War* (Cambridge, MA: Harvard University Press, 1985), 241.
35 Oliver Belcher, "Data Anxieties: Objectivity and Difference in Early Vietnam War Computing," in *Algorithmic Life: Calculative Devices in a Digital Age*, ed. L. Amoore and V. Piotukh (Abingdon: Routledge, 2016), 127–42.
36 Arendt, "Lying in Politics," 39.
37 Mayer-Schonberger and Cukier, *Big Data*, 168.
38 Andrew Johns, *Vietnam's Second Front: Domestic Politics, the Republican Party, and the War* (Lexington: University of Kentucky Press, 2010).
39 Arendt, "Lying in Politics," 42.

40 *Public Papers of the Presidents of the United States*. Lyndon B. Johnson, 1967, Book II. Washington DC: Government Printing Office, 1967, 495.
41 "What alternative was there to a war of attrition? A grand invasion of North Vietnam was out, for the U.S. policy was not to conquer North Vietnam but to eliminate the insurgency inside South Vietnam, and president Johnson had stated publicly that he would not 'broaden' the war." William C. Westmoreland, *A Soldier Reports* (New York: Doubleday, 1976), 152. On Westmoreland and the war of attrition, see Andrew F. Krepinevich, *The Army and Vietnam* (Baltimore, MD: Johns Hopkins University Press, 1986), 164, and Gregory A. Daddis, *Westmoreland's War, Reassessing American Strategy in Vietnam* (New York: Oxford University Press, 2014).
42 Viet Thanh Nguyen, *Nothing Ever Dies: Vietnam and the Memory of War* (Cambridge, MA: Harvard University Press, 2016), 158.
43 Phạm Hồng Tung, "40 năm sau vụ thảm sát Mỹ Lai lật lại hồ sơ một tội ác chiến tranh của quân đội Mỹ tại Việt Nam." [Forty years after the My Lai Massacre Revealed the Record of American War Crimes in Vietnam], *Tạp chí Nghiên cứu Lịch sử /Historical Studies*, 3 (2008), 26.
44 George C. Herring, *LBJ and Vietnam: A Different Kind of War* (Austin: University of Texas, 1994), 4.
45 Arendt, "Lying in Politics," 149–50.
46 James J. Wirtz, *The Tet Offensive: Intelligence Failure in War* (Ithaca, NY: Cornell University Press, 1991), 2.
47 Ibid., 2.
48 James J. Wirtz, "Intelligence to please? The order of battle controversy during the Vietnam War," *Political Science Quarterly*, 106:2 (1991), 240.
49 Gregory A. Daddis, *No Sure Victory: Measuring U.S. Army Effectiveness and Progress in the Vietnam War* (New York: Oxford University Press, 2011), 105.
50 Quoted in Edwin E. Moise, *The Myths of Tet: The Most Misunderstood Event of the Vietnam War* (Lawrence: University Press of Kansas, 2017), 43.
51 Jake Blood, *The Tet Effect: Intelligence and the Public Perception of War* (London: Routledge, 2005), 44.
52 Arendt, "Lying in Politics," 32.
53 Ibid., 45.
54 "*Bài phát biểu của đồng chí Lê Duẩn*" [Comrade Le Duan's speech], January 1968. Đảng Cộng sản Việt Nam, Văn kiện Đảng toàn tập, v. 29 (Hà Nội: Chính trị Quốc gia, 2004), 28.
55 James S. Robbins, *This Time We Win: Revisiting the Tet Offensive* (New York: Encounter Books, 2012), 69.
56 Quoted in Merle L. Pribbenow, "Vietnamese Sources on Tet." Vietnam Wars Tet Offensive 50th Anniversary Panel, CSPAN May 28, 2018.
57 Huỳnh Công Thân, *Ở chiến trường Long An: Hồi Ức* [On the Long An Battlefield: A Memoir] (Hà Nội: Nhà xuất bản quân đội nhân dân, 1994), 60.

58 Phillip B. Davidson, *Vietnam at War: The History, 1946–1975* (Oxford: Oxford University Press, 1991), 475.
59 Kolko, *Anatomy of a War*, 334.
60 Bùi Tín, '*Chiến thắng Mậu Thân' của Hà Nội chỉ là 'ảo tưởng cay đắng*'" [Hanoi's 'Tet Victory' was only a "Bitter Illusion"], *Người Việt* (February 8, 2018). https://www.nguoi-viet.com/dang-duoc-quan-tam/nam-muoi-nam-mau-chien-thang-mau-chi-la-ao-tuong-cay-dang/. Last accessed July 22, 2019.
61 Quoted in Letter from Ed Moffitt to Walter Cronkite re: media influence on military decisions. VCA. 20740102003 January 15, 2009. Box 01, Folder 02. Ed Moffitt Collection.

Conclusion

"Ngo-dinh-Diem's views on democracy are ... the least understood of all his ideas. He has been accused of dictatorship, autocracy, authoritarianism ... The communists claim to be ... better democrats than, the Westerners. A communist concept of 'popular' democracy has been opposed to ... western democracy, which is essentially a parliamentary one. And it is according to either of these that President Ngo-dinh-Diem has been judged."[1]

"[T]here are ... no liberals in Việt Nam, and it is a continuing error of both war supporters and war opponents ... to seek them."[2]

It is commonplace in historical works on the war to condemn the South Vietnamese government for its lack of democracy while minimizing the crimes committed by the openly undemocratic regime in the North. The arbitrary arrest, detention and execution of thousands of suspected communists in the South is cited, for example, as evidence that the early Republic was an irredeemable "quasi-police state."[3] On the other hand, the murder of countless opponents by the Communist Party in the 1940s and 1950s, and its assassination of over 35,000 Southern local officials, are excused as an unfortunate means towards the legitimate ends of consolidating political power.[4] State censorship of the media, and the absence of effective political opposition in the South, is viewed as indicative of the illegitimacy of the early Republic in the eyes of its own population. Yet the same lack of democracy in the North is explained as a justifiable constraint upon individual freedom, imposed on a people at war for the sake of its very survival.

This unequal treatment has been defended on the grounds that the Communist Party cannot be accused of failing to conform to the ideals

The unimagined community

of a bourgeois democracy to which it never subscribed. In contrast, the Republic, because it proclaimed itself to be a defender of freedom, is rightly condemned for betraying its own political principles. Hence, the charge of "diemocracy" in the American media against "the government's make-believe guarantees of civil liberties and fair elections."[5]

This reproach continues a well-worn Western tradition of liberal outrage and irony. In his critique of capitalism, Marx attributed this liberal sensibility to a "utopian inability to grasp the necessary difference between the real and the ideal form of bourgeois society," the difference between the principles of bourgeois democracy and the reality created by the capitalist mode of production. Against the "foolishness" of those who upheld the "ideals of bourgeois society articulated by the French revolution," Marx maintained, therefore, that the "realization of equality and freedom" in capitalism "prove to be inequality and unfreedom."[6] For the Personalists, who inherited Marx's critique, this bourgeois society is one in which the establishment of a juridical system of individual liberty and the political institution of majority rule served to perpetuate the tyranny of production for profit. As Foucault pointed out, in a similar vein, the "'Enlightenment' which discovered the liberties also invented the disciplines," which conditioned the rise of industrial capitalism.[7]

In the twentieth century, the same liberal irony, which Marx recognized as an obstacle to the abolition of capitalism, would be appropriated as a moral critique of colonialism. The "French imperialists, abusing the standard of Liberty, Equality, and Fraternity," as Hồ Chí Minh famously declared, "have acted contrary to the ideals of humanity."[8] European colonialism, therefore, according to this moral critique, was based on what Sartre described as a hypocritical humanism that "never tires of talking of Man," even as it denied the humanity of the populations it colonized.[9]

This account of colonialism, however, elides the historical complicity between European imperialism and the ideals of bourgeois democracy. As officers in the French expeditionary forces announced at the imperial court in Huế in 1859, the aim of the conquest was not to impose the Christian religion. Rather, the mission to civilize was an attempt to defend "*les droits sacrés de l'humanité et ceux de la civilization*," on behalf of a non-Western people subordinated to the tyrannical rule of an absolute sovereign.[10] Early colonial administrators, who were "decisively shaped by doctrines which were, at base, anti-colonial,"[11] spoke of "French intervention in Vietnamese life to redeem the Vietnamese peasantry from the rule of an 'aristocracy of scholars.'" In accordance

Conclusion

with this noble ambition, French imperialism imposed a program of "social revolutionism,"[12] aimed at "calling [the colonial subject] to enjoy the rights of the citizen." "This program," as Le Myre de Vilers described, "conforms to the policies of France, which does not conquer in order to exploit the vanquished by reducing the latter to serfdom, but strives on the contrary to penetrate its new subject with its ideas."[13]

Contrary, therefore, to an anti-colonialism that opposes the imperial project in the name of the principles of its own bourgeois democracy, imperialism was not defined primarily, in the Vietnamese context at least, by the denial of "the ideals of humanity." Rather, its most destructive effects were a consequence of the very attempt to extend the inalienable rights of man to a non-Western society. During the colonial era, the introduction of a juridical system of individual liberties, enforced by the disciplinary machinery of the colonial state, would serve to establish the impersonal rule of the market, transforming the structure of Vietnamese civilization itself. Under the civilizing mission, the despotism of the imperial court and the communal democracy of the Vietnamese village were supplanted by the apparatus of a centralized state and the abstract domination of capital.

In the South, this imperialist project would be continued, in a more spectacular form, by the American government. During the early part of the war, "idealistic Americans ... in their ... zeal to impose their own Western concepts of right and wrong," helped to destroy the early Republic, in order to rescue its image as a bastion of democracy (an image to which its leaders had never aspired).[14] The imperialistic attempt by US officials to impose the norms of liberal democracy, in an effort to appease American public opinion, would help to determine the later course of the war and the fate of the American intervention. "What the United States did was to allow itself to forget that it was in Vietnam as an ally, not as a conqueror." In the "worst mistake we ever made," the USA "conspired to replace the government of an ally in the middle of a common war against the Communist enemy, thus plunging South Vietnam and the war effort into a steep spiral of decline."[15]

With the collapse of the early Republic, the social revolution in the countryside to establish a decentralized system of politically autonomous communities would be supplanted by a high-tech war of attrition, which produced an immense displaced population dependent on American aid. In the cities, the policy of economic and political liberalization would encourage a vibrant artistic and intellectual culture while precipitating the rise of a mass consumer society, increasingly detached from the war in the countryside. The freedom that prevailed in the later Republic, then, would engender what one South Vietnamese observer described as a modern bourgeois society that, while largely indifferent to the appeals of the Communist Party, was incapable of sustaining itself without the support of its neocolonial patron: "You thought that by giving us an easy life, a television, a washing machine, a car, that we could fight Communism better. That is not true. ... We have become bourgeois, although we were not born to be bourgeois."[16]

In recent years, this bourgeois society has been portrayed in a more positive light, as the product of a "Republican experience of nation-building." From "beginning to end," this project was purportedly aimed at creating a "viable nation based on traditional culture ... Republican ideas on popular sovereignty ... the separation of powers and ... an economy based on private enterprises."[17] This representation, however, which emphasizes the "agency" of the South Vietnamese people, not only appears suspiciously to resemble an exact mirror opposite of the conventional portrait of the Republic as a corrupt puppet regime, incapable of creating a stable democracy. It also assumes a common understanding of "freedom" among the South Vietnamese from the beginning to the end of the war.

For the leaders of the early Republic, however, it was precisely the attempt to impose a Western ideal of popular sovereignty that threatened to undermine the war against the insurgency, as well as the project of creating a Personalist democracy at the base. Thus, the Ngos attempted to develop the Strategic Hamlet Campaign as an instrument against the Americans as well as the urban elite who "in the name of liberty were trying to crush the social revolution."[18] After the collapse of the First Republic, moreover, the economic liberalism of the later regimes would help to perpetuate economic underdevelopment and dependence on American aid. But as such, it was precisely the agency of later South Vietnamese leaders, in the project of creating a nation based on liberal democracy and free-market capitalism, that ironically would deprive the Republic of its economic and political sovereignty.

At the end of the war, the Communist Party would dissolve the bourgeois society that had emerged as a result of the massive American military intervention and its economic and political program of liberalization. This event would not only erase a rich and uniquely Southern national culture, which had evolved over the course of two decades of war. It would also serve to obscure a remarkable and improbable political experiment against capitalism and liberal democracy, an experiment that

Conclusion

sought to establish a non-Western form of modernity, carried out in the South under the shadow of US imperialism.

This experiment was originally created in part as a "copy of the form of organization" employed by the communists (*sao chép vụng về hình thức tổ chức đảng*).[19] The use of this organization by the early Republic, however, fundamentally distinguished its doctrine from that of the Party. For the latter, the decentralized system of semi-autonomous villages, which supported the insurgency in the South, was a temporary emergency measure, one that would be dissolved at the end of the war with the establishment of a dictatorship of the proletariat. This dictatorship in turn, according to theorists in the Communist Party, would then direct the transition toward a withering away of the state. For the Party, therefore, the creation of a stateless society was a task that could only be realized after the proletarian revolution. During the war, according to Ngô Đình Nhu, this "meant that people in the present" were compelled by the Communist Party "to sacrifice themselves for … the future."[20] To use Walter Benjamin's account of the vulgar Marxist conception of history, the Party, therefore "preferred to cast the working class in the role of a redeemer of future generations."[21]

After the war, however, the "so-called socialist Party-State," as the activist Ngô Văn Xuyết has described, inexplicably refused to "disappear … on its own," to dismantle its state apparatus of discipline, "its army, police, jails, laws and institutions."[22] Instead, the dictatorship of the Party would devolve into a "totalitarian regime based on privilege."[23] This failure, according to Ngô Văn Xuyết, confirmed that the communist regime was not an "actually existing socialism" confronted with the practical task of constructing a real socialist society. Its program, rather, was that of an "actually non-existing communism," a communism that preserved the capitalist institutions of the centralized state and the exploitation of labor: "[W]e now know that what they called 'communism' was not communism … [I]t was nothing but a ghastly, criminal simulacrum, a state capitalism, a species of economic-political monster administered for the benefit of a greedy and unscrupulous bureaucracy." Having defeated US imperialism, the Party, therefore, would establish a centralized state that was far more repressive than the one that the French had imposed in the colonial era. Thus, Trần Văn Giàu, who had participated in the wave of repression against non-Stalinist Vietnamese militants during the Party's ascendance to power, would condemn the communist government as an instrument of oppression, exploiting the people whose popular sovereignty it was supposed to embody:[24]

> Why have we, revolutionaries and resistance fighters, created such a bureaucratic State? The province of Thanh Hoa alone has more government officials than the entire colonial apparatus of old Indochina. How can the peasants allow such a State to exist? ... I have never in my life seen peasants as impoverished as they are now ... The reason for this is that they allow the continued existence of a State that is as oversized as it is ineffective.

If the early Republic, therefore, had failed in the eyes of its critics as a liberal democracy (a form of government that its leaders had expressly repudiated), the Communist Party would fail to conform to its own conception of communism.

But as such, the sacrifice imposed by the Party during the war had been made for the sake of a future society that would never materialize. "The future," as Bảo Ninh described in the *Sorrow of War*, "lied to us, there long ago in the past." "There is no new life, no new era, nor ... hope for a beautiful future."[25] This failure on the part of the Communist Party is consistent with what the philosopher Giorgio Agamben has characterized as the fundamental "weakness" of orthodox Marxism: The "dictatorship of the proletariat as the transitional phase leading to the stateless society ... is the reef on which the revolutions of our century have been shipwrecked."

In the case of the Vietnamese Revolution, however, the failure has been largely obscured by what Ngô Văn Xuyết has described as the "image disseminated by the Stalinist-orchestrated leftwing propaganda." In this image, which excludes the experience of the South Vietnamese, the war is portrayed as a struggle between US imperialism and the indomitable will of the Vietnamese people, rooted in an ancient nationalist myth: "[E]veryone is revolted by the destruction ... the sufferings of a population cruelly afflicted for the past twenty-eight years; and everyone naïvely applauds ... the combatants without realizing that warmongering heroism can mask every type of enslavement and ... tyranny."[26]

This image has successfully served to conceal an unlikely experiment directed against the institutions of capitalism and the constitutional state, as well as the non-existing socialism of the Communist Party. In contrast to their counterparts in the North, the leaders of the early Republic had expressly repudiated the weakness of orthodox Marxism: "You and I want totally different futures for Vietnam," Diệm exclaimed to Hồ Chí Minh. "[Y]ou will ... try and impose a dictatorship of the proletariat."[27] While the early Republic, therefore, in the war against the insurgency, would copy its political organization, this organization, for the South Vietnamese government, was not a transitional phase. Rather,

Conclusion

the establishment of a decentralized system of semi-autonomous communes, which the Party regarded as a temporary emergency measure, was understood as the aim of the revolution itself. For Nhu, the possibility of a stateless society was one that was already present in the political form of the hamlet. Whereas the Communist Party, therefore, compelled the people to sacrifice themselves for the sake of a communist future that would never arrive, the Republic had sought to impose a democracy from the base as an end unto itself, or a means without ends: the "people in the present possess the same value of those in the future. Therefore, we propose to savor whatever we attain in our struggle" (*đặt vấn đề tranh đấu tới đâu hưởng tới đó*).[28]

If this experiment, which has been portrayed as an instrument of repression employed by a reactionary puppet regime, was compromised by its complicity with US imperialism and bourgeois democracy, its design, nevertheless, was more radical than the program imposed by the Communist Party. In the end, the early Republic's attempt to establish a socialism without the state would be undermined by the American government in an effort to rescue its image as a liberal democracy. On the other hand, the failure of the Communist Party and its actually non-existing communism would be transformed by the "image disseminated by the Stalinist-orchestrated leftwing propaganda" into a powerful and enduring symbol of world revolution.

With the persistent decline of liberal democracy in the era of "post-democratic spectacular societies," the image, perhaps, will continue to outweigh the reality.[29]

Notes

1 Phuc Thien, *President Ngo-Dinh-Diem's Political Philosophy* (Saigon: Review Horizons, 1956), 8.
2 Neil Jamieson and Terry Rambo, *Cultural Change in Rural Viet-Nam: A Study of the Effects of Long-Term Communist Control on the Social Structure, Attitudes, & Values of the Peasants of the Mekong Delta* (New York: Southeast Asia Development Advisory Group of the Asia Society, 1973?), viii.
3 Thomas L. Ahern, Jr., *The CIA and the House of Ngo: Covert Action in South Vietnam, 1954–1963* (Washington DC: CIA, 1999), 100.
4 See François Guillemot, "Au Coeur de la fracture vietnamienne: l'élimination de l'opposition nationaliste et anticolonialiste dans le Nord du Vietnam (1945–1946)," in *Naissance d'un État-parti: Le Vietnam depuis 1945*, ed. Christopher E. Goscha and Benoît de Tréglodé (Paris: Les Indes Savantes, 2004), 175–222.

5 Deepe Keever, *Death Zones and Darling Spies*, 87.
6 Marx, *Grundrisse*, 248–9.
7 Foucault, *Discipline and Punish*, 222.
8 Spencer C. Tucker (ed.), *Encyclopedia of the Vietnam War: A Political, Social, and Military History*, vol. 3 (Santa Barbara, CA: ABC-CLIO, 1998), 889.
9 Jean-Paul Sartre, "Preface," in *The Wretched of the Earth*, ed. Frantz Fanon, trans. Constance Farrington (New York: Grove Press, 1963), 9.
10 Philippe Héduy (ed.), *Histoire de l'Indochine. Tome I. La Conquête, 1624–1885. Tome II. Le Destin, 1885–1954* (Paris: Henri Veyrier, 1983), 68.
11 Barnhart, "Violence and the Civilizing Mission," 241.
12 Woodside, *Community and Revolution*, 8.
13 Le Myre de Vilers, *Les Institutions Civiles De La Cochinchine*, 50.
14 Higgins, *Our Vietnam Nightmare*, 287–9.
15 Moffitt, The Vietnam War 1954–1975.
16 "The World: THE U.S. AS A SCAPEGOAT," *TIME Magazine*, 98:2 (1971), 30.
17 Toung Vu, "Nation Building and War: The Republican Experience, 1955–75." Symposium: Vietnam War Revisited, September 14, 2018, Washington DC. National Archives Research Center.
18 *Times of Vietnam*, July 7, 1960, 1.
19 Nguyễn Xuân Hoài, "*Đảng Cần lao Nhân vị*" [The Cần Lao Personalist Party] Luutruvn.com, January 4, 2016, http://luutruvn.com/index.php/2016/04/01/dang-can-lao-nhan-vi/. Last accessed July 21, 2019.
20 Meeting Minutes (#36), Uỷ-Ban Liên-Bộ Đặc-Trách về Ấp Chiến-Lược tại Dinh Gia Long [Intra-Ministry Committee for Strategic Hamlets], 14.
21 Benjamin, "On the Concept of History," 394.
22 Ngo Van, *Viêt-nam, 1920–1945: révolution et contre-révolution sous la domination coloniale* (Paris: Nautilus, 1995).
23 Quoted in ibid.
24 Ngo Van, *In the Crossfire: Adventures of a Vietnamese Revolutionary* (Oakland, CA: AK Press, 2010), 122–4.
25 Bảo Ninh, *Nỗi Buồn Chiến Tranh* (Hà Nội: Nhà xuất bản Hội Nhà văn, 1991), 49–50.
26 Ngo Van, *In the Crossfire*, 121.
27 Quoted in Higgins, *Our Vietnam Nightmare*, 215.
28 Meeting Minutes (#36), Uỷ-Ban Liên-Bộ Đặc-Trách về Ấp Chiến-Lược tại Dinh Gia Long [Intra-Ministry Committee for Strategic Hamlets], 14.
29 Giorgio Agamben, *The Time That Remains: A Commentary on the Letter to the Romans* (Stanford, CA: Stanford University Press, 2005), 58.

Index

Page numbers in italics indicate figures.

Adorno, Theodor 25, 26, 201, 229–30, 231, 232, 233, 234, 235, 236, 248
advertising 18, 75, 104, 178, 193, 194, 195, 196, 198, 199, 202, 214, 216, 221, 222, 225, 235, 248, 250, 251, 254
alienation of labor 71, 98, 105
inalienable Rights of Man 55–7
Althusser, Louis 85n12
American aid 2, 17, 18–19, 126, 133, 146n163, 147n180, 169, 176, 177, 179, 180, 181, 198, 206n34, 216, 267, 268
    Strategic Hamlets against 117–25
American embassy 2, 5, 16, 190
American liberalism 75, 100
American Revolution 99, 100, 105
Anderson, Benedict 6, 27, 28, 46n32
Annamites 24–5, 28, 29, 32, 33, 38, 66, 68, 69, 70, 77, 155
anti-colonialism 51–82, 267
    Personalism 69–71
Aragon, Louis 75
Arendt, Hannah 6, 19, 97, 99, 100, 101, 104, 105, 114, 158, 163, 168, 249–50, 251, 253, 254, 256, 258, 259
Armus, Seth 86n26

autonomous organization 67, 69, 90n120, 97–8, 99, 110, 134

Baez, Joan 190
Bảo Đại 37
Bảo Ninh
    The Sorrow of War 181–2, 270
Barrows, Leland 120, 121
Baudelaire 197
Baudrillard, Jean 215, 223
Benjamin, Walter 196, 200–1, 216–17, 227–8, 230, 239, 240
Berman, Larry 174n72
black market 176
Browne, Malcolm 7
Buddhism 1, 6, 8, 52, 171n32, 186, 187, 217, 247n103
    militancy 146n163
    protests 63, 161
    treatment 164
Buddhist Affair 2, 6, 7, 127, 135, 163, 164
Bùi Anh Tuấn 18
    avenging the nation 235–42
    career 217–18
    Case of the Stolen Atomic Documents 218, 223
    Cold War and deterrence of sovereignty 222–4

Index

Bùi Anh Tuấn (*cont.*)
   Cold War balance of surveillance and spectacle 219–22
   domination without discipline 233–5
   free time and leisure 228–32
   Golden Regret in India 219, 221, 229
   mass culture and temporal mastery 233–5
   Specter over Red Square 215, 219–20, 221, 222, 223, 225, 230, 231, 235, 236, 237, 240
   surveillance and spectacle in Z.28 novels 214–42
   surveillance and style 225–8
   Z.28 novels 214–42
   see also Văn Bình (fictional character)
Bundy, McGeorge 254–5

cầm kỳ thi họa 25, 26, 45n19
Cần Lao Party 20n20, 38, 40, 64, 71, 135, 136, 151n260
Catholicism 52–3, 58, 63–4, 86n17, 186, 239, 246–7n103
   Personalism 52
Catton, Philip 40, 41, 74, 77, 122–3, 134, 164
Cavaillès, Jean 85n12
Césaire, Aimé 63
Chakrabarty, Dipesh 40, 77
Chandler, Robert
   War of Ideas 154
Christianity 7, 49n82, 53, 64, 74–5, 84n12, 187, 266
   against capitalism 58–62
   Personalism 63
   see also Catholicism
CIA 96, 133, 135, 158, 171n32, 181, 182, 196, 222, 229, 231, 240
civilization and culture 24–7
Civil Rights Movement 1
Clairmont, Frederic 89n98
Colby, William 126, 158–9
Cold War 5, 10–11, 13, 18, 215

   balance of surveillance and spectacle 219–22
   deterrence of sovereignty 222–5
colonialism, surveillance, and media 27–8
Commodity Import Program 122, 124, 131, 176
communal production 43, 55, 57, 60, 69, 70, 76, 78, 79–80, 82, 102, 105, 107, 112, 125, 133
   autonomous 107
   direct 62, 64, 97
Communist Party 4, 8, 12, 14, 17, 35, 42–3, 44, 53, 71, 72, 82–3, 96, 97, 98, 102, 103, 105, 108, 109, 117, 125, 126, 155, 156–7, 159–60, 165, 175, 178, 180, 181, 182, 183, 184, 190, 192, 204, 219, 258, 259, 265, 268, 269, 270, 271
   French 85n13
   Nghệ Tĩnh soviets 99
Conein, Lucien 133
Confucianism 53, 62
   elite 26, 28, 45n20
   examinations 27
   hierarchy of occupations 169, 239
   literati 26, 45n20
Contemporary Culture 183
counterinsurgency 4, 16, 41, 42, 101, 104, 108, 116, 130, 131, 136, 153, 158
   American 251–4
   anticommunist 105, 114
   British 14
   see also Strategic Hamlet Campaign
Counterpart Funds 123
   see also Commodity Import Program
coup (1960) 51
coup (1963) 137, 149n208, 151n260, 172n59, 194
   Johnson 166, 167
   Kennedy 4, 173n60
   Lodge 127–8, 133, 164–5
   media 7, 190, 195
   newspaper industry 195

Index

Personalism 16, 51, 127–8
   social revolution 5
   "talented men" 188
   US support 2, 4, 5, 9, 15–16, 127–8, 130, 134–5, 136, 164–5, 166, 173n60, 187, 188
   Creator and Creation 58–9
   see also Personalism
credibility gap 257, 259, 260
Cronkite, Walter 249
cultural policies in the North 190, 207n47

dân tộc (national people) 12, 29, 30–3, 43, 184
   nam tiến (Southward Advance) 109–13
   see also avenging the nation
Đảng Cần Lao Nhân Vị *see* Cần Lao Party
Đào Duy Anh 45n20
   Chinese-Vietnamese Dictionary 72
Debord, Guy 10, 23, 215, 222
   Society of the Spectacle 37, 199, 221, 248, 251
Declaration of Independence 30, 69
decolonization 84
democracy, discipline, and second Southward Advance 37–44
dependency 89n98, 123–4, 160, 206n34
Derrida, Jacques 84n12
detective fiction 244n55, 246n77
de Villiers, Gérard
   Son Altesse Sérénissime 192
dictatorship of the proletariat 15, 60, 72, 77, 103, 105, 139n45, 140n61, 269, 270
diemocracy 40, 74, 106, 160, 161, 266
Dommen, Arthur 129–30, 189
Dương Nghiễm Mậu 186, 195
Dương Thu Hương 182
   Novel without a Name 34
Duong Van Mai Elliott 122

École Normale Supérieure 85n12
economic liberalism 39, 121, 159, 268
egoistic man 56, 65, 71, 80
Enlightenment 33, 39, 61, 266
Ernstfall 223, 224
Esprit 51, 75, 85n12, 86n26

Fanon, Frantz 23, 26, 31, 32, 63, 179
feuilleton see serialized fiction
Field, Michael 38
First Republic 5, 6, 13–14, 15, 16, 101, 136, 268
Fitzgerald, Frances 51, 104
Fleming, Ian 18, 214, 219
Foucault, Michel 34
   biopolitics 244n43
   dark side of the parliamentary state 39, 43
   Debord critique 222
   discipline 65, 68, 111, 228, 232, 233
   Discipline and Punish 222
   Enlightenment 33, 39, 61, 266
   "enslaved sovereign" 29
   Marxism 85
   Napoleonic character 35
   sovereign subject 29, 61
   surveillance and spectacle 215
Fourniau, Charles 114
Fourteenth Central Committee Plenum 259
Fraleigh, Albert, 116, 121–2, 130, 166–7, 172n59
fraudulent liberalism 76
freedom of religion 171n32
French imperialism 53, 69, 266, 267
French Revolution 57, 70, 71, 75, 99, 228, 266
   Rights of Man 7, 11, 56, 65, 69, 70, 71, 74, 77, 100, 267

Geneva Accords 33, 118, 184
Goburdhun, Ramchundur 133
Goldman, Emma 102
Great Depression 98
guerrillas 115, 117, 119, 177, 260
GVN Television 193

Index

Hammer, Ellen 105
Hegel, Georg Wilhelm Friedrich 84n12, 111
Heidegger, Martin 84n12
Herr, Michael 251–2
Herring, George 13
Hesse, Hermann 191
Higgins, Marguerite 76, 129, 135–6, 162, 163
Hoàng Đạo Thành 32
Hồ Chí Minh 155, 270
  ceasefire 130
  cult of personality 35, 37
  "cultural front" 34
  "culture of the masses" 34
  deposition 159, 165
  French imperialism 266
  independence 8, 46n40, 69; *see also* Declaration of Independence
  quotations 83
  war's end 117, 129, 130
  writings 204
Học Tập, 175
Horrox, James 101
Husserl, Edmund 84n12

IBM computers 252, *252*
idealistic Americans 135, 267
image of God, liberation of labor in the 58–62
see also Personalism
imagined community 12, 15, 17, 18, 28, 203
see also Anderson, Benedict
imperialism
  French 53, 69, 266, 267
  US in Strategic Hamlet Campaign imperialism 96–137
  US in Vietnam War 6, 19, 248–60
  intelligence 19, 38, 106, 116, 117, 156, 229, 251, 258
  communist 231
  faulty 166
  phony 162
  RVN 158, 189
  secret 164, 223, 236, 253, 254

  US 116, 135, 153–4, 240, 257, 259, 260
  Western 219
  see also Văn Bình (fictional character)
image-making and US imperialism in Vietnam War 248–60
International Control Commission 111, 133

Jamieson, Neil 238
Jefferson, Thomas 99, 100, 104, 138n24
John Paul II, Pope 55
Johnson, Lyndon B. 129, 166, 167, 173n72, 249, 250–1, 254–5, 256, 257, 259, 260

Kant 25, 187
Kennedy, John F. 116, 127, 128, 148n208
  assassination 158
  coup 4, 173n60
  "networks of resistance" 158
  suspension of aid 133
KGB 219, 222, 225, 230, 231
kibbutz 100–4
Kim Dung 196, 212n174
knowledge 60, 84n12
  forensic 230
Kojève, Alexandre
  Phenomenology of Spirit 85n12
Kolko, Gabriel 82, 102–3, 180

Lacroix, Jean 85n12, 88n61
Lansdale, Edward 104–5, 162, 168
Lê Duẩn 100, 259, 260
Lê Lợi 30, 31, 67, 154, 155, 156, *157*
Lemur Nguyễn Cát Tường 244n55
Le Myre de Vilers, Charles 68, 69, 70, 267
Lenin, Vladimir 63, 82, 98, 100, 101, 204, 219
Lê Văn Nghĩa 194
liberalism 17, 18, 40, 51, 53, 64–5, 68, 74, 81
  American 75, 100
  definition 89n98

Index

economic 39, 121, 159, 268
fraudulent 76
Occidental ideology 70, 71, 77, 78, 104
political 6, 89n98, 267–8
liberation of labor in the image of God 58–62
Li Tana 41
literature 25, 27, 29, 32, 175–6, 181, 183, 185, 186, 187, 191, 193, 196, 197, 200, 202, 207n55, 210n115, 218
 cultural policy 210n115
 economic 89n98
Liu, Lydia 25–6
Lodge, Henry Cabot, Jr. 127–8, 131, 162, 163–4, 165–6, 249
 covert operations 133
Logevall, Fredrick 128–9, 149n216, 173n72
 Choosing War 174
Luttwak, Edward 253
Lý Thường Kiệt
 "Mountains and Rivers of the Southern Court" 46n40
Lý Chánh Trung 75, 100, 137n8
 Understanding America 97

Magsaysay, Ramon 105
Mai Thảo, 195, 197, 199–200, 207
 Creation 183
Maneli, Mieczysław 1, 2, 3–4, 5, 130
Manifest Destiny 42, 109
Maoism 157
Marr, David 28, 29, 98, 99, 184
Marshall Plan 74–5, 119, 124
Marty, Louis 27, 32
Marx, Karl 58, 100, 112, 204
 capitalism 55, 56, 62, 266
 commodity 196
 "economic *fictio juris*" 225
 free individuality 80
 Grundrisse 79
 liberal state 118
 modernity 79
 "On the Jewish Question" 56
 orthodox 270
 personal independence 107
 "representation of wealth" 239
 socialism 57, 72, 103, 108
 Marxism 3, 5, 9, 14, 16, 52, 83, 85n14, 89n98, 97, 98, 101, 102, 269
 anti-colonialism 70
 bourgeois democracy 74
 capitalism 58, 62, 63, 64, 67, 82
 commodity 229
 free individuality 82
 liberal democracy 136
 modernity 60
 Mounier, 13, 53, 55, 56, 57, 59, 75, 81, 104, 132
 praxis 59–60
 revolutions 103–4, 135
 Sartre 84n12
 socialism 135
mass culture in later republic 175–204
 decline of culture in South Vietnam 183–4
 passing the time 190–204
 people and national media 184–7
 popular culture escalation 187–90
 regime of freedom 181–2
 US neocolonialism 175–81
 see also withering of the state
McCarthy, Eugene 166
McNamara, Robert 116, 151n260, 158, 250, 251, 255
McNaughton, John T. 250
media
 collapse of early republic 160–7
 colonialism and surveillance 27–8
 coup 7, 190, 195
Miller, D. A. 233–4, 235
Miller, Edward 37, 106, 146n163
Miller, Henry 191
Minh Võ 122, 129
"misalliance" 15, 153
modernity and Personalism 77–84
Mounier, Emmanuel 54, 85n13, 96
 bourgeois society 64
 capitalism 59, 62
 democracy 62, 67, 74–5, 78, 80, 81, 136
 market economy 64

Mounier, Emmanuel (*cont.*)
   Marxism 13, 53, 55–6, 57, 59–60, 75, 81, 86n26, 103–4, 132
   Personalism 13, 51, 52, 53, 58, 60–1, 65, 73, 86n26, 101, 120, 132
   praxis 60–1, 71
   responsible liberty 80
   sovereignty 76
   surveillance 106
   see also Esprit

nam tiến (Southward Advance) 14, 41–2, 50n101, 50n103, 99, 110
Napoleonic character 35, 37
National Assembly 38, 118, 147n180
National Cinema Center 109
national culture and war 33–7
National Liberation Front 133, 157, 158
NATO 75
neo-colonialism 3, 17, 178, 179, 181, 219
Nghệ Tĩnh soviets 98–9, 101
Ngô Đình Diệm 8–9, 64, 74, 129, 149n216
   ascendance to power 38
   assassination 2, 4, 9, 134, 164–5, 166, 173n60, 187–8, 189, 218
   autonomy 124
   Buddhist crisis 6, 7, 135, 171n32, 217
   Catholicism 52, 63
   coercion 161
   commodities 122–3
   coup 9, 51, 101, 127–8, 135, 164–6 172n59, 187, 194
   cult of personality 48n71
   demise of regime 6
   democracy 13, 38, 40–1, 67–8, 73–7, 78, 97, 106, 108, 111, 118, 123, 126, 128, 146n163, 160, 164, 185, 188, 265
   diemocracy 40, 74, 106, 160, 161, 266
   discipline of communal production 107
   early career 48n74
   economic accord 118
   freedom of religion 171n32
   ignorant of state of affairs 162–3
   independence 83
   Maneli meeting 1, 2
   Mounier's Marxist humanism 75
   national culture 185
   "national discipline" 39–40
   pacification programs 137
   Personalism 38, 51, 75–6, 77, 80, 108, 119, 120, 123, 127; see also Personalism
   propaganda 189
   Republic of Vietnam establishment 37
   resistance to 6, 7
   sovereignty 124
   Strategic Hamlet Campaign 8, 13–14, 112, 116, 133, 134, 151n260, 160; see also counterinsurgency
Ngô Đình Nhu 3, 37–8, 63, 83, 90n107, 149n216, 160
   assassination 2, 4, 9, 134, 164–5, 166, 173n60, 187–8, 189, 218, 269
   autonomy 67, 68, 120, 124
   Cần Lao Party 20n20, 38, 40, 64, 135, 136, 151n260
   capitalism 3, 71, 72–3
   Christianity 49n82
   communism 76, 82, 104, 150n229
   communitarianism 82, 97
   coup 2, 9, 51, 101, 127–8, 130, 135, 136, 164–6, 172n59, 187, 194
   democracy 3, 13, 38, 40–1, 64, 67–8, 73–4, 76, 78, 81, 97, 103, 105–6, 107–8, 110–14, 118, 123, 126, 127–9, 146n163, 160, 164, 185, 188, 265
   inauguration of Strategic Village of Củ Chi 83
   labor and praxis 71–2
   Maneli relationship 1, 2, 3, 4, 5, 130
   Marxism 3, 63, 104
   national discipline 39

Index

Personalism 3–5, 14, 38, 49n82, 51, 52, 62, 64, 65, 70, 75–6, 77, 80, 96, 106, 107, 108, 119, 120, 123, 127; *see also* Personalism praxis 71, 96
socialism 4–5, 40, 65, 71, 81
Strategic Hamlet Campaign 8–9, 13–14, 42, 81, 97, 100–1, 102, 103, 104, 105, 108, 109, 110–15, 116, 117, 125, 126, 128–9, 132–3, 134, 135, 151n260, 160; *see also* Strategic Hamlet Campaign
surveillance network 172n58
syndicalism 20n20
US aid 131–3
Ngô Văn Xuyết 9, 10, 269, 270
Nguyễn Ái Quốc 155
see also Hồ Chí Minh
Nguyễn An Ninh 23, 44n1
Nguyễn Cao Kỳ 121
Nguyễn Công Hoan 207n55
Nguyễn Đình Hoà 45n19
Nguyễn Đình Toàn 195
Nguyễn Đức Cung 73
"*Từ Ấp Chiến Lược Đến Biến Cố Tết Mậu Thân*" (From the Strategic Hamlet to the Tet Offensive: Historical Falsehoods in the Vietnam War), 86n30
Nguyễn Đức Cường 177
Nguyễn Đức Son
"*Một mình nằm thở đủ kiểu trên bờ biển*" 201
Nguyễn dynasty 45n19
Nguyễn Hiến Lê 183, 198, 199, 201, 232
Nguyễn Khắc Viện 177
Nguyễn Ngọc Lan 186
Nguyễn Ngọc Thơ 64
Nguyễn Trãi 30
"Proclamation of the Pacification of the Marauding Ngô" 46n40
Nguyễn Văn Lục 175
Nguyễn Văn Trung 27, 31, 32, 75, 186, 190

Nguyễn Văn Vĩnh 226, 244n55
Nguyễn Văn Xuân 186
Nguyễn Vĩnh Long 232
Nguyễn Xuân Hoài 101
Nguyễn Xuân Lai 124, 176, 232
Nhã Ca 186, 195
Nhân Dân 117, 184
Nhất Hạnh 186
Nhất Linh 211n136
Self-Strength Literary Group 183
Nighswonger, William 104
Nolting, Frederick 38, 42, 73

Occidental ideology of liberalism 70, 71, 104
Oriental Personalism 62, 64, 77, 80

pacification 16, 41, 127, 135, 136, 137, 168, 252, 256
Paine, Thomas 104
Paris Commune 97, 98
Parrel, Fernand 49n82
periodicals in the North 207n64
Personalism 14, 16, 70–1, 72, 73, 96, 97, 101, 107, 111, 112, 113, 127–8, 131, 135, 136, 137, 145n151, 146n163, 188, 199
American liberal democracy 73–7
anti-colonialism 69–71
capitalism and communism 51–4
Catholic 52–3, 58, 64
Christian 63, 64
Diệm 38, 51, 108, 119, 120, 123, 124
economic system 64
French 52, 75, 81
Lacroix 85n12, 88n61
Marx 3, 5–6, 13, 52, 53, 64, 266
modernity 77–84
Mounier 13, 51, 52, 53, 58, 60–1, 65, 73, 86n26, 101, 120, 132
Ngos 41, 268
Nhu 49n82, 64, 65, 66, 102, 106, 108, 114, 119, 130, 133
Oriental 62, 64, 77, 80
see also Esprit
Personalist Labor Party 3, 71, 106

Index

Phạm Cao Củng 246n77
Phạm Công Thuận 186
Phạm Duy 169, 181, 185, 187–8, 200
Phạm Quỳnh 70
Phạm Văn Đồng 30, 117
Phạm Văn Lưu 111
Phạm Văn Sĩ
   Literature of Liberated South Vietnam 176
Phan Bội Châu 29
Phan Chu Trinh 244n55
Phan Nhật Nam 167
Phan Quang Đán 123
political liberalism 6, 89n98, 267–8
popular culture 34, 178, 194, 197, 201, 202, 203, 217, 232, 248, 255
   escalation 17, 187–90, 192
   see also Z.28 novels
popular sovereignty (*dân quyền*) 12, 13, 29–33, 39, 43, 76, 77, 268
   Diệm 40, 67, 163
   Hồ 36
   "illusion" 57, 60
   Lê Lợi 30, 67
   Lodge 163
   Marx 56
   Mounier 56, 57
   Ngos 80, 111
   Trần Văn Giàu 269–70
praxis 14, 59–61, 96
   labor 71–3
primeval democracy 77, 78, 80, 110, 114
"The Proclamation of the Pacification of the Marauding Ngô" 30, 31, 46
proletarianism 36, 60, 69, 72, 82, 91n129, 97, 98, 103, 269
psychological warfare 16, 104–5, 135, 153–69, 181, 185, 192, 195
   campaigns 153, 180
   US 209n108
Puzo, Mario
   The Godfather 192
PX (post exchange office) 176
   see also black market

Quê Hương 89n98

Reader's Digest 102
religion, freedom of 171n32
Rights of Man 7, 11, 56, 65, 69, 70, 71, 74, 77, 100, 267
Rostow, Walt Whitman 248
RVN TV 193

Sacred Sword Patriotic League (SSPL) 153–60, 157, 180
Sagan, Françoise 191
Salinger, J. D. 191
Sartre, Jean-Paul
   existentialism 52, 59, 63, 84n12, 266
   freedom 59–60
   littérature engagée 186
   serialized fiction 18–19, 194–6, 200
   see also feuilleton
Schmitt, Carl, 223–4, 240
   Concept of the Political 224
   Theory of the Partisan 215, 224
Segal, Eric
   Love Story 192
self-criticism 157
self-glorifying publicity 35, 36
Self-Strength Literary Group 53, 183
Shaplen, Robert 96
Situationist International 96
socialism 14, 43, 53, 57, 92n144, 119, 169, 269, 270
   definition 60
   difference from capitalism 11
   Personalist 65, 97
   state 43, 72, 102
   stateless 15, 102, 271
South Vietnamese Literature 175
South Vietnamese view of war 4–7
Southward Advance (*nam tiến*) 14, 41–2, 50n101, 50n103, 99, 110
sovereign indecision, theory of 216
sovereignty 35, 55–6, 58, 59, 61, 65, 82, 107, 112, 113, 130, 159, 165, 166, 167–8, 215, 240, 241
   authority 39
   civilized 67
   conception 12, 110

Index

consumer 220
deterrence 222–4
national 12, 15, 24, 30, 33, 42, 43–4, 57, 110, 223
political 18, 109–10, 124, 216, 217–18, 254, 268
popular 12, 13, 29–33, 36, 39, 40, 43, 56, 57, 57, 60, 67, 76, 77, 80, 111, 163, 268, 269
public 57
territorial 42, 66, 110
weak sovereignty of the Vietnamese court 11–12, 65–8
spectacles
Cold War balance of surveillance 219–22
surveillance in Z.28 novels 214–42
Vietnam War 221, 249, 257–60
SSPL *see* Sacred Sword Patriotic League
Stalin, Joseph 219, 220
Stalinism 5, 7, 10, 14, 16, 51, 82, 83, 269, 270, 271
Sternhell, Zeev 86n26
Stoessinger, John 173n72
Stone, Loren 192, 193
Strategic Hamlet Campaign 14, 16, 42, 81, 84, 160, 161, 166, 168, 188, 268
against American aid 117–25
communist revolution against the communist revolution 113–17
council democracy 96–100
decentralization and the urban elite 125–34
destroying democracy for the name of democracy 134–7
dictatorship and democracy 104–8
kibbutz 100–4
philosophy 4
Southward Advance as an anti-nationalist myth 108–13
US imperialism 96–137
Vietnamese village and council democracy 96–100
Strategic Hamlet Program 8, 41, 42, 81, 82, 84, 97, 101, 102, 109, 111, 112, 113, 116, 117, 125, 126, 133, 134, 149n225, 151n260, 160
underdevelopment 143n106
Strategic Technical Directorate 155, 157
surveillance
Cold War balance of surveillance and spectacle 219–22
colonialism and media 27–8
spectacle in Z.28 novels 214–42
style in Z.28 novels 225–8
US counterinsurgency 251–4

Taberd, J. L.
Dictionarium Latino-Anamiticum 72
Tam Lang 183
Tạ Văn Tài 65
Taylor, Keith 9–10, 91n129
Taylor, Maxwell 76, 114, 116
Taylor, Milton 64, 73
Tết Offensive 7, 161, 249, 257–60
Thanh Châu 207n55
Thanh Lãng 186
Thế Lữ 226, 228–30, 244n55, 246n77
Thích Nhất Hạnh 190
Thích Quảng Đức 1, 6, 7, 161, *161*
Thompson, Robert 14, 103, 107, 108, 114, 115, 122, 127
Trần Đức Thảo 35, 72, 85n12, 190
Trần Lệ Xuân (Madame Nhu) 107, 129, 149n225, 166, 175
Trần Thái Đỉnh 186
Trần Văn Giàu, 269
Trần Văn Minh 114
Trịnh Công Sơn 190
Turley, William 31
Tze-Ki Hon 26

United States Operations Missions 114
urban elite 15, 119, 121, 123, 136, 137, 146n159, 268
decentralization 125–34
indigenous 178, 244n55
US Aid Information Center *252*

Index

US intelligence 116, 135, 153–4, 240, 257, 259, 260

Văn Bình (fictional character) 219–23, 225–6, 229, 230–1, 235–8, 239–40

VanDeMark, Brian 174n72

Văn Học 175

Văn Nghệ 175

Văn Nguyễn Dưỡng 164, 166

Versailles Conference 155

Vietcong 103, 115–16, 129, 257

Vietnamese Secret Affairs Bureau 219, 229, 231

Vietnam War 7, 10, 12, 217, 232, 238
American public opinion against 19, 166
Buddhist Affair 6
escalation 187
image-making and US imperialism 248–60
media 33, 217
propaganda 33
sovereignty, information, and image of omnipotence 254–6
spectacles 221, 249
surveillance and US counterinsurgency 158, 251–4
US imperialism 6, 19, 248–60
victory of the spectacle and defeat of the people's war in Tết Offensive 7, 161, 249, 257–60

Võ Nguyên Giáp 260

Võ Phiến 175, 181, 182–3, 185, 186, 187, 188, 190, 192, 195, 196, 197, 201, 203, 214, 218

Vũ Khắc Khoan
"Spirit in the Tower of the Tortoise" 187

Vũ Quốc Thúc 120, 123, 124

Vuving, Alexander 46n40

Warner, F. A. 149n216

Welles, Orson
War of the Worlds 156

Westmoreland, William 249, 257, 259, 260, 263n41

withering of the state 15, 103

wuxia novels 212n174

Yang Dongchun 45n20

Yizheng, Liu 26

Z.28 novels 18
avenging the nation 235–41
career 217–18
Cold War and deterrence of sovereignty 222–4
Cold War balance of surveillance and spectacle 219–22
domination without discipline 233–5
free time and leisure 228–32
mass culture and temporal mastery 233–5
surveillance and spectacle 214–42
surveillance and style 225–8
see also Bùi Anh Tuấn; Văn Bình (fictional character)

Žižek, Slavoj 238

CPSIA information can be obtained
at www.ICGtesting.com
Printed in the USA
JSHW031806180322
24008JS00005B/36

9 781526 162502